HUNTINGTON LIBRARY PUBLICATIONS

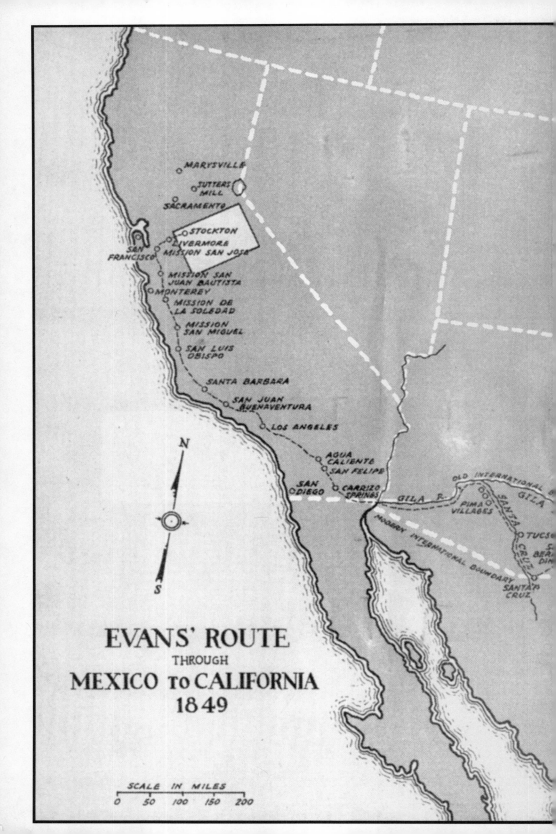

MARYSVILLE

SUTTERS MILL

SACRAMENTO

STOCKTON
LIVERMORE
MISSION SAN JOSE
SAN FRANCISCO

MISSION SAN JUAN BAUTISTA
MONTEREY
MISSION DE LA SOLEDAD
MISSION SAN MIGUEL
SAN LUIS OBISPO

SANTA BARBARA
SAN JUAN BUENAVENTURA
LOS ANGELES

AGUA CALIENTE
SAN FELIPE
SAN DIEGO
CARRIZO SPRINGS

GILA R.

OLD INTERNATIONAL B
GILA
PIMA VILLAGES
SANTA CRUZ
TUCS
S. BEA DIN
MODERN INTERNATIONAL BOUNDARY
SANTA CRUZ

N

S

EVANS' ROUTE
THROUGH
MEXICO TO CALIFORNIA
1849

SCALE IN MILES

0   50   100   150   200

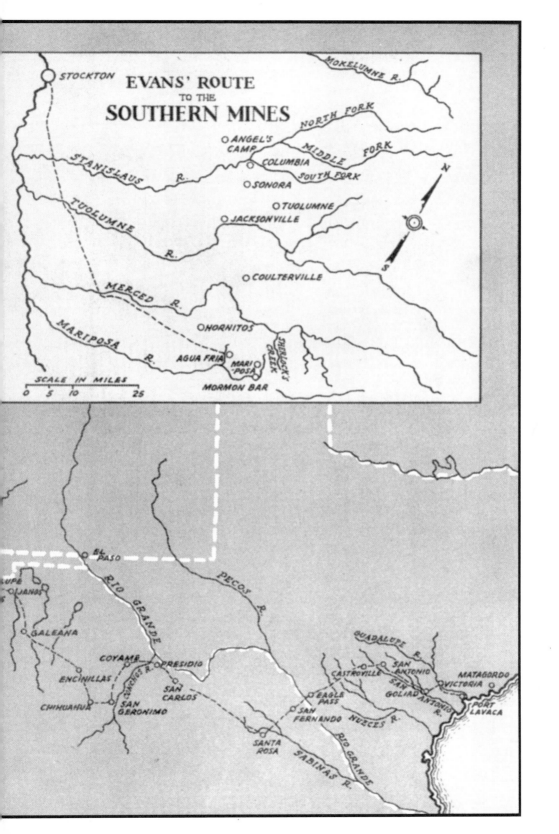

EVANS' ROUTE TO THE SOUTHERN MINES

STOCKTON

MOKELUMNE R.

ANGEL'S CAMP

NORTH FORK

MIDDLE FORK

COLUMBIA

SOUTH FORK

STANISLAUS R.

SONORA

TUOLUMNE

JACKSONVILLE

TUOLUMNE R.

N

S

COULTERVILLE

MERCED R.

MARIPOSA R.

HORNITOS

SHERLOCK'S CREEK

AGUA FRIA

MARIPOSA

MORMON BAR

SCALE IN MILES

0   5   10   25

EL PASO

RIO GRANDE

PECOS R.

LUPE

JANOS

GALEANA

GUADALUPE R.

COYAME

CONCHOS R.

PRESIDIO

CASTROVILLE

SAN ANTONIO

ENCINILLAS

SAN CARLOS

EAGLE PASS

MATAGORDO

VICTORIA

CHIHUAHUA

SAN GERONIMO

SAN FERNANDO

NUECES R.

SAN ANTONIO R.

GOLIAD

PORT LAVACA

SANTA ROSA

SABINAS R.

RIO GRANDE

MEXICAN GOLD TRAIL

The Journal of a Forty-Niner

BY

GEORGE W. B. EVANS

~

EDITED BY GLENN S. DUMKE WITH
A PREFACE BY ROBERT GLASS CLELAND

Huntington Library   ~   San Marino, California

Henry E. Huntington Library and Art Gallery
1151 Oxford Road, San Marino, California 91108
www.huntington.org

Cover design by Doug Davis

Front cover: "Emigrant Party on the Road to California" from *California,
Its Past History, Its Present Position, Its Future Prospects,* London, 1850,
RB 2606. Huntington Library. Images from items in the Huntington's
collections are reproduced by permission.

Library of Congress Cataloging-in-Publication Data

Mexican gold trail : the journal of a forty-niner / by George W. B. Evans ;
edited by Glenn S. Dumke ; with a preface by Robert Glass Cleland.
    p. cm.
  Includes bibliographical references and index.
  ISBN 0-87328-222-1 (pbk. : alk. paper)
  1. Evans, George W. B., 1819–1850—Diaries. 2. Pioneers—West (U.S.)—
Diaries. 3. Overland journeys to the Pacific. 4. Frontier and pioneer
life—West (U.S.) 5. California—Gold discoveries. 6. Chihuahua (Mexico
: State)—Description and travel. 7. Mexico—Description and travel.
8. California—Description and travel. 9. Southwest, New—Description
and travel. I. Dumke, Glenn S.
  F593.E85 2006
  978'.02092—dc22
  [B]

                          2006014825

Errata:
In the lower-right corner of the map of Evans' route, Port Lavaca should
be located south of Matagordo, and not at the mouth of the Guadalupe
River. In the same area, there should be no river shown between the
Nueces and Guadalupe rivers.

CONTENTS

Preface, by ROBERT GLASS CLELAND   xi

Introduction, by GLENN S. DUMKE   xiii

Introduction to the Second Printing and Supplemental

    Bibliography, by PETER J. BLODGETT   xxi

February, 1849: OHIO TO THE ARKANSAS   3

March, 1849: THE ARKANSAS TO SAN ANTONIO   8

April, 1849: SAN ANTONIO TO THE MEXICAN BORDER   28

May, 1849: THE MEXICAN BORDER TO SAN CARLOS   43

June, 1849: SAN CARLOS TO CHIHUAHUA   75

July, 1849: CHIHUAHUA TO JANOS   106

August, 1849: JANOS TO THE GILA RIVER   139

September, 1849: THE GILA VALLEY TO SANTA BARBARA   160

October, 1849: SANTA BARBARA TO THE MARIPOSA

    DIGGINGS   195

November, 1849: THE MARIPOSA DIGGINGS   218

December, 1849: THE MARIPOSA DIGGINGS (CONT.)   228

January, 1850: THE MARIPOSA DIGGINGS (CONT.)   240

February, 1850: THE MARIPOSA DIGGINGS (CONT)   256

CONTENTS

March, 1850: THE MARIPOSA DIGGINGS TO

    SAN FRANCISCO   267

April, 1850: SAN FRANCISCO   275

May, 1850: TO SACRAMENTO AND BACK BY RIVER   286

June, 1850: REMOVAL TO SACRAMENTO   295

July, 1850: SACRAMENTO CITY   302

August, 1850: SACRAMENTO CITY (CONT.)   309

September, 1850: SACRAMENTO CITY (CONT.)   316

October, 1850: SACRAMENTO CITY (CONT.)   321

November, 1850: SACRAMENTO CITY (CONT.) AND THE

    END OF THE TRAIL   327

Bibliographical Note   329

Appendix   333

Index   335

LIST OF ILLUSRATIONS

A FORTY-NINER AT HOME   *Frontispiece*
    (*From a pastel by J. Goldsborough Bruff, December, 1849*)

                                              OPPOSITE PAGE

PATIO OF A MEXICAN MINING HACIENDA;
    THE PATIO PROCESS   120

GUADALUPE PASS, SONORA   136

JUNCTION OF THE GILA AND COLORADO RIVERS;
    LOOKING UP THE GILA   152

WARNER'S PASS FROM SAN FELIPE   168

SOUTH END OF SANTA INEZ MOUNTAINS AND SAN
    BUENAVENTURA VALLEY   184

SAN JOAQUIN VALLEY   200

VIEW OF AGUA FRIA TOWN   216

SACRAMENTO IN 1849   232

PREFACE

IN PUBLISHING the Evans Diary, the Huntington Library is rendering a service both to the historian and the layman. The diary, as Dr. Dumke clearly brings out in the Introduction, is a vivid—at times, indeed, an intensely dramatic—human document. It is also extraordinarily rich in detailed and authentic information on many phases of the gold rush, some of which are rarely or never mentioned in other journals of the period.

Evans made three unusually valuable contributions to the literature of the gold rush. His account of the overland journey, especially along the wild, little-used trail from Eagle Pass to Chihuahua, is far above the average of the gold-rush narratives in vividness and realism of description. Despite a very limited experience in the mountains, he gives a better picture of mining practices and mining camps than one finds in some of the best-known journals of the forty-niners. Finally, Evans' account of conditions in Sacramento in 1849 and the early part of 1850 adds a valuable chapter to the history of that important gateway city.

The George Evans Diary was written by the great-uncle of its present owner, Mrs. Elbert Walker Shirk, of Kimberly Crest, Redlands, California, who has kindly given permission for its publication.

The diary has been edited by Dr. Glenn S. Dumke with his usual scholarly and painstaking care. Part of the editorial expense was met from the grant of the Rockefeller Foundation to the Huntington Library for a regional study of the Southwest.

ROBERT G. CLELAND

The Huntington Library

INTRODUCTION

MANY Argonauts of 1849, realizing that they were partaking of history, kept journals of their travels and experiences in those crowded years. Of these, some are interesting and readable, some dry as dust; a few are painstaking and accurate, many sketchy and unimportant. It would be unfair to claim that the "Evans Diary" lacks most of their faults, for Evans, like other diarists, had his human failings. But it would be equally unfair to omit mention of the things that make the Evans Diary worth reading.

Only a few of the journals, for instance, were written by men who liked to write, who enjoyed putting pen to paper. Evans reveled in the joy of expression, and although his spelling is, to say the least, original, his thoughts are crystal-clear. Many diarists were keeping only a perfunctory record to refresh their own memories in later years, while others wrote expressly for publication. Evans, however, was doing both—keeping an accurate, painstaking, day-to-day record of happenings on the trail and in the diggings for the benefit of himself and his family, but withal producing a readable, running account with at least half an eye to eventual presentation to the public. The combination was a pleasant one, and adds to the diary's value. Evans, moreover, traveled by one of the least-known of the overland trails—the route through northern Mexico. And even there he was unsatisfied to follow the beaten path via Parras and Saltillo, but insisted on embarking, with his companions, on a dubious wilderness cutoff, which took him through the waterless waste of northern Coahuila in a region untraversed and unknown to the majority of emigrants.

Throughout his adventures, Evans demonstrates a flair for poetic description: he sees the beauty of a Texas campfire, the picturesqueness of the valleys of Mexico; he is fully aware, despite his gnawing illness, of the majesty of the California landscape. He was well-read for a man of his day, and evinces a

xiii

knowledge of historical background that makes easy the task of the annotator. Finally, the Evans journal has all the elements of great tragedy. Here was a young professional man of feeble physique, urged on by the lure of gold to win a fortune for his wife and family, passing through all the terrible vicissitudes of the emigrant trail—cholera, Indian attack, death by desert thirst, scurvy in the diggings—merely to gamble on a chancy fortune in the temperamental southern mines. He failed to win the fortune, and his health grew progressively worse. Waiting for the mail became an obsession—news from his dear ones the greatest pleasure in an empty life. Men died around him, and he watched them die with full appreciation of the horror of death on a frontier, far from home and family. And finally, the thing which he dreaded most came to pass—his feeble body gave out at the age of thirty-one, less than two years from the time he had left Ohio for the diggings with such high hopes and energy. Truly this is an American epic, set down for posterity in the graphic prose of a pious, middle-class, middle-western Yankee—an odyssey in which the hero perished.

On February 20, 1849, Evans left Defiance, Ohio, and his wife Cornelia, with a party of fifteen persons—the original "Defiance Gold Hunters' Expedition"—and the group traveled by steamboat down the Ohio and Mississippi to New Orleans, which place they reached on March 3. They spent six days in the interesting old town—days in which Evans marveled at the quaint customs, the water-filled graves in the old cemetery, and the Negro population. Here Evans first came in contact with the terror of the trail—cholera, the horrible disease which struck and killed without warning and which carried so many Argonauts to untimely death. On March 9 the party left by boat for Texas, transshipped at Galveston, and arrived on the 13th at Port Lavaca, in Matagorda Bay, ready for their long overland trek. Now came difficulties inherent in all overland migration, although they crept upon the Argonauts so gradually that their approach was hardly noted. Evans enjoyed the trip through Texas by way of Victoria and Goliad to San Antonio. He was sufficiently educated and patriotic to appreciate the scenes of historical interest on both sides of the trail, and stirring incidents of the Texan War for Independence lived again for him as he passed the Alamo and Fannin's battleground. His love of incident betrayed itself in a vigorous sketch of the difficulties of mule-skinning, and his pious Protestant soul expressed its frank disapproval of the remnants of Mexican Catholicism that persisted near the border. Via Castroville, the little Alsatian emigré village west of San Antonio, the party journeyed to Eagle Pass and the Rio Grande, where the Mexican portion of their journey began.

They crossed the international boundary on April 21 and trudged through fertile lands made memorable by General Wool's Mexican War expedition. Here, on the threshold of a foreign land, they reorganized their little group into the "Ohio Company,"—losing some members and gaining others—and joined another Argonaut band, the "Mississippi Mining Company," for the Mexican jaunt. At this point one of Evans' companions was seized with a fatal attack of cholera, and the journal contributes a gem to gold-rush records by listing in detail the equipment of the unfortunate victim, which may be taken as typical of the paraphernalia of most southern emigrants.

It was the next section of the trek that made Evans important among forty-niner diarists. Refusing to follow the beaten trail southward to Parras and Saltillo, Evans' group hired a guide to take them directly west over the barren uplands of the Serranía del Burro by way of a little-known pass called Santana. Here the real hardships of the journey began. The country grew drier and more barren as they pressed into the bleak uplands, and in one place the party had to travel eighty tortured miles without water. Evans' constitution did not crack under the strain, as did those of many others, but the hardships probably laid the foundation for his later illnesses and early death. The sufferings of the animals affected the kindly Evans almost as much as did the distress of his companions, and, to cap the climax with tragedy, one member of the party separated from the group and was never heard from again. Added to their bodily discomfort was the mental gnawing caused by doubts of their guide, whom they baselessly suspected of being in league with the Indians and conniving to lead them astray for capture and plunder. Eventually, however, they approached the valley of the Rio Conchos, and arrived at the Presidio San Carlos on June 7.

Their original intention was to go directly to Chihuahua from the presidio, but an error in reckoning took them northward to Presidio del Norte, and forced them to double back down the Conchos Valley. The land grew more attractive, and they finally camped in the outskirts of Chihuahua, the metropolis of northwestern Mexico. Evans leaves us an interesting description of the city—its churches, streets, and people—and emphasizes the importance of American contacts in northern Mexico at this significant period. The group left Chihuahua on July 18 and traveled across the vast estate owned by politician Don Angel Trias, past the sinks of Encinillas and the willows of Sauz, to Galeana and the majestic ruins of Casa Grande.

All through northern Mexico the Indian danger dogged the travelers' heels. Apaches, Comanches, and Lipans terrorized the northern settlements, and brushes with small bands of roving savages were a common occurrence. Evans' disgust was directed violently against the passive Mexican policy of letting the Indians run roughshod over the rights of frontier settlers, but the Indians interested him as well, and he described their appearance and habits in his usual picturesque style. Near the Gila River the sedentary Pimas and Maricopas presented themselves for more detailed observation, and he examined their villages thoroughly— less impressed with their appearance than he was with the Yumans' farther on. The wild cattle of the San Bernardino area that had so troubled Colonel Cooke on his earlier journey were still lively, and Evans pronounced them "as dangerous as the buffalo."

Human interest was not lacking in this portion of the journey, for near Chihuahua two of the emigrants engaged in a knife battle which resulted in the death of one and the disablement of the other. Evans was properly aghast at this deed of violence, and his journal fully expresses his horror—which was not, however, so great that he neglected to report the skirmish in detail. Also, Evans himself suffered symptoms of heart trouble near the Maricopa villages, another danger signal that the hardships of the journey were proving too much for his enfeebled constitution.

The Argonauts descended the Gila River and on Sepember 2 crossed the Colorado. Thence they plodded across the dry flats of the California desert, and eventually rested briefly at Warner's Ranch, near the hot springs of Aguas Calientes. Evans' joy at being at last in California was supreme, and he describes the improvement of the climate, his mistaking a fog bank for smoke of a brush fire, the local Indians, and the Californios' vast herds with every evidence of eager interest. The travelers decided to reach the mines by land rather than by water, and trudged northward to Isaac Williams' Rancho Chino (where they left evidence of their stay in the ranch record book), and to the pueblo of Los Angeles, where they arrived on September 26.

They did not hesitate in the pueblo, but persisted northward by way of the coast trail, hearing, from a distance, the celebration which denoted the constitutional convention at Monterey. By way of San Jose and Livermore's Ranch they crossed into the San Joaquin, which Evans pronounced one of the best game regions in the world—elk horns, measuring five feet from head to tip, were seen "all along the road." Footsore and weary, Evans followed his healthier companions past the diggings of the Merced, Tuolumne, and Stanislaus, and finally settled, after additional misadventures which included the loss of his mule, in the little mining camp of Agua Fria, on the Mariposa.

Evans' account of the Mariposa diggings is a classic of detailed description. He started enthusiastically to pan gold, but when his health declined, first with "liver trouble," then with dysentery and scurvy, he reverted to his former profession and became a mining-camp lawyer. His descriptions of mining law and organization, the election of an alcalde for the rough little village, the gambling, fights, and carousals of Irish and Chilean immigrants, the Catholic solemnity of a Latin-American funeral bring to life again the rowdy, serio-comic existence that prevailed all along the western slope of the sierra in that boisterous year of 1849. Disease and human violence proved not the only dangers which threatened the miners, for Evans recounts the death of a young hunter attacked by a bear in the slopes behind the camp. Again he contacted history when remnants of the Jayhawkers' party staggered into camp half dead from their tragic Death Valley adventure.

During all these months Evans was prey to gnawing anxiety, for no mail arrived from home, and he heard, through other miners, that cholera had struck the East and Middle West with fierce intensity. He sent continually to the cities for mail, and always he was disappointed. He was panic-stricken when news of the death of his father, uncle, and cousins from the dread disease was transmitted to him through a friend's letter, and his worry over his wife and son became frantic. He finally decided that mining was overly detrimental to his health, and left the diggings in March of 1850, having gathered, during his months of suffering and toil, only "eighteen ounces and one penny-weight" of gold—worth about $288.

In San Francisco he took a job with the customs service as inspector of incoming vessels, and spent his spare time haunting the post office. Finally, to his great delight, a letter arrived on April 26, and he hurried to a secluded spot to open it—only to discover that it was from "a Miss Henry, with whom I have never had the slightest acquaintance." In May he was sent to Sacramento in the course of his duties and, a short time after his return, resigned his position and went to that city to live. On July 11 he received his first letter from home, discovering that the laxness lay not with his family but with the postal and express service which had neglected to deliver his letters. He commemorated the event with the heartfelt sentence—"This is . . . the happiest day to me in California." A short time later another Argonaut brought him a picture of his wife and son, and his happiness was complete.

He was still determined to make his fortune in California—by trade if he could not mine—and he investigated business possibilities in Sacramento with much interest. The famed "squatter riots" took place during his residence there, and his account furnishes interesting details of that event. Evans finally went to work for a commission house as an auctioneer, but overwork soon broke down his health again, and in October he reflected bitterly that his average earnings during a year in California amounted to only $62.48 per month. Despite ill-health and the ever-present fear of cholera, which broke out in the fall of 1850, he maintained his interest in contemporary events, and helped to celebrate on October 19 news of California's admission to the Union. The diary ends with the entry of November 6, a brief statement of the poor condition of his health, and an appended note adds that he died in Sacramento on December 16, 1850, at the age of thirty-one.

The diary is thus a human and moving story as well as a historical document of no mean value. If Evans had lived to polish his work, the journal would probably have been in print long ere this. As it is, it represents the crude but enthusiastic account of a man who wrote in the first flush of eager interest of things and events along the Mexican trail to the diggings of '49, and, as it stands, is probably much more gripping and sincere than if its writer had discarded the sweat-stained pages and made calm history of what is actually a news report of the first magnitude.

I wish to express my appreciation to several people who aided me directly or indirectly in the preparation of this diary for publication. The staff of the Huntington Library were of great assistance. The confidence of Dr. Robert Glass Cleland was of primary importance in my being given the responsibility of editing the document, and his aid and suggestions have been invaluable. The first task—that of transcribing the diary from a photostat—was done with marked fidelity by Mrs. Lindley Bynum. Láter, Mrs. Marion Tinling helped greatly in editing and checking the details. Mr. Godfrey Davies and Dr. Cleland both aided in selection of the plates, and Mr. Roland Baughman helped design the map of Evans' itinerary. Mr. Willard O. Waters called the attention of the Library authorities to the value of the manuscript.

Mrs. Elbert Walker Shirk, grandniece of George Evans, kindly provided important biographical data.

In transcribing the manuscript, spelling and punctuation have been modernized and contractions expanded with the exception that names of persons and places are spelled as written by Evans. Dating has been regularized, and division of the journal into chronological chapters was done to facilitate annotation and analysis of Evans' travels.

GLENN S. DUMKE

Occidental College

INTRODUCTION TO THE SECOND PRINTING AND SUPPLEMENTAL BIBLIOGRAPHY

T
HE WHOLE COUNTRY, from San Francisco to Los Angeles, and from the sea shore to the base of the Sierra Nevadas, resounds with the sordid cry, 'gold, GOLD, GOLD!' while the field is left half planted, the house half built, and everything neglected but the manufacture of shovels and pickaxes." So saying, the San Francisco–based newspaper *The Californian* sourly announced suspension of further publication on May 29, 1848, due to a lack of subscribers, proclaiming itself the victim of gold fever. From our perspective a century-and-a-half later, we can easily forgive *The Californian*'s disgust at its situation, for it stood in excellent company. Barely four months after James W. Marshall's discovery of gold on January 24, 1848, in the tailrace of John A. Sutter's mill at Coloma on the American River east of present-day Sacramento, news of Marshall's find had inspired thousands of Californians to abandon their prior occupations and depart posthaste for the canyons and streambeds of the Sierra Nevadas.

In the months that followed, as further details of California's golden possibilities spread in every direction, an international migration of steadily mounting proportions unfolded, attracting fortune seekers from the Oregon Territory, Mexico, the Sandwich Islands (modern-day Hawaii), Peru, Chile, and Australia. By the winter of 1848–49, with confirmation of the golden harvest received in the United States from officers serving with its army on the Pacific Coast, the lure of California's wealth ignited yet another wave of frenzy, greater than all its predecessors. Throughout all the American states, family members in innumerable households debated the desire of fathers, sons, brothers, and husbands to pursue their fortunes in the golden land of El Dorado.

Among those whose choices propelled them westward, George W. B. Evans of Defiance, Ohio, joined the procession near its very beginning. Setting out by sleigh on February 20, 1849, with fourteen fellow Buckeyes, Evans began a journey that would carry him by railroad, steamboat, wagon, and eventually mule to California's gold mines. Though Evans' diary reveals nothing about the planning of his expedition, the date of his departure dictated the routes that he and his companions would follow, down the Mississippi River to New Orleans, across the Gulf of Mexico to Port Lavaca, Texas, and then overland through western Texas and northern Mexico before crossing the Colorado River into California.

Americans residing in the states that abutted the Atlantic Ocean had the opportunity to leave for California by sea through any deep-water port not clogged with ice as soon as vessels could be rigged and fitted out for the voyage. By contrast, Southerners and Westerners from Michigan to Mississippi and Ohio to Arkansas could not begin the trek overland across the continent to California until winter had given way to spring and spring in turn gone nearly to summer. Only then, with prairies covered by lush grasses that would feed the mules and oxen hauling the wagons and with mountain passes in the Sierra Nevadas cleared of snow, could thousands of other gold hunters set foot on the trails to California broken by earlier westering emigrants during the 1840s.

For the more impatient, determined, or adventurous among the argonauts, however, various trails forged by commerce, exploration and conquest also crisscrossed Texas, New Mexico Territory, and Mexico's northern states of Coahuila, Chihuahua, and Sonora. Further south, yet other trails brought Americans from Mexico's Gulf Coast to its Pacific shores, from whose ports they might embark by ship for California. These trails, unhindered by winter storms, presented the alluring prospect of earlier departures and quicker passages west to the mines. In hopes of profiting from prospective overlanders in need of everything from harnesses to hardtack, frontier entrepreneurs in Texas, Arkansas, and Missouri aggressively promoted the possibilities of different southern routes throughout the winter of 1849. By spring, thousands of argonauts such as George Evans and his fellow Defiance gold hunters were already making their way across northern Mexico and the southwestern deserts of the United States.

Evans' account of this journey furnishes us with a marvelously detailed narrative of his adventures. In doing so, it illuminates both those aspects of his travels common to California-bound overlanders in general and those peculiar to the southern trails. Furthermore, after describing his arrival in the Mariposa mining district in October 1849 (eight months after leaving Ohio!), Evans also relates his subsequent labors in the Golden State as a miner, a customs inspector, and an auctioneer over the next twelve months. Though Evans proved as unsuccessful in seeking his fortune as did most argonauts, his chronicle of the era is a treasure in its own right.

As Evans and his peers headed west by south to reach El Dorado, his diary recorded their constant encounters with what seemed to them a thoroughly alien world. A careful observer and a vivid writer, he seemed to possess an omnivorous curiosity as reflected in the descriptions of flora, fauna, landscapes, climate, commerce, architecture, agriculture, cuisine, social customs, and domestic life that flowed from his pen. Laden with the prejudices and presumptions of his age, he could celebrate the anniversary of American independence and the blessings of democracy in one passage while decrying what he considered Apache savagery or Mexican thievery in others. Though never reticent about the hardships that he and his companions endured, whether on the trail or in the mines, he also had the capacity to be struck by scenes of great beauty arising, as the Romantics would have understood them, from the sublime and the terrible in nature.

During these same months, Evans captured a cavalcade of peoples in his pages, reminding us that, contemporary mythologizing notwithstanding, many parts of the trans-Mississippi West were far from empty in the mid-nineteenth century. Beside his fellow gold hunters, Evans reported Germans, Mexicans, Apaches, Comanches, Yaquis, Pimas, Yumas, and Californios; his own emigrant party frequently took sustenance and sometimes shelter in towns, villages, and haciendas throughout their travels. Parties of Mexican gold miners, met while homeward bound after their efforts to exploit California's bounty, demonstrated how quickly and how widely the fever for gold had spread. In like fashion, the presence of various Americans engaged in ranching, trading, or mining in northern Mexico emphasized the permeable nature of the international boundary and the opportunities available in the borderlands.

As a resource for the study of the past, Evans' diary represents an exceptional contribution to our understanding of the history of the Far West at this crucial moment. The breadth and depth of his depiction of the rush to California via the "southern" trails, for instance (a topic that occupies quite a bit of space in the six original manuscript volumes), bolsters our knowledge of that important but overlooked dimension of the overlanding experience. Though routinely caustic in his comments about all the inhabitants of northern Mexico, he captures many lively vignettes of their existence as well as of the effects of the unremitting hostility between native peoples such as the Apaches or Comanches and the Mexicans who had come to occupy the land. Finally, in reciting his unsuccessful attempts in California to triumph in the mad scramble for wealth, he not only documents the familiar story of the miner's harsh existence but also testifies to the adaptability and doggedness required of each player in what many argonauts described as "Nature's great lottery."

In following Evans' saga to its poignant conclusion, the reader in the end learns much about the author, beyond perhaps what the author expected to reveal. A man of some education, exhibiting a familiarity with history and literature, he often peppered his sentences with the kind of emotional flourish common to many writers of the age. Perhaps anticipating that the frenzy following the discovery of gold would generate a demand for chronicles of the search for it, he apparently wrote with an eye to eventual publication, addressing each volume to the "dear reader" who followed his story. Though he could be irate or vituperative or melancholy, his darkest moments of depression came only as the months of unbroken silence from his loved ones back home exacerbated his sense of isolation and his fears about their safety. On the whole, Evans seemed to have a deeply embedded streak of optimism, perhaps the very quality that led him to cast his lot with the pursuit of golden dreams in California. He clung to that sense of life's possibilities right up until his death in Sacramento, California, on December 16, 1850, at the age of 31.

Lacking access to other documents about his life, his family, his aspirations, and his expectations, we must rely on the occasional hints that Evans offers us in the diary to find out what inspired him to set out on this grand venture. Perhaps the most significant of them are the words he wrote on April 27, 1849, just outside of San Fernando, Mexico: "Here I remain overnight for a load of provisions, and then I start for camp and the wide, unbounded West. California, the land of my search, still lies many leagues in advance, but with the blessings of a just and righteous God, I expect to reach its limits and be enabled to reap its benefits and assist in alleviating the wants of misery consequent upon the misfortunes of my fellow beings" (page 41).

The eminent western historian Dale L. Morgan, endeavoring to establish "the significance and value of the overland journal" in his 1962 essay bearing that title, asserted that "in their journals westering Americans set down a collective self-portrait, a mosaic in words. The mosaic can never be altogether filled in, never amount to a fresh creation. Each journal that is found alters some detail, and gives fresh play to our imagination as well as our understanding." This splendid diary amply measures up to that standard, opening a window into a moment in our past that still fascinates and captivates us. New generations of readers will find, in this new edition of *Mexican Gold Trail*, an opportunity to explore George Evans' story and its place in our national history.

SUPPLEMENTAL BIBLIOGRAPHY

When Professor Glenn Dumke of Occidental College transcribed and edited the diary of George W. B. Evans for publication in 1945, he drew on the research of early twentieth-century scholars in the fields of California and Western American history as well as accounts written by other participants in the rush for riches. The next six decades, however, witnessed a seemingly unending procession of publishing about the gold rush era. Fueled in part by the celebration of the centennial (1948) and sesquicentennial anniversaries (1998) of gold discovery, this proliferation of scholarship also drew inspiration from a revitalization of popular and academic interest in the history of the trans-Mississippi West following World War II. At the dawn of the twenty-first century, individuals wishing to learn more about various aspects of the gold rush decade may choose from a host of volumes that, taken as a whole, would fill a sizeable library. As a starting point, therefore, readers seeking further illumination might wish to consult one or more of the following titles that have been published since 1945, as well as relevant titles from *Mexican Gold Trail*'s original bibliography. Readers should also be aware that this list is highly selective and makes no attempt to be comprehensive.

FOLLOWING THE SOUTHERN OVERLAND ROUTES
TO CALIFORNIA

BROWNLEE, ROBERT. *An American Odyssey: The Autobiography of a 19th-Century Scotsman, Robert Brownlee, at the Request of his Children,* edited by Patricia A. Etter. Fayetteville, Ark.: 1986.
CLARKE, ASA B. *Travels in Mexico and California,* edited by Anne M. Perry. College Station, Texas: 1988.
COUTS, CAVE J. *Hepah, California!: The Journal of Cave Johnson Couts from Monterey, Nuevo Leon, Mexico, to Los Angeles, California, during the years, 1848–1849,* edited by Henry F. Dobyns. Tucson, Ariz.: 1961.

ELLIS, GEORGE M., ed. *Gold Rush Desert Trails to San Diego and Los Angeles in 1849*. San Diego, Calif.: 1995.

EGAN, FEROL. *The El Dorado Trail: The Story of the Gold Rush Routes across Mexico*. New York: 1970.

ETTER, PATRICIA. *To California on the Southern Route 1849: A History and Annotated Bibliography*. Spokane, Wash.: 1998.

HAGUE, HARLAN. *The Road to California: The Search for a Southern Overland Route, 1540–1848*. Glendale, Calif.: 1978.

HARRIS, BENJAMIN BUTLER. *The Gila Trail: The Texas Argonauts and the California Gold Trail*, edited by Richard H. Dillon. Norman, Okla.: 1960.

HUNTER, WILLIAM W. *Missouri '49er: The Journal of William W. Hunter on the Southern Gold Trail*, edited and annotated by David P. Robrock. Albuquerque, N.M.: 1992.

LAMAR, HOWARD R. *Texas Crossings: The Lone Star State and the American Far West, 1836–1986*. Austin, Texas: 1991.

THE OVERLAND EXPERIENCE DURING
THE CALIFORNIA GOLD RUSH

HOLLIDAY, J. S. *The World Rushed In: The California Gold Rush Experience*. New York: 1981.

MORGAN, DALE L. "The Significance and Value of the Overland Journal" in *Probing the American West: Papers from the Santa Fe Conference* edited by John Alexander Carroll, A. R. Mortensen, K. Ross Toole and Robert M. Utley, pages 29–36. Santa Fe, N.M.: 1962.

UNRUH, JOHN D. *The Plains Across: The Overland Emigrants and the Trans-Mississippi West, 1840–1860*. Urbana, Ill.: 1979.

OVERVIEWS OF THE CALIFORNIA GOLD RUSH

BLODGETT, PETER J. *Land of Golden Dreams: California in the Gold Rush Decade, 1848–1858.* San Marino, Calif.: 1999.

CAUGHEY, JOHN WALTON. *Gold Is the Cornerstone.* Berkeley, Calif.: 1948.

HOLLIDAY, J. S. *The Rush for Riches: Gold Fever and the Making of California.* Berkeley, Calif.: 1999.

PAUL, RODMAN W. *California Gold: The Beginning of Mining in the Far West.* Cambridge, Mass.: 1947.

ROHRBOUGH, MALCOLM. *Days of Gold: The California Gold Rush and the American Nation.* Berkeley, Calif.: 1997.

PETER J. BLODGETT

Huntington Library

Mexican Gold Trail

{ February, 1849 }

OHIO TO THE ARKANSAS

BOOK FIRST

John Terry, Benjamin F. Hutchinson, Rinaldo Evans, George W. B. Evans, Hiram Crittenden, Elias Bruner, Milton Cameron, S. L. Cameron, Asa Womsley, A. T. Parker, Charles Speaker, W. A. Haller, Jacob Teats, J. G. McCauly, and T. Laubenheimer[1] left Defiance, Ohio, February 20, 1849, in three sleighs. Found snow plenty to Gilboa, in Putnam County, after which sixteen miles, was hard. Made this day fifty miles, arriving in the evening at Finlay, Hancock County, weary and exhausted. Stayed at Wing's hotel, kept by a Mr. Reed, a perfect gentleman. Left Finlay at 4 o'clock A.M. and arrived at Carey on the L. E. and Mad River Railroad, at 8 o'clock, having made sixteen miles. We had an excellent breakfast at Mr. Plumber's hotel. Expenses thus far $4.37. At 11 o'clock started down the road, passing through Kenton, Bellefountaine, Liberty, Urbana, to Springfield. Here we laid over till 2 o'clock A.M. The distance made this day was ninety-six miles. Left Springfield and arrived at Cincinnati at 10 A.M. Distance eighty-four miles. I was very sick the most of the day. This is February 22, dark, dreary, and smoky, with rain. I can say but little for Cincinnati, having been sick all this day and consequently housed up. The boys are out making every preparation to start for New Orleans tomorrow. Expense from Carey by railroad to this city is $5.75.

Feb. 23. This day has closed our business. We have been joined by our president, John Terry, and T. Laubenheimer and W. A. Haller, the last two having taken different routes. Terry, Laubenheimer, R. Evans, A. C. Parker, and myself are now just leaving the Cincinnati landing for Louisville, Kentucky, on board

[1]George Evans was a practicing attorney. See below, journal for January 1850. Evans later changes the spelling of one name from Womsley to Wamsley or Walmsley, and gives Parker's initials as A. C. instead of A..T.

3

of the steamer "Martha Washington." The other members of our company are on board of the steamboat "Marshall," about [?] hours in advance, with all our trunks, traps, and provisions. My trunk is gone with all my clothing and $117 in specie.

Feb. 24. I was aroused from my uneasy slumbers this morning by the cry, "Here is the steamer 'Marshall,' " and hastily dressed, went on deck, and found the boat at Madison, Indiana—and, what was better news than all, my trunk safe and all well. The country generally presents the picture of a river winding through a mighty ravine. The banks on both sides are very high and abrupt, and in places presenting the appearance of a mighty wall of solid rock, crowned here and there with stately farmhouses, mostly brick. We have been thus far supplied with wood by slaves from the Kentucky shore. These poor darkies are meanly clad, but appear well fed. We arrived at Louisville at 11 o'clock and there left the steamer "Martha Washington" and stopped at the Ohio House, kept by a Dutchman. Here we made further purchases for the company and at 2 o'clock went on board steamer "Chief Justice Marshall," which has just arrived. This is a very commodious, well-finished boat, with gentlemanly officers. Here we found a company of Californians from Xenia,[2] one from Cincinnati, and our own company. There is yet but little fellow feeling between the several parties. The water is too low to pass the canal at this place and we lie over till morning.

Feb. 25. As was said by a man on board, "They made up a good fire in the stove down cellar" this morning early, and, having been detained at Louisville by boats coming through the canal, we did not get off until after 3:00 P.M. Several of us called on Porter, the Kentucky Giant, one of the wonders of the "bloody-ground" state.[3] He is truly a man of many inches.

[2]Xenia, Ohio; sixteen miles east of Dayton.

[3]James D. (Jim) Porter, the famed "Kentucky Giant," was born in 1810 in Portsmouth, Ohio, and during adolescence moved to Shippingport, Kentucky, where he made his permanent home. His phenomenal growth started at the age of seventeen, and interested neighbors recorded one inch in seven days as his

His gun measures nearly his length, being seven feet, eight inches. This tall specimen of humanity has built him a new brick house with doors and windows corresponding with his height. We are now under way. Albany City,[4] a pleasant-looking place, has been passed, and we are swiftly gliding down La Belle River. There is now no drawback excepting a want of knowledge touching the health and happiness of those we leave behind. Fare at Cincinnati and passage to New Orleans $15.

Feb. 26.   This is the first clear day we have had on our journey, and, having passed several towns through the night—among which are Owensborough, Kentucky,[5] and New Burg, Indiana[6]—we are gradually getting into wider water, and passing larger and better-cultivated farms. Our time has thus far been spent in lounging, sleeping, thinking of the past and trying to dive into the future, and eating and reading. These are our only means of recreation. Sometimes a conversation springs up, sprightly in its nature, but not always attended with that freedom from restraint that we find [on] other great thoroughfares. The only reason I can assign for this is that we have on board several professional men—to wit, pickpockets—and every man having any money keeps his hands on it.[7]

----

best record of increase in height. He was variously a cooper, a hackdriver, and a tavern keeper. To satisfy his needs he built an eighteen-room house, on a scale proportionate to his size, which became a tourist attraction. He was seven feet, nine inches tall, and his shoes measured fourteen and a half inches in length. Evans' estimate of the length of his rifle is conservative; other records place it at seven feet, ten inches. He was renowned enough to attract the attention of Dickens, during his visit to America in 1842. Porter lived to the age of forty-nine, and was buried in Louisville. See Federal Writers' Project, *Kentucky, a Guide to the Bluegrass State* (1939), pp. 191-92.

Samuel McNeil, another forty-niner, visited the Kentucky Giant a few days before Evans. He says: "He is more than eight feet in height, and he looked down upon us little mortals with the feelings of a Goliath when he gazed on David of old. If he is not a temperance man he cannot flourish in his establishment, for his huge corporocity would speedily oblivionize whole oceans of porter, ale, and brandy." *McNeil's Travels in 1849* (1850), p. 4.

[4]New Albany, Indiana.   [5]Owensboro.   [6]Newburgh.

[7]References to gambling on Mississippi River boats during this period are numerous. The card-sharps and pickpockets knew that those starting for the

We have passed during the day Evansville, Owensborough, the mouth of the Wabash River, and Shawnee-town. The last is an old town in Illinois, said to be very sickly. A few miles below this place is a place called Cave in-Rock,[8] famous as the head-quarters of a noted band of robbers and murderers in the early history of this country. This we will not get to see, as we will pass it during the night. The gamblers are at their work. Money has been lost and won. There is already a very perceptible change in the weather. The forest trees begin to look heavy topped, and buds are becoming more perfect, as we proceed.

  Feb. 27. Passed Metropolis, Illinois, early this morning, and called at Cairo about 10:00 A.M.; and now we are on the Father of Rivers, and have already passed Columbus and Mills-point in Kentucky.[9] The canebrakes look quite green. We passed this evening New Madrid, a place that has suffered slightly from earthquakes in times past.[10] I have read of those places, and naturally expected to find large and beautiful cities, but find them very small and the buildings old and in a dilapidated condition. I also find the banks of this river very low and subject to inundation; consequently there are few inhabited spots. Everything

---

gold fields of California were supplied with funds at the outset of their journey, and large sums were lost by inexperienced travelers. See *McNeil's Travels*, p. 4.

 [8]For the story of the river pirates who laired at Cave-in-Rock, see Otto A. Rothert, *The Outlaws of Cave-in-Rock* (1924).

 [9]Mill's Point became Hickman in 1937.

 [10]Evans' depreciatory reference glosses over the true importance of the New Madrid catastrophe. On the night of December 6, 1811, violent earth tremors were felt, which roiled the Mississippi, sank sand bars, crumbled cliffs, and upset river boats. Fissures appeared and closed again in the earth's surface, and mud fountains, impregnated with black, bituminous shale, spurted up and left broad sinkholes when they subsided. An unpleasant, sulphurous vapor filled the air and added to the terror of the inhabitants, many of whom fled their homes. The shocks occasioned heavy loss of life, and continued into February of the following year, when another severe tremor was felt on the 7th. The disaster was important enough to attract the attention of both Humboldt and Sir Charles Lyell, and the event had political repercussions in the famous "New Madrid claims," in which refugees, given land scrip by the state

seems wisely ordered by a kind Providence, for if the banks of
this noble river were high and easily cultivated, Yankee enterprise would soon clear away these mighty forests, and, that once
done, it would become very difficult to procure a supply of
steamboat wood for consumption on this mighty thoroughfare.
I this evening heard the piping of the first frogs, an evidence
that winter is past in this region.

Feb. 28. A splendid, heart-inspiring morning. We all
find ourselves in comfortable health and good spirits, for which
we feel that thankfulness due to our Creator. We have passed
several towns during the night and are now approaching
Memphis, Tennessee, which city is almost in sight. The state of
Tennessee is on our left, and Arkansas on the right. Cotton
plantations, with their Negro quarters, are becoming more numerous and of a better character. Memphis has been passed, and
looks like a place of business. Plantations are now opening
before us and everything improves as we go south. The weather
is very warm indeed.

---

for the purpose of obtaining a fresh start in unoccupied areas, lost it to speculators and thereby caused a series of involved lawsuits. A good account can
be found in Walter B. Stevens, *Missouri, the Center State, 1821-1915* (1915),
II, 545-50.

{ March, 1849 }

THE ARKANSAS TO SAN ANTONIO

Mar. 1. We passed the mouth of the Arkansas River and the town of Napoleon[1]—also Hellena.[2] Along here the river seems to lie higher than the country on each side. We stopped to wood a mile above Napoleon, and found that it was necessary to bank up to keep the water out of the wood man's house. And here we noticed the first peach blossom. The mistletoe is also seen in great abundance. We have just overtaken the "Martha Washington"—and now for a steamboat race on the Missi-[ssi]ppi.[3] Both boats are cracking on steam. Here we go! Hurrah! The guns are firing and the steam on both sides is getting up some. Now, now we are within fifty feet of each other, neck and neck, the engines working with all power, with smoke as black as midnight belching from the chimneys of both. Side and side they move, like two mighty, living things, sometimes one gaining a few feet, and again losing as many more. This way we continued to run for perhaps twenty miles, when the "Chief Justice Marshall" glided about ten lengths ahead of her competitor, when a hail from the town of Collumbia[4] caused the "Martha Washington" to give up the chase. We are now between the states of Arkansas and Missi[ssi]ppi and on either hand, at short intervals, pass some of the most splendid plantations. Everything connected with them looks tidy and comfortable, and I am satisfied that abolitionists of the North are, when upon the

[1]Napoleon, Arkansas, was situated on the Mississippi at the mouth of the Arkansas River. The two streams shifted their beds and encroached on the town to such an extent that it was permanently abandoned in 1874. The community was formerly an important shipping point; its population in 1850 was 239.

[2]Helena, Arkansas; about three times the size of Napoleon.

[3]See Mark Twain, *Life on the Mississippi*, chap. xvi, and George Byron Merrick, *Old Times on the Upper Mississippi* (1909), chap. xix.

[4]Unlisted in census of 1850.

8

subject of emancipation, meddling with a matter with which they are little acquainted, and if called upon to advise them as to the proper application of their pent-up sympathy, I should say, turn your attention to the alleviation of the wants or miseries of your next-door neighbors, who stand vastly more in need of your money and your tears than do the blacks bordering upon the Missi[ssi]ppi River. Here the peach and china trees are leaving out, and the peach blossoms falling off. The forest trees are also putting on their livery of green.

We stopped this evening at a very extensive wood yard, in the edge of a forest of cottonwoods, and found the master, overseer, and a number of male and female slaves from the adjoining plantation ready to sell us wood for fourteen shillings per cord. Our boat took on about twenty cords. Here we received information of the burning of the steamer "Convoy" below Vicksburg, on Monday or Tuesday last. There, that bell is sounding again, and we lose another passenger, who gets off.

Mar. 2. Vicksburg[5] has been passed. I can say nothing for the place, for we passed it before day, this morning. The passengers are amusing themselves this morning shooting at wild geese. They are very numerous. The river is very high—so much so that the woods and plantations on both sides are covered with water as far as the eye can reach. Another halt for wood. About noon we passed the scene of the late burning of the steamboat "Convoy," and soon after came into a more diversified and picturesque country. At 3:00 P.M. landed at Natchees,[6] under—not on—the hill. We did not get to see the city proper, for want of time, but the Natchees under the hill is such a place as will scarcely ever enter into the imaginations of any mind. It is composed of a row of low, dingy building[s], with one or two exceptions, admirably adapted to the wants of such low, vile, and degraded characters as are here met with. The country immediately in the vicinity of this city is better than farther up

[5] Vicksburg, Mississippi; population, 3,678 in 1850.
[6] Natchez, Mississippi; population, 4,434 in 1850.

9

the river. There is here and there some splendid scenery. Steep and high banks, washed by the descending rains into miniature representations of conical mountains, studded with evergreen trees, and a variety of shades and colors present to the eye a much more splendid picture than that in the up-country. Soon after leaving Natchees, we began to overtake portions of the wreck. Numerous bales of cotton, some partly burnt, were found on the banks of the river, having been taken out by the inhabitants. One passenger and one hand are reported drowned. The former is said to have lost his life in trying to save a bag of gold; when last seen he was floating, with the gold in one hand, and paddling with the other.

Mar. 3. This morning we found ourselves a few miles south of Baton Roche,[7] the late quarters of our distinguished president-elect, General Z. Taylor. After a quick passage, through a splendid country, one every way entitled to the name of the Sunny South, we arrived at the Crescent City[8] at 6:00 P.M. Here the most that needs be said is that this is a very neat and would be handsome city if the streets running to the steamboat landing were wider. Here we saw and heard some of the Negro melodies from the real darkies, as happy as kings.

Mar. 4. Still in New Orleans and no prospect of getting off. The weather is growing warmer every day.

Mar. 5. Another day past and gone and we are still in the Crescent City, making every preparation to accomplish an overland journey to California from [Texas].

I have been better able today to see this city in part, and find that the river is from five to ten feet higher than the foundations of this city, which adds much to the convenience of the inhabitants, for water is passed from the river in pipes to every house. The streets are very narrow, which detracts from the

[7]Baton Rouge, Louisiana; a little larger than Vicksburg.

[8]New Orleans was nicknamed the "Crescent City," because of the conformation of the river banks at its original site. It was a fair-sized metropolis, containing more than 110,000 persons at the time Evans passed through.

THE ARKANSAS TO SAN ANTONIO

beauty of the place. The buildings on the levee are occupied by the small dealers and boarding (private) houses by Mrs. So-and-so, all widow ladies. I have remarked one thing, perhaps peculiar to sickly cities only, and that is, a large majority of the business men of this city wear upon their hats the mourning weed. So with the ladies. But listen, a female's voice in song! Now let's see from whence come those sounds. Ah! yes, here they are, in full promenade on the balcony in the story below our room, singing, "Come, oh, come with me" and "I come from Alabama, with my wash-bowl on my knee." Great gals, these!

Mar. 6. We have at last secured a passage in the steamer "Palmetto," to Fort Lavaca, Texas, to sail on the 9th instant. We numbered, on board of the steamer "Chief Justice Marshall," thirty-six Californians. Some are going round Cape Horn, others by way of the Isthmus, and twenty-one of us are going over-land, by way of the Rio Grand and Gila River.[9] Our party now includes five men from Perrysburg, Ohio, a Mr. Johnston, Mr. Carpenter, Mr. George McKnight, and two others. I was told this evening, by a Mrs. Corteniho, that the ground was so low that in their cemeteries they had to erect tombs. This is expensive; and strangers are interred in graves of water because the grave fills before the interment takes place. When these in-terments take place, the coffin is deposited in the water and sunk by heaping the earth upon it. The cost of a place in the tombs is $60 in the French cemetery in this city.

These people are in the annual habit of assembling, on a day set apart,[10] and decorating the graves and tombs, and at night illuminating this resting place of the dead. This is certainly paying a noble tribute to the departed friends, a testimonial worthy of the heart that conceived it.

[9] See the Introduction to *Southern Trails to California in 1849*, ed. Ralph P. Bieber ("Southwest Historical Series," V; 1937); and Mabelle Eppard Martin, "California Emigrant Roads through Texas," *Southwestern Historical Quarterly*, XXVIII (1925), 287-301.

[10] All Saints' Day, Nov. 1.

One poor fellow on his way to California was called to a halt this morning, having been taken with the cholera,[11] from some imprudence in eating fruit. His remains now lie entombed in this city, far from friends and home, and perhaps by his death the sacred ties of husband, father, son, and brother have been snapped asunder. There are many coffeehouses in this city and but one place that can be termed a hotel. This one is the St. Charles Hotel,[12] a very large building and pleasantly located. I find that the courts are fully occupied with the trials of persons for murder and larceny. Two murders and one suicide have taken place since we came into the city.

    Mar. 7.   Very warm. Some rain during last [night] and the night before. All that has fallen, however, is speedily evapo-

[11]Cholera was the scourge of the western traveler, and with the increased migration of gold-rush years the disease took a huge toll of victims. The epidemic was especially virulent in Louisiana and Texas during 1849, claiming more than 3,000 lives in New Orleans alone. Brownsville, Laredo, and San Antonio were also foci of the disease, and there many emigrants turned back, discouraged. The disease has usually centered in British India, whence it was carried by means of flies, infected clothing, food, and water to many parts of the world. The lightning speed of the attack was what made cholera so terrifying, deaths having been known to occur within one or two hours after appearance of the first symptoms, which included alimentary discharges, cramps, and weakening of the pulse. Modern methods of treatment have robbed the disease of many of its horrors, but in 1849 the principal treatment consisted of large doses of a mixture of calomel, camphor, and red pepper, with mustard footbaths and strong brandy. Strangely enough, this heroic treatment often served its purpose, and cures have been recorded which were almost as sudden as the first seizures. But where resistance was low or treatment unavailable, the victim usually progressed to typhoid fever, even if he managed to shake off the cholera virus. See William Dunbar Jenkins, "The Cholera in 1849," Mississippi Historical Society *Publications*, VII (1903), 271-79; *Standard History of New Orleans*, ed. Henry Rightor (1900), p. 213.

[12]The St. Charles Hotel was first opened in 1837 as one of the most magnificent hostelries of the South. Cost of construction amounted to $800,000, and its columned façade and huge dome formed an imposing landmark. The hotel was usually tenanted by wealthy planters, and it maintained its own slave exchange. Two years after Evans visited the building it was destroyed by fire and rebuilt. In 1896 it was again burned to the ground, and the present structure is a second replacement of the original. See Federal Writers' Project, *New Orleans City Guide* (1938), pp. 108, 313.

rated when the sun once shines. This delay seems interminable, but Friday will come and then, life and health permitting, we are off. I visited this morning the lower part of the city, in which the French part of the population reside. The shops and stores are many, and their goods displayed with taste. Every article wanted by man, woman, or child can be found here.

Mar. 8.   This day has been characterized by a busy preparation on our part. Our saddles—thirty-six in number—for packing have all been purchased and are now in the hold of the steamer. We have also each purchased a riding saddle and the necessary straps. The weather has been very warm indeed. Our meals are composed in a great degree of what we had to eat when we first came. All the members [are] in what may be called good health.

Mar. 9.   Breakfasted lightly, and hastened on board of the "Palmetto." At half past eleven o'clock, we turned our faces once more to the south, and our noble ship, panting and pawing the water as if eager to depart, soon caused houses, ships, and trees to pass swiftly by; and now the sea breeze fans our warm foreheads and we are leaving the city of the Sunny South far behind us. No one who has not experienced the confinement of city can realize the feelings of each of our little band. All were anxious to leave New Orleans and now that we are out and once more blessed with fresh air and permitted to see the beautiful green trees, the smiling of nature on every hand, our hearts are lifted in thankfulness to that Being who has so kindly granted these things for the well-being of His creatures. It is now nearly midnight, and we are lying at anchor in the middle outlet of the Mississippi River, about fifty miles from the city. Our lying here is in consequence of a dense fog, which prevents our running. We have had during the evening a regular Negro dance by some slaves on board. I must say that these happy fellows are not often surpassed in this accomplishment and, to them, happy relief from the fatigues of the day.

We enjoy on board of this vessel kind attentions from the officers and an abundance of the good things of this life—with butter and soup unmixed with hair.

Mar. 10.   Early this morning our vessel got under way, after receiving on board a pilot, and in one hour we had passed the Balize,[13] and we are moving rapidly over the rolling waters of the Gulf. In a short time pale faces were to be seen on board, and some sickness ensued. This afternoon was employed by a few of us in an attempt to capture a shark, and, after having two hooks and a portion of our line taken off, we gave up the attempt. During all this time, shoals of the porpoise were playing around the vessel, some springing out of the water as much as three feet and again disappear[ing] head-foremost in the briny deep.

> The land is no longer in view,
> But the clouds they do not frown;
> For fear I get sick too,
> I'll go straight off and lay down.

Mar. 11.   Once more the Sabbath has dawned upon us, and with it some alarm. The cholera is now in our midst. This alarming disease has broken out. A slave on board is now suffering the agonies of that disease. 10:00 A.M. The slave is now in the deep, deep sea, having died about an hour since; distance from nearest port—Galveston, Texas—about sixty miles, and from land, about the same. Another case has made its appearance—Judge McQuarter, of Montgomery, Alabama. He also is sinking fast. The sea is not very rough, just enough so to keep the boys on the sick list. 5 o'clock P.M.—in sight of port. The judge has just expired. Time with him has closed. He has left a large family and numerous friends to mourn his untimely end.

Mar. 12.   This day has been employed in transshipping our goods from the "Palmetto" to the steamer "Yacht." No new cases of cholera have yet appeared. We are now at sea again, considerably tempest-tossed. Wind pretty high. Galveston City

[13]Balize, Louisiana; the cape at the end of the Mississippi River delta.

is the handsomest place seen on our route. It [is] situated on Pelican Island, in Galveston Bay. This island is noted in the history of the Gulf as being the place of residence of the much-dreaded pirate, Lafitte.[14] The city is regularly laid out into large squares and wide streets, and [is] partly planted with the palmetto trees of native growth.

Mar. 13. The past night has been one fraught with anxiety and care on the part of the passengers on the "Yacht." It stormed all night, accompanied with thunder and vivid lightning. At ten o'clock A.M. [we saw] the breakers across the mouth of Matagorda Bay. This boiling flood had to be passed ere we left the Gulf for the last time. Soon our noble little steamer was plunging in the midst of this foaming abyss, and one little error in our wheelsman would launch us in Eternity. Nothing is heard but the roaring of the angry waters and the hurried commands of our captain. All is breathless suspense and anxiety. For twenty minutes this state of anxious care lasted, and then all was over, and we were again in smoother waters in Matagorda Bay. Having passed up this twenty miles, we were again reshipped on board of a government lighter, and at 8 o'clock in the evening safely landed at Port Lavaca.[15]

Mar. 14. This day has been disposed of in frequent at-

[14]Jean Lafitte led a colony of pirates and smugglers on the coast south of New Orleans from 1810 to 1814, managing to stay in business despite the capture of his ships by a United States naval expedition in the latter year. When the British, attacking New Orleans in 1814, offered him money and a commission to aid them, he refused and turned over their communication to General Jackson, who enlisted Lafitte among his forces defending the city. In return for his military service, Lafitte was pardoned, but unwisely resumed his piracy from a base at Galveston three years later. Pressure was once more brought to bear by the United States government, and he finally fled in 1821. See Charles Gayarré, "Historical Sketch of Pierre and Jean Lafitte," *Magazine of American History*, X (1883), 284-98, 389-96; repr. by Louisiana State Museum as *The Story of Jean and Pierre Lafitte, the Pirate-Patriots* (1938). See also Lyle Saxon, *Lafitte, the Pirate* (1930).

[15]Port Lavaca was founded by the Spanish in 1815 and was named after the La Vaca River, christened by La Salle. Once a principal port of entry, the harbor facilities were destroyed by incursion of sand spits, and the town stagnated until oil development revived its waning population.

tempts to procure wagons and mules for the transportation of our goods. The town of Lavica contains about 300 inhabitants.

Mar. 15. Took a stroll off into the country on a hunting expedition this morning. Passed over a very fine prairie,[16] decked with flowers of every color and altogether presenting a splendid appearance. Asa Wamsley, who has been sick, is reported better—he, however, thinking that he must die. This evening the lighter again approached the wharf, and our provisions are once more under our control, with a loss of only one box, containing candles. Part of the goods are now on the wagon, and tomorrow morning we start for San Antonio. We pay $150 for two wagons to carry our goods to Antonio, a distance of 140 miles.

Mar. 16. Our goods were all loaded by 9 o'clock and we started on our journey. We passed over a prairie country a distance of twelve miles. This is truly a magnificent country, interspersed with little groves, looking like islands at sea, and apparently boundless. Game of every kind abounds here. We are now at the house of Mr. Malden, a gentleman of intelligence. His lady has prepared for us a substantial supper, the only good meal we have had since leaving the "Chief Justice Marshall."

This public house is the only residence between Port Lavica and Victoria, and [is] called the half-way house. This is the only place where water can be obtained between those places. There is no doubt that water can be had by digging wells in this prairie, if not too near the coast. This day's journey was accomplished on foot. The sensitive plant[17] grows here in its beauty and prime.

Mar. 17. Started on foot early, and reached a camping ground about eighteen miles. Here we halted and had the pleasure of taking a cup of coffee with an old Texan, in the open air and boundless prairie. This old man was also a traveler, of kind and generous disposition. One of our wagons was broken down in sight of our first camp, almost out of water and about

[16]Throughout his manuscript, Evans uses the word "perarie," a natural result of Yankee affection for the letter *r*.

[17]*Mimosa pudica,* whose leafstalks droop and whose leaves close when touched.

five miles out to the river Guadaloupe, or, as called by the inhabitants, Warloop.

Mar. 18 (Sabbath). We have just had our breakfast, composed of fried ham, prairie chicken, and pilot bread. The only water we have had this morning was obtained by dipping from the ruts and wagon tracks. This water, although thick, tasted well, and made glad the hearts of us poor, famished, Californians. Our horses were considerably alarmed last night by the approach of wolves, which disturbed our rest and caused me to turn my other side to the hard bed I occupied. We have made this day only seven miles, to Victoria.[18] Our wagons have not yet come up. This town is not in a flourishing condition. The only gristmill seen in Texas on our route is at this place. It is composed of a large flutter wheel and one cogwheel. The stones or burrs are small and run in a half barrel or tub, surrounded by pilot cloth, and the whole mill floats on four small boats, two on each side of the water wheel. This simple structure is moored in the rapids of this stream, and the action of the water, without dam, sets the whole in motion. Of the Texan character, I can say that a more open-hearted and open-handed people never lived. They are hospitable in the extreme, ever ready to give any desired information and to feed the penniless poor. That selfish feeling so inherent in the breast of our northern men is not met with here, unless in trade between man and man. The country passed today is prairie, and under a sun as hot as our July. The banks of this river are high, and on the opposite side is a thick forest. We have been threatened with rain for several past days, but none yet. Our teams reached here just at night, and we pitched our tents on the banks of the Warloop and took a supper of fried pork and bread and tea. I occupied a blanket in the tent of our Perrysburg friends, and enjoyed a comfortable night's rest.

Mar. 19. Broke up camp at 10 o'clock this morning and

[18]Victoria, Texas, about twenty-six miles northwest of Port Lavaca. The town had a population of 806 in 1850.

commenced crossing the river. The ferry at this place is kept
going constantly, crossing Mexican and other teamsters. These
Mexican teamsters resemble our northern Indians and are of the
same copper color and all slaves to other men of that nation.
They use nothing but the broad-wheeled cart, drawn by three
and four yoke of oxen. The only iron used in making a cart is
in the tire of the wheels. For a mile and a half from Victoria we
traveled through a thick woods, in which I found the live oak
and other trees hung with the Spanish moss,[19] giving, in contrast, youth and hoary-headed old age. This moss hangs in beautiful festoons from the underside of the limbs, and the whole
[is] surmounted by the beautiful green leaves of the tree. The
moss is of a gray color. We are now in the edge of another
prairie, feeding the mules and awaiting the arrival of the wagons.
Soon after the wagons came up, we ascended a hill about sixty
feet, and continued on over a beautiful, open, rolling country
a distance of four miles from our starting point, and encamped
on Dry Creek, where we found good standing water. The grass
is good everywhere. The houses are of brick or wood, generally
frames and log in the country. No plastering is done in these
houses, being sufficiently warm without, at all seasons. The
cattle are large and handsome. I have seen some few oxen, measuring five feet between tips of horns.

Mar. 20.   Our breakfast was prepared early this morning,
and, after the tents were struck, we took up our line of march.
This forenoon we passed over a rolling country, called, with us,
oak openings, and at noon halted on the banks of Coletto River,[20]
a beautiful stream. Here we filled our vessels with water to do us
until tomorrow noon, the next water being at least twelve miles
in advance. We found this day a solitary grave in the openings.
This was indicated by a cross planted right over the breast of

[19]*Tillandsia usneoides*, a long, gray moss in horsehair-like fronds, which
droops from the limbs of live oaks in southwestern United States. Often called
"Old Man's Beard."

[20]The Coleto River joins the Guadalupe south of Victoria.

the corpse. That species of the cactus known as the devil's tongue[21] is found growing wild here. We saw one this morning, measuring three feet high and spread out in every direction. The new growth has just started. After going about seven miles from the water, we encamped for the night on the ground known as Fanning's battle ground. Here Col. F. and some of his men were taken prisoner by the Mexican forces in 1836, and carried off to Goliad and there massacred. The place occupied by F. is easily distinguished by the ditches dug for the security of his men.[22] After supper we all retired to rest in good health.

Mar. 21. This morning, as soon as we were up, flocks of deer were seen in every direction around us. Several of the men started out, and in a short time J. Teats came into camp dragging a very fine young buck. This was hailed with joy, as it afforded a change of diet. Soon after getting under way, one of the men shot a fine wild goose. By this change of fortune, we can live for several days on the fat of the land. We traveled this day about eleven miles over a beautiful and diversified country. We passed the deserted Mexican city of Labardee,[23] built of stone, and which was reduced to ruins by the Texans in their war with Mexico. The ruins of a stone church measuring 50 by 180 feet are still to be seen, a part of which is at this day occupied by Judge Lee, a Texan lawyer. Our Ohio lawyers would smile at the idea of such a residence. Opposite these ruins

[21]Ordinary prickly pear.

[22]Colonel James W. Fannin, Jr., with a force of more than 300 men, was intercepted in a retreat to Victoria by the Mexican general Urrea, commanding a much larger force, in March, 1836. Fannin erected a makeshift fort with units of his baggage train and held off the Mexicans until the latter were reinforced to the point where further resistance on the part of the Texans was useless. Fannin then unwillingly surrendered, and he and his men were taken to the presidio at Goliad, where most of them were executed. See George Lockhart Rives, *The United States and Mexico, 1821-1848* (1913); Chester Newell, *History of the Revolution in Texas* (1935), chap. ix; *Official Correspondence of the Texan Revolution, 1835-1836*, ed. William C. Binkley (1936), Vol. II.

[23]La Bahia, from Presidio Nuestra Señora de Loreto de la Bahia, the original Mexican site of Goliad.

is the town of Goliad,[24] a very small and wild-looking place. It contains a public house, one store, and a grocery. They grind their corn on windmills, with which every family is provided. The hopper is about twice as large as a common coffee mill. We found large patches of cactus of the prickly-pear variety, saw some at least five feet high. Several of the Texans have come into camp with mules for sale. The[y] ask from thirty to a hundred dollars and generally take much less than they ask. One of these Texans is suffering with chronic dysentery, contracted while a soldier in Mexico. He is a living skeleton, reduced to skin and bones, dragging out a miserable existence. After much jockeying, our party bought of him two mules and paid him $40. The night was cold.

Mar. 22. After making a few repairs to a wagon, all under way. Dr. Hutchinson and myself went in advance and, after traveling six miles, stopped at the only dwelling by the roadside. The owner, Mr. Lott, formerly of Mississippi, invited us to dinner with him, which proved to be a good one and for which he would accept of no pay. Here we found some of the company for Mississippi encamped, living upon the best the land affords. Our committee sent out to purchase mules returned to us at this place with twenty-one mules, having paid for each $35. Soon after leaving Mr. Lott's hospitable home, we passed through a rolling country grown up with *montes* of bushes, and at one place found acres of the prickly pear, some of which measured eight feet high. We encamped this evening on the prairie and each stood guard two hours, to keep our wild mules in camp during the night.

Mar. 23. I did not get to bed last night till 12 o'clock, and slept until aroused from my blanket by a call to breakfast. This over, we struck tents and started nearly all our mules to San Antonio for safekeeping. I mounted one of the tamest and

[24]Goliad was originally an important link in the mission-presidio system of Spanish Texas, but declined in importance when troops were withdrawn following the Mexican war for independence. See Federal Writers' Project, *Texas* (1940), pp. 648-49, for a brief description.

soon felt secure upon his back. They are, unless constantly used, the most treacherous animal in use. After riding about five miles, we halted in a small shade and waited for the teams to come up. This did not take place until 2 o'clock P.M., in consequence of a difficulty in finding the work cattle. We passed over a picturesque country of prairie nature, about thirteen miles this day, and found no water on the road. Encamped on Spring Creek, where we found a little standing water. The Spanish moss has wholly disappeared, and we now find occasionally some live oak and the percon [pecan?] tree, with bunches of the prairie willow.[25] Coffee is worth in this region eight cents per pound. Flour has been worth here, in the days of the Republic, $50 per barrel, but costs now $6.00.

Mar. 24. Cloudy, threatening rain. This is the first cloudy weather we have had in Texas. At noon we crossed the Claytto,[26] a small stream of good, cool water. To the next good water is fifteen miles. One of our men shot a small alligator in the Clayto, but the shot only proved a wound and he did not succeed in capturing the reptile. I have seen a number of the swifts, a species of the lizard. They are as quick as an arrow from the bow, and are found only in the sand banks. We have made this day twelve miles, and are now encamped in the edge of a large growth of prickly pear. Several other varieties of the cactus have appeared today, among which is found the ball cactus. The weather has been very hot.

Mar. 25 (Sabbath). Last night we experienced a very heavy squall, which lasted about two hours. We thought that our tents would be pulled from their moorings. This morning it is again cloudy, and some wind. The weather is much cooler than yesterday, and, in fact, fire is not unpleasant. R. Evans and O. H. Carpenter are cooks for today, and a fine figure they cut, in the preparation of our pork and coffee. At 8 o'clock our teams began to move, and shortly after Mr. Crittenden came up

[25]*Salix humilis*, a dwarf willow.
[26]Cleto Creek, a tributary of San Antonio River.

and reported all the mules escaped during the night from the corral, or yard. Horsemen were dispatched in every direction, and on our arrival on the Seevilla River,[27] we found them all in camp again, which was fortunate to us, as the government is now gathering them in for army use. The Seevilla is a clear and cold stream of water, but not very deep. It served the purpose of a bath for our wearied limbs, and well did we enjoy it. After the wagons came up we pitched our tents on the banks of this bubbling stream, and at nightfall stationed a guard, and all others retired to their several couches.

Mar. 26.   We were all up early and, breakfast over, we proceeded to filling our water vessels preparatory to passing sixteen miles of country destitute of wells, springs, or running water. We found on the banks of the Seevilla several families— one American woman living among men promiscuously. The others were generally white men with Mexican women. These women were dressed in the very cheapest manner, having generally nothing but a chemise and skirt to hide their charms, and this dress often failed of its desired object, being in rather a dilapidated condition. However, blushes were scarce in the faces of these almost nude damsels. They, the women, all smoke the *cigarettos*—a small quantity of fine tobacco rolled in a piece of corn husk—which is the only means of smoking enjoyed by the natives. I found today a splendid and new species of the cactus. It was a ball about as large as a pint cup, fluted, and bore a splendid pink blossom, and grew in the midst of stones and large rocks.[28] Another deer was killed today by one of the hunters, and now for a little more high life! The country passed over today is rolling and pretty well timbered, but no living water. This whole prairie country, particularly western Texas, is well adapted to an outdoor life. Everything necessary to sus-

[27]Cibolo Creek.

[28]For description of Texan and north-Mexican plants, see Frederick Adolphus Wislizenus, *Memoir of a Tour to Northern Mexico, connected with Col. Doniphan's Expedition, in 1846 and 1847* (30th Cong., 1st Sess., Sen. Misc. Doc. No. 26; 1848), pp. 87-115.

tain animal life is found here in great abundance excepting water, and this I think could be procured by digging wells. After traveling fifteen miles we again encamped in a mesquite[29] grove and here we were joined by Mr. Terry McKnight, Clark, and Spafford. Asa Wamsley and Dr. Bunnell left Lavaca on Friday last for [San] Antonio, and when we get there our company will number twenty-four persons. There was great rejoicing when these men came into camp, they being some of the few white men met with while on this journey. After supper we had a dance on the green to the music of the violin, upon which our friend Terry drew his scienced bow. At 10 o'clock, the camp sank to rest and we passed a night uncomfortably cool.

Mar. 27. Cloudy and windy. Broke up camp and traveled over a country of tolerably thick timber and traversed by deep, but dry, ravines. A pleasant dream of home and its pleasures was terminated this morning by a call to get up, and from the heighth of happiness I was aroused to the stern realities of a camp life in Texas. Several took dinner with a Castilian gentleman who resides on the banks of the San Antonio River. After dinner we traveled about five miles, making twelve miles this day. We encamped this night in view of a Spanish rancho. We passed the residence of Cassianno, a son of one of the daring men in the command of Lafitte, the pirate.[30] The father of this man now resides in San Antonio, having accepted of the pardon offered to those who would fight against the British at the battle of New Orleans. This house is very ordinary, but still the best on the road this side of Victoria. Robinson, who was tried in New York for the murder of Hellen Jewitt, is undoubtedly still living.[31] He was recognized by a New Yorker at the town

[29]Spelled by Evans, "muskeet."

[30]See above, p. 15, n. 14.

[31]On April 11, 1836, Helen Jewett, boarder in a house on Thomas Street, in New York City, was murdered, and the killer, in an effort to destroy evidence, burned bedclothes around the body. A clerk, Richard P. Robinson, was indicted, but was freed by means of a jury disagreement caused by testimony of a highly unreliable witness. The case was celebrated because of the im-

of Goliad, where a person fully answering his description is selling goods. To complete his disguise he now wears a tremendous beard. But all will not answer the purpose of one branded with crime and he was openly told in the presence of others that he should "go away, he was a murderer." This morning I had the pleasure of eating an excellent breakfast, at which a Spanish lady presided with much dignity.

Mar. 28. Cloudy, and slight rain. Traveled over broken and prairie country fourteen miles to a creek called the Slough.[32] Here we encamped, to await the return of our men sent forward to select a camp at San Antonio. Haller killed this evening a very large rattlesnake, numbering nine full rattles. The tea for this evening is over, and our plates, knives, and forks pushed to one side without the ceremony of a baptism in soap and water. Whilst some are engaged in angling, others are playing a game of euchre. This is done by first spreading a gum elastic coat upon the ground, and then the players are seated around, tailor-fashion, and much pleasure arises to the party engaged in this harmless manner of passing time in a dull, monotonous camp. Darkness is fast approaching, and we are seriously threatened with a thunder shower. This is the first thunder we have heard in Texas. The weather has been very dry and roads deep in dust. About half a mile from our camp is a camp of soldiers engaged in breaking cattle and mules to work. They are part of General Worth's command, preparing to open a road to Passo Del Norte,[33] with the intention of extending it through to California during the summer. Should this work be accomplished this will be one of the safest roads to California.

Mar. 29. Day broke, but we could not say, as did a happy fellow, "Let it break and be d——d; he owes me noth-

---

passioned plea of the defense attorney, Ogden Hoffman. See Charles H. Haswell, *Reminiscences of an Octogenarian of the City of New York (1816 to 1860)* (1896), pp. 319-20.

[32]Salado Creek, a tributary of San Antonio River.

[33]El Paso, then known as El Paso del Norte.

ing"; for it was our fortune—or misfortune—to meet daybreak drenched to the skin and our tents, hats, clothes, and every light article blown to a distance. We have, in Texan words, been overcome by a norther, in all its terrific fury. This terrible storm came on at 12 o'clock last night and lasted only half an hour, but so sudden was its approach that our tents and loose clothing were flying with the tornado before we could spring from our beds to secure them. I have experienced strong winds and very violent storms in Ohio, but they were nothing compared with this terrible norther. After the wind abated the rain began, and at daylight not a blanket or coat remained dry. Some of our men slept the after part of the night on ox yokes around the fire, and were thankful for this bed and the comfort they had in prospect. This storm was attended with thunder, loud and almost deafening, and vivid flashes of lightning. The roaring of the wind was so loud as to drown the noise of two trees that were thrown down by the wind in pistol-shot of the tents. After breakfast, we moved on to San Antonio River, distance seven miles, and encamped, for the last time in the river bottoms, on Camp Walker.[34] Here our wagons were discharged and paid off, and now comes packing by mules. The ground is covered over with pecans, which grow very plenty and of a superior kind. This fruit is much esteemed, and brings readily one dollar per bushel. An active person would gather from two to four bushels of these nuts a day. Another snake, measuring six feet in length, was killed in this day's march. It is of a dark brown color, slim, and extremely quick in its motions.

Mar. 30. A glorious morning. Cooks are washing dishes and the men airing and washing clothes. After my clothes were ready to hang out and take an airing, we started to town, mounted on horses and mules. San Antonio is situated on the banks of the river of the same name, with narrow, irregular streets all

[34]Named after Captain Samuel H. Walker, who, serving under Persifor Smith, was killed in action at Huamantla, Mexico, October 9, 1847.

terminating on the plaza.[35] The houses are chiefly of stone and cement, with level roofs and only one story high. The Catholic church, or cathedral, is a stupendous work of solid masonry. There are two ruins, of immense masonry work, within three miles of San Antonio, of which a more general description will be given hereafter. About two miles northeast of the town is the powder house, also of stone and cement. It is a square tower, perhaps a hundred feet high, tapering to the top. Near this place is the site of the encampment of Texans from which the bombardment of Antonio, then in Mexican possession, took place. At the edge of the town is the burial place of Walker and Gillespie,[36] who fell in an engagement in the Mexican War. A row of fine trees, called alamo,[37] are growing near the graves of these heroes. Myself, Mr. Carpenter, and R. Evans, a committee appointed for the purpose, procured the assistance of a guide to Chiahuahua, [and] discharged that duty by employing Mr. Charles Clark, a gentleman of good address, and said to be well qualified for the discharge of this duty. After making a few purchases we again returned to camp at sundown and found all well.

Mar. 31.   This day has been attended with some excitement, consequent upon the effort of our guide and selves in trying to tame our wild mules. This is always a job of some consequence, as the mule is a stubborn but cunning animal and never submits until brought under by the treatment they always get from persons accustomed to breaking them. The first thing done by our guide was throwing the lasso or lariat over the head of the mule he wished to handle first, and then the kicking and pitching by the animal followed, as a matter of course. If the mule did not submit, he next threw a lasso so as to catch him around one or both forefeet, and if he continued to kick, strike,

---

[35]The site of San Antonio was named in 1691 and settled in 1718 by the Spanish. The first settlement consisted of the Mission San Antonio de Valero and the adjoining Villa de Bejar, later spelled Bexar.

[36]Captain R. A. Gillespie.   [37]*Alamo* is the Spanish term for cottonwood.

and pitch, the leg lasso was passed over so as to inclose both hind legs below the fetlock joint and by a sudden jerk the mule was thrown on his side. This generally answered, yet some of our mules required further and harsher treatment than this. Our efforts thus far have been attended with partial success. Ten o'clock, and I am out on guard. Another evening in camp has been passed, and camp stories and camp songs had their time. Dr. Bunnell is one of the sweet singers of Israel and the songs from him are all good. His "Would I Were a Boy Again," is a song of much merit, and was sung by him with much applause. One of our party saw an elk, within a half a mile of the camp, but, for want of his rifle, failed in bringing his honor in. Wolves are the companions of our travels; at all events, they are heard every night. Sometimes they approach very near; at others they are heard at a distance. Texas is blessed with a fine climate and beautiful, moonlight nights. I love the night, the glorious night, when the camp is hushed and its fires low; 'tis then that thoughts of home and its domestic pleasures steal over our minds and with its balm softens man's harsh nature and hushes the tumults of his breast. Under such influences who can be unhappy—at least while he feels as if to forgive and forget real or imaginary wrongs is divine. Such are my feelings, and I wish them ever to be.

{ April, 1849 }

SAN ANTONIO TO THE
MEXICAN BORDER

Apr. 1. The day of rest, set apart for the good of mankind, is again upon us. The day opened warm and sultry, but towards noon became cooler. We have been engaged in hunting the lost mule, but so far without success. Some of our party returned this afternoon, the guide in advance, leading in a young heifer by the lasso. The animal, a splendid beef, was furious, and in a bold push to escape was thrown and broke its foreleg, and demolished a good saddle by the sudden check on the lasso, which was fast to the saddle of our guide. After the fall, this noble daughter of the prairies was permitted to rest and cool off a few hours; after which its life was cut short, and its flesh now is being jerked for the use of the boys in the mountain regions of the Far West. The tallow is used in softening boots, shoes, and straps, and the hide is speedily converted into ropes, straps, etc. The doctor is again singing his sweet songs, and "A Life on the Ocean Wave," in all its beauty, ravishes the senses and swells the breast. Who can remain unmoved amidst such scenes, and under the influences of such sweet sounds? All are in perfect health, at present, and good spirits.

Apr. 2. Cloudy, and slight rains. Some of our boys have gone to town, and the rest of us have been engaged in breaking mules. Some are brought under subjection by once throwing, while others are quite wild and furious. Carpenter and myself undertook to lead one out by the halter, a rope about thirty-six feet long, and we had rare sport. The mule took fright, and without a moment's notice we were towed up through the chaparral in double-quick time. Luckily for us, however, a tree in our path served as a snubbing post, and we brought our long-eared horse to an anchor, glad to get off so well.

There is excitement in the camp of rather a political character; at any rate, we have opposing candidates for the post of W.P. and W.A.[1]—terms used by us to escape the question in Mexico, "Are you a military organization?" For we have been told that no body of men answering in the affirmative to the above question will be permitted to pass through that territory.

While this election is pending, the friends employ every leisure hour to gain friends or votes for his favorite candidate, and logrolling is as well done here as at home. Evening came, and with it the election. Cameron, Carpenter, and F. Laubenheimer were the competitors for the post of W.P. On the first ballot, neither having a majority, a new vote was taken, and Carpenter of Perrysburg was elected by a majority of seven votes, and George McKnight, W.A., by a majority of four votes. By this election my party triumphed, and all parties submitted with a good grace and becoming cheerfulness.

Apr. 3.   Opened very pleasantly, and all hands went to work—some on mule harness, others to breaking animals to pack, and some in errands to town. The day passed free from any hard feelings, the result of our final organization, having a common head to look to. George McKnight has been sick with fever and diarrhea.

Apr. 4.   Morning cloudy, with heavy dew. One of our mules escaped from his moorings during the night, and after some time spent in hunting was brought into camp by Mr. Haller. The day was spent in making preparations to pack and depart.

Apr. 5.   A very warm day. Dr. B. F. Hutchinson, a member of our association, applied for leave to withdraw, which was granted. The doctor has no enemy in the camp, and this determination to withdraw and return home is much regretted by the whole camp. It gives me the pleasing opportunity of sending some things home. Work same as yesterday. Good news by a late arrival from Chiahuahua, in relation to the route. A

[1]Unknown terms. The usual title was "Captain" for the leader.

Californian died in San Antonio with the cholera last night.

Apr. 6.   Clear and very warm. Still in camp, but start tomorrow for the Far West. This day has been occupied in writing letters home and making other preparations for our departure from the frontier.

Apr. 7.   Aroused early and went to work. Packing mules and marching is not always as quickly done as is supposed by persons unacquainted with the nature of those animals. The whole day was spent in trying to conquer and to move on our journey, and when night came we had got from Camp Walker just two miles. And our trouble did not end with this. Rain set in, and the night was spent with nothing but the canopy of heaven for a covering.

Apr. 8 (Sunday).   Began the tedious operation of packing our mules at 6 o'clock, and word "forward" was given at 10 A.M. Some of the mules continued very unruly, and several packs were kicked off and then kicked to pieces. After some difficulty we encamped twelve miles west of Antonio at a tolerably good water hole. After the party had got in, a vote was taken and a wagon dispatched to Antonio with a part of our bread and one barrel of apples, with orders to sell at any price, the company being well satisfied that our load was too heavy. At 2 o'clock A.M. we experienced another norther, with considerable rain.

Apr. 9.   Lying in camp, awaiting the return of our wagon and party. Mr. Carpenter, our W.P., is very sick with bilious cholic. I had another turn at washing shirts, and, if I had warm water, could make a very good washer. At 4 o'clock P.M. it became cloudy and soon after a heavy rain set in, with loud peals of thunder and almost constant flashes of lightning. The rain continued at intervals until late at night, and although ditches were cut around each tent, the water fell so fast as to soak every tent—and pack saddles made good bedsteads. This is the life of soldiers and Californians, and all these freaks of fortune are borne with resignation. This camp is surrounded by some of [the] handsomest elevations of land that it has been my fortune to see. Handsome farms and gorgeous buildings spring up and are seen in the prospective future teeming with busy thousands. Here friends will part and meet with kind greetings and smiling faces and the welcome hand extended to the weary traveler in days to come. But adieu to fancy's pictures, and I will retire to my damp blankets, upon the saturated ground, and sleep sweetly and perhaps dream of my home and its many comforts.

Apr. 10.   Encamped, after traveling about nine miles, on a beautiful dip in the prairie on a small stream called, in Spanish, Royea in Madu,[2] or Middle River, but now dry, with the exception of the deep holes. Mr. Haller was taken today with the smallpox, and there being no way to avoid the contagion, we submit with the best possible grace.

Apr. 11.   This night we are on the Madena, upon which stream is the small town of Casterville,[3] a German town. It is of low buildings and contains perhaps forty or fifty families, and [is] only five miles from the Middle River and twenty-eight west of San Antonio. From one of the denizens of this town I learned that nearly all these Swiss came into Texas under the administration of President [Houston], second president of the Republic of the Lone Star, and consequently they were freeholders by virtue of the law granting to every head of a family a portion of the public domain on condition that he should settle upon and improve the land. These titles to land are called "head rights," and vexatious lawsuits have sprung up between Mexican and Texan claims to the same land. The banks of the Madena on the opposite side are very high and broken and covered with short, thick underbrush, presenting a very fine view. We find here the cypress tree, decked in its beautiful green, and

[2]Probably Medio Creek (*Rio Medio*).

[3]Castroville, Texas. Settled in 1844 as a colonization venture by Count Henri de Castro and twenty-seven emigrants, mostly Alsatians. The town struggled through famine, insect plagues, and cholera, and emerged a pleasant little Alsatian village, retaining many characteristics of its Rhenish origin. Population today, 865. The river Evans mentions is the Rio Medina.

'tis said to be very abundant and of large growth forty miles above us. The stealthy, crawling snake, of various kinds and sizes, is found on the ground and on the trees, and if a man wishes to fasten his mule to a tree he first looks up. It is raining now and has been during the afternoon. Our sick tent is about a half mile south of us, and the smallpox case is better. Mr. C. Speaker, who has been sick, is also reported better by our doctor. Our guide has lost favor among the boys—so much so that we will stay at this camp until we can be joined by a company now coming up. He is strongly suspected of being in league with either the guerrillas or Camanch[4] Indians. Of this we were notified by a person well [acquainted] with the guide, and his own conduct looks like treachery. But we have an eye on him, and he falls, at the first false step, without judge or jury.

Apr. 12.   Laid in camp all day and had our mules herded on the adjoining prairie. Dr. Bunnell, while out hunting, found an abundance of ripe mulberries. Game appears abundant, as the gobbling of turkeys is heard every morning. Sick some better.

Apr. 13.   Camp aroused at 4 o'clock and, after a breakfast made on coffee and pilot bread, packing commenced, and in a short time we were on our way. Four Texans joined us, but soon after halted, one of their company having been taken with the cholera. Camped thirteen miles from the Madena, at the side of a water hole, adjoining a colony of Swiss. They understand the Spanish language perfectly, and in fact have little use here for any other. The houses are all made of upright posts or sticks, placed with care about ten inches apart, crossed with small sticks and plastered with mud, and the house is then thatched with wild straw and the whole is ready to be occupied. The fences are of upright sticks. Corn is now about knee-high and looks well, and nothing else is seen growing. We have now

---

[4]Comanche. Most travelers through northern Mexico at this period were greatly impressed by the Indian danger, and yet very few actual encounters took place. Most of the warfare was between Mexican troopers (guerrillas, irregular provincial infantry) and Indian rangers.

twenty-four persons in our company, and our bread has been reduced to three barrels by sale and consumption, and in place of the bread we use pinole. This is ground corn, first parched and after being reduced to meal, two pounds of sugar added to each bushel of meal.[5] It is used in place of bread by all persons on a journey in this country, and a Mexican never drinks without mixing pinole in water. It is much esteemed and is pleasant and palatable as food or drink. We encamped early this day to rest our sick, and one company on its way to California has just passed us. They go with wagons and four months' provisions. Distance thirteen miles.

Apr. 14. Passed a night of rain and storm. Another norther, with all its chilling effects, paid us a visit of five, long, weary hours, without the ceremony of an invitation. We had chosen a fine spot for camp, and I anticipated a fine snooze after my guard hours, but my happy anticipations were dampened, at the moment the relief guard was called, by a perfect deluge of water. The rain descended for five hours, and the only protection we had was our saddle and other blankets, as we had no tent pitched. But we wore out the tedious hours and when day dawned our misery was complete. The day so far has been cloudy, with an occasional streak of sunshine. The country encamped on is chaparral, and stones (or, rather, rocks) make their appearance at the surface. I mentioned in my notes that our guide was strongly suspected of being leagued with robbers, and am happy to say that those suspicions have measurably subsided and comparative quiet and a feeling of security has taken its place. We pack as soon as our beds and saddles dry and move forward. The rain has raised the water in the holes of the Wee Hee,[6] a small and rather insignificant stream passing between our camp and the German colony spoken of. This colony is Catholic in

[5] A.B. Clarke (*Travels in Mexico and California* [1852]) describes a variation in the method of preparation: wheat soaked in hot water was put into frames to drain, then spread on hides to dry in the sun. It was then parched or baked in an oven and ground into flour, usually by a crude mule-mill.

[6] Quihi Creek, a tributary of Hondo Creek.

religion. Traveled over a broken and stony road about ten miles, and encamped on the banks of the Rio Hoonda or Deep River. This name is at present a perfect contradiction, as the bed is now dry, with the exception of a few holes. In these water is found, cold and clear. Our guide says that when he first became acquainted with Deep River there was a constant current of water, but that within a few years no water run in the channel unless in a very wet time. Every evidence of a subterranean passage for the water exists. These holes are often found with a current, although dry above and below, and some of them were filled to the depth of four feet by the last heavy rains, yet there is now no water in the most of them.

Apr. 15 (Sunday). The past night has been very cold, with a north wind, but luckily we passed it in tents. The morning is windy, but a cheerful sunshine dispels the sharpness of the wind. I visited a portion of the Rio Hoonda, half a mile below the camp, and found it a natural wonder. The water in past days has worked various channels through a barrier of rocks that cross the river here in a direction east of northeast, and in two places chambers, varying in depth and breadth, are left. These rise one above the other, and outside they form a perfect circle, with bold, projecting rocks. These chambers have been used by the wild-horse hunters and by them called corrals. The mustangs are surrounded by the hunters and gradually driven into these holes, and when once there are easily taken with the aid of the lariat or rope. I intended in these hasty notes to give a general description of Mission San Hosey[7] and Mission Conception, near San Antonio. These immense structures present the appearance of large and well-finished churches, at a distance, and when so seen are more charming than when [one is] actually in them. This arises from the fact that the many broken and fallen parts cannot be seen until the traveler is actually at the walls. San Hosey I did not get time to visit, but am told by those who did that it is superior in its construction to Mission Conception. The

[7]San José.

latter mission is a very large building, constructed of stone and mortar, or cement. The walls are four feet thick and about twenty feet high, with flat roof of [the] same material and same thickness. The main building, or body of the church (or cathedral), is finished off with a stone font for the holy water, and pulpit (of the same material), and Christ's image—also made out of stone and cement. There are also paintings in a rude state on the walls, representing the Virgin Mary, and another called by our boys the Ace of Clubs. Wings [are] of same material and construction, and each roof is supported by stone arches and partition walls. This immense pile of ruins once served as a prison and a place in which to worship, not God, but the Virgin, the mother of God. This is the building in which about 600 Texans, taken by the Mexicans in one of the battles of the revolution, were confined and afterwards barbarously shot by order of the tyrant dictator, Santa Anna. And even at this late day the signs of that inhuman massacre remain. On entering the church through the high, arched doorway the traveler is led to believe that he is walking on decayed chaff, when his steps are actually leading him over the dust of these noble sons of the Republic of the Lone Star. But they fell, and the city of San Antonio again passed into the power of that cold-hearted dictator, and for the twenty-fifth time in the past twenty-seven years did she change her masters. But the cry, "Remember the Alamo; remember Fanning, boys," was not heard in vain. It nerved hearts for battle, and after much suffering and many privations they had the proud satisfaction of flinging to the breeze the flag of the Lone Star, and to see its independence acknowledged by other nations.

Apr. 16.   Started at 7 o'clock, and after traveling about ten miles encamped on the banks of Peach Creek. After staking my mules, I took my gun and, after starting some turkeys, only killed a deer. Shortly after my return to camp a Mexican came in and reported 105 Camanche Indians within a mile or two, and the reader of these notes may well say, or think, that our camp was in a perfect state of excitement. At the same time this

35

Mexican had his camp a mile below us, and he had scarcely told of this menaced danger before the rifle's sharp crack and the dreadful Indian yell were distinctly heard by all in camp. Immediate preparations were made for our defense. The mules and horses were all brought in and closely picketed, and the pack and other saddles piled in the center for a breastwork. Double guards were stationed, and we awaited in suspense the expected attack. The attack on the Mexican camp below did not last long, and the only injury done was two horses shot by the Indians. Eight o'clock came, and a party of horsemen came up to the line, and I challenged. The answer was, "Californians," and we found them Texan Rangers,[8] and [they] were welcomed with gushing hearts and open hands. Their encampment was five miles in advance, and they had that day received a visit from these redskins. A consultation was called, and orders given to pack and march forwards. At 1 o'clock A.M. we arrived at the Texan camp, and, after staking mules and putting out a full guard, the camp became quiet. Our second camp was therefore on the banks of Rancho Creek, where we found tolerably good water but short feed.

Apr. 17. Moved forward at 8:00 A.M. and crossed the Rio Frio, and a very broken country and poor soil. The Indians hovered on our path all day, but did not attack us. We crossed this day some very high hills and met with several mounds or needles, and, after traveling about eighteen miles, encamped on a stony ridge, with poor grass. Our mules are getting very much fatigued. At 10 o'clock, after the camp had become quiet, the Indians, by way of a little sport, shot several arrows into camp and then left us.

Apr. 18. Started early and in a short time we crossed a beautiful stream called Rio Leona or Lioness River, and from thence to the Neueco River.[9] This river was low, but the water we found clear [and] cold, and [with] a beautiful, pebbly bot-

[8]See Walter Prescott Webb, *The Texas Rangers* (1935).
[9]Nueces River.

tom; and, after traveling about twenty-two miles, encamped in a mesquite thicket, grass short. A member of Captain Harvey's company died and was buried on the banks of the Neueces, without winding sheet or coffin.

Apr. 19. Started from our encampment at 1:00 P.M. and traveled ten miles, and again encamped on a beautiful rise of ground with good grass and poor water. This beautiful and productive spot we will call Camp Ohio, in honor of our own noble state. Here our jaded mules and horses were again permitted to eat all they required. Our camp was alarmed by a challenge and the firing of a gun at a thieving Indian who had come to the lines to spy our strength and equipment, but upon such a reception he did not think proper to stay long or make further observations. After the alarm subsided, all went to their blankets but the guards, and passed the night without further molestation.

Apr. 20. Pulled up stakes early, and in a short time passed the encampment of the Mississippi Mining Company, and, after about six miles' further travel, our advance guard was brought to a halt, and by the timely arrival of the train were probably saved bloodshed and death. Bullsheart, with his twenty-five warriors, was in our path, ready, as he said, to fight or keep peace. Our men were soon dismounted and the mules and horses quickly and strongly tied in the chaparral, and the men were drawn up for war. Our guide, who speaks their language, then held a parley with these redskins, and, after some time spent in this manner, they approached each other and the usual civilities were exchanged and presents given and a formal treaty of peace entered into, after which each party was permitted to proceed. After traveling twenty-seven miles this day, we encamped on a small grass plat by the side of a water hole, in a basin formed by the bleak and dreary-looking hills around us. Our horses were permitted to pick the short grass until dark, and then they were picketed down and a strong guard stationed around, and the rest of us went to bed on the ground and had the benefit of a little rain and—with the guard excepted—undisturbed slumber.

Apr. 21. Aroused at 4 o'clock, and soon after sunrise we were again riding along the road towards the Rio Grande, or Grand River, which stream we reached about 1 o'clock P. M. and found it very muddy and high. The stream here is about 150 yards wide. We had to go up this stream to the station occupied as a military station by the U. S. troops. We here found a healthy, cleanly, and gentlemanly set of fellows and were at once invited to charge on a pork barrel pointed out by one of these generous men. His invitation was politely declined, and we at once proceeded to fording the Rio Grande. This name has become intimately associated with the glorious victories achieved by our victorious troops, and every schoolboy has heard of and spoken the name of the Rio Grande and sung the praises of the old man in the brown coat,[10] under whose direction those battles were fought and won.

And this name, with that of the Rio Neuces, has been proclaimed from every stump, one party claiming to the Neuces and the other to the Rio Grande. But aside from this difference of opinion between the two political parties of the United States, the river now forms a part of the boundary line between our government and that of Mexico.

But I am digressing, and must say that we found a quick current and the stream just low enough to pass. One man lost his pistols and holsters and other things nailed on his saddle. Jacob Teats had some difficulty, lost his oilcloth overcoat, and waded out of the river. After all our mules, horses, and men had got over, we passed down the river two miles and encamped on Mexican soil, and now I must go on guard two hours and then to my blankets to dream and tomorrow I will tell you more of Mexico and its productions.

Apr. 22 (Sunday). Breakfast at daylight, packed and moved forward about three miles and here encamped on Hidden

[10]Zachary Taylor.

River—and a more appropriate name could not be given. This river runs in a deep, narrow channel, the banks are thickly studded with sycamore, mulberry, mesquite, and other trees, and the water is of a sky-blue color. Here we remain to feed our horses on the parched grass and to recruit our own weary energies. We find here, and for several days past have been admiring, the wonderful arrangement of our Creator. From the bleak, barren, and worse-than-unproductive hills is made to grow cacti of various species and beauty, one of which has been praised by every man. It springs from the earth in clusters and grows about a foot in length and resembles a large cucumber. The plant is now in bloom, and a handsomer flower or body of flowers never blessed the senses or graced a lady's window. Turkey, deer, and the Mexican lion and wildcat are found here. The shepherds are out on the plains with their sheep and goats, and we had a very fine kid roasted, which proved to be the best roast I ever ate.

Apr. 23.   Our wagons have all come up, and the Mississippi Mining and Trading Company is also encamped close by. It is reported that a company of Californians, numbering thirty, had been cut off by the Indians, only seven having escaped. This has induced us to join the above company, and negotiations are now going on for that purpose. We had another kid for dinner, and some goat's milk. Hail, as large as pullet's eggs, fell in camp. Four miles from here [there was] much injury to persons during the storm, several having been knocked down and horses stampeded or broke away.

Apr. 24.   Spent this day in camp to recruit our mules. Our own provisions are short.

Apr. 25.   Started at 8 o'clock in the morning, and in crossing a small brook my mule, with several others, mired down, but no injury but the mud. Encamped this evening late, one mile west of San Fernando,[11] a Mexican city containing

[11]For a general description of this section, see Francis Baylies, *A Narrative of Major General Wool's Campaign in Mexico* (1851).

about three thousand inhabitants. In this camp we found grass very scarce, but were compelled to adopt this for want of better. Threatened rain, with thunder and lightning.

Apr. 26. Still in our poor-grass camp, and feed our mules corn to keep them up. We stay here to provide for the five hundred miles of wilderness that lies between here and Chiahuahua. Extra mules, half a bushel of pinole, one peck of *bizcocho* (or Mexican hard bread), some beef and some pork, will complete our arrangements, and then we are off. I am truly sorry to be called upon again to record the determination of seven of our company to return to their homes, after having accomplished more than half the distance. I commenced this record with the firm determination to write out the history of every important transaction, and to this end I will give the names of those who, at the eleventh hour, see fit to abandon this enterprise. They are the following named gentlemen: Rinaldo Evans, H. Crittenden, S. L. Cameron, M. M. Cameron, John C. Terry, Asa S. Wamsley, and George W. Clark, the last named from Perrysburg, Wood County, Ohio. But joy go with them, and, if life and health are spared, I go to California. I am now in the city of San Fernando, where I shall remain during the night. This is a place similar to San Antonio, Texas, built in the same order of architecture. My intercourse with its denizens has thus far been pleasant, they in all cases far surpassing me in politeness, consequent upon my habits of real Yankee don't-careativeness. I had the high honor of dining with, and at the table of, the Alcalde, or mayor of the city. The first course consisted of a saucer of rice boiled with onion tops and mixed with eggs; next followed a saucer of hashed meat; and the third and last course was bean soup. Our guide told me while eating that, to follow the customs of the Mexicans, a knife, fork, and spoon were unnecessary, [and] that I must drink the soup as I would coffee. The bread in general use here is *tortillas*, or thin cakes of corn, eaten warm. I witnessed the custom of a funeral procession today. Two little boys in red uniforms bore the Cross, followed by the priest; then came the coffin on the shoulders of four men, next the friends of the deceased, and in the rear of the procession was a person carrying the *lid* of the *coffin.* The coffin was made of rawhide, and the borders and outside traversed with tape. During the marching of the procession, the church bells were tolled, and all persons in and out of the procession uncovered their heads. The ladies are very small and generally display small, naked feet, pendant breasts, and naked arms. The[y] are fond of their *cigarettos,* and smoke almost constantly. We this day packed our clothing in sacks and disposed of our trunks at low prices. Clothing, such as pantaloons, vests, and shirts, meet[s] with ready sale. I shall once more sleep under a roof and within walls, and almost regret that I did not go to the camp. However, I will be permitted to sleep on the floor. Had some rain.

Apr. 27.   Arose early and walked out to the camp, and immediately commenced packing for a move to better grass. This we found about four miles out, and, after arranging my goods and chattels and attending to the distribution of some of the company stock and the settling of company debts, I took my mules and went to town. Here I remain overnight for a load of provisions, and then I start for the camp and the wide, unbounded West. California, the land of my search, still lies many leagues in advance, but with the blessings of a just and righteous God, I expect to reach its limits and be enabled to reap its benefits and assist in alleviating the wants of misery consequent upon the misfortunes of my fellow beings. These hasty attempts at a written description of the country and the incidents of our journey will close the first book of my notes, and I hope that its perusal will be ample payment for the time spent by the reader; and, until the appearance of the next book, adieu.

BOOK SECOND

Apr. 28.   This was a day long to be remembered, as it was accompanied with great labor in the preparation and collection of provisions and mules, and the departure of our companions to their several homes. We paid for mules from forty to fifty dollars and for *bizcocho* and pinole from two to three dollars and as high as six dollars. The men despatched for the purpose of purchasing these several necessary articles returned to camp at ten in the evening, and, after an equal distribution of the provisions, we all lay down and rested until daylight, then drank a cup of coffee.

Apr. 29 (Sunday). Started after breakfast and traveled over a barren, hilly country, with tall peaks showing their blue heads in the distance, until we struck a mountain stream, on the borders of which we halted and rested several hours. Here we found the first springs of water and a small patch of grass. After refreshing our mules and, of course, ourselves, we started for the next grass and water, and, after a fine, moonlight ride of eighteen miles, we encamped on dry grass, and no water.

Apr. 30. Arose early and saw, as if within a few miles, the tall and rugged peaks of the mountains before us, blue as the countenance of a disappointed fair one. After breakfast we packed, harnessed, and mounted, and traveled thirty miles, nearly all the way over a level, barren waste and expecting every moment to commence the ascent of the tall mountains before us. At eighteen miles from our starting point we found a water hole, and our parched tongues in both man and beast were again benefited by this liquid's cooling effects. After filling up our vessels and skins, we moved forward, crossed two fine streams of water, and again encamped nine miles east of Santa Rosa, on no grass, at 8 o'clock P.M.

{ May, 1849 }

THE MEXICAN BORDER
TO SAN CARLOS

May 1. Started early and moved forward four miles and here we found tolerably good grass and an artificial channel with fine running water. Here we remain until our mules rest and feed up. Cloudy, with slight rain in the morning. Three members of the Mississippi Company have died with the cholera in the past two weeks and another man is now lying sick. From this encampment we have a grand view of the Sierra Madre Mountains, the tops of which are veiled in mist and clouds, and we will shortly be brought to confront its rugged and shattered sides; and when we have passed this bound of our view we will be able to look into the world beyond.

May 2. After a brilliant evening it clouded up and at 2 o'clock rained a very little, and the day so far has been cloudy with some rain. Our company is now called the Ohio Company and consists of the following named men, to wit: O. H. Carpenter, S. P. Johnson, G. W. B. Evans, J. H. Chace, Dr. Bunnell, A. J. Spafford, George McKnight, D. Kinzer, F. Laubenheimer, Jacob Teats, A. T. Parker, Wesley A. Haller, Elias Brunner, Charles Speaker, and J. G. McCauley. This company is now traveling in connection with the Mississippi Mining Company, and the general duties of the camp are discharged without complaint. Sickness has been in camp and four men have been consigned to the tomb, having died from cholera, and a Mr. Steel will in all probability be called from among us in an hour. We are still lying in camp, gathering all the strength we can for the mountainous country before us. This afternoon Mr. Chace and myself paid a visit to a rancho (or farm) one mile below camp. We found four families occupying an enclosure of about an acre, surrounded by a mud and stone wall

43

with but one entrance. The ladies were dressed in the usual custom of chemise, wide around the breast and consequently open,
over which they wore a skirt. A scarf served the double purpose
of bonnet and shield of the breasts.

The men were dressed neatly with the exception of the
patriarch. He wore no shirt, short breeches, broad-rimmed hat,
and sandals on the feet. I have found several very old men and
women, several of whom were blind. They live by grazing cattle, mules, horses, sheep, and goats, and cultivate small patches
of ground. Nothing can be raised here without watering or
irrigating their farms, and to do this water is brought in ditches
for miles and discharged through the furrows over the lands
cultivated. Their plows are of the same material and pattern
used by the ancients and described in Bible history, and make
about the same impression upon the earth that one of our heavy
iron harrows make[s].

May 3 & 4.   Last night we had another short rain, with
loud thunder and vivid lightning. The morning broke cloudy,
but cleared up and became very warm. We remain in this camp
all day, but have orders to march forward in the morning. I have
in my notes but slightly alluded to Mexican customs, and shall
therefore touch lightly upon this topic. There are, as near as I
can learn, three classes. The first are the regular descendants of
Castilian or Spanish blood and are characterized by a desire to
gain knowledge, and are ambitious and industrious and generally intelligent. The next class comes from a mixture of Spanish
with Indian blood—and if an American makes anything off of
these in trade, he may be pronounced an early riser. The last
class is of Negro and Indian origin, indolent and very cowardly.
These live from hand to mouth, are very talkative but exceedingly ignorant, so much so that they must make calculations on
their fingers if inquired of *"Quanto lavos por ouva,"*[1] or "How
far to the next water?"—although they may have come from it
within the last half hour. The first class are habitually polite

[1]Probably *"Cuantas leguas por agua?"*

and attentive, and the latter is composed of peons or slaves and exercise politeness only when among their superiors. Snakes, toads, lizards, fleas, and lice are very numerous, and that abomination of Mexico, the tarantula (or very large spider), can be found here abundantly. This insect is abhorred by all persons acquainted with its habits. It is as venomous in its bite or sting as is the rattlesnake,[2] and great care is observed in spreading our blankets to know that none occupy our beds. Lizards frequently come into the tents, and can be heard running over them at almost any time.

I mentioned in my notes of yesterday a visit to a neighboring rancho, and must again refer to it in order to more fully illustrate the character of that class of Mexicans known as peons, or slaves. This rancho is wholly occupied by this order, as are all others, for the rich owner lives in town, and his slaves are on the farm. As it happened, a Negro belonging to one of the Mississippi Company went with us, and this "colored gemmen" was received by the peons with far more distinction than ourselves, although we were of a lively tinge and would not be taken in the States for white men. The only chair unoccupied was, with every demonstration of delight, handed to the Negro and taken by him, while we poor fellows were permitted to stand.

It is notorious that the woolly-headed, thick-lipped African is regarded with more favor and affection than an American by the peons.

May 5. After deciding to procure another guide before passing the mountains, this camp was broken up and we marched ten miles, with the mountains on our left, and passing through Santa Rosa. This city is of the same order with all Mexican cities passed on this route, but of greater age and in a more dilapidated condition. The cathedral is still used but crumbling to dust. A nunnery—or, rather, its walls—are still standing and look as if it had never been used. Here we found beautiful shade and fruit trees, among which may be enumerated the pecan, fig,

---

[2]The tarantula's sting was greatly overestimated as a cause of death.

45

orange, and peach trees. Here is also a nursery devoted to cultivating the century and other plants. Within four miles of Santa Rosa are rich silver mines, worked by Mexicans. Our camp is five miles west of the city and not far from the mountains, with good grass and running water. Here we shall probably remain a day or two. Mr. Steel is getting well.

Cloudy, and a strong prospect of more rain. The Sierrea Madre range of mountains lies in our front and there is a line of mist extending along the side for miles, concealing the middle but leaving the base and summit exposed to view, presenting a sublime view. These mountains are said to be rich in ores of silver and lead, but to the Mexicans afford little profit, for want of the right application of labor.

We had a camp visit from Dr. Long, who resides in the city of Santa Rosa and is a native of Pennsylvania. He has been in this country several years and could scarcely be distinguished from a Spaniard. He says that the United States ought to have as its boundary this range of mountains,[3] as it would require a less number of men and less money to defend our national rights, and that the people of this portion of Mexico were very anxious, at the close of the war, to be included as a part of our newly-acquired possessions. This gentleman once took the city of Santa Rosa with only ten men, when there was a force of Mexican soldiers to the number of 250 stationed here. The doctor's father-in-law is a Spaniard, a well-educated man, once governor of this state.

Through some act of his, political hatred and envy caused his friends to charge him with treason, and upon trial he was condemned to suffer death. Dr. Long was notified of the horrible and unjust sentence pronounced against his father-in-law, and by prompt and energetic action came to the edge of the city with ten men and two U. S. wagons, and by surrounding the herald and his escort they (the doctor's party) were enabled to provide themselves with arms and ammunition. This being done,

[3]The Serranía del Burro.

the doctor sent in one of the prisoners, an officer, with orders to tell certain families, including his father-in-law's, to march by his camp up the mountains, and that in the event of a refusal on the part of the city authorities to comply with this request, not one stone should be left lying on the other in two hours from that time. This ruse had the desired effect. Mexican cowardice came under, and at the end of the stipulated time he had the proud satisfaction of seeing his aged relative, at the head of the city authorities, coming forward to negotiate a peace, with a formal declaration of rights and full immunities to each party. This timely movement of the doctor's party saved the life of his wife's father and gave the doctor an ascendancy over the cowardly population of the city such as few men possess. He lives a nabob among them, and his word is generally of more force than Mexican laws.

May 6 (Sunday). Pleasant in the early part of the morning, but it is now *munch colora*,[4] or much warmer—indeed, quite sultry. The advance guard is just starting for the mountains to reconnoiter and explore a wagon pass. The train will move forward gradually until this guard reports, and if favorable we all march on to Chahuahua without any other than necessary stoppages. Our camp was thrown into great excitement by the report this afternoon that George Richardson had accidentally shot himself. Drs. Slack and Bunnell, Mr. Chace, Judge Tippin, and myself started for the scene of the melancholy accident. When we arrived George was dead, one ball and two buckshot having been discharged into the right side and passing out on the back, a little below the shoulder. Poor fellow, he has passed from a life full of hope and expectation, and now lies in his blanket beneath the clod of the valley. His grave is on the bank of the Rio Sabinia[5] and is fully marked by eight large cypress trees standing in a straight row and immediately on the water. At his head is a stone, marked in a rude manner by the letter R. This grave is six miles west of Santa

[4]From the expression, *Hace mucho calor.*   [5]Rio Sabinas.

Rosa. Colonel Watson, Mr. Glenn, Judge Tippin, and myself
were appointed by the company his administrators, and have
just taken an inventory of his effects. The list of personal property is small and may be found on the flyleaf of this book in
pencil mark.[6] As soon as the advance guard comes into camp,
this property will be sold, and the money held subject to the
demand of his heirs.

   May 7. Aroused the camp at daybreak and after breakfast packed and started. After traveling twelve miles parallel
with the mountain over a dry plain, we again encamped on the
waters of Cypress River, or Rio Sierrea Madre, a beautiful and
the largest stream met with thus far, excepting the Rio Grande.

   [6]Property belonging to George Richardson, deceased: 1 double-barrel shot-
gun; 1 six-shooter pistol; 1 belt and butcher knife; 1 small P mirror; 1 brass
compass; $2.25 cash; 1 comb; 1 bay mare, saddle, and bridle; 1 white mule;
1 brass key; 2 caps and handkerchiefs and satin vest; 3 check and 1 flannel
shirts; 1 pair pantaloons and 1 coat; 1 cannister powder; 1 pair boots and 1
pair socks; 1 lot of nails and buttons; 1 pair of kiacks; 5 combs; 1 butcher knife,
shot and lead; 1 pack saddle and ropes and 1 S blanket.
   Account of property sold by Watson, Evans, Glenn, and Tippin, belonging
to the estate of George Richardson, deceased. Sold May 18, 1849:

1 cotton shirt	sold at	8/-	Vaughn	Paid	1.00
1 ” ”	” ”	9/-	Laubenheimer		2.12
1 ” ”	” ”	11/-	”	Paid	1.37
1 flannel shirt	” ”	4/-	Vaughn	Paid	.50
1 cannister of tea	” ”	4/-	Floyd		.50
1 oilcloth cap	” ”	4/-	Vaughn	Paid	.50
1 ” ”	” ”	2/-	”	Paid	.25
1 pair boots	” ”	8/-	Clark		1.00
1 compass	” ”	8/-	Vaughn	Paid	1.00
1 P flask	” ”	2/-	Wm. Lott		.25
1 frock coat	” ”	8/-	D. J. White		1.00
1 panama hat	” ”	8/-	Watson		1.00
1 pair kiacks		16/-	Coleman	Paid	2.00
1 knife		3/-	Calcote	Paid	.37
1 pair pantaloons		4/-	J. Lott		.50
1 six-shooter knife & belt			Watson		5.50
1 bag of traps		4/-	Jimison	Paid	.50
1 double-barrel shotgun			Clark		7.50
1 riding saddle			Haller	Paid	3.50
1 bay mare			Howell	Paid	15.50
1 pack saddle & blanket			R. White	Paid	5.75
1 white mule & rope			Howell	Paid	19.00
handkerchief & vest		2/-	Coleman	Paid	.25

At this encampment, and along the road, we find the ball cactus, bearing a beautiful ripe fruit of purple color and about the size of the egg plum. Here game exists. The wild turkey's notes were heard but a short distance from camp at an early hour this morning, and fish of the bass and sucker tribe are caught out of this noble little river. The atmosphere is very pure and healthy, and the mountains look beautiful. Some of our men started to them on a visit, and I am satisfied that if they reach them it will be at the end of eight or ten miles' travel, although the distance does not appear more than one mile. We have good grass here, and the water is not very warm, pure as crystal. The wind was very high this evening, with a few drops of rain, but it all passed off, and the night was illuminated by the reflection of the burning prairies beyond the mountains.

Our road has come to an end, and now for several hundred miles we will be wholly dependent upon the knowledge and sagacity of our guides, two of whom go with us to Chiahuahua, and for their services we pay $380.

May 8.   Glorious morning, indicating, however, a very, very warm day. 2 o'clock P. M.: warm, with little air. Three men of the advance guard have just returned with the cheering news that the mountain pass is practicable and that they had gone through—concluding, however, that some hard work would have to be done in order that wagons might pass. Tomorrow morning we move to the mouth of the pass, and when this is accomplished one thing can be said: that Yankee ingenuity has prevailed and that a work, considered impossible by Mexicans, has been accomplished by a small squad of Americans—and that, too, with wagons. This road (or pass) shortens the distance to Chahuahua about five hundred miles, with good grass and occasionally a water hole. The Natches California Company have gone by way of Saltillio,[7] and will require at

⁷Saltillo. This route, as taken by McNeil and others, avoided the long, waterless stretch of mountainous desert due west of Santa Rosa. According to McNeil, the town contained a population of about 8,000 in 1849. *McNeil's Travels*, p. 15.

least twenty more days than we do to reach the same point—
provided both parties have good luck. The fires burning along
the mountains are the result of some of the acts of our advance
and not (as was supposed) of Indian origin. No Indians have
been seen by our advance.

May 9. Very warm, but with considerable wind. Commenced our march at half past eight for the mountains, and are
now just six miles from the mouth of the pass, about half surrounded by a raging fire, but measurably protected by the river,
which forms a semicircular side to our camp. A capful of wind,
bearing a single spark over the water, would be certain destruction to us, and should we be so fortunate as to escape with
our lives, our mules and property must be lost to us. But to
retreat were madness, and with the blessing of God we may yet
escape. Should the wind fall, the danger is over, but should it
increase, we are then indeed dangerously situated. It is now
sundown and the smoke is rolling from our side of the mountains in large clouds. The wind has fallen, and the fire bordering on our camp is smouldering, not out, and we feel that our
threatened danger from that source has disappeared. We found
some very fine and large fish in this stream, although we are now
within a few miles of its source and one mile from the base of
the mountain. This mountain is not less than three nor over five
hundred feet high, and its sides are cut into cones, caves, and
ravines by the action of the descending waters—waters that have
rolled at intervals for ages past.

May 10. The camp was called at 4 o'clock, and, as soon
as breakfast was over, we took up our line of march, crossing
Cypress River at the camp, and then traveled with the mountains on our left for five miles over the burned district, at the
end of which we turned to the left and entered a very stony
but dry bed of a river, which introduced us at once to the pass
called Santana Pass by the Mexicans. Here every variety of
scenery presented itself to the eye. The sides of the pass were
in places over two hundred feet high, perpendicular, and looked

as if a master mason had put up the walls. In the crevices grew the cucumber cactus, robed in its beautiful purple blossom, and at the end of the dry bed could occasionally be seen a new and beautiful variety of this plant, bearing a rich yellow flower. Ten miles from the entrance of this wild and unfrequented pass we found good, warm water and good grass, and encamped on the stony bed of the river in the shade of the lofty, the mighty, peaks of the Sirrea Madre Mountains. The wagons in our train may be said to be the first that have passed through this key to either world since the Spanish crown held dominion over Mexico. Our Mexican guide pointed to the top of one of those lofty, natural walls and said that if California was on top Americans would reach it, in spite of walls or anything else. They feel perfectly secure when a train such as ours passes through their country, and no one man of Mexico could be induced to guide the same number of men of their own nation over this or almost any other route. The[y] repose no confidence in their people, whether civilian or soldier, but Americans with money can command their services on almost every application. There is music to my ear, as Jacob is calling to tea. Tea over, J. Teats and myself started for the mountains. After walking about a mile of tolerable level plain, we gradually ascended for a short distance, and then came the tug, as we had to go up, upward and onward to reach the lofty top of this peak. But, with the declaration that "a faint heart never won a fair lady," we began to ascend, and after a toilsome march, over rocks and through brambles, we gained the top and enjoyed a splendid view of the mountains, valleys, passes, ravines, and rivers within reach of vision. I tied a handkerchief to a stick and waved it in triumph over the valley below. Our two camping grounds were in sight, and the horses and men looked as mere toys. The river or dry bed through which we had passed looked as a small ravine in the depths below, of silver-sanded bottom, and wound in graceful form through the pass into the plains beyond. Glorious sight, refreshing view, and heavenly picture, worthy of every effort

that man could make to obtain but a glimpse of this surrounding
paradise! This mountain is rounding on the top, having at each
end a slight elevation, one of which I called Jacob's and the
other George's Peak, believing that no other white men ever
stood on their tops before.

May 11.   After breakfast a few men were detailed to go
up the pass and clear a road over some of the tableland. Myself,
Judge Tippin and son, and Levi started for the top of a neighboring peak. We walked as fast as circumstances would permit,
and at 11 o'clock reached the top of a peak which we judged
to be five hundred feet above the dry bed in which our camp
was located. Here we had another glorious prospect, one that
delighted and instructed. But we did not gain this immense
height without labor, but found ourselves there after much toiling, fatigued and almost powerless. After resting and recovering our wind and a full enjoyment of the exciting scene before
us, we reluctantly began our descent and in a few hours arrived
safely in camp and partook of a good dinner: coffee, pancakes,
and fried pork. Orders were issued at 2:00 P. M. to pack and
march, and by 3:00 P. M. the train was under way and in a very
short time passed Giant's Castle, an immense pile of perpendicular rock, forming a circular opening inwardly; the height
of these stupendous walls were supposed to be at least a thousand feet and surmounted by rocks, turret-like in their appearance. The road passes in the water at the foot of this work of
nature and the traveler shudders at the thought of the loose
rocks, suspended, as it were, by a hair, many, many yards over
his head. The road traveled over today has been very rough,
being over a very rocky portion of the pass; we only made five
miles, or fifteen from the entrance, making half way, and encamped on tolerably good grass and excellent water opposite
Word's Tower—named in honor of our gentlemanly commander. Word's Tower is a perpendicular wall of tremendous
height and a gentleman in our company said it favored the castle
of Chepultepec in all its parts. It is truly a wonderful and awe-

inspiring work of nature, and I exclaimed in my heart: "How wonderful, how sublime are Thy works, oh, God! showing how diminutive man is when compared with this." At the foot of this immense tower flows a beautiful stream, which is found only at intervals, as it runs part of the time in subterranean passages and in all probability is a part of Rio Sabinia or Cypress River.

May 12. Broke up our camp early and started up the pass over a very rough and rocky road. The morning was clear but very warm, and at 8 o'clock the sun appeared to us. This was our sunrise, caused by the high mountains on each side of our narrow passage. Man is incapable of realizing the beauty and sublimity of scenery in this pass unless he has had the experience—unless he has had a soul large enough to attempt their passage and see and feel the force and effect of Nature's teachings. This camp is now about three thousand miles from my much-loved home and the dear ones I left behind, but my goal lies still upward and onward, and many weary days will pass before I can taste the sweets of home again, even if life should be prolonged. Twelve miles this day, full of rich and glorious and delightful scenery. Found the century plant growing wild and was told that it furnishes a drink[8] similar to our whisky, and that bags are manufactured from its fibers by the Mexicans. We are very much annoyed by the buffalo gnat in this pass—an insect that needs no description here.[9] A shower of hail, with some thunder and lightning, is the closing event of this day—and now to bed, to dream of home and its pleasures.

May 13 (Sunday). Sun rises directly in our path this morning and at an earlier hour than it did yesterday. The weather is much cooler, so that a coat and vest are indispensable articles and had to be taken from their place in a bag where they have reposed for days past. We keep the Sabbath here, and have good grass and fine water for our jaded animals. We are

[8]Pulque.

[9]Genus *Simulium*. Sometimes caused the death of livestock by their voracious stings.

now encamped about four miles from the south end of this wonderful pass and see a change in the appearance of mountains and valleys. This is caused by our ascending at every step we take; the ranges of mountains seem to be lower and the valleys wider. But all this arises from our elevation, and when traveling on the tableland we are at times from one to two hundred feet above the river below. Fish are abundant—of the speckled trout, bass, sun, and a few catfish, with other varieties. They afford fine meals to our epicures and sport to the angler. Bears are very numerous and occupy as their beds the yawning caverns and caves in these rocks and hills. The Mexican lion, panther, and Mexican hog are also found in these wilds. This hog is dangerous, although small, and fights everything that will stand and give battle; but the lion and panther are rather shy of man and but seldom seen. 12 o'clock M. and our advance guard has just returned to camp without discovering water. Clark, the guide, left the guard under the pretense of making further search for water, but has in all probability left the company and gone over to the Indians. But whatever scheming he may do will be promptly met by us, unless taken in ambush. The company now numbers eighty-four men, all able to do duty, and is headed by men experienced in Indian fighting. The advance found a fresh Indian trail leading to the north, crossing our path. At 4:00 P.M. we had a very heavy rain with some hail. This may prove a blessing to us in more ways than one. Grass will improve and the holes in the plains may be filled by this much-needed beverage. According to the best of our information, it is now twenty-four miles to the next water hole and a strong probability that this is dry—and should this be the case, the distance to the next water will be eighty-four miles, under a burning sun. Our India-rubber bags, canteens, gourds, and goatskins have been prepared to supply our wants with this very much needed beverage, needful because very scarce on this route. At 4:00 P.M., the rain having ceased, we struck tents and moved forward one mile, and here found tolerable grass and the water extremely hard to get at. The river here runs through the wildest and most dense thicket I ever saw, so thick that men with axes could scarcely penetrate. After much labor we got a road sufficiently wide to lead mules and horses to water, and here, it is said, the last water is found for eighty-four miles. In this narrow passage we met with a plant, the leaves of which stick to our pants as well; the attachment is as strong as Hutchinson's Salve, and is equally green in color, and we look as if we had been patched with green. Had another little rain, and lightning all night.

May 14. Moved one mile further up the creek and loaded water. Our mess consists of F. Laubenheimer, Jacob Teats, A. T. Parker, and myself, and three men with a wagon, having in all fifteen horses and mules to provide for. We have therefore taken on about sixty gallons of this pure element, and if fortunate can get through to the next water without much suffering. Left the head of this water and traveled about twenty-four miles east and encamped on good grass. Myself and ten others went two miles east of the camp after night and dug for water until midnight, but without success.

May 15. Were aroused at 2:30 o'clock, and after a very hasty breakfast moved forward. The night was a cold one, with some dew, and our poor mules were much benefited by it. At length the sun shone over the mountain to the east of us, and in a few hours woolen coats were cast aside and shirt and pants alone remained. After traveling about sixteen miles we halted to graze our horses, and sent a company forward to dig for water—and if ever a poor, suffering community prayed for God's special interposition, we are jointly that community. Our mules are much in want of water, and we have given them but about one gallon each, not daring to venture too deeply. Forty, and perhaps fifty, miles more remain to pass ere reaching the water, and this cannot be done before tomorrow night, under a broiling sun. Our path (for ours is the first wagon train) is but a trail or Indian path, and over a rough road. A party of Indians have just gone to their homes from a robbing—and murder-

ing—expedition over this trail, and we have consequently found
a dead colt and two bulls, all having perished with thirst. They
committed their depredations at Monclova,[10] and then started
a party off with their cattle and horses, and the others remained
at a short distance from our pass, in ambush, awaiting their pur-
suers. Twelve Mexicans followed—and one was left to return
and tell of the bloody butchery of his companions. This is but a
sample of the treatment these poor, cowardly Mexicans receive
from the Camanche Indians. This tribe has sworn eternal enmity
against Mexicans, and they are executing their threats; and the
poor, miserable, driveling Mexicans must meet their fate, for
they have no American government to protect them. We are
now upon a large plain with no shade but our wagons and a few
flaming-sword trees, the latter affording but very little of that
comfort. Our guide is in the bordering mountains searching for
water. 3 o'clock P. M.—guide has returned without finding any
water, and again we march. After marching through a narrow
pass, we landed high above and passed over a very dry and beautiful plain, and at dark encamped on good grass, without water,
hoping that the dews of heaven would fall and supply our animals' wants. Half a gallon of water to each of our mules has
been this day's allowance, and our animals are almost perishing
with thirst.

May 16.   Started at 6 o'clock and marched on as fast as
the jaded condition of our poor animals would permit, and encamped in a point of the mountain, and here we found water,
but extremely difficult to get at. We found it in holes worn into
the rocks, at least two hundred feet above our camp, and to
this elevation, over rocks and difficulties of every shape, we
made our way, our famishing animals following at our heels.
Here all were satisfied in a measure; but when through there
was not any left.

Mr. Bullock, of our mess, went into a deep, dark ravine, and
found excellent cold water, in a hole to which the rays of the

[10]Now known as Coahuila.

56

sun have never penetrated. To us this was a blessing, for many of our men were in a famishing condition, ready to lie down and die. I was under the painful necessity of refusing a drink to my fellow-traveler today, not having any to give. Mules were begging in their peculiar manner for a drink, but none to give. Poor men and animals! I hope it may never be my case to see so much suffering for water. We passed two dead cows, having perished within a few miles of this water. The[y] belonged to the stolen caveyard,[11] and were left by the Indians. Three miles from our camp, and just over a small mountain, is a stream of running water, strongly occupied by Indians. To this we must go, and a fight will probably be the consequence—and the result cannot now be told. This day's march has been over a beautiful plain, with good grass, and our camp is this evening about seventy-five miles from the last water. It is useless for any set of men to think of supplying themselves or animals with water on this route by digging wells, as the country is too high and dry to yield anything like water. The water here is found only in the ravines that pierce the sides of these two mountains, and only in holes in the rocks. Colonel Watson, Charles Clark, and several others who had gone in search of water have not yet returned to camp, and serious apprehensions for their safety are entertained. If they have not reached the water beyond the mountain, they will in all probability perish.

May 17. Stood guard two hours last night, after which I slept until daybreak, when the whole camp was aroused by the coming in of Colonel Watson, Clark, and others, all in a famished condition. The last day had been passed by these poor men and their animals without a drop of water, and Colonel Watson's tongue was so much swollen that it was almost impossible for him to articulate the word "water." All were rejoiced to see them come in alive, and everyone was ready and willing to supply their wants and ease their sufferings. They

[11]From Spanish *caballada*, or group of horses. The American cowboy corrupted this term into "cavayard," or "cavvey-yard."

found water, but could only see it at the distance of many miles, they being a thousand feet above it and on the edge of a perpendicular precipice, and could only imagine how delightful its taste would be. Their sufferings were much increased by this sight, and torment became a double torment. After breakfast, we started with our mules for the newly-discovered water. We passed down the side of the mountain about two miles and then turned in at the mouth of a ravine grown up with various kinds of brambles and underbrush. Here our labor began—and a more tedious piece of work I never assisted to perform. We led our horses and mules up the side of this ravine as far as they could go, and then, with sacks, kettles, and canteens, carried them water—a distance of about four hundred yards, over rocks, stones, wood, and obstacles of every kind. In this labor four of us were engaged constantly for three hours, and had only ten horses to supply. The pass was in the narrow bed of a dry ravine, many places having to climb up and down large piles of rocks which had fallen from the heights on each side. Trees of various kinds grow in this dry bed, and are completely hidden from view by the perpendicular walls that tower above them at least eight hundred feet. These walls almost touch each other in places at the top, and are pierced so as to form large caves in the side, large enough to be occupied as a second-rate hotel. The water, and the only water found in this ravine, is contained in a hole at its head, and measures from three to eight feet in depth, cool and pleasant to the taste, but contains some of the embryo mosquitoes. These we strained through our teeth, well satisfied with this good fortune. To the weary traveler or emigrant taking this route, I would say in all the earnestness of my soul, provide yourself well with water before leaving Santana Pass, and let your vessels be ten- and twelve-gallon kegs. Leave the last water early in the morning and travel diligently. At night, after camping, give each horse or mule a gallon of water, and two next day noon, if very warm. The third and last day out, give them all you can safely spare and your journey will be accomplished, without danger to yourselves or animals, over this dry and hot plain. When you arrive here on the banks of this dry ravine, you must adopt our course—search in every ravine on the side of the mountain. Go well up towards the head of each, and your labors will be rewarded with a sufficiency at least for all immediate wants. We found good water and an abundance for our wants this evening, at the head of a ravine about one mile from camp, and all in view if it were not concealed by small growth. Dr. Slack came in this evening and reported two Indians taking note of our movements, position, strength, etc. As soon as they saw the doctor the Indians ran for the chaparral and were soon lost to sight. They have been in our path for several days but do not let us get too near them. We find animals at intervals along their trail—cattle and horses that were broken down and left by them. One of their horses is now in our camp, and several head of cattle were killed and prepared for provisions by some of our company yesterday. I had a supper and breakfast of this beef and found it good, though not very fat.

May 18 [& 19]. After an early breakfast our camp was broken up and we started over the mountain. This was a work of no small magnitude, and for three hours we packed and drove, and at the end of that time found ourselves just three miles from the last camp, having traveled over a ridge, or backbone, of the mountain, very rough and steep, and lost only one wagon. Our entire day's travel of fourteen miles was over a mountainous and stony road and in the heart of an Indian country; and, contrary to expectation, we have seen but few of these children of the plains and mountains. We, or rather one of our mess, found a neat pair of buckskin moccasins, and another picked up a flat stone upon which were paintings of Indian characters, very rude, but still in keeping with their knowledge of the arts, not sciences. Our camp is on the top of a high mountain, overlooking a pleasant valley, in which there is running water, and here we are, dipping water out of small holes

in the rocks, and carrying it in sacks and canteens up the side
of a steep mountain and then down the side of the same, crossing over a deep ravine and up the side of the steep and rocky
mountain upon which our camp is located. Kind reader, this
is work, labor that requires the strength and exertion of every
muscle of the body, and nature almost sinks under these repeated trials and privations.

Our limbs are sore and stiffened by this continued labor, and
God only knows when we will find ourselves again upon the
plains below. At 3 o'clock P.M. orders came to march forward
to the mountain, and [were] willingly complied with. Found the
pass to the jumping-off place tolerably good and when we
arrived there Mr. Haller, one of the Ohio Company, met us
with the gladdening news of their having discovered water in
the edge of the plains below. The consequence was a general
rush for the pass. The pass is an Indian trail, winding its course
in a zigzag manner down the side of a mountain measuring in
height about 350 feet; and at different places the trail lies on
the immediate edge of a perpendicular cliff, and the traveler
and his mule can have the satisfaction of looking into the depths
below and shudder at the [thought] that his fate is suspended
upon a hair or that one false step would hurl him and his animals into the awful depths below. But these difficulties did not
prevent famishing men and horses from going down, and at sundown I found myself safely down and my animals enjoying a
little grass after a good watering. The water we found in a hole
in the ravine, and not enough for all the train, numbering about
250 horses and mules. Our drinking water *is living*—that is, it is
composed of one third green, fine moss, one third polliwogs,
and one third embryo mosquitoes—and but a little of that, or,
in other words, we do not get as much as we need. As soon as
the train gets off of the mountain we move forward to the next
water, a distance of fifteen miles.

May 20 (Sunday). In the multiplicity of troubles and
difficulties, I missed all of Saturday but recorded the doings as

of Friday. Sunday was therefore well employed in lowering wagons and packing down provisions, goods, and wares down the side of the mountain. One wagon was left, and Dr. Howell's broke from the men and was hurled over the side of the precipice and dashed to pieces. At 4:00 P.M. some of the wagons and nearly all the packers went on their way to the next water. We traveled until midnight and encamped in a perfect desert, destitute of water and grass. Half a pint of water remained to each man and this, mixed with some pinole, constituted our supper. Our poor animals suffered very much and are really in a perishing condition, having had no water in thirty-six hours.

May 21. Started at daylight and after a march of about four hours found ourselves at the foot of a mountain of red rocks, out of the side of which flowed, in a weak stream, living water. Holes were dug and, as fast as a bucket of water accumulated, it was carried to the horses. In this way the remainder of the day and night was spent; and famishing men and horses are arriving every hour. This is suffering in fact, and how little do people in the States know how to appreciate their cold and sweet-tasting water. This mountain is strongly impregnated with silver. Rocks that will probably weigh 200,000 tons lie in a circle around this water, and ten men could defend themselves against five hundred.

Bones of cattle slaughtered by the Indians cover a large portion of the inclosure. I am writing these lines in a cave, the walls of which are decorated with figures representing the hunter in chase of the buffalo, the horse and the warrior, and other representations, rudely drawn and colored with dull dyes of various hues. I took up a coal and in large letters printed my name on the wall, and, however humble, I hope the passer-by will see and recognize the hand. A short distance and over the way are two large, round rocks with hollow tops, and I observed that in each of them was the remains of a fire, supposed to be the places upon which the Indians offer up their sacrifices and devote a portion of their time in devotion, praising an unknown

God. These large, round rocks, of which there are many, present a sparkling appearance in the sunshine, and I for a while flattered myself that riches in the way of diamonds were spread before me. But this was all delusion, for upon examination these glittering particles proved to be stone resembling glass. The distance from the head of Santana Pass to the next water is about eighty miles; from thence to this red mountain is at least twenty miles; and the next water to be reached is about thirty miles. Mr. Clark, one of our guides, visited a cave a short distance above the mountain pass, in which he found the skeleton of an Indian, without the usual accompaniments of bow and arrows, gun, and tobacco, and our conclusion is that he died on a journey without friends. Our horses were once more fully gratified with water at 12 o'clock last night.

May 22. The water has accumulated on our hands during the night, and if we had good grass we could, even here in this wild and desolate place, feel comparatively happy. I suffered very much from nervous headache, during the afternoon of yesterday, but feel much better this morning. I am now out grazing our "cavey yard"—an Indian term for a herd of horses, mules, or cattle. This watering place is called Stone Mountain, and possesses some points of interest. There is every indication of silver in a pure state,[12] and bituminous coal lies scattered over the plain at the base of this isolated mountain. If silver really exists here, it proves the justness of God's wise dispensations: coal to smelt, and water to wash the ore and quench the thirst of the future adventurer after these riches. The whole of Mexico traveled over by our company is very dry. Little rain, barely sufficient to lay the dust at any time, has fallen in the past twelve

[12]Probably the "scoria" which Gregg mentions as existing near the city of Chihuahua (Josiah Gregg, *Commerce of the Prairies* ["Early Western Travels," ed. Reuben Gold Thwaites, XX], p. 190). Bartlett refers to the Viesca silver mines of Coahuila, twenty leagues from Parras. (John R. Bartlett, *Personal Narrative of Explorations and Incidents in Texas, New Mexico, California, Sonora, and Chihuahua* [1854], II, 478.) According to Gregg, several indigent citizens of Chihuahua made a meager living by pounding free silver from these mineral outcrops.

months. But we are told by the few Mexicans in our train that the rainy season will open in a few days, and that at least two months will be a wet time. There is one consolation in this: we shall not suffer for water, as we have done in the past ten days. Mr. Chace, a member of our Ohio Company, is now posted on the top of an immense rock overlooking our stock and making a survey of this wild but gloomy region. Our company is now making preparations to send an advance guard to the next water, and this consists of bags and kegs of water and provisions cooked and ready for use. The duty of the guard will be to dig holes for the reception of all the wasting water, should there be a scarcity, and to scare the Indians away from it, should they now occupy the spring. Water has been bought and sold at $1.00 per gallon in this camp in the past week, and I offered last night $1.00 for two buckets of water and could not obtain it. Some one had had possession of these springs here ever since early day, and 10 o'clock at night has come and the labor of watering has just closed. I mentioned the discovery of silver ore in these mountains, and now I can say that I yesterday picked up a small white stone with a small but beautiful spot of pure gold in it, and Captain Swope, of the advance guard, showed me some of what is termed "gold-and-silver blossom," or bearing rock. Riches abound here, but will require much labor to disclose its place.

May 23. Beautiful morning, and, the guard having left, there is an abundance of water. Some of our horses and mules have this morning for the first time refused water. Two wagons and four packs, including myself, started for the next water, said to be a spring twenty-four miles in advance. The day was very warm, and we made all the progress we could and arrived at a beautiful green spot of about half an acre, covered with fine grass, and here our first water ought to have been found, but the sands of past years had entirely covered the spring. Here we suffered our weary mules and horses to pick a little grass, and then moved on till 10 o'clock that night, when, being unable to see the trail of the advance, we encamped on a small prairie for the night and drank the last half pint of water in our canteens, expecting to find more early in the morning. The country passed over today presented a varied aspect: first, a level sandy plain, hot, almost suffocating winds, similar to those described in Captain James Riley's narrative of his captivity on the great African desert among the Arabs.[13] Small mountains were also passed, some of stone as black as hard-burned brick; others again, in dust and stone, looked precisely like red bricks or their dust. The whole scene would again change in a few miles' travel from this dark and solemn aspect to bright and glittering gems. The ground in places sparkled—equal to a lady in her richest robes and most gorgeous ornaments. But a change came, and for the worse. We soon began to travel over ravines and rolling ground covered with a growth of something similar to the century plant, each sprig of which was as sharp and pointed as a Spanish dagger, and our poor horses suffered much.

May 24. Started onward without breakfast, and in a short time came to and passed three horses and one mule that had been abandoned to their fate, also several packs and one broken-down wagon. This, to me, indicated at least that the water was still far ahead, and Laubenheimer, Teats, Parker, and myself were suffering all the torments of burning thirst. We pushed onward, however, Mr. Parker falling in the rear—and in a few miles more he was lost to sight, his mules failing very fast. Our poor animals became more and more exhausted every hour, and I was reflecting on the propriety of abandoning my pack when we were met by Dr. Riley returning to the last water, then a distance of about forty miles. He told us that Watson's wagons were about two miles ahead, the mules all turned loose and the men scattered in every direction, and some dying of thirst. By this time I had become very much exhausted,

[13]See James Riley, *An Authentic Narrative of the Loss of the American Brig Commerce, Wrecked on the Western Coast of Africa, in the Month of August, 1815* (1818).

my mouth and tongue parched and much swollen. We reached the wagons after another hour's severe toiling, and found men in absolute despair, having abandoned the idea of immediate or prospective relief. As soon as our animals were relieved of their loads, we took such shelter as the wagons afforded from the rays of a burning sun, and here in fitful and agonising slumber passed about two hours. Our minds wandered back to the cool and refreshing streams and springs at our loved homes, and we were permitted in dreamy fancy to indulge our appetites, to cool our parched tongues and lips, and to enjoy life again—but to be called back to the miserable reality of our forlorn and apparently hopeless condition, by some one crying in the agony of his soul, "Water, oh, God, some water!" Reader, can you imagine the torments of a person burning with thirst and high fever, with water forbidden by the attending physician? or can you imagine the torments of a person condemned to die a felon's death with the rope around his neck and the burning words of his death warrant sounding in his ears? If you can imagine these horrors, and realize anything like our torments, you may easily conceive the boundless transports of our poor hearts when a messenger rode up with a half pint of water for each man and the soul-cheering news that ten miles ahead there was an abundance for both man and beast. Mr. Phipps was this messenger, and his visit saved our lives, thanks be to God in the highest, and glory to His name! Those of us able to travel saddled our riding mules, left our packs, and at sundown had an opportunity of drnking pure, cold water, and slaking thirst. We found George S. McKnight four miles from the water, raving mad, burning with fever. He had also been supplied with water by Mr. Phipps, and I rode into camp and sent Dr. Bunnell to his relief. I there learned that Dr. Riley and Mr. Holeman had gone back for water, and unless they find relief when they meet the rear train they must certainly perish, far from their homes and families and away from everyone. I have now seen trouble, I have seen insanity produced by thirst, and never do I wish to see so much

suffering again. Mr. Parker abandoned his mules and packs
about 1 o'clock and we have both sent back for them. I pay
gladly $5.00 to the person sent for mine. After eating a light
supper, being the only meal I have had for nearly two days, I
spread my blankets on the rocks and slept soundly until daybreak. Water has been sent out to the sufferers.

May 25. Morning dawned, and having been very kindly
invited to breakfast with Mr. Coleman (our provisions being
behind), which I readily accepted, and after which I went to
work and dug a few more holes in the sand and found good
water—and plenty of it. George S. McKnight rode into camp
early this morning, much better, the fever having left him.
J. Teats has been quite unwell and very much reduced in
strength, but is also on the convalescent list. The wagons have
not yet come in, and will probably not reach here until morning, but the men remaining with the advance wagons have been
supplied with water from here. Colonel Word, our commander,
came in this morning, and reports that Riley has succeeded in
turning the rear wagons back, and a week will probably elapse
ere we are all brought together again. Clark, the guide, has been
sent back to bring them up, and will do so if the men have not
lost all energy and been panic-struck and scattered to the four
winds of heaven.

Fresh Indian signs are found near our encampment, and it is
supposed to be the rear guard of the party returning from their
robbing expedition to Mexico. They keep at a very respectful
distance from us, and we have had no guard stationed for the
past several nights, in consequence of a feeling of security and
the prostration of the men. This is a very healthy climate, but
at the same time not very pleasant, because very hot through
the day, and cool nights, and no rain, although very much
needed. The men are now all in camp, excepting Riley, Holeman, and the rear wagons. In the past ten days we have passed
a mountainous region of country abounding in a troublesome
growth of cactus. Many new varieties have been discovered,

some of which are very beautiful, bearing a splendid blossom and, in some cases, delicious fruit. This fruit probably saved the lives of several of our men during their travels over the last dry plains. Another circumstance connected with the sufferings of some of the men must be mentioned here, because the remedy adopted by them went far to relieve them of thirst and strengthen their failing bodies, and may be of vast service to such persons as may be equally unfortunate. The remedy adopted was drinking their own urine, and one man actually drank that of a horse. Our strength is increasing, and our time employed in washing, sleeping, eating, watering and pasturing animals, and talking of the events of the past few days—some of which provoke a laugh at the actors' expense, although connected with immense suffering and pain. All are rejoicing in their escape from the threatened death from, at least, intense thirst. Provisions are growing scarce in camp, but we are within four days of San Carlos, where pinole and *bizcocho* may be obtained, and perhaps some dried beef. Don Muscuo, one of our guides, says that flour, pinole, *bizcocho*, and every needful article excepting bacon can be had at the city of Chiahuahua, which is now eleven days off.

May 26. This day opened somewhat cloudy, and we are enjoying a pleasant breeze. Some are washing body and clothes, others resting in the shade of the chaparral, and others again are mending pants and shirts, using buckskin leather for patches. We are now in a valley between two high ranges of mountains, and have good grass for our animals and the blessing of water. These mountains are high and very irregular; all the earth that ever lay on their tops or sides has rolled down, and the bare rocks alone stand, in singular confusion, resembling towers, castles, turrets, domes, and almost everything conceivable. The rocks are of a copper color and highly impregnated, in my humble opinion, with several rich minerals of little use to Mexicans or of very little value to any other nation or persons. The rattlesnake is frequently met with in this narrow valley, because the only water within six miles is here found.

Persons traveling over these dry and barren tablelands are cheered by the sight of these poisonous reptiles and the crow, blackbird, and hawk, because wherever they make their appearance you may rest well assured that water is not far off and that by a little exertion and diligence thirsty wants will vanish. A rattlesnake numbering eighteen rattles was killed yesterday, and another with seven crawled under the blankets of a sleeping man and by his buzzing noise started him into perfect wakefulness. There is game here of various kinds. Several deer have been killed, and an old bear and her cubs killed a broken-down mule for Mr. Parker last night. The cougar, lion, and mountain cat keep up a nightly serenade. We now support two camps. Captain Swope, with a part of the advance, is encamped about eight miles from here at a spring of excellent water, southeast of this, in a ravine in the side of the left-hand mountain.

May 27 (Sunday).   Beautiful, calm morning, with little excitement in camp. Colonel Word is now sending water to his wagons, and they will probably come into camp tomorrow evening without much suffering. This is a course that ought to be adopted by all campaigners, whether traveling with packs or wagons. In very hot weather, such as we now experience, mules and men must become exhausted, and to supply such sufferers an advance should be sent on to water with orders to bring it into camp with as little delay as possible. If this precautionary measure were adopted, much suffering and loss of property would be saved. We have found bags manufactured of India-rubber or gutta-percha the most convenient and most serviceable article adapted to that use. These articles, as well as canteens, caps, and coats, can be obtained at elastic stores in Cincinnati, Ohio, New Orleans, and other cities in the States. Nothing of this kind is found for sale on this route. The goatskin is much used by the Mexicans to carry their mescal[14] to market, but do not answer for water, as the best of them will rot in two days' use. Many of the packers have gone on to the

[14] A drink distilled from the maguey or agave plant. Mildly intoxicating.

next water, to which place we move in the morning, Colonel Watson's wagons having come into camp this morning. This is slow work, and several days must yet elapse before our whole party can get together. This advance movement is made for the benefit of the horses, as there is splendid grass, good water, and large shade trees, and deer in abundance. All are anxious to kill some of these animals for their meat, a very good substitute for bread—an article now nearly exhausted in this camp, some of the men having baked the last pinole yesterday. The clouds now so gracefully floating over our heads and crowning the mountain tops on either hand look as if rain might come in the course of this hot day and by its influence revive the grass and cool the wind, now blowing in fitful breezes through this defile in this extended chain of the Rocky Mountains. The next mountain, a link of the same range, lies west of Chiahuahua, and it comes next in order to be passed and is said to be more formidable than those already passed.

Captains Harvey and Lott came into camp this evening, reporting the rear train almost in camp with all the wagons.

At dark we had some thunder and lightning, and at bed time a fine refreshing rain set in and lasted about one hour. My bed on the rocks was not much softened by the falling water, but the air is much cooler.

May 28. Cloudy, but cool. Judge Tippin and several others left the wagons and came into camp during the night. Many of the poor fellows suffered some, and all are made happy to get in. Nearly all are complaining of a want of bread, or something to make it of, and are very anxious to go forward to San Carlos to obtain something of that kind. After breakfast we packed and marched seven miles further down the bed of this stream, and here we find good running water, good grass, and splendid shade under the tall and majestic cottonwoods growing by the side of this stream. This is a new thing, and much comfort is taken by all in this quiet and cool retreat from the rays of the burning sun. I have just been engaged in washing some shirts and socks, and find that practice makes perfect. Try it, reader, try it. The rear wagons may possibly come down to this camp this evening, and if they do we will march for San Carlos on Wednesday and reach there on Sunday next. Colonel Watson came in from the upper camp since our arrival and about two hours after us, and reports that further advices have been had from the wagons, that Dr. Riley had left the wagons yesterday morning, intending to reach our camp last night, since which time he has not been seen or heard from. Mr. Lynch, of Capt. Swope's company, started with him, and the fate of both of these men up to this hour is wrapped in solemn mystery. It is evident that they have taken some by-trail and have been lost or taken by the Indians. How much uncertainty there is as to the final result of men's acts! Lynch and Riley had both passed over the wagon trail from one watering place to the other twice, and had the trail of nearly the whole train to be guided by; and after all these favorable circumstances, they are lost. This is truly an accident of no ordinary character and creates a serious impression in camp. This evening we have more clouds, with thunder and lightning, and strong indications of more rain. Our horses and mules are recovering strength and flesh, and this good grass and fresh water will make our "Richards feel themselves again." The pending storm hangs in the east, and a glorious sunset lingers still in the west, the god of day just sinking from view over the tall and rugged peaks on our left. This camp, I have already said, is located on running water in the shade of these noble trees, and I can say that for beauty and the combination of everything for man and beast, it has not been surpassed nor equalled by any camping-ground on this route. Oh, for a continuation of such places! Here that rest so absolutely necessary can be enjoyed, and our animals grow in strength and be prepared for the tedious and laborious marches yet before them. I have often thought that if my family and friends at home, in the full enjoyment of the luxuries of life, could but take a bird's-eye view of our camp arrangements, our mode of traveling, and for one moment realize a small portion of our troubles and sufferings, it would be pleasant to me; yet when I reflect, I am truly thankful that they are deprived of this privilege, for I do not wish them one moment's pain. 'Tis now bedtime, the wind has lulled, and—without rain—the moon is casting her silver rays over our camp, and in a short time nothing will be heard in the deep stillness of the night save the sentinel's measured tread, and the hooting and screaming of night birds. This stream is called Altarias or Spring of the Heights.

May 29. Day opened very pleasant, and after breakfast I again went to my washing and continued at this until 10 o'clock. At 12:00 M. the rear train came rolling in, and at this time nearly all the men are in excepting Dr. Riley and Mr. Lynch. There is now no doubt in the minds of the men as to their fate. They have been taken by the Indians and marched through the mountain pass northeast of the one taken by our train. This view is taken from the fact of a trail crossing ours in that direction, on which were fresh pony tracks and the shoe tracks of a footman, which must have been Riley's, as his horse had given out and he was on foot. It is impossible for us to render them any assistance, as the Indians can out-travel us in the present condition of our mules and horses, and hopes are entertained that they may escape and reach San Carlos. I mentioned the scarcity of provisions in camp, and can now say that Captain George Scott of Texas, having more of pork, flour, rice, and pinole than he needed, sold rice at 37c a pound, and retailed flour at the round sum of $74 per barrel. This is taking advantage of the necessity of men, and he is a member of this company standing alone, without a personal friend, despised by all. The day closed pleasantly, and its cares would have been less if Riley and Lynch had come into camp, but nothing has yet been heard of these unfortunate men.

May 30. This morning all the wagons and men excepting

the two lost are in camp, and at a meeting we concluded to
remain here, and permit our horses to eat, drink, and rest until
tomorrow evening, when we start for the next water, said to be
distant twenty-four miles. With this arrangement all seem to
be well satisfied, because our horses and mules are growing fat.
The whole appearance of our camp has changed. Men look
clean, washing has been done, looks are brighter, and confidence
in our eventually reaching Chiahuahua spreads pleasant smiles,
over every face. There are times, on an unexplored route like
this, when the heart sinks at the prospect before it, and man
loses all his ambition, becomes in a manner reckless, particularly
when water is "few and far between," but all these feelings give
place to new and livelier hopes, and sympathy and commisera-
tion form a large part of his feelings when surrounded by the
blessings of water and grass. This has been fully verified by the
conduct of men in this company who had gone in the advance,
and, in an exhausted condition, found water, satisfied their
wants, and then without any rest and in a hot sun returned immediately to the men in the rear with water. Again, but few of
the several messes reached the water with any provisions, and
those men opened their eatables and invited all to partake, until
further provisions and messes came in. There was truly a liberal-
ity of heart displayed on the eventful 24th day of May—a liberal-
ity that will be treasured and remembered to the latest hour of
the recipients of its benefits. Among those who contributed to
alleviate the sufferings of those in the rear, I may name, in addition to those already recorded, Colonel Watson, Mr. Coleman,
O. H. Carpenter, and Dr. Bunnell. The doctor went on foot
six miles out with gourds and canteens of water and his medicines to relieve the sick and despairing. I have referred again
[to] these things in order that simple justice might be done
those who by their promptness contributed so much to the comfort of others. Our guide, Charles Clark, deserves particular
notice here. He rode day and night, and exerted every energy

to get the scattered train out of the confusion and panic into which it had been thrown by Riley and Holman on their return; and manfully did he discharge that duty by a ride of about eighty miles, alone and in an Indian country.

Evening came again—and, with it, Dr. Riley! After all hope of his ever returning had been given up, he came in this evening, in good health and condition. It seems he had taken the trail before spoken of and followed it to the northeast for many miles before he discovered his mistake. He lived upon mesquite beans [and] grains of coffee, and on his way back found some of the pork and bacon thrown away by some of our men, and upon which he designed to subsist until he overtook us at San Carlos. Now if Lynch was in camp, we could be better satisfied. Riley has not seen him in his wanderings, nor did he see a single Indian, although the trail before him was fresh with passing Indians making homeward. This arrival was hailed with pleasure, and could poor Lynch get in, our camp would no more wear so gloomy an appearance.

May 31. At 7 o'clock A.M. we packed and marched forward. At about four miles out, we accidentally stumbled on a good spring of water, nearly concealed by a thick growth of chaparral. We drank, and our horses followed suit, and then for nine more long hours our path lay over a sandy, broken chaparral country. At the end of this time we came to some water holes in the deep-washed ravines, and encamped near some more alamo, or cottonwood, trees. This water is muddy, but makes good coffee and, when thirsty, is good to drink. Bear, deer, antelope, and hares have been seen all along the path of today. The hare is excellent food, and several tables have been supplied by our rifles during the day. The valley we are now in is narrow, with small, conical-shaped mountains, and bordered by a high range on either hand. The distance traveled this day ranges from twenty-five to twenty-seven miles, over deep sand a great part of the way. We are now in the territory of the Muscalara tribe of Indians and have passed over the Lapaches, Comanches, and Lapan ground, and, strange to say, we have not seen an Indian since leaving Santa Rosa.[15]

[15]Evans refers to the Mescalero Apaches, Comanches, and Lipans. (See Frederick Webb Hodge, *Handbook of American Indians North of Mexico* [1907], I, 63-67, 327-29, 768-69.) The Lipans were an Apache tribe who raided the Texas border during the eighteenth and nineteenth centuries, and then were nearly exterminated in the Texas Indian wars of the middle 1840's. They made the mountains west of Santa Rosa their headquarters, but by 1903 were reduced to nineteen individuals. Recently they have been removed to the Mescalero Reservation in New Mexico, and are again slowly increasing in numbers. Bartlett's frontispiece map (*Personal Narrative*, I) shows the Lipan territory as consisting of the barren lands between Guajuquilla, Chihuahua, and the Rio Sabinas, Coahuila.

⟨ June, 1849 ⟩

SAN CARLOS TO CHIHUAHUA

June 1. Opens very warm and quite sultry. We remain in camp a few hours until our advance returns. We sent forward several men to look up a good camping-ground to occupy until the rear train comes up. Our object in traveling in detached parties is to find water and prepare it so that all may be equally benefited. Another small advance has gone on to San Carlos to make purchase of necessary provisions. For the first time I have a sore-backed mule. My poor packer is really suffering with that very common disease, if it may be so called, and it makes it necessary for me to effect an exchange of mules at San Carlos, if possible. Mr. Parker has sent forward to purchase one for himself. Our mules are all much jaded, and, if others can be procured, it will be the policy of all to do so. This afternoon we moved down the trail two miles. Here we found more water holes, with very poor water impregnated with copperas, which acts as a cathartic upon several of the company. We had to dig holes to obtain water fit to use as drink. We also found the grass very thin and much dried up. Here we remain until tomorrow, when we will again move forward to the next water, said to be twenty miles. The reader will have observed ere this that our late marches have been entirely governed by the water holes, and should any of you follow me in my wanderings among these mountains the[y] may be controlled by the same circumstances. The fact is, a water hole measuring in depth two feet, length twelve feet, and breadth ten feet, is of more importance to us than the mines of silver in the State of Chiahuahua, and we rejoice more over such a discovery than we would to have this state's riches open up before us. Our guide has just returned in company of another Mexican from San Carlos. We have very unexpectedly got within ten miles of this town without the knowledge of the fact. Our camp is on the same ground occupied by the Victoria California Company about a month since. They came by the Gavia Pass, and were so unfortunate as to get lost, wandered in the mountains until their provisions were exhausted, and on this ground they killed and ate one of their mules, having previously converted seven mules into provisions. This company numbered thirty men when they left Victoria, Texas, and they too, have had their share of suffering. They have reached Chiahuahua ere this and have, I hope, passed the worst part of their route.

June 2. Left camp early this morning, and after traveling about three hours we struck San Carlos River, a fine stream with cold and running water. On the banks we found good grass and small patches of ripe wheat ready for the reaper. With the exception of this wheat and a very few beans just ripening, there is nothing to supply our wants, and eighty-four men must live five days longer without bread. We encamped on the banks of this river, and, after making a few preparations, I started on foot to the military post of San Carlos. Arrived here, I presented myself and passport before the commandant and met with a kind and polite reception. This little duty attended to, I strolled from hut to hut and made a personal inspection of the state of provisions, which, I have already told, were found extremely low, and with one or two exceptions the citizens occupied the same level. The three miles between this place and our camp is rolling, and I found a grave by the side of the road upon which a cross had been erected, and the whole cross was covered with rosettes placed there by the hand of affection. Behind the cross was a structure upon which vines had been trained but now were in a withered condition. One more mile, crossing the stream once, brings us again to my strolling among the huts, and in a few words I can convey a perfect idea of this almost forsaken town. A few of the houses are built of dried mud, the others are constructed of upright poles plastered with mud. There are no streets, but everything of or concerning this town is arranged in admirable confusion. There are some soldiers of tolerably genteel appearance, and a constant guard is kept on the flat roof of their quarters. The rest of the inhabitants are very loosely clad, and seem to be of the very lowest order of Mexicans. They rub all their wheat into flour on a stone, and the flour is then sifted and converted into dough in a large wooden bowl or trough. The next step was to spread a blanket on the ground, roll out the cakes, lay them on the blanket, and cover with another. After all this had been done, an oven was heated and the process of baking was gone through with. Their children go without any clothing and are trained from infancy to endure the heat of the sun. This town is one of the most impoverished on the whole route. The most of the inhabitants have for several months past lived on the leaves and pith of the maguey plant.

June 3 (Sabbath). Stayed in town last night, lodged on corn husks, and arose tolerably early this morning; found the ladies busy in carrying water from the river to town. This they do by filling up a vessel and then carry it on the head a distance of a quarter of a mile. This is truly labor of the most slavish character, and the females do it all, and the whole truth is told when I say that the females support the family by the most slavish labor. Our camp will be moved up this evening to a place about four miles in advance, and tomorrow we make a vigorous start for Chiahuahua, where we expect to arrive in eight or ten days. There, we are told, provisions can be obtained, and, if so, I shall take at least enough to last to the Pacific coast. A few days more, and the water will run the other way, and we shall be tending downward again. Our camp is this evening nine miles from town; poor grass and no water.

June 4. Started early and traveled twelve miles to a small water hole in the sand. I took five horses half a league to a hole in the red rock and found water sufficient for many more. We met a Mexican lancer, who told us it was thirty-nine miles to the next water, which will be found incorrect, as we think, for his information is based on a knowledge of the mule path only, and we take a road leading in a different direction and through a different country. At 4:00 P.M. we set out and traveled until ten at night and then encamped without supper, water, and good grass.

June 5. Started at daylight, intending to reach the water in time for an early breakfast, and after pushing on for twelve miles we met a Mexican who told us that we were on the road to Presidio Del Norte, instead of the city of Chiahuahua road. Here then, we have lost ten miles' travel and suffered much for want of the water which we missed; however, we turned back, retraced our steps, and, under the guidance of the Mexican, soon left the road, and at the end of seven miles' travel arrived at a large reservoir of water, of very bad taste in consequence of its being the only watering place for all the Mexican cattle within miles of it. Our guides both returned to Santa Rosa, and having again a broad and broken wagon road before us, we felt perfect confidence in our ability to keep it—with what success the reader may judge. At this watering place we found tolerably good grass, and our mules are making good use of it. Here we will remain for a short time, to allow our mules to fill up again for the next dry plains, a distance of forty-five or fifty miles. Here we met with the first trouble from mosquitoes, which we found very numerous.

June 6. Found better water higher up the ravine; Mexicans are coming into camp with flour and *tortillas*, or cakes, for which they ask a bouncing price, and our necessities compel us to pay it. Flour, with the bran in it, sells for $1.00 for four quarts, and *tortillas* from two to three dollars per peck. You may judge from this as to the expense on this route. Our stock is recruiting finely on this grass and water, and tomorrow we move twelve miles to a deserted rancho, where we again rest a day.

June 7. Instead of leaving Presidio Del Norte to the

right, as we intended yesterday, we are now in Presidio, in the
enjoyment of everything but good grass. There is plenty of provisions to be had—at the usual high prices—and the best of water,
but the only feed we have for our mules is a little grass brought
in by boys. Presidio Del Norte is considerable of a mud-built
town; the only respectable building in town is the Catholic
Church. This is a large mud building, of mud brick, neatly
whitewashed. The town is laid out with some little regularity
on a hill, at the bottom of which flows the Rio Conchas, a stream
of fine water and considerable size. On this river's bottoms are
small gardens, closely cultivated by the Mexicans. One mile
north again brings us on the banks of the Rio Grande, which
here makes a long bend to the south: near the most southern
point is this city, which is large enough to get a name on the
maps. With the exception of the small fields on the Conchas,
the whole country is a pebble bed, with nothing in the world
growing upon it but small chaparral. This town numbers about
2,500 inhabitants, the most of whom are almost naked and of a
copper color; and in each house may be seen a revolting image,
representing the crucifixion of our Savior, which is worshiped
instead of God. Mary, the mother of Christ, also occupies a
conspicuous place at the family altar, and a rude picture of
St. Wan,[2] or St. John, and the other apostles fills up the background. On our arrival, we were escorted to the customhouse,
where our packs underwent the scrutiny of those at the "Public
Crib," and when night came on, a guard of soldiers was placed
around our camp to prevent smuggling. Preparations were made,
and our boys enjoyed themselves at a Mexican fandango, or Spanish dance, where rude things were indulged in, although the
fandango was held at the residence of the city alcalde, or mayor.
In addition to the ornaments of each house, there is a gamecock
kept to fight.

June 8.   Moved out of town two miles, to good grass
and excellent water, but find this encampment very warm, be-

[2]San Juan.

cause the land is covered with a thick growth of mesquite bushes. Beans grow on these, and our mules are very fond of them, and they are highly beneficial to them, as the beans are equal to corn when ripe. We are now within seven days' drive of Chiahuahua, but unless we change our minds we will not arrive there for twenty days, for we intend to allow our animals to recruit and wait for the rainy season to set in. All the routes west of the city are said to be destitute of water, and if this is the fact we must stop until rain falls and fills up the dry ravines, rivers, and water holes. There has been no rain in the last eight months in this range of country, and no one not intimately acquainted with a sparsely-watered country can form any idea of the utter destitution. Some places are vastly benefited by dews, in times like these, but it is very evident that the curse of God rests upon this country in a marked manner, for no moisture is found or derived from that source. This camp has the first well and scoop we have met with in Mexico. 4:00 P.M.— left camp and went one mile further up the river, and again encamped on open ground, good grass, and running water, and enjoy a perfect shade of alamo trees, tall and noble—sweet, delightful shade! On our arrival here we—that is, Teats and I— found that the Ohio boys had left the day before, and we are now here alone, with the middle wing of our company. Laubenheimer and Parker, members of our mess, are gone, and with them our coffee and pork, but we have them still in our power, for we have the most of the bread and the coffeepot. This separation was caused by two water holes and the branching road to Presidio, and we can only say, "Go ahead, boys, we are in possession of the machinery for boiling, if we do fall short in the coffee."

June 9.   After a night of trouble from mosquitoes and red ants, the morning opened fine and clear, although we had a fair prospect of rain last night, which, however, passed over our heads without so much as a sprinkle. The day continued very warm, and the Texas boys have been making pack saddles, hav-

ing disposed of all the wagons excepting those belonging to
Colonel Watson; and he has taken the other road,[3] upon which
he will have to travel sixty miles without running or standing
water. It is expected that the members of our company will
again be united at or near Chiahuahua, provided no accident
should happen to any of them. We will probably remain in this
camp until Monday morning. Our mules are doing first rate,
and I flatter myself that this will be vastly to our benefit, and
that those who have pushed on so rapidly will find it a step
much to their cost. We have one more mountain to cross ere
we reach Chiahuahua, and when I get to it I will be better qualified to speak of its grandeur and the toil and labor of passing it.
Mexicans from Presidio and the adjoining country are constant
visitors at our camp, and bring with them gourds, curd, milk,
and *tortillas*, for which they ask a high price. I went into Presidio today, and while there was much assisted by a young American by the name of Hall. This gentleman has spent some time
in trade in this country and is master of the Spanish language
and ever ready to interpret for those who do not understand
this tongue, and is very obliging and affable in his manners. The
alcalde was seeking to make me pay the sum of *dos pesos* (or
$2.00) for countersigning my passport, when Mr. Hall told him
that he had no right under the sun to do it; and by this inter-
ference my $2.00 were saved and Mexican rascality exposed to
the scorn of strangers. Conscience has nothing to do in a
Mexican's estimate of the value of his property or his services,
and when an attempt is made by any of these harpies to extort
money for real or imaginary services, the only thing necessary
to be done is to take a firm stand at your own price and give
them that or nothing. I have said that with few exceptions the
Mexicans met with on this route are of the lower order, of
Negro and Indian origins, and if they seek to do you a kindness,
you may rest assured that there is a motive and that your con-

[3]Watson probably traveled directly to Chihuahua, without making the side
trip to Presidio del Norte for supplies.

fidence will be misplaced if you place any in their acts. I have
met with perhaps twenty men, Mexicans, that I would be willing
to trust with any of my property, and among these I will name
first Gonzalles,[4] a man we hired in San Antonio; next, the alcalde
of San Fernando; Don Muscus, our guide from San Rosa to San
Carlos; and the customhouse officer at Presidio. These men I
believe to be perfectly honest and every way well-disposed
towards Americans, and I know them to be gentlemanly in their
intercourse with others.

Two or three men who have hitherto traveled with us left
yesterday on the Passo Del Norte route,[5] whilst others from that
route are coming into our camp and are going to Chiahuahua
with us. Poor Lynch has not yet been heard from and no person
in our company thinks of seeing him again.

June 10 (*Domingo*, or Sabbath). Still in camp and as
busy at preparations for the march tomorrow. Colonel Word,
our commander, is sitting in the shade sewing up the side of a
bag or wallet, Parson Hill, a minister of the Methodist persua-
sion, is engaged in stuffing pads for his pack saddle, and here sits
Judge Tippin keeping his needle active, whilst Shrieves, Calcote,
Jimison, Adams, and Major Ball are engaged in making the
woodwork of several new pack saddles. This is not the general
way of spending our Sabbaths, but [we] are compelled to this
for want of time, wishing to go forward and overtake the several fragments of our company at Santa Aronomo,[6] thirty miles
this side of the capital of the State of Chiahuahua. Mosquitoes
are very bad, and we are anxious to get away from them.

June 11. Opens warm and sultry. News came into camp
this morning that forty wagons were about crossing the Rio
Grande. This is a party of emigrants for California consisting of
families, male and female, and I can only say that I wish them

[4]Probably Gonzales.
[5]The usual route through El Paso followed the Rio Grande to that city; then
several alternates offered. One struck due west to Tucson; another looped
south through Guadalupe Pass.
[6]San Gerónimo.

safely through it. Men must be destitute of proper respect for females, or it must be a necessity absolutely compelling them to move their families, to introduce them to the many hardships of a journey like this. There is on the American side of this river a fort owned and established by a Mr. Seaton for trading purposes. The amount of business done at that fort is said to be very great, and he pays his clerks from forty to sixty dollars per month, and controls almost the entire Indian trade. He is an American, has a Mexican wife, and lives in his stockade, protected by a few heavy pieces of artillery and his own bravery. This man employs several Mexican men in herding mules and cattle, and assigns to each his duty, which must in all cases be discharged by these servants. Our preparations for a departure are drawing towards completion, and we will soon be on our winding way once more. The day so far has been very warm, and were it not for the little wind blowing, it would be hot. The mountains are still around us and the Ruler of the Universe only knows when they will be behind us, and we once more permitted to breathe the free, pure air of the western world. The monotony of camp life is almost insupportable, and were it not for the bright and glittering prospect ahead, we would all sink under the repeated trials we are daily called upon to encounter. The only advantage we derive from this long stay in this camp is that accruing to our mules and horses, and if a few days' continued rain should fall, much good would be the result. Oh for some rain; oh, for a distillation from the clouds of heaven to cool the burning earth and to fill up the dry holes, rivers, and ravines along our path! This would indeed be a blessing incalculable, such as has not visited this accursed route for many months, and is seen in every plant or tree we meet with. Corn is just in roasting-ear condition, and the people are just cutting and gathering in wheat. The wheat crop is light, the grain very small and much shrunken and all of a very inferior kind, only growing to the height of a foot, or not to exceed eighteen inches. Tomorrow morning we start, and with good

83

fortune we will again be on the wagon road in two and a half days on our way to Chiahuahua. I might mention the name of Torrey, who is engaged in trade through this country, and is making vast profits on his merchandise. A few men, and these chiefly Americans, are the money-making men of this region, and are in fact looked up to by the whole population and regarded with much favor. This is the result of education. These northern towns are, in fact, nothing but colonies; the wealthy owners residing in the large and rich cities of the south, whilst the people here are peons—poor, miserable slaves of their rich and noble masters, toiling and risking life and limb, that they and their families may roll in wealth and luxury. But such is the case. Shut out from the mind of man the truths of the Bible, the knowledge derived at school, the intelligence gained from, and widely disseminated by the free, untrammeled press, and you at once blot that people, as it were, out of the world; you shut them from everything like an intelligent existence, and open the door to abject slavery and fully prepare them for the fetters ready for them. Thank God that my fate has been cast among the free and intelligent of the earth, that I am an American by birth and in feeling, and can fully appreciate the blessings conferred by our Republic.

June 12. Breakfasted early, and all hands began packing, and at half past seven [we] were under way, as the sailors have it. We traveled parallel with the Rio Conchas for twelve miles and encamped on its banks, under the shade of some fine alamo trees, near several Mexican ranches.[7] Shortly after our

[7]Clarke characterized the ranchos of northern Mexico as follows: "Many . . . are built like forts, and may be considered as such. Their form is the following: A strong adobe wall, in the form of a square, from 200 to 400 feet on a side, and 15 or 20 feet high. There is sometimes a small chapel at one corner, with its chime or bells; it has one strong gate in the centre of one side; the rooms for the proprietors are on each side of the entrance within. There are built against the walls on the inside a range of rooms for the peons; these have but one door which opens into the court. There are no windows and no chimneys, but a hole is left in one corner for the smoke to escape. There are no floors and no furniture, except a few earthenware pots and occasionally a brass kettle for cooking; their beds are principally of ox-hides and sheep-

arrival at this camp, the Mexicans came in with horses to sell, and, always wishing to make the most of a trade, no bargains were struck. Our road today lay through a broken, hilly chaparral, and we are now at the foot of a very high mountain which remains to be passed on tomorrow. Our water is tolerably good, and the grass is very good—much better than we usually find, and only found by the side of water. I have observed that we scarcely ever find water, grass, and wood on the same ground, unless on the borders of considerable streams. We were passed today by an Indian in some way or other connected with Torrey's trading establishment. He is a young man of fine form and features and beautiful black hair, which he wore very long behind but cut short before and on the temples. The hair was not braided, but suffered to float at pleasure over his back. His dress consisted of a shirt and pants, belted, and in which he wore his scalping knife. He had on neither shoes nor hat, and was well mounted on a mule. This son of the plains looked altogether superior to the peons, and saluted each packer in good Spanish as he passed. There was a party of Muscallaras at Presidio last night, having come in for a little *aguardiente* or liquor. The Commanche tribe are now represented at Chiahuahua by their chiefs, who meet the authorities of this state for the purpose of forming a treaty of peace. How well they may have succeeded in this attempt remains to be seen. The Indians know full well that they have these people in their power—that, in other words, the Mexicans dare not do anything other than to concede to such terms as they may deem fit to propose; and should the authorities refuse the offered peace, Santana[8] will return to his home in the mountains, gather his warriors, and

---

skins; the roofs are of the height of the walls, nearly flat, and made by laying poles and twigs upon the rafters, upon which is laid a layer of mud or clay, nearly a foot thick, which becomes hard by being dried in the sun, and sheds the rain. Upon the tops of the roof sentinels are placed when Indians are in the neighborhood." A. B. Clarke, *Travels in Mexico and California*, pp. 39 f.

[8]Santa Anna.

descend upon them, kill all he can, drive off their mules, horses, and cattle, and carry into captivity their wives and children. This has been his course, and he deems it sport to come from his retreat and like an avalanche, roll upon his confused, dismayed, and cowardly foe. This is the character of this wily chief, and when his mind once matures a plan, it is faithfully executed by his followers. The population of this tribe is said to be 125,000 souls, headquarters being at a town on Green River many days' journey north of this route. I have not learned the number of the Lapan and Musculara tribes, but they are said to be very strong in fighting men.

June 13.   Left yesterday's camp early, and moved forward to the mountains. Here we again struck the Rio Conchous, watered, and crossed, and in a few minutes began to ascend its steep and rugged sides. For ten long miles we continued to ascend and descend some of the steepest and stoniest roads I ever saw; but after much toiling and risk of life and limb, we were safely landed at the side of the river again, and here found wood and water, but no grass, for which we substituted mesquite beans, which we found tolerably abundant. We find camp signs here made by our boys ahead, and one fresh grave. Blood was seen along our path for the last four miles, and it is conjectured that some poor fellow has come to his end by a fall from his horse or the accidental discharge of some firearm. We will probably learn the particulars at Coyammi,[9] which is fifteen miles from here. We also struck another trail just below our camp made by Americans. This we know by the shoe tracks, the only tracks made by American horses or pack men, and we are also certain that they were strong in number, but we do not know where they came from, or who they are. Our company now numbers only twenty-five men, and we feel secure enough to sleep without a guard. This day has been cloudless and very warm, but the sun is covered with a haze or smoke, indicating the preparations for rain.

[9]Coyame.

June 14. Arose very early and picked mesquite beans for our horses, and after breakfast started "over the mountains and far away," and at 1:00 P.M. halted to feed on a small patch of green grass, or *sacate*, but had no water. We passed in the morning a very steep and rocky mountain, the south side of which we found extremely difficult of descent, in some places falling off abruptly for two and three feet right in our path and not to be avoided. Over such roads we wound our slow course for two miles, when we struck the plains, in which we found the grass. After resting an hour we again packed, and traveled *siete* (or seven) miles, when from the top of a small mountain the town of Coyami was first seen by us. In all our travels, we have not met with a Mexican town and surrounding country that looked so pleasing to the eye from the mountain; and I could not repress the "Huzzah!" that almost involuntarily broke from my lips. Here, then, lay before us small patches of wheat, some of which had been already garnered; fields of waving corn; large and splendid trees near the town; and good water breaking from the side of one of the molehills, and our path was frequently crossed with ditches of water used in irrigating the lands. The view from the hill was soul-cheering, perfectly enchanting, and lost none of its effects on our nearing the town. We encamped on the side of a small mountain, half a mile from town, by the side of several good springs of water, and in a short time had corn for our mules (at $2.00 per bushel), eggs, *tortillas*, and milk and pinole for ourselves. Everything needful was brought in to trade with, and, in fact, we found this town a perfect El Dorado when compared with others already passed through. We passed a mountain of singular formation this afternoon. Stratas of quartz running vertically across our path almost every twenty feet were seen projecting from the earth and measuring not to exceed four inches in thickness. Besides these glittering walls there was strewn over the side large and small lumps of silver ore mixed with iron. These we examined, and found them much heavier than ordinary stones of the same size,

and came to the conclusion that a large outlay of money and
labor would be necessary before a harvest could be realized
from the silver extracted. Gold blossom also was seen at this
mountain in very small quantities.

June 15.   Breakfasted, having milk, eggs and slapjacks—
a rarity—after which we moved our camp to better grass, east
of town half a mile. Here we found the grass some better. After
unpacking and turning my mules out, I wandered into town.
I here met with Mexicans far more intelligent and courteous
than at any other place visited by us, excepting San Fernando.
The town is wholly of these sun-dried mud blocks, buildings
but one story high and rather inferior in their construction; but
it is a clean place: the inhabitants are well dressed, there is an
air of comfort thrown around them, and the few gardens cultivated are laid out with much taste and ingenuity. Water is
constantly passing around these gardens, and by means of small
sluices it is let upon the roots of every plant, shrub, and tree
within the bounds of the garden—not to say inclosure, for all
is open. I visited the largest garden in company with Colonel
Word, and we found almost every variety of fruit and some
vegetables. Here for the first time apples are found, peaches,
plums, pomegranate, and a variety of grapes [in] beautiful vineyards, with a very heavy crop of grapes now nearly ripe.

Provisions can be had here abundantly, and when a man has
money he need not want in a place like this. The old madonnas[10]
cultivate saffron and superintend the weeding of their gardens,
whilst the aged *hombres*, or old men, are acting in the capacity
of shepherds. Colonel Watson's train, or rather our left wing, is
now up, and at Santa Aronomo[11] we will probably all be united
again. We were visited this evening with a very heavy rain
accompanied with vivid lightning and heavy peals of thunder.
This was very refreshing and much needed, and the only complaint we had to utter was this, that it did not rain long enough,
although we were exposed to the whole of the storm without so

[10]Probably what Evans meant was *duennas*.   [11]San Gerónimo.

much as a tent for shelter. But we felt thankful for the beneficial effects of this short but violent storm. It will supply water for our use on the road to Chiahuahua and the grass will grow green again. I found a sick man in town today, and prescribed for him [and] gave him a dose of medicine, and he returned the compliment by bringing to camp a bowl of chicken soup and some *tortillas* for *El Doctor*. I am therefore an M.D. unexpectedly and undeservedly, having but little knowledge of medicine and no desire to gain fame in that line of business. Every town passed has its sick, and at all places our physicians are called upon to administer medicine.

June 16. My Mexican friend brought us milk and eggs this morning, and, on invitation, remained to breakfast with us. The morning was clear, with a fine breeze, which continued to blow for several hours. At 3:00 P.M. we again packed and moved forward ten miles to good grass but no water. We met ten American wagons, drawn by ten splendid mules each, and loaded with corn and whiskey for Presidio Del Norte, intended by the traders to hit the California emigration. These men are making a speculation upon their wares and merchandise, and should there be as many emigrants on the Sante Fee route as have already gone through here, they are in the way of realizing a splendid fortune.

June 17 (Sabbath, or *Domingo*). Aroused camp early, and found that the grass had been slightly dampened by dew. Baked a few cakes and, without coffee, breakfasted and moved for the *escondido*—next water; this we found after hard pushing until about 2:00 P.M. This water, the coldest spring found on our route, we detected by a mule track turning square to the left from the road and passing down a ravine between two mountains; which path we found to lead down, down, and up, over hill and dale, for three miles, when, at the bottom of a deep and small valley, we found the much-sought-for water. The spring is strong and the water cold, being for the first time such water as we were accustomed to find at almost every spring in the

north. The road so far has been a very good one from Coyammi, no rough, rocky, and broken road, but one as good as any
need be. We met this morning eleven American wagons, a part
of the train passed last night. They were each drawn by ten
mules, in fine order and high-spirited. Our camp is at the spring
and well shaded by a thick growth of small willows, and entirely shut in by mountains. This water is called Hidden Spring
by the Mexicans—a name full of poetry and well applied—and
is distant from the last water about twenty-five miles. The next
water is said to be twenty-seven miles from this, and also one
that we must seek for, it being a hole in the rock. Our animals
are improving slowly, and when we get to San Aronomo, the
grass will suffer some, for we cannot avoid feeding and resting
our stock there, as they stand much in need of it.

Dr. Riley presented me with some dried antelope meat. He
had been successful in killing one a day or two before our arrival
here, and I found the meat very good, and fine eating. We were
again blessed with a shower of rain this evening, which continued long enough to wet our blankets through and refresh
the air.

June 18. Delightful, refreshing morning. Breakfast over,
we went to work to dry our wet blankets, and some of us cleaning out new gourds, an article found indispensable on this route.
Each man carries at least one gallon of water, and some of us
have from one to four gallons strung upon our mules in gourds
and canteens. Thus provided, we suffer but little ourselves on
a thirty-mile stretch, but we cannot, with that quantity, give
any water to the mules. I have found indications of gold and
silver in these hills and mountains, and, if the materials necessary
for extracting it were found here, do not doubt but that money
could be made here by mining. There is here the remains of an
old mine worked for silver, which has been abandoned, in consequence, probably, of the Indians, this being their place of
resort, there being no other water for miles around. But they
have gone into the more northern mountains, and at this time

only come down to rob and steal from the Mexicans when a supply of horses, mules, and cattle became necessary to their comfort and convenience. 'Tis said that the Muscalara tribe now have about two thousand head of mules alone, not including cattle and horses, and this is substantiated by those of the tribe who occasionally come in and trade these animals for other necessaries of life with the traders constantly traveling through this region of country. A large business of this kind is now carried on by these parties, and money is made on both sides. We have now several mules in our train which have passed through the hands of the Indians within a short time. I now own a regular Comanche mule, known by their mark, a slit in each ear. 4:00 P.M.—packed, and move on. After traveling until about ten o'clock, Colonel Watson and Captain Scott being in the advance searching for water, they were charged upon in the open plains by five Indians, without an injury to either party excepting the loss of a gourd to the Indians. The Colonel and Captain were sitting in the grass, waiting for the train to come up, when this party rode up, and on being hailed in Spanish they answered "*Munches Amego,*[12] *Spaniola, Mexecano,*" and on being ordered to halt and not complying, Captain Scott fired a pistol, which confused them a little. They then came on a second time, and Scott fired his rifle, when they broke and made off in a northerly direction. Soon after this little rub the train came up and encamped a quarter of a mile from this field of scrimmage. The gourd is covered with Indian paintings, the only thing going to contradict the presumption of these men being actually, as they professed to be, Mexicans. It was dark and their nationality could not be distinguished.

June 19. Broke up camp early and moved on until 12:00 M., when we again turned from the road, and at a short distance entered a ravine to the left, in which we found the Friend, or "Amigo" Springs, one of which is very hot, and other a cool, sulphurous spring. Just above the latter is the foundation

[12]*Muchos Amigos,* or many friends.

and part of a heavy stone wall built in early times to protect the watering place from the mountain torrents. This is the probable cause for this water and wall, and this reasoning is strongly supported by the scarcity of water on this route and the absolute necessity for its protection on the road. The distance to the last spring is not over twenty-four miles.

The grass found here is good, very good; and we may remain until tomorrow evening. 3:00 P. M.—one of our hunters has just come into camp, with the information that three men of our company are now encamped half a mile west of us, at another spring and that five men, citizens of Chiahuahua, had left that camp for Presidio Del Norte last evening. Here, then, is the key to the Indian fight between Colonel Watson, Captain Scott, and the supposed Indians. These two valiant men concluded that the Indians were upon them, yet laying aside all the answers being Spanish and well understood by Captain S., they must fire, and scare the poor, cowardly Mexicans, who were making every effort to escape from their daring foe. Happily, no injury resulted from this almost fatal mistake, and [it] will, I think, put men on their guard and prevent them shooting when answered "*Amigos.*" It was the result of a misapprehension of the term "*Vamos,*" which means "go along."[13] Colonel Watson told these men to *vamos*, after they had declared themselves friends and Mexicans, and accordingly they took the road, intending to pass our men; and they, thinking that it was nothing but a second charge, fired the rifle, or second shot, and then the party of supposed Indians did *vamos*. This error may prove troublesome to us yet, and is to be regretted. There was no intention on the part of our men to disturb Mexicans, or in any way to interfere with their rights, but on the contrary, to treat them with respect, but we are among strangers, and it would be hard to prove our innocence, if arraigned on an indictment for disturbing the peace of the country and of Don— somebody in particular. Evening

[13] *Vamos*, meaning "Let us go," corrupted into a third-person command by Texans and other border-dwellers.

has again closed in upon us, and we have a fair prospect of another storm of rain. Such blessings have been few and far between, and I feel [tempted], when wet to the skin, to bless the hand that showers it upon us, for it is much needed. We have now traveled about three days since leaving Coyammi, and at no time has the distance between waters been less than twenty-four miles and the next is the same. The three men of our party mentioned above were waylaid by ten Indians, but the redskins, having discovered them to be Americans, came forward and made friendly demonstrations. The rascals said they were on the alert for Mexicans, but they will yet wake up the wrong boys. These Indians were perfectly naked and poorly armed, and seemed destitute of all the necessaries of life, and depend almost entirely upon their thefts from Mexicans.

June 20.   We had a very heavy rain in the night, and have now every prospect of an abundance of water on the road. The morning is clear, and the sun is growing warmer every moment, and in a short time it will again be as warm as usual. I suffered much from heat yesterday and think it the warmest day we have experienced in Mexico. Our horses and mules are doing very well on this grass and the mesquite beans we pick for them. We picked up in this camp cups, coffeepots, and spoons left by our boys now in advance, and there is every indication of their having been forced to leave here in a hasty manner. This is further indicated by the marks of a large camp of horses and mules a short distance back from this water, and the probability is that our boys occupied the water when the Indians came upon them, and that they thought it advisable to decamp. In doing this they, in their excitement and hurry, left these articles. The train leaves this evening at four, and I have just baked the last of our Grahamite flour. We have just four cakes each all told, and these will have to, with a slice of bacon, constitute the next three meals, in which time we will reach San Aronomo, where they have mills and an abundance of grain and other provisions. Some of the messes in this train neglected

93

to supply themselves with flour at Coyammi and they are now
without bread. This is right; men must learn wisdom by experience, or they never will do to make long campaigns in
Mexico, particularly in sparsely-settled portions of this country.
The camp has been well supplied by the hunters with fresh meat,
the chaparral being alive with hares. 4:00 P.M.—started forward,
and traveled until 10 o'clock, when we found a little dry grass
but no water, and with a few bites of bread and a little pinole
and water, we went to our blankets, and slept soundly until
daybreak.

June 21. Started early, and at the end of two hours' ride,
we entered the town of Santa Faronomo and encamped in the
street, under fine cottonwood trees, and having fed our mules
corn, we commenced the preparation of breakfast. This over, it
will be proper to tell the reader of what this consisted at this
new town on our road, and to attempt, in my feeble manner, to
convey to him, or her, some faint idea of the locality and appearance of this city. First, then, as to our first meal here. Coffee, hot
and well cleared, sweetened with Mexican sugar, or "Pelonca,"
fried pork, onions, and ripe tomatoes—the first met with on the
journey—and good wheat cakes, or, in the Spanish tongue, "Panda
Arena." For our dessert, we had splendid ripe figs and for those
who relished [them], mesquite beans. This comprehends our
bill of fare, and when thus blessed, who so base as to complain,
or murmur a word of discontent? And now, a hasty word or
two for the town of San Faronomo—not Aronomo, as I have
heretofore been led to call it. This place is located at the head
of a range of small mountains, in a mesquite thicket and on the
edge of a plain upon which nothing else grows without cultivation. A short distance from the town flow the waters of the
River Puerko,[14] a good stream, supplying water and setting in
motion the machinery of a gristmill, the first since leaving Victoria, Texas. This place has rather a handsome plaza or square,
around which water is constantly running, and is further orna-

[14]Rio Puerco.

mented with a fine row or double sets of cottonwood trees, between which is the promenade. On one side of this plaza is a neat and clean market, in which we found candy, bread, cakes, melons, milk, etc., ready for sale and to be had on reasonable terms. Several of the principal streets are also benefited by running water. There are many small shops, where bread, *queso* (or cheese), and cakes and liquors are sold. And cockfighting and gambling amount to a passion in the most of Mexicans. The dress of the ladies is but little better than that already described but the gentlemen are habited with better clothing. A few of the poor are poorly clad. I saw a man driving an oxteam through the streets, having nothing on to hide his nakedness but a short shirt and wide-rimmed hat. The buildings are of sun-dried brick, and have already been noticed, in the description of others. Four churches, all Catholic, are sustained in this town. One and a half miles out there is a large building looking very neat at a distance. A very heavy cloud is seen hanging over our road and up the river, and we may expect to get wet tonight, although our camp is in the principal street, and just in the edge of town. But notwithstanding our favorable situation, and the convenience of shelter, we do not seek it; having become inured to those hardships, and accustomed to look upon the wide world as our home, and the canopy of Heaven as our shelter.

June 22. After some preliminary preparations, and a little pork, coffee, and bread, with a dish of Jake's cooking consisting of eggs, tomatoes, and onions all fried together, we packed and moved forward. We passed the building mentioned in my notes of yesterday, and found it to be an old church constructed in a better and neater manner than those in town. This building is large, with arched roof and well-finished steeple, and looked more Americanized than any we had seen. But it, too, has had its day; the voices accustomed to chant *Te Deums* there are no longer heard within its walls; the sound of the dome bell no longer calls worshipers together, nor is the silence broken, unless by an occasional visitor. We passed on, and in a few

95

hours encamped on the bank of the river, where we found a little coarse grass. Here we rested until 2:00 P.M. and then again moved forward, and at 4:00 P.M. encamped ten miles from Chiahuahua, having good water and the open fields of a rancho for the feed of our horses. Here we overtook five of our Ohio boys—viz., Chace, Bunnell, Brunner, Parker, and McKnight. They have been in this camp waiting for us about a week, in good health, and their animals doing very well. I must now enter somewhat into detail in order to throw light upon some matters recorded on our journey from Presidio to San Faronomo. It will be remembered by the reader that I spoke of a new-made grave, of blood in the mountain path, etc., and the conjectures that this circumstance gave rise to. Of the death and burial of the deceased there mentioned, the reader must remain in as much ignorance as the members of our company, save this, that he was a member of a California [company] several days in advance of our advance; further there is nothing known connected with his death. The blood on the mountains came from an injured mule. The finding of tin cups, coffeepots, etc., will also be remembered, and the boys say that they saw no Indians, and these articles must have been forgotten. The caveyard camp spoken of was made by the large train of wagons. It will therefore be seen that our conjectures were wholly groundless, and I am happy to know it. This is a delightful camp, having good grass, little wood, and fine running water, and only nine miles from the capital of the state of Chiahuahua. The Indians stole from San Faronomo last night one hundred horses, and we have been strongly solicited to go in pursuit. This we of course refused to do, not wishing to get up hostilities between them and Americans. There is much diversity of opinion relative to routes from this city to the Pacific coast. Some of the Americans, including the most of our company, have gone to Yanos, from thence to Piemo Village, and then to pass the great American desert, alike destitute of water and grass for ninety long miles. Others have gone by way of Durango, thence

to Mazatlan, there to take shipping. I go to the city in the morning to investigate the feasibility of these several roads, and the
opinion then formed will be my guide as to future traveling.

June 23. Beautiful morning. Mr. Parker has been, and
is still, quite unwell with the bilious colic. I am now ready to
start for the city with the long name and the reader will please
wait for further comments until I return. 2:00 P. M.—still in the
city, and now for another hasty description of the capital. First,
then, the road from camp is good, crossed at quick intervals with
acequías (or canals) of good, cool water. About one league from
the city we came to a hacienda, or village, at which the best
flouring mill is met with on this route. It is of rude construction
and rude material, the burrs being large stones and whole, with
straight furrows and not hooped. The building is *blanco* (or
white) and looks neat outside. A short ride further brought us
to the entrance of this renowned city. The buildings in the environs are low huts of sun-dried brick, and are occupied by the
many poor. A few moments more, and you are suddenly thrown
into the richer portion of the city, and find buildings corresponding in length with the best of city buildings at home, but
in height do not. The public buildings are the residence of the
Spanish minister, the American Hotel, public offices, and the
several churches. The churches are splendid buildings, and [are]
of stone, and pass my power of description, and unless I can
have time and opportunity to visit the inside of these churches,
I shall not attempt to convey to the mind of the reader a just
conception of the magnificence of these edifices. Another building not heretofore named is the state prison, or *la cárcel*. This
we passed coming in, and through the iron-secured windows,
saw the faces of many prisoners, some of whom were serving
out a term of years for crimes committed. The law is severe in
its punishment of crimes. For instance, a pistol was stolen by a
Mexican from Mr. Vaughn, a member of our company, and on
his trial for the offense he was found guilty and sentenced to
four years' imprisonment. But I am digressing. The streets are

narrow and short, making many turnings to arrive at a given
point, and laid out in this manner for ease and convenience in
barricading the city on the approach of a hostile army. The
public buildings are nearly all situated on the main plaza, or
square, in the center of which is a neat fountain continually
spouting forth from four jets the cool and sparkling water. This
falls into a larger circular basin, from which there are men and
women dipping at all hours of the day. Shows and cockfights
employ the attention of the sportsmen when not engaged in
dealing *monte*,[15] a game at cards, and a favorite with Mexican
gamblers. The national army, or that portion quartered here,
looks better and the soldiers are better dressed than those met
with at Presidio and San Carlos. To close this short history of
the city, I must say that nearly everyone is engaged in small
trade, selling cakes, melons, figs, and confectionery. There are
men, Americans, here, who are merchants and gentlemen, and
whose stores are not easily surpassed in the beauty of arrangement and the quality of the goods. Tomorrow is San Wan's
Day,[16] and proper arrangements are being made to celebrate this
day in a becoming manner. I have now said as much of the town
as is necessary, and will only add that it is located on the headwaters of Conchas River, the only lands cultivated being those
bordering upon its waters and so situated as to admit of irrigation. In this way the water is spread along for miles, through
gardens of pepper, onions, corn, and potatoes (sweet), and
thence into fields of corn, barley, wheat, etc.

June 24 (*Domingo*, Sabbath). After a breakfast on bread
and milk, Dr. Bunnell and I mounted our mules and rode to
camp and found all doing well, etc. Colonel Watson's camp was
entered during the night and several guns and pistols stolen
from it by the *ladrones*, or Mexican thieves. In camp, and our
animals grazing, we indulged in such amusements as fancy dictated until the hour of 4:00 P.M., when I again rode into the

[15]Monte bank, a favorite card game of the gold-rush period.
[16]San Juan's Day.

98

city, accompanied by J. Holland Chace. On our arrival we met
the citizens in great number going out of the city, some in fine
carriages, some on beautiful horses, and others on foot, and all
seeking exercise on the public avenues. The ladies were generally well dressed, some richly; but the *bussle*-ing fashion of
the north is just in its infancy here, and great care is taken by
the fashionable lady to get skirts enough on at one time. The
day has been passed with great ceremony, it being the great
festival day of St. John, and a day devoted to church ceremonies
and services by all Catholic countries, and particularly by this
priest-ridden country. This evening, I took a dry bull's skin and
laid in the back yard, preferring it to a bed of the same kind in
the *casa* or house. I was aroused by a great tumult in the street
shortly after retiring, and, on inquiring the cause, learned that a
mule had dragged a small boy along the street in full speed, and
that the child had been killed. I did not again sleep soon, for
my bed was alive with fleas, a thing I expected to avoid by
sleeping outside.

June 25. I went into the street early this morning, and
there saw the trail marked by the blood of the unfortunate boy
dragged by the mule. In a few moments after, Laubenheimer,
Chace, and myself passed into the plaza, and from thence into
the large and splendid Catholic Church, already slightly noticed.
This church measures 180 feet in length, and a corresponding
width. On each side of the front entrance, in niches carved for
the purpose, are two figures representing four of the Apostles,
as large as life and cut out of a stone found in this region. The
inside of this magnificent building has been, in days past, of the
very first order of architecture, and the gildings and mouldings
have been superb, but now look old, rusty, and dusty. The roof
and gallery are supported by three immense arches on pillars
cut from the stone alluded to. This immense building has two
high steeples on the front end, with a large clock between them,
which keeps good time and when striking can be heard in any
quarter of the city. On the end opposite there is a large dome

surmounted by a steeple of smaller dimensions. This once beautiful and still stupendous building was erected under Spanish rule and dominion and from money levied as a tax upon the miners then gathering silver out of the mines here. This tax amounted to six cents on each mark of silver, and out of this, and in this manner, one and a half millions of money was raised and the church built and paid for. This was the cost of this church. When we entered, we found an old madonna kneeling on the floor near the entrance, and on casting my eye into the body of the cathedral, I saw many engaged in devotional exercises in every quarter of the house, all of the votaries being women excepting two. Six chairs, looking like boxes with an open front and occupying as many places in the room, were devoted to the use of the priest and the penitent in confession. The priest took his seat, and on giving a signal, a small door opened either on the right or left of his holy head, and his ear was graciously inclined to hear the words of the lady making her confession and asking him to intercede with the Holy Virgin and other saints in her behalf. As soon as he had drank in all that was deemed necessary, he waved his hand as a token of silence, gave the signal at the other door, and the same ceremony was again gone through with. There is an older church, which I did not enter, but saw some of the ceremonies. As I was riding out of the city and came in front of this building, I found the doors wide open and saw the tapers burning brightly at the farther end. On the steps and in the doorway there were about twenty persons on their knees gently approaching the Ark of the Holy Covenant in this humble position. This church was hung with rich tapestry similar to the other and presented a fine appearance. In the evening, as soon as the matin bell strikes, you can see every man take off his sombrero, or hat, and remain uncovered until the sounds of the bell cease. To the behests of the priest all Mexicans pay attention, in no case violating his commands or transgressing the requirements of their religion.

In this respect they are always true, and by their blind devotion
are easily kept poor and ignorant, and few arise to eminence or
distinction. Among the lower order theft seems to be a trade,
and extremely well followed. McKnight lost his pistols, belt, and
knife yesterday, having been absent from his pack but a few
moments.

June 26.   Breakfasted and moved nearer the city to fine
shade, good water, and stubble field pasture. This camp is now
just five miles from the city, and here we will probably remain
another week. Our animals are improving very much, and by
the time we get away from here, they will be as good as new.
Our camp has been very throng[ed] today. We are on the edge
of a wheat field, and there are fifty men and boys, all peons,
reaping and hauling home the wheat. Two men, a major-domo
and his secretary, stand over these slaves and keep them at work
from 8:00 A.M to 12:00 M. and again from 4:00 P.M. to sunset.
The most of these copper-colored chaps have nothing but a covering for the loins and hat. They have all been with us during
their hours of rest and all wish to purchase a quarter's worth of
tobacco, or tobacco for 3¢. I sold two pounds of the southern
smoking tobacco for $1.00, and Cavendish is sold for $1.50 per
pound. This is an article used by both male and female, and is
in much demand because it is a government monopoly and only
four shops in the city of Chiahuahua are licensed to sell tobacco;
and persons purchasing of these agents of the government are
compelled to pay extremely high, and large revenue accrues to
the government by the enforcement of this law. While [I was]
writing the above lines, three Mexican ladies came up, and had
the doctor exercise his gallantry in handing them fire with which
to light their *cigarettos*. Ladies of the States, do you hear that?
If not, I really wish you could be with us for a few moments,
only for comparison, and that you might see with your own
eyes the strange and indeed singular ways of this part of the
world. At 4:00 P.M. we were visited by very heavy gusts of

wind which lasted, at short intervals, until 10 o'clock in the evening. We are in a valley and still between the mountains, which are low here.

June 27. Up early and attended to the wants of our mules. Mr. Shrieves came down and reported that a thief of Mexican birth had entered Colonel Word's camp and had taken out a bag of clothing belonging to Judge Tippin, and shirts, with a variety of small articles, from others. This is a very common occurrence, and every Mexican needs watching. This inherent disposition to steal is inherited by these people from their ancestors, the Indians, and in it they are as expert as their forefathers. The evening was attended with the threatenings of rain, but passed over with much wind.

June 28. Fine morning, with a pure atmosphere. It may be wondered that we should lay in this camp so long. This is easily explained. We are making up another train for a direct overland route to Puebla Los Angeles, and from thence to San Francisco, the train to consist in part of wagons and the trip to be performed to the California settlements in forty days. Colonel Ward, a resident of the former city, is at the head of this expedition, and he charges $50 per 100 lbs. freight to San Francisco, payable two months after our arrival at that place. This is an opportunity embraced by many for want of funds to go on, and is an actual relief to men thus circumstanced. Our company has been divided. The Perrysburg boys have gone to Mazatlan, there to take shipping, and Haller, McCauley and Speaker have taken our intended route, and are now ten days in advance. It is feared that they must suffer when they get to the ninety miles' plain upon which there is no water, and for want of provisions—having gone on without making necessary arrangements to supply these several wants. But if men will push ahead without reflection, they must suffer the consequences. We have the Mexicans now engaged in manufacturing leather canteens, pinole and beef, for the journey of sixty days. I have already given the manner of making pinole, and now, for the information of others traveling through Mexico, I will tell how beef is prepared for a long journey. Take twenty-five pounds of beef and   pounds of lard and   of pepper, and procure the assistance of one or more Mexicans, and they will, by the process of cutting and pounding, so mix these articles that no fear need be apprehended of its preservation in all kinds of weather, and salt and pepper and lard become useless, as those ingredients are already a part of every meal you make on this mixture. A small pinch of this meat, thrown into a pan or kettle of boiling water with a little flour or corn-meal thickening, will satisfy the wants of six men at any time; and it is a dish much relished by all. They charge high for it: we pay them $1.00 for three pounds, or $33 per hundred. Good flour can be bought in the city at $11 for 300 lbs. and pinole for $1.25 per peck. The distant thunder is again heard this afternoon, and we are looking forward to the time when it will rain almost constantly. Captain McNeal, with his company of sixty men, has just joined our camp, and all, or nearly all, will join this Ward expedition. There is one thing of which I have not spoken, in the vain hope that the reports might prove unfounded, as I could not bring my mind to believe that Americans could be bought to shed blood, even if it did flow from the veins of an Indian. Men, Americans, have been induced by offered rewards to go out in companies and kill Indians who are known to be at peace with the Government of the United States, and drive off their mules and horses, women and children, the latter to be placed in the hands of the Mexicans at from one to two hundred and fifty dollars to be condemned to a life of slavery and wretchedness. It is admitted by all that the Indians have dealt with the Mexicans on this frontier without mercy, but, at the same time, does this furnish the shadow of an excuse for men of my own nation? I think it does not, and I blush for the perpetrators of acts like these, and hope that no evil will result to those little bands of Americans now wending their way through Indian territory.

June 29. I was confined to my couch nearly all day

103

with an attack of the nervous headache which lasted until late in the night. Rain set in at nightfall and continued until daybreak.

June 30.   Very wet and disagreeable morning. Our bedding all wet, and it was with difficulty that we raised a fire and at 9:00 A.M. breakfasted. The Appache Indians are at work. An American by the name of Vaughn was found horribly mutilated and scalped a short distance from the city, and it is reported that three hundred of the redskins are waiting for our train. This we have expected, and had it not been for the attack made upon them by those Americans, we would have had nothing to apprehend but the loss of horses, and now we may expect to fight our way to California. Our new train already numbers about sixty men, and by the fifteenth of July, our appointed time to start, it will swell to two hundred men. With this number we can go over the territory without danger to the men, and probably without loss of property. But, to change the subject, let us now refer for one moment to the condition of things in the valley of Chiahuahua. This valley is not very extensive, being hemmed in by surrounding mountains, and the whole of it is irrigated. The entire water of the river is diverted and conducted by ditches through every part of the bottoms, having first been used in propelling the machinery of a gristmill. The property we are now encamped on is owned by an old Spaniard, very wealthy, and who now has on this plantation 150 peons, men, women, and children. They have just cut and harvested their wheat, and are now plowing for a corn crop, making two crops in one year. This lord of the land has his major-domo, or overseer, and his secretary, who have charge of the slaves. Some are sent into the pepper and garlic gardens, others into the fields, one with the cattle, another has charge of the goats and sheep, another, of the hogs, and one, of the caveyard of horses and mules. In this manner all are kept employed, yet they all together do not accomplish more than twelve able-bodied men in the north would do in the same number of hours. There is no timber in this valley, excepting a few cottonwood trees growing along the ditches, and [these] are valued very highly by the owner. The plains are covered with mesquite of very short growth, the twigs of which are cut and carried upon asses to the city market. In this way that place is supplied with fuel for cooking, none being necessary to heat the rooms. When it becomes cool enough for fire, a blanket serves the purpose, and this article is found over the shoulder of the rich and poor, and is at night substituted for a bed. All the mountains passed by our train have been found destitute of vegetation, wholly barren and unproductive, excepting here and there a century plant or maguey stalk and a few stinted bushes in the ravines. It will not be amiss here to recapitulate the several distances from town to town on our route, and by so doing, show at a glance the distance from Port Lavaca on the Gulf of Mexico to the city of Chiahuahua, or, as pronounced, Chewa-wa.

From Port Lavaca to Goliad *via* Victoria, Texas	60	miles
” Goliad to San Antonio, Texas	100	”
” San Antonio to San Fernando, Mexico	260	”
” ” Fernando to Santa Rosa, ”	80	”
” Santa Rosa to San Carlos, ”	300	”
” ” Carlos to Presidio del Norte, ”	60	”
” Presidio Del Norte to Ceyammi, ”	55	”
” Ceyammi to San Faronomo, ”	80	”
” San Faronomo to Chiahuahua, ”	20	”
Total number of miles	1,015	

Three hundred miles of this route was found to be over plains and mountains, without the sign of a wagon trail and almost destitute of water, and of late years traveled only by Indians and their stolen caveyards, and almost destitute of water, and grass only sufficient to keep up our animals.

{ July, 1849 }

CHIHUAHUA TO JANOS

July 1 (*Domingo*). In camp, and a wet, dreary day. We had a very heavy rain at noon, and no shelter to retreat to, having neglected to pitch our tent. But I feel thankful for all this, having the assurance that there will be water on the plains this side of the coast range of mountains. The rainy season has, in fact, set in, and everything like vegetation is fast assuming a new dress; and when once on the road again grass, and good grass, may be confidently looked for. This is a great desideratum, for we have no other feed when away from the Mexican settlements. We live well here, having good flour and vegetables (save potatoes) in any quantity. Fruit can be had, such as pears, figs, and melons, and a few apples. The apples and pears are very small, but the figs grow large and delicious and are found very palatable to persons fond of sweet fruit. Tomatoes form a staple article at our mess table, and can be had at a reasonable price at the adjoining gardens. The peons living upon the ranchos below us have all gone to the city to attend religious service. They passed our encampment in droves, the ladies with skirts high above the mud and water, and shoes in hand, and the men with pantaloons rolled up to the thigh, and their shirts in their hats. Such is their custom, at least among the peons, and there are yet other customs of which we need not speak here. At sunset Dr. Bunnell was called for by a Mexican, who stated that his presence was much desired by an aged Mexican at the hacienda. The doctor on his return stated that his patient was better but had been very sick.

July 2. Fed my mule corn, and after breakfast rode to town, where we found things quiet as usual. I bought a leather water tank, and left orders for more. These vessels are put together in a very rough manner, but are made out of thick leather, [and] therefore will answer a very good purpose. While in the city, I took an outside look at the large church, the building of which cost the Jesuits much expense, much labor, and exceedingly great trouble, and long before they could finish this grand undertaking they were by force compelled to abandon the work, and the walls now stand in about the same state of preservation in which they left it. The front of this building was finished in the very best style, with pillars and carved work of their best order, and the niches and recesses are all filled or, rather, occupied with the statue of some saint, one of which is, as usual, devoted to one representing the crucifixion of our Savior. Had they been permitted to finish this immense building, it would without doubt have outshone in splendor any other building devoted to religion in the city. But this, too, is but a monument of things intended.

I am happy to be able to record the fact that the rains have already had a decided influence upon the grass, which is particularly shown on the road between the city and our camp. A decided change has taken place, and a few more weeks will give us all the feed we want and an occasional water hole. We hear every day of some new depredation by the Indians. A Mexican was killed within a mile of San Aronomo, and within eighteen miles of this city. Turn to the west, and you find the same news repeated, and money, mules, and packs driven off; and notwithstanding these repeated injuries the government makes no effort to rid her people of the *Appache wrongs*, although they have many soldiers quartered in the city without employment or activity for the body or mind. These reports of countrymen having been waylaid, murdered, and scalped afford food for an hour's conversation, and then the subject, with all its horrors to an American mind, is dropped and rests with the things of the past. Would this be the case in our government? Could Indians come within eighteen miles of the city of Columbus, and there commit wrongs of this character, and the whole transaction [be] passed by our people without more than a murmur? Would Americans, on the receipt of such news, ride to the seat of disaster, and there look upon the gory, gaping wounds of the body before them, and hear the sounds speaking from every gaping gash, "Revenge me, my countrymen, revenge," without a swelling heart, a fixed determination, and a vow registered on high that this night's bloody deeds should return in a fourfold manner upon the heads of the perpetrators? I answer confidently for my countrymen, "No, never." Cowardice is not inherent with us, but here it is—hence the difference. I traded my aparejos,[1] and Laubenheimer his saddle, for Mexican saddletrees, and we now think that something has been gained. The Mexican saddletree is generally as good as any made, because it is made to fit almost any horse without so much as touching the ridge of the back, and are preferred to our American saddles by every one.

July 3.   Clear and calm but bracing morning, the rain of last night having refreshed the air very much. Our tent had been erected ready for our reception on the occurrence of another shower; and about midnight we were compelled to move from the out- to the inside of this protection from the pelting storm, which continued for several hours. Captain McNeel's company is moving on to a ranch about ten miles south of the city, where they expect to dry their beef and wait for our train. This company left San Antonio after we did, and went by way of Fredericksburg, intending to go to El Passo and thence down the Gila River, but, when they got to Presidio Del Norte, changed their views, and sixty of the men are now here. I am now writing these lines under the wide-spreading arms of a beautiful cottonwood on the left of the road leading to the city, and about two hundred yards from our camp. I have chosen this spot for several reasons: one is the want of wood, which is carried along this road to the city upon the backs of the gentle ass, and by being here I can make a purchase of a cargo which would otherwise pass by unnoticed, our camp

[1]Harness.

being under the alamos to the right and over a small ridge concealing it from the view of the passers on this road. Another
reason is that I am removed from the humming noise of the
camp, and can here take greater comfort than is usually found
among the mixed multitude. When I look back and reflect upon
all that has passed in our journey thus far, I wonder that life
has been spared to so many of us. Disease has done its share, and
accidents resulting in the death of several of the members of our
company have occurred. The cholera has terminated the existence of five or six men; George Richardson accidently shot
himself whilst attempting to mount his horse; and poor Lynch
was undoubtedly taken by the Indians, and perhaps inhumanly
put to death. But, by and through the goodness of an over-
ruling Providence, all others have been spared and permitted
the enjoyment of perfect health and the comforts, if not the
luxuries, of life. For these blessings I feel thankful, and could I
but hear at this place of similar blessings enjoyed by my family,
I could be contented and measurably happy. A gentleman (Mexican) with two ladies has just passed on horseback, and to give
the reader an idea of how things are done, I will attempt a
description of this party. The gentleman and one of the ladies
sat upon one horse, the lady behind—which order of riding is
frequently reversed. The lady was dressed in the usual style, and
wore her scarf in such a manner over her head as to conceal all
but the nose and eyes. The second lady was on a horse, with a
child in her arms, and upon her head wore a scarf and a wide-
rimmed hat made in the manner of a gentleman's hat. Men's hats
or none are worn by the ladies here. The gent wore a pair of
wide-legged double pants, a vest, and his wide sombrero or hat,
with a pair of immense spurs on his feet, which were in continual motion. These are some of the absurd customs of the land
of the Montezumas, and nothing short of a total revolution
could effect a change. Although wagons are used by the American residents here, the Mexicans adhere to the heavy, wooden-
wheeled cart, the wheels of which are a load for any one pair

of oxen. Their plows are still the same in form and material [as] were those used by the agriculturists of ancient times, without the addition of a single point of improvement. Reader, we have toiled along together thus far, and as tomorrow is the anniversary of our nation's birth and freedom, we will open with a new book, and, I hope, one of greater merit.

BOOK THIRD

  July 4. This is the anniversary of our national freedom, when the tyrant's chains were shaken from strong hands and willing hearts and Liberty was proclaimed throughout "the land of the free and the home of the brave." Little did I dream of my present situation one year ago, when I was surrounded by friends and all the endearments of home. But being here, and intending to be far from this in one year from this date (if life is spared), I must speak of things here, and leave the event to the future. Yesterday in the afternoon a very heavy rain hung over the mountains in the south, and in a short time it descended in torrents, which we could see but did not feel until this morning, when the water in the canal passing by our camp became very muddy and the river opposite was foaming and roaring down the valley. It is now cloudy, and we expect more rain, which is now of daily occurrence. Colonel Watson came out to the camp this morning, and our mess has arranged with him to carry 300 lbs. of freight to San Francisco, for which we pay as freight 50¢ per pound when the contract has been fulfilled. Laubenheimer and myself have been busy this morning, in preparing pads and blankets for our mules, and Teats, Brunner, and others have gone into the city. Colonel Word's mess bought and killed a beef, and are now engaged in drying it for the journey. We were presented with a fine cut of this beef, and having purchased onions and tomatoes went to work and in a short time our table was groaning under one of the best dinners on this fourth in Mexico; and well did the soup relish in this land of saints and angels. It is in this manner that we passed this great national Sabbath, quietly, without ostentation, but to the entire satisfaction of everyone. In the afternoon another small shower of rain visited this section, and added its blessings to those already enjoyed.

In the evening an oration was delivered at the upper encampment which elicited much applause; after which the party came down to our tent, and we were favored by the doctor with "the Star-Spangled Banner," "Would I Were a Boy Again," and other songs of a kindred character. The doctor was accompanied on the violin by Colonel Word.

July 5. This morning before breakfast two men of the Mississippi Mining Company disagreed on some private matter and came to blows, but were parted without much injury to each other. News of further Indian depredations came into camp, of the following purport. Six Mexicans are said to have been killed last night ten miles south of the city, but this needs confirmation. The major-domo, or overseer, of this hacienda took dinner with us today and from him we learned that the peons were nearly all single men and women, although living together as man and wife. When asked the reason for this violation of the doctrine taught by the Bible, and regarded with so much reverence by other denominations of Christians, he answered that they never could get money enough to pay for the celebration of the marriage ceremony; consequently, they were compelled to adopt each other without the performance of that ancient rite. He told us that the priest charged the rich for his services on such occasions from twenty-five to forty dollars, and when called upon by a poor couple his fee was in all cases fourteen dollars. He was asked whether the padre ever interfered with, or preached against, this practice of self-marriage, to which he answered no. These are actions that would be characterized as sins by our clergy, but here, where sins are so easily disposed of, such conduct is winked at by those in charge of the spiritual interests of the people, so long as their blind devotion keep[s] the church purse well filled and a cunning priesthood in absolute power and dominion. This day has been passed in refitting and padding our saddles, and repairing the strapping to our pack saddles. Laubenheimer and Parker are in town making further arrangements for a start on the fifteenth, and in the meantime our horses and mules are growing fat and wild again—so much so that it is with much difficulty that they are caught at night. Rain commenced falling about dark, and continued all night. We found our tent very serviceable on this occasion, as it kept off all the water, and we slept soundly. We ascertained that a party of Indians had passed through this valley with a number of stolen animals last night. They passed within a few miles of our camp, but did not disturb our slumbers.

July 6. The rain ceased at break of day, and the weather is cool and pleasant. Two Mexicans came into camp this morning and laid claim to a mule belonging to Mr. Ball. This is of frequent occurrence. Our party has already lost several mules and horses under such claims, the Mexicans claiming that these animals had been stolen by the Indians and that they were marked with their brand. These men presented a paper, pretending it to be a warrant from the alcalde, which was of course disregarded, for it lacked a seal and amounted to nothing. Ball told him to bring the horse he had traded for the mule, and he has gone in search of the thief and horse; and in the meantime Ball will ride the mule off to the advance camp and conceal him. Some such measure must be adopted, or Americans will suffer under this new system of thieving whilst traveling in Mexico. Drs. Bunnell and Ogburn are now cutting a wen out of the cheek of a Mexican, which operation was quickly performed. The patient bore it with remarkable fortitude, never suffering a sound to escape his lips whilst suffering intense pain. The owner of this hacienda has taken it into his head to have us removed, and sent his major-domo down with a written order for us to leave his domains, alleging as a reason that he wishes to work his slaves, and if our goods and chattels should be stolen by them, he would not be responsible. We sent Dr. Bunnell, who is our interpreter, to reason the case with him, and to demand a satisfactory reason for this arbitrary order. The doctor came back after an absence of about two hours and told us that our mess had permission to stay but that others must leave the ground on account of disrespectful and even threatening language used by a few of the wagoners. The evening was very cloudy and [there was] vivid lightning.

July 7. Although very cloudy and threatening last night, morning came and no rain had fallen. The heavy body of clouds that arose in the south turned off to the eastward, where the sharpest flashes of electricity escaped that I have ever seen. In the south and east we could see heavy waterspouts from this cloud, and much water must have fallen about ten miles from us. During the night a horse was stolen from our camp by a Mexican, and, though diligently looked for, has not yet been recovered. The Appache Indians passed our camp last night and went into the hacienda above, and there shot a Mexican and killed him instantly—and this, too, at his own door. A few nights since, they compelled five Mexicans to dismount, took their horses, and rode on to a sheepfold, where they killed those in charge and drove off about a thousand head of sheep and goats, all of which took place not to exceed five miles [out] of the city of Chiahuahua, where they have a large military station, etc.; yet such acts do not arouse the cowards quartered there, and no notice is taken of them. The whole country seems to be governed by the Appache nation, and those pretending to rule dare not say that they are masters. Gomaz, the Appache chief, is said to be a Mexican, and they have offered the Americans a reward of $1,000 for his scalp. But he is too smart for his brethren, and, unless he should be taken by Americans, he will live to a good old age, honored and respected by his followers because of the many Mexican scalps dangling at his belt. This daring chief has laid the town of Ceyammi under an annual contribution, and draws from that and other, similar sources a large amount of revenue. 'Tis said that this city makes him an annual payment as a peace purchase. Would Americans suffer this? No! not if every tree in the forest served to shield an Indian, and they stood upon the ground as thick and numerous as the blades of grass. It may be thought that too much is claimed for Americans, but a moment's reflection, a retrospective view of the fields of Lexington, Bunkerhill, Monmouth, York-town, and later still, of [Resaca] de la Palma, Sacrimento, Buena Vista., etc., will convince any doubter that Americans will not submit to injustice from any source but under all circumstances defend their rights manfully. 4:00 P. M.—prospect for more rain. The water in the river has been so high as to break away the dam, and for the past few days our supply of water in the ditch has entirely failed, and in the morning we move eastward about one mile to new grass and water. A small company of soldiers passed our camp this morning, armed with a gun and sword, well lashed to the saddle, and in one hand they held the bridle reins, and the other held the handle of a long spear, at the top of which floated a small streamer. I thought that now these marauding bands of Indians would be hunted down, and proper vengeance visited upon them for the lives they had so recently taken. But in this I gave them credit for more than they deserved, for this company of valiant men, well mounted, *were in charge of a drove of mules and horses* which they had brought here to pasture under government orders. This, then, is the country where *one mule* is worth more than the lives of *many citizens*.

July 8 (Sabbath). In accordance with previous arrangements we moved our camp early this morning to a camp having a little of all the necessaries but infested with ants, or, as expressed in the Spanish language, *hormigas*. We lost nothing last night, and our camp remained undisturbed under the guardian care of a strict watch, relieved every two hours. A few yards below our present camp is a large and well-cultivated garden of pepper, melons, tomatoes, and corn, and, regardless of this being a day set apart as a day of rest, the owner is working in it, hoeing down the weeds and drawing the earth into ridges along the rows. In the middle of his work he has stuck down a "Santa Cruz" or sainted cross, which he told us he had placed there to keep off his Satanic Majesty, the Devil, but which he offered to sell us if we desired it. This offer we declined, believing perhaps as little in the virtue of this cross as any other body of men. The grass is very good here and covers a level, open plain, upon which we can see our horses for several miles, and we have the promise of more water on tomorrow. In the afternoon it became cloudy in the west, and towards evening we had some thunder and lightning in that quarter and a slight sprinkle of rain here.

July 9. Stood guard last night; consequently, I slept late this morning. When I came out of the tent, the sun was peering over the eastern mountain with great warmth, and the sky was almost unveiled with clouds. All our horses and mules were found in their places, nothing having been taken during the night. No Indian alarms, save at the hacienda above us, where the guard contended strenuously that two Appaches had made an attempt to steal the mules in his charge. The day is growing warmer every hour, and unless a wind springs up it will be unlike the days of the past week, cool and comfortable. We are now beginning to long for our departure from this place, and, as it approaches, activity in preparation takes place and all are trying to procure such things as are deemed necessary for a journey of seventy days over an Indian territory. The party of Americans out after the Appaches have not yet returned, and nothing has been heard of them since they left. It is possible that they may never get in again, because this tribe is in arms against the Americans, and nothing but the scalps of some of the men will appease their appetite for blood and plunder. Through this section our train has to pass; and it may yet be our misfortune to meet them in large bodies and be compelled to fight our way through. They, like their descendants (the northern Mexicans), are cowardly, not well-armed, poorly mounted, but thievish in their dispositions; and, unlike the Camanche nation, fight in ambush.[2]

The Camanches[3] are braver, have better arms, and are generally well mounted and make their attacks on horseback, and are, perhaps, as a nation the best horsemen in the world. To fight them successfully, it is necessary to dismount them by shooting their horses first, and then take them while running from you in an ungainly, waddling gait.

This day has almost closed, and no water has yet been passed to our camp, and unless it comes in the morning we will be compelled to abandon the camp and retreat to the city. This we dislike, on account of the difficulty of procuring feed for our

[2]Jacob Robinson, with Doniphan in 1846-47, remarked on the Apache menace to farmers near the Rio Conchos. "The climate here is delightful," he said; "and the cultivator is in no danger from the storm nor the drought; but sometimes the dreadful Apache Indian comes down from the mountain, and drives off in a moment the increase of years." (Jacob S. Robinson, *A Journal of the Santa Fe Expedition under Colonel Doniphan*, ed. Carl L. Cannon ["Narratives of the Trans-Mississippi Frontier"; 1932] p. 83.) Bartlett said in 1853 that "two of the largest and most widely spread tribes, the Comanches and the Apaches, are as actively hostile to the Americans and Mexicans as they were before the country occupied by them, became a part of the Union. At no period have the incursions been more frequent, or attended with greater atrocities, than at the present time. . . . The depredations of the Apaches are less serious [than Comanche raids] only because their numbers are less, and they have a more thinly settled country for their operations. In Mexico these are confined to the northern portions of the States of Sonora and Chihuahua. These regions, once inhabited by a peaceful and happy population, are now deserted, and the fertile valleys they tilled are reverting to the condition of a wilderness. . . . The Apaches, whose number does not exceed 5000, extend from the vicinity of the Pecos through the States of Chihuahua, Sonora, and the territory of New Mexico, to the confines of the Colorado of the West. They are less nomadic in their habits than the Comanches, and have districts in which their families permanently reside. This tribe, from the time they are first mentioned by Father Kino, in the year 1694, have been a nation of robbers. Their hand is against every other tribe, and that of all others against them. It was they who drove out the peaceable people and semi-civilized tribes from the Gila, and destroyed the builders of the ancient edifices. . . . Every account we have represents them as a treacherous and bloodthirsty people, living by plunder alone. They have made repeated treaties with the States of Sonora and Chihuahua, only to be broken on the first favorable opportunity; and the treaties recently made with the United States have been as little regarded." (Bartlett, *Personal Narrative*, II, 385-87.)

[3]"The Comanches," said Bartlett, "pass across the Rio Grande into Mexico,

mules, there being nothing but hard corn and dry grass to be found. But we hope for the coming of water, which has been frequently promised and always delayed. Our letters have been dispatched by a Mr. Owens, who returns to the United States by way of Parras and Monteray. There is an arrangement between Dr. East of this city and our consul at Monteray by which letters and packages are transmitted at a cost of half a dollar to the person sending. At 8 o'clock another heavy rain passed over, with but a slight fall here.

July 10.   Our guard was hailed in the night by a company of ten Mexicans, who came into camp and reported that nine mules and twenty horses had been stolen from the caveyard in the adjoining hacienda by three Apache Indians. The guard stationed over the animals fired on the Indians when they came up, but did them no injury; and they drove off the animals, after which these men came down to notify us of our proximity to danger, and perhaps thought that by being with us a greater measure of security was afforded them. This morning a small company started in search of the property and Indians, and a short distance below our camp found the mules, but the horses had been driven off; and with the recovered property they returned, well satisfied to get so much back without having to fight for it. After breakfast I mounted and went to the river for water, passing over the now dry canals or ditches, and a field of corn just high enough for the first ploughing and dressing. The gardens looked as if water was highly necessary; all the plants were in a drooping condition, and the inhabitants generally

in bands of 300 or 400, and penetrate the very heart of Chihuahua; they have passed into Durango and Zacatecas, and have traversed Coahuila and Nuevo Leon. The extent of the depredations and murders committed by them would be appalling, if summed up. . . . Their range is from the Mexican States alluded to, to the Buffalo region, north and east of Santa Fe. In the fall and winter season their home is near the Rio Grande in the *Bolson de Mapimi*, a vast basin shut in by high mountains at the west. Here they enjoy uninterrupted possession of a wide extent of country, whence they make their sallies into the heart of Mexico." He estimated them to number about 12,000. (*Ibid.,* pp. 385-86.)

[were] at work on the dam, by which water is thrown over the broad acres of this valley. Without irrigation nothing could be raised, and this land, of a coarse, sandy nature, would be entirely useless for agricultural purposes; but by the adoption of this ancient practice, nearly all the grains are raised successfully, and tolerably abundant[ly], although all of an inferior order. It is now near sunset, and cloudy, and the promised water has not yet come down the canal. Tomorrow we will go into the city and finish laying in our supplies. This arrangement once completed, we move forward to another camp, where we will remain until the train comes up—and then, by steady marches, for the Pacific shores! At 8 o'clock I came on guard, and during my two hours' watch, the most intensely vivid lightning was playing from the clouds at all the cardinal points of [the] compass. I never saw such blinding flashes of electricity as were almost constantly darting, like the tongues of fiery serpents, across the frowning sky. During this time Heaven's artillery was constantly roaring, and each cloud, however small, seemed but a part of this apparently great storehouse of storms, and contributed largely to the general roaring of the storm. There was, however, but little rain at our camp; the most fell at or near the mountains.

July 11. Quite cloudy and cool this morning. We are preparing to move and try a city life, of which I entertain a horror. Fleas, lice, and vermin of other names generally infect the towns, and but little comfort can be taken in a visit. But it must be done, and the sooner we get through the better for us, as we can then bid *"Adios"* to the city of Chiahuahua and betake ourselves to the camp which is pitched wherever circumstances compel us to halt. Camp life, although pleasant to many persons, is not the life for me. When compelled to lie by, to rest and recruit our animals, it becomes exceedingly irksome, but yet far more agreeable than confinement to the narrow streets and adobe houses of a Mexican city or town; and only when pushing on our winding way, and only when compelled to stop at night does this kind of life become pleasant.

But a change will come in a few more days. The country will soon slope to the west, and the waters pass on and mingle with those of the Pacific. A new country, new productions, and a new climate will claim our attention, and drive dull care away; and if fortunate, a few more months will permit us to see the land, to which all eyes are now so anxiously turned. In this camp we have been very much annoyed with a host of houseflies.

1:00 P.M., and now we are in the city,[4] without any accident, although our mules had become quite fractious from long rest and high feeding. Here we bought bread and eggs and had a fine tea, with sugar in it. These are some of the luxuries not enjoyed by the commonalty, as eggs sell at 25 ¢ per dozen. No rain this evening.

July 12. Breakfast on bread and milk. The church bells are almost continually sounding, and prayer books, beads, and sainted images are constantly f[l]itting before us. Our first care this morning will be the mules, and then comes the purchasing

---

[4]Good descriptions of Chihuahua city at this period may be found in Bartlett, *Personal Narrative*, II, 431-41, and in Julius Froebel, *Seven Years' Travel in Central America* (1859), pp. 342-46. Almost every traveler through northern Mexico mentions the city at some length. The chief points of interest were its altitude (nearly five thousand feet), its picturesque site on a plain surrounded by rocky mountains, its cathedral of cut stone, a graceful stone aqueduct, the *casa de moneda*, or mint, and the bullfight arena. Chihuahua was originally a silver center, the rich mines of Santa Eulalia, a dozen miles east of the town, supplying the ore; with the decline of the mines, the town's population decreased, until, at the time Bartlett passed through, it amounted to only 12,000. The name, said Froebel, was derived from the Tarumare language, and meant a place of pleasure. See also Robinson, *Journal of the Santa Fe Expedition*, p. 76 *passim*; George F. Ruxton, *Adventures in Mexico and the Rocky Mountains* (1847), pp. 151-58; Gregg, *Commerce of the Prairies*, II, chap. vi. Clarke (*Travels in Mexico*, p. 51) stated that the town was well built, and had "wide clean streets, and handsome buildings. . . . The plaza or public square, is large and imposing, adorned with a splendid fountain and seats, and pillars of white porphyry. On one side is a large and splendid cathedral, and the other sides are occupied by spacious public buildings and stores. There are a large number of American merchants here. Dry goods are bought from the states, by the way of Santa-Fe. . . . I am of opinion, it would make a pleasant place of residence." See also the diary of Cave Couts (MS, Bancroft Library).

of *carne seca,* or dried beef, with such other things as our journey will require. For dried beef we have to pay $18 per 100 lbs., and even this we are glad to get, worms and bugs not thrown in. To secure it from further gnawings of this insect, we, after procuring [it], cut it into small pieces, tie it up in a good bag, and expose to the sun, which generally effects a removal of the moth and bug. To give persons an idea of the cost of articles in the city of Chiahuahua I will here enumerate and give a list of such as are generally used.

First on this list of necessaries, is the article of

Flour, per *arroba* (25 lbs.)		$1.00
Corn, per bushel		.75
Corn pinole, per peck or *almud* [1/12 bushel]		1.25
Beef on foot		16.00 & 18.00
Pork, 250 lbs. weight		16.00
Lard, per lb. or *libra* [36 oz.]		.31
Beef, dried, per 25 lbs.		4.50
Beef, *higote* or prepared, per 25 lbs.		10.00
Sugar, per lb.	15¢ to	.25
Coffee, per lb.	25¢ to	.31
Horse shoeing, from	2.50 to	4.00
Men's shoes, goatskin dressed		1.50
Spanish saddles from	12.00 to	100.00
Bridles, from	2.00 to	20.00
Double palm hats		1.00
Buck and cloth pants, usually		10.00

This is a summary of such things as the traveler may need on a journey of this kind, and I am well convinced that cheaper routes to California exist than this. Mexicans must be paid a high price for all they sell to Americans, or there is no trade; and if anything is offered for sale, it hardly ever brings first cost from any of their pockets.

This day has come to a close, and the most of our mules have been shod, and other preparations in a way of completion. No rain, but slightly clouded.

July 13. Began operations early this morning and find

PATIO OF A MEXICAN MINING HACIENDA; THE PATIO PROCESS

H. G. Ward, *Mexico in 1827* . . . (London, 1828), II, 438

much to be done preparatory to starting for the third time on our journey. It becomes necessary to take provisions for the entire distance to Puebla Los Angelos, and, to meet this, one more mule must be taken to carry the extra hundred pounds to each man. Mules are extremely high and but few in the market, and we have therefore availed ourselves of the opportunity of loading all on the wagons in our train, excepting the provisions, which, with our blankets and a change of shirts and water canteens, will be the load for each of our packs. This will by daily consumption be reduced, and when arrived at the dry plains our mules will be loaded with water to do them for a hundred miles, which is said to be the distance from water to water. Our powder has been dealt out to each man, and some of the smaller necessaries collected in, and by tomorrow evening we will be ready to put our goods aboard of the wagons, and at the end of eight days we shall probably be at the frontier town of Yanos and ten more will place us on the Rio Gila, if fortunate. During my rambles over the city this morning, I unexpectedly found myself in the market space, where I found a variety of vegetables and a small quantity of meat for sale. Onions predominated, and in every purchase but my own they formed the largest portion. The market men and women were nearly all very aged, some so old that they supported themselves on sticks while dealing out their wares, and pocketing "the change." I noticed that the pork was all neatly skinned, excepting the head, which was always laid on the wooden bowl containing the meat as an index to the kind. Meat of every description is sold at a certain price for the piece, and not by the pound. Different kinds of melons, prickly pear, pears, and figs composed the greater part of the fruit offered for sale, together with a very small acorn relished as much here as are our chestnuts at the north, but with no comparison to us Americans. We have now procured our supply of flour, pinole, and beef, and a few articles only remain to be added to our outfit. In addition to our old mess, we have taken in Dr. Bunnell and E. Brunner—making

our number six; and we get along swimmingly, living on fresh
meat, bread, milk and coffee, and when we wish to be sociable
in the highest degree, we use tea. There is one thing creditable
amongst this people. I noticed the approach to the market of a
host of beggars who never applied to anyone without receiving
alms. Many of these are blind and live upon the gifts of others
from day to day.

July 14. A number of errands have been done, and we
can now say that we are nearly ready. Our loads have been
weighed out to each, and other indispensable arrangements
finally concluded. Tomorrow (being the greatest day in Mexico) we load our goods on the wagons. The Sabbath is devoted
by this people to religion and amusements, among which bull-
fighting stands the most prominent, and we are compelled to
devote a part of tomorrow to the duties above referred to, in
order to get an early start and accomplish a journey to water and
grass on Monday. The Indian depredations have ceased, in consequence of a chase now in progress between them and the Americans who have gone in pursuit. It is reported that two hundred
warriors are being hotly pursued by the company, all going
northward. This, however, needs confirmation, as this is a country given to rumor and the old Madam is constantly moving and
wagging her thousand tongues to the infinite annoyance of the
cowardly population. Cloudy, with a little rain in the morning.

July 15 (*Domingo*). Having shared my bed with a host
of fleas, I arose early and found that it had clouded up thick
during the night, and the rain set in at 8:00 A. M. and continued
at slight intervals all the day. After breakfast, I went to the
American Hotel, which is situated but a few yards from the
church. A chime of bells was ringing at the time, and this was the
first call—a call designed for the poor of the city, inviting them
to come up to the temple and have their sins forgiven. And this
call to the needy did not pass unheeded, for many hundreds
passed the portals and knelt to the gods of their own making.
While these poor people were blindly contributing their mite

towards the support of a crafty priesthood, others in the enjoyment of a little more wealth were in the market, selling clothing
of every description, with such other articles as are bought and
sold here. At the end of an hour another deep-toned bell was
heard, and in a moment the streets were filled with human beings, the poor just leaving the church, and the second class, or
common traders, going to it. With these I observed many mid-
dle-aged women, who carried in their hands a small tin frame,
with glass door and neatly decorated with rosettes of various
kinds, and in this they had their hearts—their religion—for the
image of Christ crucified was *there*.

At the end of the next hour these worshipers departed and
the neat but old-fashioned carriage came rolling up with its load
of wealthy lords and ladies. Those who went there at this hour
on foot were well dressed and wore the appearance of being
wealthy. These, too, departed with hearts at ease—to all appearance—having in their opinion spent all the time necessary with
God. Few Mexicans ever pass the doors of the church, even
when walking in the street, without uncovering their heads, and
assign this as a reason for the act: that God is in the church, sees
them as they pass, and that He will be highly offended if they
neglect to do this act of reverence while passing in His presence.

Our goods are now loaded, but we are still unwillingly confined to the city. We concluded to take some extra provisions,
and there being a horse race this afternoon, the flour store is
shut up, and we are compelled to remain till morning. Our provisions, 100 lbs. per man, cost us each $17, and other messes have
been compelled to pay much higher rates for pinole and *higote*.
As our day of departure draws near, the Mexicans begin to
charge higher for everything, for they take for granted that we
are the last Americans who will be here this season, and that
their only chance for enlarging their means is to charge these
"Diablo Americanos" well for every article purchased.

July 16. Made our purchases early, and at 1:00 P.M.
encamped on a fine grass plat six miles northwest of the city,

amongst the farmers or rancheros. Our camp is beautifully
situated in a fine valley on a branch of the Conchas River, with
a range of mountains on either hand, and command[ing] a view
of the city we so gladly leave behind us. There are American
residents in Chiahuahua whom we regret to part with, and among
these I will name Dr. East, Mr. Riddle,[5] and Mr. Anderson,
whom I found to be perfect gentlemen, and men who by several
years' residence have become well qualified to impart to their
countrymen knowledge of importance. On repacking, we found
our pepper box, containing about a pound of that necessary
article, a hatchet, tin plate, and ropes gone, and we were well
satisfied that the owner of the corral or his boys had stolen them.
But they could not be found, and we came away very much
dissatisfied with the thieving propensities of those in whom we
placed a slight confidence only. The train has not all come up
but will be here this evening, and tomorrow morning, or *mañana*
or *mañanita*[6] we move on to the Sacrimento, the battleground
between Colonel Doniphan and the Mexicans, one of the most
bloody engagements during the war.[7] This field of strife we

[5]Bennet Riddells, American consul at Chihuahua.

[6]Tomorrow, tomorrow morning.

[7]Robinson's account of the Battle of Sacramento was as follows: "Took up
the march early on the morning of the 28th [February, 1847], and were soon
informed that the Mexicans were coming forward to meet us; but it proved to
be only a body of about 500, moving to our right with the intention of cutting off our wagons, but as we marched our wagons by fours and the troops
between them, it rendered their effort fruitless. At about 12 o'clock we came
in sight of the enemy, about one mile distant, when we turned from the road
toward the left, in order to gain an eminence which the Mexicans occupied.
In this movement we were completely successful and our line formed instantly,
and commenced firing by our artillery upon an advanced body of Mexican
cavalry, who had formed for the purpose of charging upon us. Our first shots
fell directly among them, and threw their ranks into confusion, but they soon
retreated behind their artillery, which then opened a fire upon us, without
doing much damage, the balls passing over or falling before us.

"It was soon perceived that a charge would be necessary, to rout the enemy
from their forts; and it was accordingly made by Capts. Reed and Barstow,
sustained by Capt. Hudson and the First Battalion. The result was the complete discomfiture of the Mexican forces. Their artillery retreated in order to
occupy a high and commanding point, and their cavalry and infantry retreated

will reach tomorrow. The train came into camp late in the evening, in consequence of the unruly disposition of some of the mules. Fleas very numerous, and exceedingly annoying.

July 17. Very warm. The water at this spring is pleasant and cool, but our mules refuse to drink it. The wagons have to be reloaded this morning in consequence of a neglect on the part of those whose duty it was to see that everything had a place and that everything was in its proper place; and we will not get out of this camp until near noon. But here comes a lady, bearing in her arms a box containing an image of Mary and the infant Jesus, and many worship this by the wayside. They have many gods in the city and now there is also one in the country. There never existed a people on the face of the globe so completely, so emphatically, the worshipers of idols, and so entirely controlled in all their acts by priestly dictation as these Mexicans. They uncover their heads or bend the knee to every cross, wherever met with, and all persons who neglect or refuse to bow to these absurd notions are looked upon as heretics and regarded with disdain. Dr. East informed me that social visits between Americans and Spaniards were rare occurrences, and that the foreigners formed a distinct and separate class or social circle, into which a Spaniard rarely ventured. Mr. Riddle, keeper of the American Hotel and an American, has a Spanish wife who cannot speak a word of English, but is a perfect lady, and accomplished. I have observed that the women in Mexico do

in disorder. . . . During the charge a cross fire was kept up by five pieces of Mexican artillery already occupying the high point abovementioned. Another charge was now necessary to dislodge them from that point, which was almost inaccessible, except by a road cut through the rocks directly in front of their cannon. An ascent in the rear was therefore attempted by the First Battalion and with difficulty accomplished; the men forcing up the howitzers over rocks which at other times would have been deemed impassable. The Second Battalion was in the mean time ascending the road, and the artillery kept up a continual fire across the valley. When we reached the summit we were astonished to find the Mexicans had all fled or were flying. We pursued them over the rocks and ravines, and succeeded in getting their cannon, ammunition and stores. The victory was complete. . . ." (Robinson, *Journal of the Santa Fe Expedition*, pp. 74-76.)

nearly all the buying and selling, and when so engaged rarely consult their husbands or those who are nominally so. When a woman is engaged at needlework, she scarcely ever sits in a chair, but squats upon a skin or mat and leans upon the wall for support. In this position she will sit and work for hours without changing. I have also seen them sitting in this manner in front of their dwellings during the shady hours, and when disturbed by the sun they would walk across the street and lean against their neighbor's *casa*, or house, during the remainder of the day.

3:00 P.M.—We are still in camp, and will remain here until tomorrow. This delay is unpleasant, but could not well be avoided, as the men had not been settled with yet, and the wagons had not been loaded conveniently in town.

5:00 P.M.—A serious rencounter has just taken place in our camp between a Mr. Jones and Mr. Parker, strangers to us. They had a misunderstanding and came to blows, and before many minutes Parker fell, mortally wounded, his right side cut open and his intestines gushing from three large gashes in the abdomen. In three minutes after he fell, his last breath passed the opening in the side, and he lay there, a monument of human folly and human wickedness when unrestrained by laws and social compact. Jones received a large gash in the left side, close under the arm, the knife having cut through the ribs and penetrated the lungs. The surgeons in our company pronounce his case hopeless, and in a week or perhaps ten days he too will pass to the silent tomb and enter upon the untried realities of another state of existence. While the fight was progressing a pistol was fired at Jones by a young man belonging to Parker's mess, but did not take effect. Thus it is with men who lay aside all restraint and allow passion to govern in place of reason.

Great God! what a sad spectacle, what a sad reality, what a sad consummation!

The grave was dug a few yards to the left of the road among the mesquites, and at 12 o'clock in the night the remains of Parker were lowered to their last home, and he was left to the worms and his God. A funeral by candlelight throws a melancholy feeling over any observer and had a solemn effect upon me, as I had a full view of the rigid corpse as the[y] bore it to the grave, being on duty at that hour. He was neatly buried, with his blanket for a winding sheet. Jones was much affected with the result of this awful tragedy. After Parker fell, Jones retreated to his tent and called for the surgeons. Shortly after, he inquired whether Parker was dead. The answer was yes. Jones replied that he almost wished that Parker had killed *him*, and that this was the first blood he had upon his hands to account for at the final day.

July 18. The sun steals from his bed of roses with considerable warmth beaming from his glowing countenance and I think there is a warm day in reserve for us. Our camp has been visited by our Mexican neighbors with milk *tortillas*, or "torteas," chickens, and milk curd—by them called "good cheese" or "*bueno queso*" but not found "*bueno*" by us. A carriage was sent for this morning to convey Jones to the city, and is expected every moment. At 8:00 A.M. the carriage arrived, and Mr. Jones was carefully placed in it and conveyed to town, accompanied by Colonel Watson and others, who went in to testify before the authorities and to place him in the charge of some of the resident Americans. At 9 o'clock we were once more moving onward, and at 1:00 P.M. arrived at the head of the Sacrimento Valley upon the battleground of the Sacrimento. We found here a large hacienda, well prepared for defense against Indian aggressions, which have been of late very frequent. On the hill to the right of the river and spring are the remains of the fortifications constructed by the Mexicans, where they expected to give Colonel Doniphon a *warm* reception. The battle opened at about 1:00 P.M. and continued untill after nightfall, and during this sanguinary conflict about a thousand Mexicans were made to bite the dust, and only one American died on the field. The next day many of the poor Mexican soldiers were found badly wounded, and some dead, in the neighboring mountains. The hill on the left was crowded during the conflict by thousands of women and children, looking on this meeting with beating hearts. But Doniphon was not so easily repulsed, and the Mexican general retreated to the city after a resistance of several hours. John [   ], the colored man, who rallied and brought into action the Negroes belonging to the Colonel's train, and who fought with a valorous determination to conquer or die, is now in our train and on his way to California. At 2:00 P.M. we left this battleground and water, and moved forward to better grass, and encamped without water or wood about eighteen miles from the dueling camp and twenty-four miles from the city. The valley we are now in is one of great natural beauty. It is probably fifteen miles wide, green with young grass, and at the distance of a mile there is a large herd of antelope, regaling themselves on the new and tender grass. As far north as we can see, this noble valley lies extended between a low range of mountains and bounded on the west by the rugged and tall Sierra Madre, or mother of mountains.

July 19.   Left our antelope camp at sunrise, and traveled about ten miles, and encamped on good grass and the finest stream of water found in the State of Chihuahua. The ground traveled over today is one of beauty, partaking of a prairie nature, grown up since the rains with fine, tender grass and flowers of various kinds and colors. But there is a total absence of everything like wood, and we have been compelled to resort to *bois de vache* or cow wood, which we found abundant, being only one mile south of a hacienda called Souze. Cattle in fine order are grazing a short distance from our camp. We noticed coming up large herds of antelope, and the prairie wolves were in sight nearly all the time. The white rabbit was also scared from his concealment and ran off over the meadow. I must say for this valley that a handsomer spot has not yet been passed by us in Mexico. 3:00 P.M.—moved forward, over a level and excellent road, eight miles, and at sunset encamped at the Lone Tree—a name given to this camp because of a single, and the only, tree within ten

miles of it. We found saltpeter apparently strewn along the
road and a number of small pools of water, some of a saline taste,
others strong of sulphur. We here topped the lone tree for wood
to cook with.

July 20. Aroused camp at daylight, and moved forward
to the hacienda of Ensineas,[8] eight miles. Here we halted and
sent to the mountains for wood to cook with. Ensineas is handsomely located in this valley and is supplied with water from
tanks or large artificial basins. This hacienda is noted for its fruit,
several varieties of which are cultivated here in a large garden;
peaches, pears, apricots, apples, quinces, and figs are raised here
and can now be obtained of the gardener, and a cherry much resembling the wild cherry, only much larger. Our wood from the
mountains did not reach us, and Dr. Bunnell procured from the
garden or orchard some dry limbs of the apple tree, and with
it prepared a good dinner. The wood left was then placed in a
wagon and carried to our next camp for our half[?].

At 3:00 P.M. a meeting was called, and Colonel J. H. Watson
was elected commander of the expedition and I had the honor
of being appointed second in command. At 4:00 P.M. we again
marched forward ten miles and at night encamped on good grass
and an abundance of standing water. Our encampment was
formed during one of the hardest rains we have yet experienced
in Mexico, and we were completely drenched by the fast-
descending shower. As soon as the storm struck us our mules
wheeled and took a stand, and during the hardest part turned
only to accommodate themselves to the change of the wind.

We are now in sight of a tolerably large lake called the
Second Sous.[9]

[8]The Hacienda Encinillas, including the town at the southern end of the
salty lake, belonged to Don Angel Trias, governor of Chihuahua. The town
consisted of a church and a group of adobe dwellings. See Bartlett, *Personal
Narrative*, II, 416, 418; *Southern Trails to California*, ed. Bieber, pp. 192-93;
Ruxton, *Adventures in Mexico*, pp. 161-62.

[9]The lakes and rancho in this area, the latter belonging to General Trias,
were called Sauz, meaning "willow." The Mexican village mentioned below
was El Sauzillo.

July 21. Notwithstanding the wetting we got last night, I enjoyed a good night's rest, and breakfast is once more over. In front of us, at a distance of about three miles, lies a fine sheet of water, with cottonwood trees on its borders, and another hacienda or Mexican settlement. This beautiful lake is about six miles long and probably three in width. The head of the lake is near the head of this noble, enchanting valley, and we regret to pass from a region so beautiful and so well adapted to the wants of the traveler. At 8:00 A.M. we marched, and are now encamped about a mile from the lake at a beautiful and very strong spring of good water. It rained nearly all the forenoon, and has become necessary for us to halt and dry our wet clothes and beds. Just back of our camp are the ruins of a deserted rancho, and the whole face of the valley is well covered with excellent grass. Our mules are improving very much on this change of food to them and fortune to us.

We are now about to leave the valley, to pass beyond a range, or rather a spur, of the Rocky Mountains, and are well assured that after traveling twelve miles we will again have good grass for our stock to the Rio Gila. At a hacienda three miles below our camp, Gomez, at the head of 150 Appaches, night before last, killed a large number of cattle and drove away all the horses belonging to Governor Treas,[10] now ruler of Chihuahua, who owns many leagues of this valley. His possessions include the hacienda of Ensineas and extend within a few miles of the city

[10]Don Angel Trias, for several years governor of Chihuahua, was, according to Bartlett (*Personal Narrative*, II, 426-27), "a gentleman of large wealth and fine accomplishments. After receiving his education, he went to Europe, where he spent eight years travelling in various parts, although he remained most of the time in England and France. He is well versed in several of the European languages, and speaks English with great correctness. . . . With large estates, a cultivated mind, and elegant manners, General Trias cannot but exercise a great influence in the State. . . . There are not many such patriots in Mexico; if there were, she would not be in the position she now is. There is no doubt that General Trias detests the Americans as a people; yet American gentlemen and officers who stop at Chihuahua, are always treated by him with great politeness and attention. He is ardently devoted to Santa Ana, and is considered at the head of the war party in his State."

of Chihuahua, covering very many of the best acres of land that I have yet seen in this republic. Near the head of this lake are two passes through the mountains. The road through that on the right, leads to Passo Del Norte and Santa Fe and our road passes through the left;[11] and we may possibly reach the pass tomorrow.

While [I have been] engaged in writing, the clouds have broken away and the sun is pouring its warmth into our wet blankets. El Rio Sauz is the name of a rapid mountain stream we crossed this morning, and which discharges its water into this lake, called by the Mexicans, Laguna Sauz, or Lake Sauz.

Ensineas, the name of the hacienda passed yesterday, means "live oak," and had its origin from the fact that at the mountains near it this oak, ash, and cottonwood grew abundantly. I observed lying on the pebbly bottom of Rio Sauz the conical seed pod of the pine tree, which was deposited by high water. This is proof of the existence of this wood in the Rocky Mountains bordering on this plain, and would reduce the price of pine and other boards if the fear of Indians did not prevent the Mexicans from procuring the logs. [Of] saw mills there are none, and when a board is wanted they *hew* it out of a suitable stick.

Consequently an ordinary-sized drygoods box will sell in Chihuahua for from $1.50 to $3.00 and boards at a still higher rate. 4:00 P.M., and a heavy rain falling between us and the Alta De Deos, or "mountain named of God," which is the spur on the east side of this valley. Rain falling in this way produces a beautiful view to the beholder, and one that changes almost constantly. At times the mountains are wholly concealed by the sheet of falling water, and then again a part of it may be seen through the curtain suspended from the clouds. Such changes are frequent among these mountains in the rainy season. Cloudy and some lightning.

July 22 (Sunday). I left my blanket at break of day

---

[11]The "left" road to which Evans refers passed through Galeana, then went northwest to Janos, while the cutoff to El Paso del Norte probably followed the Rio Carmen north-northeast.

and called the camp. A very heavy rain fell in the night, but we had a tent to keep us from getting wetter than we had been and passed the night comfortably. At 8:30 A.M. the train left camp and traveled forward briskly for eight hours, having made twenty-four miles. We were told that this day's journey was on a dry stretch of thirty-five miles, but we have found water in abundance, and are encamped on a swift and noisy stream of good fresh rain water. Indian trails, fresh—that is, made since the rain this morning—cross the road a mile or two below our camp. We traveled over a splendid road leading through a pass in the mountains, and we are now out of the Sacrimento Valley and upon another plain or valley of equal beauty. Several kinds of grass, a strange variety of flowers, and among the herbs I noticed lobelia just in blossom. The mountains on our right are smooth and covered with fine grass, and those on the left rugged, broken, and apparently well-timbered with large pine trees. I was informed that water of the very best was to be found in great abundance in these pine mountains. Two rains this afternoon and more in prospect.

July 23. Started at 8 and crossed the arroyo, which we found had risen during the night and was now a very rapid, roaring stream. A mile further on and we came to the basin or spoon of this valley and found the water running and spread at least a mile wide. The mud was consequently very deep in places, and, with much difficulty and doubling teams, we found ourselves once more on high ground at about 11 o'clock A.M. Three miles further brought us to innumerable springs or marshes, upon the borders of which a mule could not safely venture for fear of bogging. From this marsh we moved two miles over land of the same nature, all having been probably made by the encroachments of the mountain sands upon the water of the marsh, and then we commenced the ascent of a narrow pass, between conical formed hills, which gradually led us into another valley, and our camp is on good grass but without any water excepting such as we dip out of holes in the road. With these favors we are well pleased; to find this additional water is an unexpected fortune, for, without it, we would have been compelled to water all our horses at a very weak spring—and this, too, the only water in a distance of seventy-five miles. Just before breaking up camp this morning, three Indians made an unsuccessful attempt to appropriate three of our mules, which had escaped from the lines during the night. When they saw the boys, they thought it advisable to go back to the mountains and leave the wandering mules to their owners. We are now encamped about eighteen miles from Carmel, a small Mexican town, which place we will reach tomorrow.

July 24. Broke camp at 7:30 o'clock and after passing a rolling country, with several water holes and tolerable grass, at 12:00 M. encamped half a mile from Carmel, a small but old-looking Mexican village, containing probably one hundred inhabitants and one Catholic Church. This town is located at the head of another valley, opening to the north, and on Carmel River, the banks of which are well studded with large live oak and cottonwood trees. At 4:00 P.M. we crossed Rio Carmel, which we found much swollen, and encamped on grass alone, after traveling over a stony road from Carmel, making about twenty-two miles this day. The Indians are now thick around us, in consequence of repeated American and Indian wrongs. They have collected here for the purpose of destroying Carmel. The Indian hunters, or Americans who went out in that capacity, all returned to Carmel last night, and to their shame and the shame of all Americans, it must be told that the only prisoner taken was a very aged squaw, whom Glantin,[12] the captain, inhumanly ordered a Mexican to shoot and scalp. Out upon such bravery, out upon such inhumanity, such barbarous cruelty! The heart must be corrupt that could inflict such a wrong upon the aged and infirm. Savage barbarity does not in wanton cruelty exceed this infamous transaction.

[12]Either John Glanton, mentioned by Bancroft as co-proprietor of the Yuma ferry in 1850 (_History of Arizona and New Mexico_, in _Works_, XVII [1889], 488), or John Galantin (_ibid._, n.).

July 25. Moved at 8:00 A.M. and found a heavy road, and encamped at night upon the site of an old Spanish Mission, now in ruins. Here we found good grass, good wood, and good water—a spring of very excellent water and great strength—and rattlesnakes in abundance. We killed one last night within ten feet of the campfire, and many others have been captured in and near this camp. We made yesterday twenty-two miles, over a rolling country and [one] in which there is in dry weather a scarcity of water—and, in fact, none for thirty miles at a stretch. We, however, found every hole full. Gomaz, the Appache chief, has offered a reward of a thousand dollars for each American scalp, so we may be watching and praying. This is Rattlesnake Camp.

July 26. Rained very hard in the night, but is clear and pleasant this morning. I observed on the rocks above the spring characters that may safely be classed as Aztec and will here copy them for the benefit of the reader. These letters or characters were neatly cut in the face of some large, soft rocks that lay piled on each other near the springs, and insensibly lead a person into the past ages.

The Aztecs have passed away, but they have left their impress upon many a rock and many acres of land. Could we but trace out their habitations, and spread upon canvas a full view of their means of defense and the articles used in those days by this ancient race, together with the likeness of the gods to whom they did homage, such a picture of the past would be presented as is rarely brought before the world.

After having dried our blankets and partaken of a breakfast, we again took the road and at 12:00 M. encamped one mile north of the town of Galliana,[13] on poor grass and bad water. This

[13]Galeana.

place contains perhaps two hundred inhabitants, and considerable corn, wheat, etc., is raised on the bottoms of a good-sized
river running to the northwards. On the borders of this stream
stand fine, healthy-looking cottonwoods, and I observed a very
thick growth of willows back in the low bottoms. These people
have few cattle and less sheep, as they, too, suffer from the
thieving disposition of the Indians and are constantly exposed
and ever liable to lose everything in the shape of stock. No man
ventures out of town without his gun ready for immediate use.

     July 27.   Broke up Camp Galliana at half past seven
and moved over a plain of good grass twelve miles and then
passed a chain of low mountains and in one hour found ourselves
in the large and fertile plains of Cassa Grande, or large castle;
and after traveling all the afternoon we encamped on Cassa
Grande River. Here the grass is not so good, being much coarser
than that on the plains. We traveled over plains of extreme beauty, and almost all of which are surrounded by spurs of the
Rocky Mountains, and find them fertile and bearing several
kinds of grass and flowers of extreme beauty of color and shape.
The poppy and the white lily graced the borders of [the] prairie
path and enlivened the scene. This valley, river, and a small
town all take their names from a large, deserted castle, now
in complete ruins, and of which the Indians have little or no
traditionary history.[14] It was undoubtedly erected by the Aztecs,
and now stands a monument of their knowledge of the arts.
One of our wagons broke down last evening, and our movements will be delayed some few hours, perhaps, and an opportunity may be given to examine this noted ruin. In the meantime
I will give the reader a view of a group of Mexicans who can
be seen in this dress and this very position at any time. These

---

[14]The ruins of Casas Grandes were, at the time Bartlett visited them, about
800 feet from north to south and 250 feet from east to west. They consisted
of adobe walls from five to thirty feet high, and Bartlett identified several
of the buildings as granaries or storehouses (*Personal Narrative*, II, 345-65).
Hardy was not overly impressed by the ruins, but he mentioned that Apaches
had excavated there to obtain artifacts for sale.

drawings were made by Monsier Rondé, a French gentleman and an expert draftsman.

July 28. Left camp Cassa Grande at 3:00 P.M. and at 7:00 P.M. again went into camp, half a mile north of the town of Barranco, on Cassa Grande River. This is the place established by the late Robert McKnight[15] and is a mining town of but few inhabitants and yet of considerable importance, owing to the richness of the silver ore taken from the mountains. The business is now carried on by a Mr. Float,[16] an American, who married a daughter of McKnight's, and he told us that the yield this year was equal to four marks of silver from each 300 lbs. of ore. Little or nothing is raised here in the vegetable line, the inhabitants depending upon Gallianna, or, as named on the maps, Buenaventura, and Cassa Grande for their supply of grain and other necessaries. One of the wheels of our wagon having given way, we must again lie by some time to make the necessary repairs. How long this detention will last is yet a matter of uncertainty, and the time will be occupied in an examination of the furnace and smelting preparations of this place.

[15]Robert McKnight was one of the founders of the Santa Fe trade, in 1812.
[16]Lewis Flotte.

GUADALUPE PASS, SONORA

J. R. Bartlett, *Personal Narrative* . . . (New York, 1854), I, 296

July 29 (Sunday). Having breakfasted, and watered my mules, I walked into the town of Barranco, and here had an opportunity of inspecting the silver works of the place. We found five smelting furnaces and two separating fires in full blast, all blown by large bellows worked by mule power. The rich metal was constantly oozing from its bed of fire and deposited in holes made to receive it. Here it was suffered to cool, and then the cakes were transferred to the furnace, where it, by the application of intense heat, again assumed the liquid state and the silver was separated from the lead and other ores, and again run into cakes weighing from five to twenty-five pounds. These cakes are taken to the mint and once more pass the ordeal of fire before assuming the form of coin.

The products of these mines will enrich Mr. Float, as the whole of the labor applied here or at the mines is peon or slave. He now legally owns every man, woman, and child in the place, and can at all times command their services. Eight dollars is a month's wages, and out of this the poor Mexican must live, and the consequence is, he is at the end of the year deeply in debt, which is synonomous to slavery. The mines are described as very rich, and this is sustained by the specimens now in our possession. Silver ore, in its purest state, is found attached to quartz, a very white stone, the exposed part of which is rough and of a yellow color. This quartz is a certain indication of silver or gold ore and is the guide of the miner in his search after the riches of the mountains. Besides the furnace there is but one place of business, and that is the wagon shop. Here all necessary repairs to the wagons belonging to the mines is made, and boards for that purpose are sawed out with whipsaws. But night is upon us, and a very heavy rain, with almost incessant thunder and lightning, is now drenching us to the skin.

July 30. The rain continued falling until near 12 o'clock last night, and a more dismal night has not been passed by us. Our repaired wagons were brought into camp at 9:00 A.M. and at ten we were leaving the town of Barranco behind us and moving rapidly towards Carraletus,[17] which place we reached, and, after crossing Cassa Granda River, encamped on good grass at 1:00 P.M. Here we will remain until morning when we move on to Yanos, the frontier town. This town (Carraletus) is another mining town, and the description given yesterday of Barranco will well answer here. I find that there is a very perceptible change in the extent and variety of grasses and plants on our approach to mineral regions, all being materially diminished in quantity and quality, and it may be truly said that in places grass is not to be found where the minerals exist. This scarcity causes us to wish ourselves roaming the wide and fertile plains, as these alone afford the best of food for our mules.

July 31. Broke up camp early, and after traveling over a broken and apparently unproductive country we again went into camp, one mile east of the town of Yanos, and distant from Barranco about thirty miles. In this camp we have grass and small wood, but are distant from water one mile. We are here because grass is very short on Rio Yanos, or, as pronounced by Spaniards, Hanos. This town is going into decline fast, and is as handsomely located as any west of Chihuahua.[18] They have a church but no *padre* or priest, and, the shepherd being gone, the presumption is that the sheep will also forsake the fold. This place once contained about eight hundred inhabitants, and these plains were once covered with cattle, horses, and mules, and the mountainsides with sheep and goats; but all of these comforts have been appropriated by the Indians and many of the inhabitants killed or forced to seek safer asylums. The southern horizon is black with clouds, from which the electric fluid is darting in fitful moods, but so far off as to do us no harm.

[17]Corralitos.

[18]Janos was one of a series of frontier forts established by the Spaniards, the others being Galeana, Carrizal, Norte, Coyame, San Eleazario, and San Carlos. It was in a state of decay in the 1850's, its streets almost deserted, and its garrison composed of a handful of raw militia. The population was about 300. (Bartlett, *Personal Narrative*, II, 338-40.) Clarke (*Travels in Mexico*, pp. 61-72) was incapacitated in the alcalde's house in Janos from April 28 to May 13 of 1849. He emphasizes the friendliness and helpfulness of the people.

{ August, 1849 }

Aug. 1.   We found a wheel needed repairing this morning, and consequently we moved to the banks of the river and again encamped and set men to work on the broken wheel. This consumed the greater part of the day, and in the meanwhile we will look around and see what kind of a place we are now in. Of the town of Yanos little more can be said. The inhabitants burn charcoal for the use of the furnaces at Corralletus. This is made from the roots of the mesquite growing in these plains. The bush never attains, in this country, a greater height than seven feet, and is of many branches, or rather shoots, none of which are larger than a man's wrist, but the roots are enormous and very lengthy. The river should properly be called a creek, and is well shaded with large cottonwood trees along its borders. It discharges its waters into Rio Cassa Grandes, and they flow on together in a northerly direction through a plain of rich land, all in a state of nature, and empty into the Rio Grande. The mountains now in sight are not very high to all appearance, but might be found so if we had to ascend them. But here is an order from below, and pack up it is. At half past three P.M. we took Major Grayham's trail, the open and wide wagon road having measurably disappeared, and went forward about seven miles [and] encamped on good grass bordering on mesquite, but without water.

Aug. 2.   Started from camp at 7:00 A.M. and at ten arrived at a spring stream of excellent clear water, with ash trees growing on its borders. We found this creek of a marshy nature, and had the misfortune on crossing it to break a wagon tongue, and almost lost a mule. This delay is unfortunate, and yet it is well that it occurred where timber can be had. This break might have occurred in a place where no timber could have been pro-

cured short of forty miles' travel, and were it not for the delay
we would be content. A few hours will mend the broken tongue,
and then we shall take on water for a dry stretch of forty miles,
'tis said, and again move forward. The valley of this creek is not
very wide but lies much below the surface of the plain and the
land is well grown with grass (rather coarse) and plants of
various kinds, among which I found the wild lavender—called
soapweed here, from the fact that the natives make soap out
of ashes of this resinous plant. This ash timber is the first we
have met with in Mexico and is of good growth and measures in
height probably forty feet—top bushy and well spread. At 3:00
P.M. we again got under way, but soon found that the dry
stretch had not yet been reached. After traveling in a northwest
course for five miles we began to descend from the hills to the
plains and found these covered with water for many miles and
our road very deep and heavy. At night, after traveling about
twelve miles this day, we lay on good grass and had no wood
but an abundance of water in every hole. This plain may well
be called a very wet prairie, for it has now more water on its
surface than I saw on the whole route east of Chihuahua. Another heavy rain this afternoon.

    Aug. 3.   No rain last night, but some thunder and light-
ning. Left camp at 8:00 A.M., and in a few hours found ourselves
out of the mud and once more upon ascending ground; but after
a mile or two we passed over the hill and again rolled down into
a beautiful but narrow valley. Here we found water impregnated with soda and very warm and muddy. The regular watering place is about three miles ahead and in full view. Here we
halted to rest and let our mules feed on good grass and at 5:00
P.M. we move on to the next water, above mentioned. At 4:00
P.M. we started for camp, and at dark drove on the banks of
Cedar River, a small but beautiful stream, making but fifteen miles
this day. We are now about to pass this mountain, which will
occupy all of this day at least. The head of this valley is crowned
with many little hills, of beautiful forms, and better grass can

not be found than we have at this beautiful valley. The wild sunflower bloomed here and lavender grew in great abundance. This day wound up with much thunder and lightning and some rain. Just before going into camp, we crossed two large and fresh trails of Indians leading in the direction of the Gila River.

Aug. 4. Well, reader, we have now traveled through a country of varied scenery together, and at 10:00 A.M. this day, we find ourselves six miles from camp and entering the Warloop pass of the Rocky Mountains.[1] A mere glance of the eye will determine this to be a romantic place, wildly so. At the entrance of this pass we crossed a few dry ravines over a very stony road, and shortly after strike St. George Cook's trail, which here connects with our road. These ravines are known at a distance from the trees—seen in lines running from the mountains into the valley, and are post oak, very low with wide-spreading branches. Two miles further up brought us to the main mountain, very steep, but practicable for wagons. Here I observed the maguey plant and the Spanish dagger, also cedar, oak, and red ebony. In consequence of the recent rains, there is good water in great abundance in all the small ravines, and the train was halted here to rest prior to making the great pull. While they lay below, I ascended the mountain and here had the long-wished-for opportunity of looking upon the Pacific slope of this great continent of ours. The sight is a sublime one. Five or six miles below lies a wide and beautifully green valley, and here on either hand are chasms and deep and dark ravines, down the side of one of which winds our giddy path, which gradually leads us into the valley below. At 3:00 P.M. the wagons began to ascend, and at the dusk of evening we were all safely encamped upon the side of the ravine and in the pass, on good grass and some water. Traveled this day fourteen miles.

Aug. 5 (Sunday). Having found this morning that our ravine water had entirely failed at camp, we resorted to a spring on the mountain side, and to a place farther up the ravine, where

[1]Evans anticipated Guadalupe Pass, which was not reached until the next day.

we found a good supply of cold, clear water. On consultation
of the maps and authorities, I find myself laboring under a mistake as to Warloop Pass. The pass of yesterday is not Warloop
Pass, but a high and very heavy hill to pass with wagons. The
reader will not be led into error, therefore, when I say that
we left our ravine camp and moved forward to the edge of the
plains below. Here the trails separated. It is evident that Major
Graham's moved directly across the plains and the emigrant
trails follow the high ground on its edge. We made the attempt
to follow Graham's trail[2] but found it too spongy and deep;
consequently, we turned and took the emigrant trail and shortly
after found several prairie springs of good water, and the road
could not be better than this around this great natural basin. At
about ten miles from camp we struck rising ground which gradually led us to Warloop Pass,[3] where we arrived at about 2:00

[2]Major L. P. Graham marched from Chihuahua to Los Angeles in 1848; the
best account of his expedition is the journal of Cave Couts, a lieutenant in his
command (MS, Bancroft Library).

[3]Guadalupe Pass, pictured in Bartlett, *Personal Narrative*, I, 296. Cooke
traversed the mountains north of the pass proper, and blamed his guide for
failure to find it. He described his trail as "a very precipitous and rocky
descent of perhaps a thousand feet into the heart of a wild confusion of mountains, which extended as far as could be seen." (Philip St. George Cooke,
"Journal," in *Exploring Southwest Trails*, ed. Ralph S. Bieber [1938].) Here at
the pass, according to Bieber, emigrants "met their first disappointment and
labored hard and long to drag their wagons over the mountain trail which in
places was 'almost perpendicular.' As the emigrants proceeded they cut in-
scriptions on the trees along the route, usually noting the name of their company together with its numerical strength, its rate of travel, and its experiences
on the road. Graves of emigrants who died on the way were found along the
roadside—mute evidences of the dangers of the trail." (*Southern Trails to California in 1849*, p. 59.)
One Lewis B. Harris described the pass as follows: "After traveling about
6 miles we came to the Pass in the mountains, and I would that I had the
power of description to give you an idea of the magnificence of the scene. We
wound round the mountain we were on to get into the valley below, on the
ledge for about a quarter of a mile, and then descended by fastening a rope
behind the wagon, and all hands taking hold to back and keep the wagon
from upsetting. In this way I suppose we made a descent of at least 1000 feet.
After getting in the valley below and looking up at the wagons winding
around on the ledge above, it would then almost make a persons head swim,
but the road is not as bad as it looks, for we were not detained with our

P. M. Here we came upon the El Passo Road, and met seven wagons and a company of twenty Californians. From this point we went about two miles over the most broken pass on the whole route, and at night encamped on poor grass but *bastante* of water and wood. This pass has an appropriate name. There never was a place better adapted to Indian ambuscades and concealment than this. The hills are steep and rugged and the deep, dark and gloomy ravines almost numberless, and the mountain sides covered with a growth of low and heavy-topped trees—white and jack oak, cedar, ebony, and occasionally wild cherry. Made this day about twenty-three miles.

Aug. 6.   Left camp early, and in a short time (and in the midst of wild and broken mountains) came to where Cook's trail comes into this road. We found this trail much worn by the emigrant travel over it, and as far as the eye could reach, the road looked better than ours.

Where these roads joined, we came upon another small spring of very good water and it may be well to say here that all the water on this side of Chihuahua is better, and more abundant. About a mile below this juncture of roads, we came upon the waters of the Hawkee River,[4] and here halted to repair a wagon and, in the language of campers, "to noon it." The mountains and hills look easier, and the valley of the Hawkee is wider and well-timbered with sycamore, cottonwood, ash, etc. At 3:00 P. M. we moved down this stony stream about three miles and encamped on good grass and water. Distance this day, ten miles.

Aug. 7.   The camp was called at break of day and at

loaded wagons 2 hours in getting the wagons over it, and there had been no work on it whatever, except throwing out the largest of the rocks. Here we passed around the Gaudalupe cliff which has the appearance of a huge Cathedral. The base of it is I suppose 5000 or 6000 feet high from the valley below, and then the cliff rises above, something in the shape of a steeple (in front) something like 1200 to 1500 feet perpendicular, of solid rock. We have been in sight of this mountain since the 7th. [It was then the 18th of June.]" See "From Texas to California in 1849: Diary of C. C. Cox," ed. Mabelle Eppard Martin, *Southwestern Historical Quarterly*, XXIX, (1925-26), 218.

4The Rio Huaqui, flowing north toward San Bernardino.

half past six we moved down the river, over a smoother road, about three miles. Here we watered, and then made an ascent of about eighty feet and bade farewell to the Hawkee. From the brow of this hill we passed over a gradually descending plain of gravel, stone, and mesquite and prickly pear a distance of about twelve miles to the small and boggy valley of San Barnardino.[5] Here are the ruins of a very extensive hacienda, and we here found a splendid spring of cold and clear water. From here we moved forward eight miles into another canyon or pass in the mountains and encamped on mountain grass but no convenient water, having traveled twenty-three miles this day. Just before arriving at camp we passed a camp of forty men. They had been here three days, resting and shooting wild cattle, found here abundantly.

Aug. 8.   Started from camp early and shortly after came to a weak mountain spring and obtained water for a part of the train. From here we went to Blackwater Creek, eighteen miles, and found an abundance of water for all. After crossing this creek we struck out for a small stream distant four miles but found little water until we encamped on this stream twenty-two miles from the last encampment. This day's journey over a rough and broken mesquite plain. At the entrance of this mountain pass we found another large camp of Californians from Arkansas, men, women, and children, who had transported themselves, goods, and chattels by means of ox teams. They were also en-

[5]San Bernardino Rancho consisted of an adobe-walled enclosure with the ruins of several ranch buildings. Some were still habitable when Cooke passed through, but they were completely abandoned by the time Bartlett saw them. They were situated on an eminence which commanded a broad valley, and were defended by several bastions. The cattle deserted by the rancheros were left to run wild, and steers became as threatening as buffalo to later travelers. Clarke (*Travels in Mexico*, p. 77) said: "Starting at sunrise we passed the extensive ruins of the rancho Santa Bernardino, the walls of which are fortified with regular bastions. They are situated on a rise of ground, with a beautiful grassy flat on each side, with a small creek running through it, upon one of which we camped last night, and beyond which is a bluff from ten to thirty feet high, which forms the level of an extensive plain; beyond these, mountains can be seen rising in the distance. It is one of the prettiest valleys I have ever seen. It has been depopulated by the Indians."

gaged in killing wild cattle and preparing the meat for future use.

The water and grass at this camp bad, but a strong prospect of rain.

Aug. 9.   The rain of last night began about 8 o'clock and continued probably three hours. During this time much water fell and in twenty minutes after its commencement, this brook was roaring and foaming down its stony bed, and threatened to go beyond the confines of its banks. Our beds were completely saturated by the water from the side hill and not a man in camp escaped a complete wetting, and it has never been my lot to experience a heavier fall of water. This camp will not be moved for several hours, giving time to dry bedding and clothing, all of which is wet to the last thread. The guns are being shot off and reloaded, many of which do not go. We have now spent three nights in passes, or canyons, having crossed during each day the plains lying between. The numerous herds of wild cattle found on these plains and in these mountain passes had their origin from those at San Barnardino. That was once a rich rancho, but by repeated Indian aggressions was reduced to a heap of ruins, and the cattle became wild and sought concealment in the plains and mountains, and are at this day as dangerous as the buffalo. Three of our men are now in pursuit of a wild bull.[6] At 1:00 P.M. we again moved over a country of extreme beauty twelve miles and encamped at night opposite what is called Santa Cruz Peak, a very tall and pointed mountain and apparently well timbered. There are many very high and pointed peaks well timbered, in the neighboring spurs of mountains.

Aug. 11.   Another very heavy rain last night, and everything wet again. After a late breakfast we moved forward over a beautiful but broken country, and encamped on good grass and running water, after traveling twelve miles. Our camp was

[6]The wild cattle of the San Pedro and San Bernardino region were exceedingly troublesome to travelers. Cooke describes an adventurous skirmish with wild bulls during which they attacked both men and animals. See Cooke's "Journal," p. 143.

made early for the purpose of drying our beds and making other necessary arrangements. It has been our fortune to find an abundance of water, some mud, and a country ever changing as we pass along. The productions are new, or rather of a new variety. Cactus of a different form spring up everywhere, and the poppy, sunflower, violet, and other varieties of flowers are, in the language of the poet, wasting their fragrance on this desert air, but lend a very welcome enchantment to our road. We left Cook's trail this morning, and took the road leading southwest to Santa Cruz, from which place we are distant probably fifty miles.

Aug. 12. Made an early start, and were nearly all the forenoon busily employed in passing a very long train of ox wagons, which was at last accomplished. While passing them the sound of the infant's cry struck the ear, and awakened reflections on the past associations of a kindred character. This train has connected with it several families, four ministers, and is conducted wholly upon strict religious principles, prayer morning and evening, and a sermon on the Sabbath. They travel very slow, and have yet provisions for six months. The road passed over today has been heavy, and in places, boggy—so much so as to require double teams. The afternoon's journey has been pleasant, and through a country of diversified scenery. Bordering upon our road were undulating hills covered with a carpet of rich, green grama grass, and occasionally groups of low, bushy trees. These hills grew higher as they rolled towards the lofty, cloud-capped mountains on the right and left, and it may be remarked here that at no place in our journey, since we entered the Republic of Mexico, have we been out of sight of some of the spurs or main chain of the Sierra Madre. But these have been more interesting since we entered the State of Sonora, in which we are now wandering like the Israelites of old. Here they are ever changing. Besides, the air is vocal with songs of the feathered tribe, which may be caused by the abundance of water daily falling. Eighteen miles this day.

Aug. 13 (Sunday). This morning we started from camp at 8:00 A.M. and shortly after found our road winding through the miry bottoms of a small stream (name not known),[7] which was kept alive by the water of marsh and springs. After several hours of very heavy traveling, we came abruptly into the mountains and began to ascend a very steep road which led from one high hill to another and over one of the most rocky roads I ever knew wagons to encounter. But by severe labor, by both man and beast, the wagons were at last landed on top of the highest peak in our path. Then came the descent, of which we only accomplished two miles, and encamped once more in the mountains. These mountains are covered with timber of much better growth than that heretofore met with, and they shut us in on all sides. Here I observed several kinds of oaks, gray ash, walnut, and willow. Made this day fifteen miles.

Aug. 14. After breakfast we left camp and again took the winding road down the hills. This we found very stony and steep, and we had gone but a few miles before we broke a wheel. This want we supplied by a pair of extra wheels attached to another wagon, and after a delay of one hour, we were once more rolling on; and at 3:00 P.M. we entered the valley of Santa Cruz and shortly after came in sight of the poor and almost deserted town of Santa Cruz,[8] situated at a very narrow point in the valley, with high mountains on the left. This is also a military post, the State of Sonora having a garrison of 150 men here. We have here determined to leave the wagons, and start out a pack train. Tupison [Tucson] is one hundred miles from here and this we will reach in five days. Our company will probably consist of about twelve men to start with. This night we

[7]Probably Agua Prieta Creek, on the headwaters of the Rio Sonora.

[8]Santa Cruz was one of the nine frontier posts established by the Mexican government to guard northern Sonora, and originally had a population of 1,500. By the time Evans and Bartlett arrived, however, the population had dwindled to about 300. The climate of Santa Cruz was notoriously sickly, and Apache incursions were greatly dreaded, the savages having lost all fear of the town's garrison. See Bartlett, *Personal Narrative*, I, 407-9.

encamped on Santa Cruz River, one mile north of this adobe town, making twelve miles.

Aug. 15.   We remained in camp until 12:00 M. this day and at that hour Colonel C. G. Word, F. Laubenheimer, Dr. Bunnell, A. T. Parker, J. Teats, William Scott, James Scott, R. H. Hill, Dr. Ogburn, and W. T. Pollard, and myself left the wagon train and pushed onward. We traveled down the Santa Cruz River, through as beautiful a valley as I ever saw. Eight miles east of the town we came to a fine rancho, around which everything seemed to be in a flourishing condition, but, like many others, it was deserted; the Apaches had driven off man and beast, and the fruit in the garden was free to all. After procuring some of the peaches, we went down this noble valley four miles farther and encamped for the night. After a supper on bacon, stewed peaches, coffee, and fried cakes, we had another rain. Colonel Word was elected director of our little company, and Mr. Browning and a Mr. Kelley were admitted members of the company. Traveled this day twelve miles.

Aug. 16.   Started from camp at 7:00 A.M. and traveled down this splendid valley eight hours and again encamped, having made this day about twenty-four miles. This is the most fertile valley we have yet traveled in. All kinds of wood grows on the hillsides, and fine towering cottonwoods mark the course of this river. This is the most important tributary of the Gila River on our route, and we have all seen what others have taken to be gold, glittering in its waters. Mica abounds here, but is easily distinguished from the solid, shining gold so much sought for at this day. We passed several trains of ox wagons this day and are now within a short distance of another large train. There are thousands now on this road. Many of these emigrants came on this road where Cook's trail joins and where the road from El Passo comes in. They say that the El Passo road is strewn with wagons, harness, and everything but provisions and firearms. This destruction of property was caused by a scarcity of grass and water in the early part of the season. All parties seem to have suffered in some way.

Aug. 17. Left camp early, and pushed forward about twelve miles, when we came to one of the best Spanish buildings I ever saw. Shortly after passing this we came to another, built of adobe, not as beautiful in appearance as the first, and at 12:00 M. we entered the walls of a large hacienda. All these buildings have been wholly deserted, their owners killed or forced to leave their homes, and the cattle, mules, and horses driven into the mountains. But the most extraordinary vegetable production seen by us on this route was passed today, and I know that many will doubt the truth of this assertion when I tell them that we saw cactus so large that they could not be put into a half-bushel measure, and covered with the most splendid blossoms. One of these astonishing growths we found had been broken down and measured eight feet in length and two feet in circumference. This species of the cacti seems to be tolerably abundant on all of the upland or mesquite openings. After marching for about nine hours we once more encamped on the river after traveling this day about thirty miles. The night set in with rain, thunder, and lightning. Dr. Bunnell was taken sick, and left in the wagon train to follow at night.

Aug. 18. Dr. Bunnell did not come into camp last night as was expected, and this morning Dr. Ogburn, Parson Hill, and myself returned until we learned that the doctor was in the care of Colonel Watson's train of wagons. On learning this we returned, and found our packs gone on. We followed briskly, and came up with them late in the afternoon, and found them in the vicinity of a party of Piemo Indians[9] who had just killed a wild bull. They were very friendly, and gave beef to some of our party. At 4:00 P.M. we encamped on good grass, nine miles from Tucson and three miles from the Indian village. We met with some cactus on the mesquite plains today that aston-

[9]Pima Indians.

149

ished every beholder. At a distance they looked like small steamboat pipes, and in places grew very numerous. In order that the
reader may have some idea of the *saguaro*, or cacti seen this day

on our road, I have here attempted a sketch of these trees,
and need only say that the
largest of these measured in
height at least twenty feet, and
in circumference about thirty
inches. This beautiful tree has
five noble branches and stands
a noble representative of those growing around it. But these
plants must be seen to be appreciated. A number of Mexicans
have visited us this evening. The distance made this day is about
twenty-two miles.

Aug. 19.   This morning we found Colonel Word's mule
missing and it became necessary for the packs to proceed without him. After moving forward about two miles we entered the
Puebla Los Indies,[10] or Town of the Indians. They have a church

[10]Travelers were almost unanimous in praising the Pimas for their relatively
high culture and peaceful habits. Cooke, for instance, says their language is
"rather a pleasant one. . . . The Pima are large and fine-looking, seem well
fed, ride good horses, and are variously clothed, though many have only the
center cloth. They have an extraordinary length and luxuriance of hair. With
their large white cotton blankets and streaming hair, they present, when
mounted, quite a fine figure. But innocence and cheerfulness are their most
distinctive characteristics."
    Bartlett said: "The valley or bottom-land occupied by the Pimos and Coco-
Maricopas extends about fifteen miles along the south side of the Gila, and is
from two to four miles in width, nearly the whole being occupied by their
villages and cultivated fields. The Pimos occupy the eastern portion. . . . The
whole of this plain is intersected by irrigating canals from the Gila, by which
they are enabled to control the waters, and raise the most luxuriant crops."
He describes their industries of blanket-weaving, pottery- and basket-making,
and concludes with the statement: "There are no tribes of Indians on the
continent of North America more deserving of the attention of philanthropists
than those of which I am speaking. None have ever been found further advanced in the arts and habits of civilized life. None exhibit a more peaceful
disposition, or greater simplicity of character; and certainly none excel them
in virtue and honesty. They are quite as industrious as their necessities require
them to be."
    Emory characterized them as "peaceful and intelligent," with irrigation facil-

here partly of adobe and part burned brick, well finished and neatly constructed. This building faces the plaza, around which are buildings of an ordinary character. Outside of these are the Indian habitations, mere huts and easily represented on paper. These are first woven into a convenient form with young willow twigs, and this frame is then covered with long grass which here grows abundantly. The most of these people were extremely poor, their dress consisting of nothing but the breechcloth and occasionally a hat. Herding was their chief occupation. They were very civil and polite, and extremely thankful for the least favor granted. Nine miles more brought us to Teusson, which we found but little better than the Indian town. Here we watered and moved on about eleven miles, found tolerably good grass, some water in the holes, and, having made about twenty-two miles, we encamped to await the coming up of Colonel Word and Dr. Bunnel. After supper Dr. Bunnell came into camp and reported that Colonel Word had not recovered his mule, and we shall therefore proceed without him.

Aug. 20 (Sunday). The night passed, but not without interest to some of the men in camp. Three of our men declare that an earthquake shook the earth so much as to make it difficult to stand. One of these men was on guard at the time, and says that he thought he was taken sick and had to seat himself, and even after being seated his body rocked to and fro. This did not awaken me and I speak only of the sensations experienced by others. We left this camp at 8:00 A. M. and proceeded

ties outstanding for their "beauty, order, and disposition." He remarked that "it was a rare sight to be thrown in the midst of a large nation of what is termed wild Indians, surpassing many of the Christian nations in agriculture, little behind them in the useful arts, and immeasurably before them in honesty and virtue."

See Cooke, "Journal," pp. 168-70; Bartlett, *Personal Narrative*, II, 213-70; and William Hemsley Emory, *Notes of a Military Reconnaissance*. . . . (1848), pp. 82-88.

onward for about ten miles and found another water hole but no grass. Our road today lay over a dry, sandy desert which is said to be the character of the country to the Gila River, although Cook calls it a hard clay soil. There is clay, but sand predominates. At noon we rested and let our mules pick the scanty bunches of grass. Half past one—started forward and drove hard until 8:00 P.M.; found a grass plat but no water. Here we unpacked and a gourd of water taken from a mudhole during the day was divided among the men having none by Dr. Bunnell, with particular instructions to set their teeth close and keep out the polliwogs. This day, thirty-two miles.

Aug. 21. Packed at dawn of day, and a little after sunrise found several holes of cool water. Here we halted to take breakfast and prepare for future scarcity of water. This we found unnecessary, for after an hour's ride we entered the pass between two mountains where there was an abundance of water in holes. These holes I think can be relied upon, unless in a very dry time. From here we struck out into a barren desert, and at noon passed the camp of the Little Rock, Arkansas, company. They were engaged in digging a grave for the interment of Dr. Fagan, a member of the company. Several others were very low at the time with bilious fever, and I have since been told that another man had died last night. After nooning we pushed forward until after night through a drenching rain and in places deep water and encamped without any grass, and without having seen a spear of grass during the afternoon. Our mules consequently fared extremely hard. We traveled this day about twenty-six miles.

Aug. 22. Packed at dawn of day, and at 10:00 A.M. halted half a mile from the Gila River and could once more look upon the territory of our government. This was gratifying and we looked upon the mountains on the other side with a singular degree of feeling and pleasure. Here we found a little grass, and our poor animals are once more feeding with a good appetite. Several of the Piemo Indians have already visited us, and in the

JUNCTION OF THE GILA AND COLORADO RIVERS; LOOKING UP THE GILA

J. R. Bartlett, *Personal Narrative* . . . (New York, 1854), II, 158

absence of an interpreter trade progresses slowly. Those who
have honored us with their presence are as well dressed, excepting a hat, as the Mexicans. They all wear their hair long and
plaited, and each has, suspended to a string of beads, the cross.
They molest no one, and look to trade to the emigrants such
articles as corn, wheat, beans, peas, and an occasional trade of
horses or mules. They brought to camp a fine lot of cornmeal—
the first we have seen in Mexico—for which they demanded a shirt
in barter. The mountains on our right and left and front for several days past are rocky and without any vegetation excepting
the cactus. The Gila River opposite our present camp is a deep,
narrow, and rapid stream of warm, muddy water, the banks covered with a dense growth of wild willow and weeds, tall cottonwoods, and the low willow tree, known as the water willow. A
dam has been constructed, and by small canals the water is conveyed over the bottoms and thrown into the fields. Here they
raise nearly every kind of grain that is usually found in a warm
climate.

But we must pack and move forward to the Piemo Village.
After riding about eight miles we came suddenly upon a number of huts, scattered over a large territory. These are built
similar to those described on the 19th instant, only the buildings
are put up with greater care and, generally, more neatness. Here
we encamped, once more without grass, but obtained half-dried
corn at 25¢ per small bundle. With this we had to be satisfied,
and soon retired to our blankets, after having stationed a guard.

Aug. 23. Before breakfast
this morning the Indians, both ladies
and gentleman, came into camp with
meal, melons, etc., for sale, and from
that time on until we left, the camp
was thronged with redskins. For
the gratification of others, I will here attempt to give a sketch
of these creatures. The first represents a female in full dress,
the second a male with his hunting bow; and the middle fig-

ure is a child. These Indians are darker than our northern races, and generally exhibit stout limbs and strong muscle, and are more given to laughing, and there is almost a total absence of that rigidity of countenance. Their toilet consists of a twist of the hair and fastening it on the head by the use of some dirty, glutinous substance and the painting of lines in the face. Several of the men were painted a dark blue. At 1 o'clock we moved down through this scattered city, and after a ride of twelve miles we passed beyond the lower settlements or lower town, and at sunset came upon a branch of the Gila so much swollen that it became necessary to lie by until the waters receded. The grass is extremely short and grows upon salt ground, spots of which are perfectly white and covered with salt. I took this to be soda, but an inspection soon established it to be (in spots) pure salt. We had the pleasure of meeting a small caravan just returning from San Francisco, having made the journey from [there] to this place in forty-six days. News favorable. Here we overtook Dr. Earl and his party, also water bound, and lying upon poor grass. Cloudy.

There are now some three or four companies of Californians encamped on this ground, and their fires burn brightly in the dusky shades of night.

Aug. 24. Morning opened very warm, and many of us passed the night without any covering over us. The dews of the mountains have left us, and very little dampness is experienced during the night. This valley is very warm, much more so than any passed since leaving Chihuahua, and the water brackish. Left camp at 8:00 A.M., and at the end of about a mile found a well of water and better grass, and, having forty miles to pass without water or grass, are encamped and remain here until this evening and will travel a portion of the desert now before us during the coming night. We met this morning a company of Mexicans, who were also on their way back from California. From them we had the assurance that there were two wells now on Cook's route, leaving only a dry stretch of thirty-six miles instead of ninety. This is cheering to us poor wanderers. At this well we used out the water as fast as it came in, but the water did not improve. We found water in holes in the plains, which proved to be highly impregnated with muriate of soda, sal soda, and nitrate of potassi[um], which was freely used by the men in wetting up bread, and it equaled any pearlash or saleratus rising ever used. After watering, and filling our gourds and canteens, we plunged into the desert, and about twelve miles from camp crossed the bed of a large stream now perfectly dry. At 11 o'clock this night we encamped, without water or grass, near a small mountain pass and lay here until the dawn of day. Two Maracopo[11] Indians passed our camp in the night, and got a drink of water. Distance to this dry camp about twenty-two miles.

Aug. 25. Saddled at daybreak, and at 12:00 M. struck the Gila River again. The reason for taking this desert road is simply this: by so doing we avoided four or five days' journey, but had to do without water and grass for forty miles. From the time we left the Piemo or Maracopa village to the river we saw nothing but cactus, a few mesquite, and some shrubs. This constitutes the only vegetation on the whole route, and there has been thus far nothing for our mules but tall, rank weeds and mesquite beans.

After striking the river we watered and came on down and at 2:00 P.M. again encamped without grass, having made this day about eighteen miles. I have often heard it remarked that it was very hot on this river and never in my life have I experienced such intense heat as this day produced. Mr. Browning and myself were quite unwell in consequence of violent exertions to reach the water through a dense growth of rank weeds, the exhalations from them producing dizziness and gen-

[11]Coco-Maricopas. These, according to Clarke (*Travels in Mexico*, pp. 90-92), "live a few miles farther down the river; they are similar in dress and manners to the Pimos, but rather more athletic, and their countenances more intelligent. They speak a distinct language. Within a few years they have associated themselves with the Pimos, having come from the mouth of the Gila. The two tribes number about two thousand."

eral weakness. The circulation of my blood was impeded to such a degree as to cause a difficulty of respiration, and great pain in the chest. Here we found an abundance of beans for our animals. Some were sent out to the trees and others we kept in camp.

Aug. 26. Breakfasted at sunrise and moved on to the mesquite beans and again fed for half an hour, and again moved forward until late in the afternoon over a dusty road and one small mountain, without meeting with a single blade of good grass, having traveled about nineteen miles. We met a few more Mexicans returning home, who all confirm the news of water and beans on the hitherto much-dreaded desert. The gold news from San Francisco is also confirmed, and if we had good grass our happiness would be much greater. This river from the Piemo village is as destitute of vegetation as any region on the continent. The river overflows nearly every acre of the bottom lands, and the soil and rocks all indicate volcanic action. The high lands over which we have passed are covered with rocks and stones of a very black and burnt appearance.

Aug. 27 (Sunday). After a tedious and hungry night for our mules (having nothing but willows) we moved forward, and on top of a bleak and black, rocky mountain, in a ravine, we found a small patch of coarse mountain grass. Here we unpacked and let our mules pick of this scanty provender until about the hour of 2:00 P.M., when we packed and at four descended again into the loam bottoms and dust. Soon after descending we came upon another patch of grass, and here halted for Mr. Laubenheimer and Dr. Bunnell, the first having been overcome with the almost unsupportable heat of the day. The soil on the river bottoms here is a yellow loam, and in the road from one to five inches deep in fine dust, clouds of which envelop us at every step whilst journeying on the bottoms. The river here is wider and better timbered and begins to look like a river. We this morning cut the sunflower to feed the mules, of which they seemed to partake with a relish. These flowers are small com-

pared with the cultivated sunflower, but the stalk attains about
the same height, and the same or about the same number of
buds expand and bend in worship to the god of day. Traveled
today about twenty-three miles. Intensely hot.

Aug. 28. Left camp early and at 10:00 A.M. again watered at the Gila. From here we pushed on till 1:00 P.M. and on
the top of one of the benches or table lands we found a little grass
and unpacked to graze. We found our poor, weary mules hungry,
and they partook of this scanty fare with a pretty keen appetite
until the heat became too great. At 4:00 P.M. we packed and
moved forward about two miles and had just descended into the
river bottoms when we met Parson R. H. Hill, who had gone
in advance several days and was in camp here feeding his mules
on beans and wild millet grass, which grew here abundantly.
These favorable circumstances induced us to camp, having left
about eighteen miles behind us. We passed the remains of a
wagon and two horses this day. On these high lands we frequently see a long animal of the lizard species and almost white.[12]
It moves with rapidity but suffers us to approach, and by way
of compliment it frequently comes into camp and occupies a part
of our beds. It is harmless.

Aug. 29. Remained in camp all day, or rather until near
sundown. The day was spent in gathering beans and supplying
the wants of our mules. The grass is not very good, but we are
extremely happy to have reached this favorable spot. The day
has been intensely hot—so much so that, if we had desired to
go on, we could not have done it, and the labor of gathering
beans was extremely hard. At 5:00 P.M. we left this camp and
shortly after came upon a water hole having good water but a
very boggy bottom. After water, Dr. Bunnell and F. Laubenheimer returned to the old camp in search of two mules that had
broken into the mesquite and sunflower thicket. The other pack
we pushed onward and in a few hours were overtaken by the
doctor and Laub with the estrays. At 12 o'clock we unpacked

[12]Probably a spotted lizard or sand lizard.

and tied our horses and mules to mesquite bushes, having come about eighteen miles.

Aug. 30.   Left camp at daybreak, and shortly after sunrise came to the grave of Mr. Christon, late a member of Captain Day's company of Cal[ifornia] emigrants, buried yesterday, aged twenty-one years. At 10:00 A.M. we came upon some scattered bunches of grass, and here unpacked to graze and let the god of day expend his heat, before proceeding farther. After dinner we rode off to the river and found it nearly two miles, through beds of sand and a dense growth of young willows. The reader of the north will smile incredulously when told that the scattered bunches of grass are all found on the high tableland, and the water miles to the right. At all of our river camps we have done without a spear of grass. At these camps we find indisputable evidence of the presence of the beaver, deer, and wolves—on the tableland, the lizard, or swift, and an animal much resembling a rat, having a thick tuft of white hair on the end of the tail, and [which] is very sociable and tame.[13] Add to this short catalogue the name of the rattlesnake, and the curtain can drop on the animal kinds of the valley of this almost desolate and destitute river. At 4.00 P.M. we dined and shortly after were once more on our winding way, and at about the hour of midnight again lay down to rest without any feed for the mules, having made about thirty miles during the morning and evening ride.

Aug. 31.   Left camp at sunrise, and shortly after descended to the river, watered, and filled our canteens, and again went to the high lands, found a few bunches of grass, unpacked, and took breakfast. Our poor mules are becoming jaded and thin, and our energies will be severely taxed to keep them up unless better feed is found soon. 4:00 P.M.—left camp and late at night struck the mountain pass, here mad[e] by the river. The mountains range north and south, are not very high and not wide, being only spurs or branches of the Rocky Mountains. Here we wound

[13]A prairie dog.

close in and out through the ravines, and on the river's side until the hour of midnight, when we went into camp, without a single mouthful of anything for the mules, having traveled about twenty-four miles over a dusty and in places a stony road. Nothing is seen along this day's journey but deep sands and dust, high weeds, a little mesquite, some rattama[14] and the cotton-woods, and if our conjectures are right, we will soon exchange this accursed and God-forsaken region for, we hope, a more favored part of creation.

[14]Possibly the rattan palm.

{ September, 1849 }

THE GILA VALLEY TO
SANTA BARBARA

Sept. 1. Breakfasted in camp this morning, and at sunrise we were on our way. At 10:00 A.M. we turned into the river and, in attempting to cut off distance and cross a slough, bogged three mules but lost none. A mile farther brought us to a mesquite orchard and found any quantity of beans. This induced us to stop, as our mules had had nothing to eat since leaving the last camp. After feeding well, we packed at sunset and again went forward until midnight, when at a short distance we saw the banks of the Colorado or Red River, and in a few moments more unpacked upon its banks. We found several persons engaged in the labor of crossing,[1] and to effect this everything that would float was brought into requisition. Wagon beds, rafts, and one very small canoe were plying these waters briskly. The river here is about two hundred yards, with a five-mile current, good sloping banks on this side but very bluff and about twelve feet high on the other. The waters from the melting of the snows above are now receding, but have for weeks past been very high. The rise of water in this river and tributaries north commences about the middle of June, and about the last of July or first of August, the snows being melted, the water recedes and a stream of two miles in width is at this time within banks, and about the distance across above spoken of. We traveled this day about twenty-four miles. 'Tis said that there are three crossings and

[1]Emory, crossing in 1846, found the river 1,500 feet wide, and four feet deep at the maximum (Emory, *Notes*, p. 99). Durivage, in June, 1849, described the river as 150 yards wide, twenty feet deep in the channel, flowing at a rate of seven miles per hour—"a booming stream, sure enough." He crossed in a boat constructed of a willow framework covered by rubber blankets and tents. (John E. Durivage, "Through Mexico to California," *Southern Trails to California in 1849*, pp. 224-25). The usual crossing-place of the forty-niners was a spot about four miles below Fort Yuma (Bartlett, *Personal Narrative*, II, 174).

that we now occupy the middle crossing. Here the water is deep all the way over and animals are frequently lost by exhaustion.

Sept. 2. Breakfast being over, we made a contract with some of the Oomah[2] Indians to swim our horses and mules. This being done, Dr. Bunnell and myself went on board of a raft and now, thank God, I am once more on the possessions of our government, gladly bidding adios to the miseries experienced in the northern states of Mexico. I am therefore in California; although upon the borders of a desert heretofore much dreaded by all travelers, yet it is a consolation to think that a few days more will place us in a fertile region where grass and water is found in abundance, and where our animals may once more rest and satisfy their now ravenous appetites. The Indians found here number, at this village, about three hundred warriors, and yesterday seemed inclined to quarrel with us American intruders, but appear very friendly today, and work hard for a shirt or long knife. They are the most expert swimmers I have ever met with, some of them swimming and leading a mule at the same time, taking the rope in his mouth. The men wear their hair very long, and are otherwise naked excepting the usual breechcloth. The women wear a buckskin covering reaching from the girdle to the knees, which is cut into strings about the size of an ordinary shoestring. These Indians are a tall and well formed race, and far superior to the Piemos and Maracopas in point of intellect, if the expression of the face or the contour of the head may be taken as an index. The females tattoo their chins, and the men do not dress their hair in the filthy manner commented upon while among the Piemos, and their address is not of an unpleasant character, their language sounding pleasantly. They are generally well armed with bows and arrows and a spear, and they have made us comprehend that they are on their way down the river to fight the Apaches, with whom they are now at war. If these men fight as well as their appearance indicates, the Apaches had better keep off. We can now say that all our

[2] Yuma Indians.

mules are safely over Red or Colorado River, and our packs will also occupy American ground in a few more moments. Hurrah! Hurrah! Shortly after dark the last of our goods were landed, and we formed a camp and remain over night under a vigilant guard. These precautions were necessary, for a more thievish set of redskins never existed. They have stolen a little of all kinds of articles from every company passed here, and horses and mules they steal and then eat them—a meat they prefer to any other. We traded them tobacco for pumpkins and fed our mules on these and a few beans we brought with us.

Sept. 3 (Sunday). Breakfasted and moved down the river two miles; found a great abundance of beans and fed until 3:00 P.M.; then packed, went back to water, and at sunset were fairly on the desert. For a few miles we traveled through and over some of the many sandhills, and at a distance could see them drifted mountain high. This caused very hard walking for our poor animals, but we soon left these and found the road much better and leading through a fine and large grove of mesquite. At 10 o'clock we arrived at the first well and found good water and plenty of it. This water is fifteen miles from the Colorado crossing, but there is nothing like grass here or on the road passed over.

Sept. 4. Concluded to remain in this camp until night, and the mules have been sent out to beans. We are very much annoyed by the large and small horse fly, finding them very numerous and troublesome. One poor fellow lost his mule this morning. It was taken with a disease similar to blind staggers. I observed the bones of horses and cattle along the road, and we not unfrequently find saddles, harness, and wagons left by their owners. For the latter these Indians know no use, and if they touch them at all, it is only to destroy. Packed at 5:00 P.M. and for a few miles continued to travel through the mesquite, and then suddenly ascended to the desert above. This we found to be a vast and boundless plain of sand and gravel, with nothing on it but a few scattering creosote bushes. Over this we traveled briskly until about 2 o'clock and then lay down to rest until daylight. We passed seven dead mules and horses, two wagons, harness, saddles, and packs—all left by some who had preceded us. Twenty-four miles.

Sept. 5. Started at daybreak and shortly after came to the second well, sunk in the edge of a large basin, the water about twenty-eight feet below the surface of the desert. This well is very weak, and it required much time to water our animals. It is called, by the Mexicans, *Alamo*, and the water is highly impregnated with sulphur; but, at the same time, it is a blessing to us. One more evidence of suffering is here supplied. The ground is covered with the remnants of property, and it is a perfect boneyard; everything but provisions and firearms can be picked up. This well is very poorly protected against the sands from its sides, and unless some large train is forced by necessity to reconstruct it, there will be little water obtained here. At this camp we met another troop of Mexicans returning from the gold region, having with them a large quantity of the gold. These men return with the intention of removing their families to the valley of the San Joacin River and express themselves well pleased with the Americans at the mines. At 8:00 P.M. we again went forward, over as good a road as can be found in any country, and at two in the morning found ourselves on the borders of a small lake of good water, but no grass yet. We found an herb growing on this plain, scenting the air for many yards with its delicious fragrance, and for many minutes [it] caused us much trouble to pass our mules over it, they being almost starved for grass or something green, and had it been longer they would have been left to eat it. This water or lake connects with New River—a stream of water but lately discovered, and by the natives is called Rio Neuava or New River. Water fowl of various kinds are swimming on its surface. Eight miles from here there is another lake of greater dimensions, of

which I will speak tomorrow.[3] Distance to this water from the
last well about twenty miles.

Sept. 6.   Left the small lake and pushed on to a larger
body of water, distant ten miles. A company of five Indians
informed us that here we would find an abundance of good
grass; but judge of our chagrin and disappointment when we
found nothing but a thick growth of bloodweed. Of these our
mules partook sparingly, but there being nothing else to give
the hungry brutes, we had to content our minds and ask them
to grin and bear it. The road last night was a beautiful and
good one; this morning, however, it became more dusty. This
lake is about a mile in length and half a mile wide, and the water
is both warm and filthy; and these considerations will force us
to bid adieu to it at an early hour this evening. After a diligent
and laborious search, a few scattering bunches of grass were
found. These were at once devoted to our mules, but we soon
found it of a strong, garlic, acid taste and the mules soon refused
it, hungry as they were. Some of these bunches were cut by the
men and carried to camp and the result was an entire change
of the color of their clothes. An Indian who speaks some Spanish
came into camp and informed us that at Carraseta,[4] distant thirty
miles, we would find some grass. This is doubtful. We left our
lake encampment at dark and pushed on until 2 o'clock in the
morning. Our road first conducted us from the basin over a small
ascent and we found that we were gradually rising in the world
and approaching the pass of the mountain before us. Onward
we went, over narrow benches of tableland, and at about 12
o'clock found ourselves among the sandhills in the pass, and on
a very heavy, sandy road. At almost every turn of the road we
found the decayed and decaying remains of some horse or mule.
In connection with this, I must here mention the doing of a
party of Indians who have traveled with us. I mentioned that at
the first well, a young man had lost his mule by blind staggers.
These redskins cut a piece of the ham of the dead mule out and

[3]Present site of the Salton Sea.   [4]On Carrizo Creek.

made what appeared to be a very satisfactory meal. Yesterday this same party arrived at the lake in a few moments after we did, and immediately proceeded to cut another piece from a dead mule where the process of decay had been going on for at least two days. It is hard to be compelled to resort to mule meat to sustain life, but when men are compelled to draw upon meat that fills the air with a sickening atmosphere, it becomes dreadful. But to the road again. This continued to wind through the sand, ankle-deep at every step, and among the hills of the pass. At 2 o'clock we unpacked, having traveled only eighteen miles. No grass nor water.

Sept. 7.   Left at dawn of day and gradually ascended into the mountain pass. At 8:00 A.M. we struck the dry bed of a stream leading from the mountain down the pass. This we followed for about an hour and came to running water but no grass, and halted for breakfast. Just above camp we found a cold spring of sulphur water, the best we have yet met with in California. After taking a dinner and breakfast, we once more moved onward through the canyon, or pass, finding the sand growing less at every step, and at 8:30 P.M., when we encamped at El Yseta—good sulphur water, and some grass. This proved a godsend to us, for our poor mules were in a starving condition and the grass, poor and short as it is, was greedily devoured by them. At this water we found over five hundred mules and horses belonging to emigrants now resting after the fatigues of the journey across the *jornada.*[5] There are also three Indian families living here. This route is the hardest and most fatiguing on the last forty-five miles, and the traveler will do well to have corn on hand when he leaves the lake encampment, for he will find nothing for horse or mule to eat from the lake to this place. We traveled today about twenty-five miles, and shall rest here one day.

To enter into a recapitulation again becomes necessary, and

[5]A *jornada* originally meant a one-day's march, but it was taken by western travelers to mean an exceptionally dry stretch of desert country.

we will now start once more from the town of Tucson, in Mexico, and in this will only refer to the condition of the country passed over, leaving the distance through from Chihuahua for some future day's work, when time will admit. From Tucson to the Piemo Village, a distance of ninety miles, water will be found only in one or two holes unless in the rainy season, grass only in a few patches on the first twenty-five miles. At the Piemo, some salt grass, more at the lower town, near and at the soda wells. When you leave this village, you will travel over forty-two miles of a complete desert, no grass, water, nor mesquite. Once more on the Gila River, you will find water and occasionally some beans, but always look for grass in the flat ravines on the high tablelands, for there is none on the river bottoms. This state of things will go with you to the Colorado, a distance of 180 miles, and your only dependence is upon the beans found in the groves, and then feed only when your animals are cool, or you may risk their lives. Cross the river and for the first fifteen miles you can gather beans, and at the end of that distance you will find yourself at the first well, good water, and a fine grove of mesquite. Here take on all the feed necessary for the journey across. The next water is twenty-five miles, and poor. The third water is twenty-seven miles, a lake, and near it some mesquite. Thirty miles to Carraseta, a watering place but no feed for animals. Next is El Yseta, good water, and some grass, eighteen miles, and this is the first that may be relied upon.

Sept. 8.   Determined to lie in camp this day and rest ourselves and mules. The sun has been hot, but we have been favored with a good breeze. The nights are without dews, and there has been, since our leaving the Colorado River, much more wind blowing than through the day. The camps here last night have all moved onward but ourselves, and we will leave in the morning. The Indians living at this water are making bread out of acorns[6] which they gather in the adjoining mountains. They

[6]The southwestern method of making acorn flour involved the complexities

are, or call themselves, Christian Indians, and are not so naked as the Oomahs. Some estimate of the destruction of animals on the last forty-five miles may be formed when I say that Mr. E. Bruner, of our party, counted yesterday afternoon the carcasses of sixty mules and horses lying along the side of the road, and how many were passed, having wandered off the road and died, is not known. It is supposed that many of these once belonged to Major Grayham's train, and were by him abandoned from necessity. What an immense amount of suffering and destruction of property, and in no case should a broken-down horse or mule be left on this desert alive, but end his sufferings by shooting or bloodletting. By doing this, perhaps five or six days of his miserable and lingering misery may be shortened, and should the mule be left alive and reach water and grass, eventually he but becomes food for the wandering Indians at last. At sunset we staked our mules out on grass and some of the men slept on the ground whilst others remained guard at camp. Yesterday we passed the water of Carraseta, cold and pleasant but all impregnated with sulphur. About five miles from this spring and in the left range of mountains we discovered smoke in several places, issuing from the side and top of this mountain, and first concluded that this was an Indian signal notifying others that there were strangers in the pass, but a closer inspection led us to conclude that the smoke really issued from crevices in the side, and that we were in fact at the side of volcanic mountains.[7] By a subsequent examination of Emory's report and surveys as Topographical Engineer under General Kearney, we find this opinion fully confirmed. All the water met with since leaving the Colorado River is more or less impregnated with sulphur, and in a high degree this is the case in the immediate

---

of drying, grinding, leaching, and re-grinding, in much the same manner that the savages of the Amazon basin prepare manioc. Acorn flour was the staff of life to many of the California tribes.

[7]Emory mentions (*Notes*, p. 106) the hot springs near Aguas Calientes, but these fumaroles were a few miles southeast.

vicinity of these volcanic mountains, and it is therefore not very surprising that combustion should take place.

Sept. 9. Left camp early, and at the end of seventeen miles found ourselves at San Phillipe,[8] an Indian town, buildings all huts or sheds. These Indians wear clothes enough to hide their nakedness, but otherwise are extremely poor, many of them having no corn and no wheat. The grass at this camp is poor and the water very good and cold, but sulphurous. Here we shall remain until morning, and then we will move forward to Agua Callientas[9]—pronounced *Ogua* slightly sounding the *g*. Agua Callientas means Hot Springs or Hot Water. I have had some opportunity during the afternoon of examining into the customs of the Indians residing at this place, and, however incredible some things may appear, they must be told to illustrate the manner of living from day to day. Acorns, pounded into flour, serve as bread, and while some are engaged at this, others are roaming over the mountains and hills searching for worms. These worms resemble such as are frequently found on the anise plant and are as much like the tobacco worm as any. They are numerous; consequently, baskets of them are brought in and

[8]San Felipe. Emory describes the village as "deserted" (*Notes*, p. 104) and surrounded with lofty mountains 3,000 to 5,000 feet high. Bartlett (*Personal Narrative*, II, 122) says San Felipe was "in a valley without woods, in the lower part of which was a marshy spot with pools of water." Many Indians inhabited the area, presumably of the Diegueño tribe. "They were a filthy looking set, half clad and apparently half starved." They wandered about gathering roots and seeds, which with acorns constituted their principal food, and the women did most of the work. "The improvidence of this people seems almost incomprehensible," Bartlett accused, and he derides their lack of agriculture. The village consisted of twenty-three "miserable old huts or wigwams built of straw and rushes" (p. 123). There were traces of irrigation trenches, showing a long period of settlement.

[9]Aguas Calientes was the name given to the hot springs and Indian village near Warner's rancho. "To the south," said Emory, "down the valley of the Aqua Caliente, lay the road to San Diego. Above us was Mr. Warner's backwoods, American looking house, built of adobe and covered with a thatched roof. Around, were the thatched huts of the more than half naked Indians, who are held in a sort of serfdom by the master of that rancheria. I visited one or two of these huts, and found the inmates living in great poverty. The thermometer was at 30°, they had no fires, and no coverings but

WARNER'S PASS FROM SAN FELIPE

Reports of Explorations and Surveys . . . (Washington, 1857), VII, plate III

form the staple of every meal, and they relish them much, smack their lips, and cry *"Buena! Mucha buena!"*

This day closed with a heavy rain, the first for us in California.

Sept. 10 (Sunday). Rained hard nearly all the past night; consequently, our blankets are all wet and we must wait until they can be dried. This will occupy several hours, if the clouds do not shower more upon us in the meantime. This little and almost barren valley is entirely surrounded by mountains, and at least one more mountain pass awaits us before quitting this very wide range of mountains. The valley is spotted with camps—men, horses, and mules all resting. The water is from springs of a very forcible kind, and after boiling out of the earth form[s] a rivulet very boggy and deep. Out of this mud we have already drawn four of our mules and several horses. These holes are about five feet deep with mud and water. Mica abundant, and makes our boots look as if some painter had, during the night, carefully bronzed them over. Ahead of us lies a high mountain upon which there is apparently a good growth of timber. This is the only timber, excepting mesquite, that we have seen for many miles. Indian señoritas have paid us a visit this morning, but we gave them no tobacco (our stores being exhausted) and they did not stay long. They were all dressed in the Mexican style, but wore dresses made to the order of some American lady and by her sold to these people. The fog is curling gracefully and rolling up the sides of the surrounding mountains, and a cool and pleasant breeze is gradually coming up.

---

sheepskins. . . . Near the house is the source of the Aqua Caliente, a magnificent hot spring, of the temperature of 137° Fahrenheit, discharging from the fissure of a granite rock a large volume of water, which, for a long distance down, charges the air with the fumes of sulphuretted hydrogen. Above it, and draining down the same valley, is a cold spring of the temperature of 45°, and without the aid of any mechanical instrument, the cold and warm water may be commingled to suit the temperature of the bather. The Indians have made pools for bathing. They huddle around the basin of the spring to catch the genial warmth of its vapors, and in cold nights immerse themselves in the pools to keep warm." (*Notes*, pp. 105 f.)

Blow, winds, blow, or old Sol will send his scorching rays upon us in a short time.

At 10:00 A.M. we marched for the head of this valley, which we reached at 1:00 P.M. and found here another Indian rancho, with some corn, peaches, and delicious grapes. We bought some [of] these, at a very high price, and found them well flavored and of thin skin and pale purple color. After leaving this rancho we descended the dividing ridge, and from this point could see into a small valley, well timbered in places and broken by small but steep hills. Over these we drove for two hours, and found ourselves in the vicinity of the hot springs, and here encamped on poor grass but very good, cold water. This cold spring is about five hundred yards below the boiling spring and is truly excellent water. Here is the residence of quite a number of civilized Indians, and from them we obtained corn in the stalk, roasting ears, and meal—also grapes of a very good kind, name not known but much resembling the Isabella.

Traveled about eighteen miles this day.

Sept. 11.　Our mules being much fatigued by past exertions to reach good grass, we concluded to remain at this camp one day and recruit. We found ten wagons here, and met some Mexicans and one American returning from the mines. They all agree in their accounts of the productiveness of the mines and cheapness of the necessaries of life. This valley is small, or rather there are many small valleys within the circle of the high range of mountains around us. These appear to be well timbered, and altogether present a romantic appearance. The road over which we passed yesterday was well shaded, and many new varieties of trees, shrubs, flowers, and plants were found. For these I have no name. The blackbird and crow are also very numerous here and this is the first place in which they appear similar to those in the north. Instead of these birds sitting moping on some dry limb or sun-heated rock, they are soaring and caroling through the air or sitting at ease above our heads on the cottonwoods. Agua Callientas is water from many springs, and all very hot,

so much so that a person cannot bathe in it. These springs boil
from the earth with considerable force and form the head of a
small stream of water, becoming colder as it flows onward. This
hot water is highly impregnated with sulphur. A caveyard of
mules is just leaving this camp, numbering about three hundred,
all destined for the gold mines and the market at San Francisco.
We have now been wandering for seven days in the Cordellera[10]
range of mountains, and they still loom up before us and promise
yet many ups and downs in this world. For the past two days
a constant change in the climate has been going on. The days
are cooler, and our blankets are damp from dews at night, and
refreshing breezes are constantly blowing through the day.
Besides this we are once more issuing from the haunts of the
thieving Indians and fast approaching the settlements of California. This is cheering, and the soul bounds like one set free
from a long and dreary imprisonment, and hears the sound of
sweet liberty. We are now at Warner's old rancho, and near the
adobe and thatch-covered dwelling of his agent are the hot
springs.[11] A short distance from this ranch the road leading to
San Diego bears off to the southwest. One hundred and thirty-
seven degrees Fahrenheit is the temperature of the hot spring
here; and above this, bursting from the rocks, is a cold spring of
45°, the waters of which may be mingled without mechanical aid,

[10]Emory's map loosely calls the southern California sierra the "Cordilleras
of California." Actually, Evans and his party had been threading their way
through the Santa Rosa range.

[11]Jonathan Trumbull (hispanicized to Juan José) Warner, of Connecticut,
arrived in California in 1831 as a fur trapper and later engaged in merchan-
dising in Los Angeles. In 1844 he applied for a grant of land in San José
Valley, and it was made in 1845. The ranch became a convenient way-station
for travelers arriving by southern trails. The Army of the West traded worn-
out animals for fresh ones at Warner's, and the ranchero was one time tem-
porarily jailed for having army mules in his possession, it being assumed that
he had stolen them. The Butterfield mail stage made regular stops at Warner's
and for many years the rancho furnished supplies to jaded desert wayfarers.
For descriptions of the ranch, see Emory, *Notes*, pp. 105 f.; Cooke, "Journal,"
pp. 227-30; *Pioneer Notes from the Diaries of Judge Benjamin Hayes*, ed.
Marjorie T. Wolcott (1929), pp. 48-62. A complete account of Warner's life
and his ranching activities can be found in Joseph J. Hill, *The History of
Warner's Ranch and its Environs* (1927).

to suit the bather. The latitude of Agua Callientas is 33° 51′ 16″. Mica abounds in all these waters and the soil is full of it.

Sept. 12. Left Agua Callientas and continued on through hill and dale and at noon arrived at water and grass. Here we halted for a few hours and took dinner near an Indian rancheria and one of the coldest springs of water met with on the entire journey. The mountains on our right and left are growing higher at every step, and the end of this pass is not yet, though long expected. We passed another Californian's grave soon after leaving camp this morning. Many a poor fellow occupies some solitary nook as his final resting place along this road, and it may safely be predicted that many more will occupy stations equally low. At 2:00 P.M. we again went forward, and at sunset entered a small valley among the many hills of the pass, and here found very good water and tolerably fine grass. Here we found two Indian families, and of them we bought corn to roast. Distance this day, about eighteen miles.

Sept. 13. Called camp early, and every man left his blankets shivering. Our elevation has become so great that heavy dews and cold nights may always be looked for at this season of the year. The sun rose clear, and shortly after we were honored with a visit from the dusky ladies of the adjoining huts. They brought *sandías*, or watermelons, which they wished to dispose of, but we did not purchase, being too early in the day. About the same time a couple of horsemen brought in baskets of fine grapes. These we bought and found very good, though not so ripe as those we got at Agua Callientes. At 7:30 A.M. we were once more rolling over the broken country of the pass and found many hills, and some of them very steep and rugged. At 12:00 M. we suddenly emerged into a fine and tolerably extensive valley, and at 1:00 P.M. encamped at the rancho of San M'Call.[12] This, we are told, belongs to an English gentleman, but he is now absent at the mines and his gardens show the want of the owner much. Peach, pear, and apple trees are left to the

[12]Probably a corruption of San Miguel.

mercy of all animals at large and vineyards are eaten off close to the ground. We had the good fortune of obtaining from these Indians some grahamite flour, roasting ears, and fresh beef, all much cheaper than at any other ranch. We therefore have had a feast, and more than a feast, and we enjoyed it much. There are many Indian huts and two adobe buildings here, and corn is cultivated pretty extensively. They dam up the many springs here and then by ditches distribute the water over the land. Here we found the first wild geese, and ducks have been seen at nearly all the waters since crossing the Colorado River. The mountains still hold us in their fast embrace, and we have abandoned the idea of an early escape. Traveled this day eighteen miles.

Sept. 14. Cloudy, with a cold south wind nearly all the night. Our general course has been west northwest, and we now go for a short distance southwest to turn a mountain. At 12:00 M. we reached the center of a fine little valley, and here we halted to rest and take dinner, after which we moved onward and passing over a small eminence, were at once introduced to another and a wider valley of extreme beauty. In the center of this valley is a lake of salt water. This sheet adds much to the wild and picturesque beauty of the scenery of this lovely spot. At the head of this body of water we encamped under some very thrifty willow trees and a short distance from the ranch. Here, and also in the other valleys passed through today, we saw large herds of the best cattle I ever met with. These were really of a superior kind, and good fat beeves could be bought for $5.00. Traveled today about nineteen miles.

Sept. 15. Started from this salt lake and at a short distance found ourselves once more in a mountain pass with a number of pretty steep hills. This pass, in twelve miles, led us to the rancho of San Maguil.[13] Here we found peaches, grapes, green corn, beef (fresh), and some fodder for our mules. There are many Indian huts here, and they raise more corn than we have seen at any other ranch. This ranch is located in a very

[13]San Miguel.

small valley and at the foot of the mountains, and may be said to be in the pass. Corn and fodder we buy here very cheap, but grahamite flour or flour and bran, is very high. For this they ask at the rate of $20 per 100 lbs. or $2.50 for one *almud*,[14] which is nearly equal to a peck in the States. Grapes 12½¢ per bunch natural. Our camp last night afforded us but little grass, and we have seen none today but are told that there is fine grass eighteen miles ahead. We therefore feed well with fodder here, and shall probably push to a later hour than usual. The road is represented as very good and we may be able to reach Rio San Antonio this evening.

Left the ranch of San McGill at 5 P.M., and at midnight encamped on the banks of the river, having traveled for twelve miles over a level plain upon which nothing was found but a short weed with a very strong perfume. Among these weeds large droves of cattle were seen, quietly picking such feed as they could find. Rio San Antonio is quite a stream of pure, cold water but there is but little grass at this encampment, and the night was cold and damp, with a heavy dew. On the banks of this river we found a large field of corn and several Indian and Mexican huts. Traveled this day about twenty-four miles.

Sept. 16. After breakfast we left our encampment on the river and started for Williams' Ranch, which place we reached about noon and found a place of considerable importance, and contains probably fifty or seventy-five inhabitants, Indians and all. Here we found the first two-story dwelling since leaving Chihuahua, and the dwellings of the best part of the population are neat. They devote their time to cattle, and have large herds. At a small store sugar of the very best quality was bought at 50¢ per pound, and we purchased the best of fresh beef for about a penny a pound. Mr. Williams,[15] the owner of this rancho, is well spoken of and has the reputation of being very benevolent and kind to his countrymen. His farm covers

[14]A dry measure, about .8 of a liter.

[15]Isaac Williams was a Pennsylvanian who arrived in California with Ewing Young's trappers in 1832. He obtained a half interest in the Rancho Santa Ana

twelve square miles of choice land, and upon this he has at large
12,000 head of cattle and 600 mules and horses, all in fine condition. He tells the emigrants that they are welcome to the beef
and that they have only to go out and kill it. If a poor man
comes along who has been unfortunate and has lost his mule,
Mr. Williams gives him one, and the poor fellow is enabled to
go on his way rejoicing and thanking God that he has such a
countryman in a strange land. They have but little grass, but
a bountiful Providence has more than provided for their wants.
The hills and mountain sides are thickly covered with wild oats
and clover, and better feed for animals never grew. This is in-
digenous to the country, and a great blessing. The last fifty miles
traveled by us has been without grass and we came in here on
mules starved and wearied and are now encamped two miles
west of Williams' Ranch, in a small valley full of oats, clover,
and two good springs of water; and here we will remain a few
days to rest and recruit our animals. We traveled only eight
miles this day.

      Sept. 17 (Sunday). After putting out my clothes to air

del Chino from his father-in-law, Antonio María Lugo, owner of the San
Bernardino Rancho, in 1841, and built one of the finest ranch houses in southern California. It was an adobe quadrangle, built around a patio, with outer
dimensions of 250 feet on a side. Williams added to his holdings, and during
the Mexican War a skirmish between Mexicans and Yankee settlers occurred
on the ranch lands. The ranch was located on a route followed by many
emigrants to California, and, like Warner's, it later became a station on the
Butterfield Overland Mail. On Williams' death the rancho came under the
direction of his son-in-law, John Rains, and it subsequently passed under the
control of Robert S. Carlisle and, later, Richard Gird. The "Record Book"
of the ranch contains an entry for September 16, 1849, which reads as follows:
"A M Browning, G W. B. Evans, Jacob Teats, F Laubenheimer, E Bruner,
A. T. Parker Dr L H. Bunnell, P S. Kelly Jas Lott. arrived at this Ranch yesterday in good health, and met with kind and gentlemanly attention from Col.
Isaac Williams, who extended to us the hospitalities of his ranch. One & a
half miles from his dwellings we found an abundance of wild oats & clover,
and our mules being fatigued & hungry, we concluded to remain here one
week and recruit; in order that we may be able to pass on comfortably. We
found the Indians quite troublesome on the colorado" (Lindley Bynum, "The
Record Book of the Rancho Santa Ana del Chino," Historical Society of
Southern California *Annual Publication*, XVI [1934]). See also George William
and Helen Pruitt Beattie, *Heritage of the Valley* (Pasadena, 1939), chap. xiii.

during the day, Mr. Browning and myself visited Rancho Chino, as Williams' Ranch is called, and found the Colonel at home. Soon after our arrival, he had a large basket of excellently-flavored grapes brought in by an Indian servant, and we once more had an opportunity of sitting upon Windsor chairs, eating grapes, and conversing with a gentleman in our own language. I found Colonel W[illiams] to be a native of Pennsylvania and from the town of Wilksbarrey, open-hearted and free as his native air, and ever ready to render assistance to his countryman. He told us that many of the emigrants had reached here with nothing in the world but the clothes they had on, and that many had suffered hunger for many days, and the only way for him to do was to relieve their most pressing wants and send them on to the mines.

He has slaughtered a beef every day for months past and frequently had no beef for his own breakfast the next morning.

The Indians who do his work are well acquainted with the manner of catching cattle, but they are poor butchers. When he wants a beef, orders are given, and in a few moments you will see an Indian galloping swift as the wind across the plains, and in a short time he has one singled out from the herd before him and the lasso thrown over his horns. The horse well understands his part of the tragedy. The moment he sees the well-directed rope fall over the head of the victim, he suddenly stops, and the next moment the beef is brought to his knees; as soon as he rises, he is led off to the place of slaughter, his feet there entangled in ropes, and then thrown, and his throat cut. As soon as he is dead, his skin is stripped off of one side, the leg and shoulder blade cut off and the meat taken from the side of the backbone, and then the same process is gone through with on the other side, and the hindquarters are removed. This done, nothing remains but the head, backbone, and entrails. These are food for the buzzards, which are here found in great numbers, and we saw sailing over our camp this morning a very large bird pronounced a vulture by all. I have seen some very good riders in Mexico, but these Californians are much better, and it is said that they will throw the lasso better with their feet than Mexicans can with the hand. The only wild animals seen along the road for several days past are wolves of the large, gray kind. Heretofore they have been the small prairie wolf, one of which was taken by a Californian a few mornings ago on horseback. The wolf had much the advantage in the start but a run of half a mile brought the rider close enough to pierce him with his sword, and the contest was soon ended. The large, gray wolf, however, is not so easily taken. Having spent an hour or more with Colonel W. I went to his mill (propelled by water) and bought some flour and a few other articles at the store, and then started home to camp, where I arrived much fatigued and well pleased with my intercourse with Colonel W. On the way back we passed by a herd of his horses, all in fine order and fat as seals. His mules he values from ten to one hundred and fifty dollars. The Colonel has a fine vineyard, and this is surrounded with thrifty bearing peach trees. At this hacienda he has in operation a large soap factory, all of which sells at about 50¢ per pound. Besides these comforts, he has cultivated by his Indians melons, onions, corn, and Irish potatoes, the last of which he now sells at $4 per bushel.

Sept. 18. Last night we slept on oat-straw beds, a luxury almost forgotten from lapse of time. After having for so long a time known nothing softer than my bed of blankets, the addition of straw seemed to increase its hardness, and I have my doubts if much enjoyment could be taken by me if immediately transferred to the soft featherbeds of home; yet I would like to taste those comforts once more, and if feathers should not suit, my blankets could be spread on the floor. But why indulge myself in thoughts of comforts far, far from here? I am now in camp, and must speak of what has transpired this day. Colonel W. sent us a fine beef this morning and the meat is now over a slow fire, smoking and preparing for future consumption. To effect this, we have built a scaffold about two feet high, and on small sticks laid crosswise, the slices of beef are hung, and a good smoke is constantly kept up. While this is doing our cook is rendering the tallow, which will serve to lighten our bread in future—or at least as long as it lasts. Our mules are enjoying the fat of the land and at the end of a week will be well prepared to go forward to the mines—a distance yet of four hundred miles. We are now only thirty miles from the city Los Angelos, and twenty from the Pacific coast, enjoying, among other things, a cool and pleasant breeze every day. The nights are cold enough to require three blankets as covering, and the dews are very heavy. The Sirra Nevada range of mountains now lies towering to the clouds on our right and are the highest mountains and the least broken of any we have passed. In making our way to this point, we came through what is called the door or passage from all the Californias to the states of Senora and Chihuahua, and from which pass we have just emerged, having entered it on the west side of the great desert or basin, and left it at San Phillipe, and in many places found it only wide enough to permit the passage of a wagon. This occupied us diligently for about eight days.

Sept. 19. I promised to give the reader the distances from Chihuahua to the coast, and, having nothing else to do, thought it well to employ this cool and pleasant morning in doing this, and shall merely premise by saying that the distances here given will not be from actual measurement, but from the combined judgment of the nine men in our small company. Where these nine opinions differed much, I took the average, and adopted that as the actual distance traveled during each day.

From Chihuahua to Yanos it is	212	miles
" Yanos to Santa Cruz " "	203	"
" Santa Cruz to Tucson	97	"
" Tucson to Piemo Village	95	"
" Piemo Village to Crossing of the Colorado River	180	"
" the crossing to El Yseta or first grass	102	"
" El Y Seta to Pueblo Los Angeles	177	"
	1,066	miles

—Total miles from Chihuahua to Los Angeles, over a good wagon road—good in all places excepting a few hard hills in the War-loop Pass of the Rocky Mountains. The water may be found at convenient distances along this road, unless in a very dry season, but on the Gila River and the great basin there is little or no grass and but few beans. Our beef is drying and smoking finely, and there are no large flies visible, so that the preparation of meat can be carried on without danger of worms or any other annoying insects usually attending the locality of slaughter-houses. This is almost the only meat used on campaign, although we have purchased bacon on several occasions from wagons going to the gold region. We bought yesterday a side of bacon weighing probably 22 lbs., for which we paid $6.00. This looks a little like California prices, yet Colonel Williams tells us that sugar, coffee, and groceries can be bought nearly as cheap as in the States on the Pacific coast, and that he had sold sugar (good Havana), and coffee at eight and ten cents per pound. But this gold excitement has raised everything in market and with the exception of beef, everything is high. The oats covering these mountains and hills has attracted the deer from the surrounding hills, and it is little work to go out a mile or two and kill deer rolling fat.

Sept. 20. Some of our mess have spent this day in washing clothes and cleaning up generally. This was much needed, as we have had no opportunity of washing up for many days on account of the muddy condition of the water along the Gila and Colorado Rivers as well as the few tributaries we crossed. Our mules are improving, and the beef is drying and smoking finely. There is one thing to be recorded of this climate, although the fact has frequently been mentioned before. The bones or parts of our beef preserved for soup have occupied a place in the sun, without salt or smoke, for the last three days, and yet this meat is just as sweet and pure as it was the first day. This is a good and healthy climate and always blessed with trade winds, rendering the days cool and pleasant and the nights not too cold for comfort and health. Colonel Fremont, J. B. Weller, and their party, appointed to survey the boundary line between Mexico and the United States, are expected at this ranch in a few days on their way home. Colonel Fremont had at one time purchased this ranch, but some misunderstanding prevented the closing of the contract at the time, and another effort will now be made to contract for the same. The California quail abounds in the ravines around our camp and differ only in color from our northern quail. We have not for several weeks past seen any of the black-tailed deer, nor antelopes, but are informed that elk abound on and near the headwaters of the San Joaquin River. There is, in fact, no necessity for much game in this region, where men raise from ten to twenty thousand head of cattle— none costing over twenty-five cents a head, and no other labor than herding once and branding. Horses and mules require more attention, now that so many persons are on the road, and on foot, too, and experience has taught us that there are scoundrels abroad. Our animals are always in sight of this camp, though at full liberty, but, being surrounded by hills, they occupy the sides, where the oats are best.

   Sept. 21.   Another very pleasant day. Many of the campers now in this valley have sold their mules and take shipping at San Pedro, a small port twenty-five miles from here. From that port they can sail to San Francisco in eight days, and it will take us about twenty-five days. We think that by being in possession of mules on our arrival, we will not be incident to delays and can pack our provisions up to the mines and be ready for the work, which we are told is better in the winter on account of the intense heat in the summer. We are also told that the heat at the mines is equal to the hot and sultry Gila River and, if true, I for one would not willingly sacrifice my health in the pursuit of riches, which is, after all, a mere bauble, a mere toy, and yet the god of some. I gathered some California oats and wild sage seed which I hope to see growing at my own dear home. There are many other shrubs and plants that might be tested in the same way, but, being out of season, seed can not be obtained. At this camp there are a few venerable oaks, and just below us willows and elder grow in groups. On the tall mountains north of us pine, cedar, and, near the base, oak timber is found in abundance. South of our camp and just over the hill tops is the head of a peak just visible, and from this point a full view of the Pacific Ocean may be obtained, and I have waited for a day clear of smoke, but so far my wish has not yet been gratified. Fogs prevail through the night and morning, and the rest of the day is smoky—precisely such weather as visits our northern homes in October and [is] known as Indian summer. We are told, however, that an Indian summer is here unknown and that there is a great similarity in the weather at all seasons. If this is the fact, I am ready to say that few places exceed the coast of California for blandness of climate, and that men here would stand in but little need of habitations. There is, however, one comfort of which Mr. Williams and others deprive themselves, notwithstanding the thousands of cattle dotting the hills and valleys, and that is, butter. They have, running over their wide acres, water pure as crystal and cold as the snows of north, and might have spring houses and in them milk and butter the year round; but as far as my observation extends, it is an article rarely seen and much less used. 'Tis true, butter, eggs, cheese, and smoked ham and other kinds of bacon may in this country be deemed *luxuries*, but they are so common a thing, and found even on the table of the poorest man in Ohio and other states, and a habit from childhood's early days of being indulged with such palatable food renders the task of forgetting them much harder in our camp life; and like phantoms of the past the memory of these palatable and pleasant dishes flit across the imagination and arouse tender recollections of the past, and with Selkirk we are ready to exclaim

> O, had I the wings of a dove,
> How soon I would taste them again!

How long this deprivation from the most common necessaries
of life is to last remains yet to be determined, but we have determined "to root it through." Dr. Bunnell and Laubenheimer
have gone down to the ranch for grapes, peaches, and melons,
and this evening we will indulge our appetites once more on the
gifts of the god of nature. If man will but exert himself, if he
will but spend one half of his time in manual or mental labor
(and by mental labor I mean to direct the Indian in the performance of his work) he may soon surround himself with every
blessing heart could desire or mind conceive, for God has here
bestowed upon him every favor he could ask for; a healthy climate, very temperate, and a good soil await but his exertions, and
soon he may be surrounded by every comfort. The Indians and
Mexicans, or rather the natives of California, are here, as they
were in Mexico, mere peons, knowing nothing but the life of a
slave and caring for nothing more than a living, and any number of these can be obtained to labor for a man if the wages of
the country are paid. Wages are higher here in consequence of
the short distance to the mines, but this is balanced again by the
price of goods and necessaries furnished by the master to his
peon; and both ends seldom meet at the end of the year, but the
slave finds himself deeper in debt, work it as he will. This is the
practice, and as long as a peon can be kept in debt to his master,
just so long is he subject to him as a slave. This has been the
law of the land and is still the law in all Mexico. There the peon
knows not of, nor cares for, a better life, and the rich owner
of large haciendas and ranchos is equally dependent, but better
qualified by education and capital to control the actions and
bind the fetters of debt and slavery upon the limbs of the poor
Mexican. I have conversed with aged peons upon this subject,
and found from their own admissions that they were still deeply
in debt, although they had labored for many years in trying to
pay a debt of a few dollars contracted in early days.

Sept. 23. We had but little fog last night, but it was quite
cool. The wolves came to the outskirts of our encampment early

in the evening, and gave evidence of their presence by sharp howls. To these we pay no attention, knowing them to be harmless. We were visited this morning by a Mr. Rose,[16] who has spent four years in this country, generally among the Umah Indians on the waters of the Colorado River. We had been previously told that this man had acquired an influence over this tribe such as not even their own chiefs possessed, and had even gone into the tribe and, for some theft or other crime, had caused some of them to be tied and whipped in the presence of many hundreds of their brethren. Rose told us of an adventure he had at the crossing of the Colorado early in the past spring. He said that on his arrival there, he met a small party of Americans who had got out of provisions and were in a starving condition. Rose divided with them until they had but little left and were then upwards of 120 miles from the settlements. This party informed Mr. Rose that a Mexican was but a few hours behind with eighty mules loaded with flour for the mines; that they had offered money and everything for some of this flour, but had been steadily refused by the Mexican.

This was enough for Rose, and at his request this small party of Americans withdrew a short distance and Rose awaited the arrival of the flour train, which came up that evening and began crossing the river. This was soon accomplished, and when the Mexican was ready to pack, Rose asked him for flour. But the Mexican refused to sell or give away. Upon this Rose sent an Indian to the top of the hill with orders to give the whoop, which had scarcely been done before the signal was answered by the prompt presence of about two hundred Indians. Rose ordered these to take sixty sacks of this flour, which was quickly done and the Mexican was suffered to proceed without further molestation. The party of Americans was then sent for, and the flour divided among them. Here was but one alternative: either to run the risk of starving, or compel this Mexican to disgorge

[16]This was neither Leonard Rose of the San Gabriel Valley, nor Louis Rose of San Diego.

some of the food he had on his mules; and when he refused to deal with these hungry men and relieve their pressing necessities for the proffered money, forcible means had to be adopted—with what success the reader can judge. Our camp was thrown into considerable excitement about sunset this evening by the appearance of heavy, black clouds of something resembling dense smoke. These clouds rolled over the hills towards our camp and all concluded that fire had broken out on the south side of the hills, among the oats, and the trade winds were then blowing a stiff breeze, and we made up our minds to pack our moveables on the nearest bare spot of ground and drive our mules beyond the mouth of this narrow valley. But before adopting this expedient, I took a station on an elevation of ground a short distance off and, being blessed with a heavy growth of whiskers and mustachios, soon determined what this meant. As soon as the wind reached the hill I occupied, my whiskers became very wet, and the fear of fire immediately vanished from my mind; for I well understood that the trade winds were only playing tricks upon us, and that this wind was only chasing from the face of the mighty deep an immense fog bank, and that we were now actually enveloped in a fog dark as midnight. This continued for several hours; after which it was clear and pleasant as usual. I spent a very tedious night, from headache to slight fever and then to headache again. O, how often I thought of the remedies resorted to and always applied by my dear wife, when [I was] suffering from such attacks at home! But here there was nothing to be done but roll and groan it out. California has already held her election, and the delegates chosen are now in session at the city of Monteray. Much good is expected from their deliberations; and the subject of a delegate to Congress is now being canvassed at every rancho and city within the limits of this territory. Colonel Fremont has good and true friends; a Mr. Stevens and Mr. King[17] are also named for the same station. Which may be the fortunate candidate, in the event of the adop-

[17] T. Butler King.

SOUTH END OF SANTA INEZ MOUNTAINS AND SAN BUENAVENTURA VALLEY
Reports of Explorations and Surveys . . . (Washington, 1857), VII, plate II

tion of a Constitution, remains for future acts of the voters to develop.

Sept. 23.   Morning dawned, and at about 9:00 A.M. the trade winds paid us another of their regular daily visits. These winds blow all day long from the west and about sunset all nature sinks into a lull and with the exception of the coolness the evenings are beautiful and, when enveloped in the folds of a good cloak or coat, they are as pleasant as any I have ever passed. Many of the packers have left camp and are now moving towards Puebla Los Angelos. Mr. Browning left our camp this morning with the intention of reaching San Francisco by water. This determination on his part will enable me to get my letters and papers eight or ten days earlier, and removes the necessity of my going to that city in person, as he will procure these and all information we stand in need of and meet us at the lower end of the bay of San Francisco. At or near this point we turn off and move for the mines direct, where we will arrive in about twenty days, if fortunate. What! twenty days only and our destination gained? It seems almost incredible, almost beyond the measure of belief, after having toiled as diligently as grass and water would permit nearly seven months of this year. But this journey, long as it has been, must end some time; and when told that only twenty more days will be required to perform it to our destination, it becomes a matter of much rejoicing and pleasure to us, who have so long sighed for its successful termination. No one not intimately acquainted with the details of a campaign can realize anything like it. Every day there is something to irritate the feelings and make man a bitter and morose being, particularly if placed in charge of mules or in any manner connected with these contrary and headstrong animals. The following cut faintly sets forth daily ocurrences. Yet if persons wish to make overland journeys, the stubborn mule is the animal best adapted to this service. They will live well on such food as horses would reject, and on a less quantity, but their manners are not the most pleasing and their tempers the most winning.

When least expecting it, they will kick or bite you and at no time can you place confidence in them, and the above stubborn position is assumed almost every time you lead up to pack. Our beef has been divided and packed away, and a sufficient quantity of grahamite flour purchased to last us to the city of Angelos, and now we are nearly ready to move forward again. This evening we had two good melons in camp, and make a good dessert of them. Our animals are well recruited, and if we get but half feed enough the distance from here to the mines will be accomplished without the necessity of any further lying by.

Sept. 24 (Sunday). Very late getting up, but blessed with another beautiful clear morning and bracing atmosphere, but had a very heavy dew. Cold nights, windy days, and heavy dews are common all along between the coast range of mountains and the coast. Yet, if a person is provided with all necessary clothing, this climate will please any one but a southern man, and would please him, were it not for the cool and dewy nights. Spent this Sabbath pleasantly, quietly, and as good citizens do spend this Holy Day.

Sept. 25. This morning after partaking of a good and early breakfast we caught our mules and commenced packing. This over, we were once more "rolling" as we call it. After traveling for nine miles over a rolling, yet pleasant country with the towering coast range on our right, we entered into a beautiful wide valley with many adobe buildings and acres of land partially enclosed with staunch mud walls. Immense herds of cattle and California horses were seen on every hand. Here we crossed a beautiful and strong stream[18] of very clear and pure water, from which these rancheros procure water to irrigate their lands. These California horses are beautiful—well made and very muscular, and all of good speed and bottom. They very much resemble in feature and form the Canadian strain of horses in our own country, only much larger and more powerful. A Californian will ride one of these noble animals from sixty to seventy-five miles per day. From this river we pushed on through the valley and at sunset crossed another very fine and clear stream of water, the banks of which were well grown with a variety of small trees, many kinds of which we knew no name for. After passing this river and the rancherias on this water, we left the road and at half a mile found an abundance of clover and here we camped for the night, and with the use of *bois de vache* and a few dry weeds (there being no wood nearer than the river), we made out to cook an excellent supper. Wild oats, which covers nearly every hill top along the road, is easily found, but the traveler unacquainted with wild clover will ride over a district of country and believe it wholly destitute of animal food when at the same time the earth may be, and here in fact is, covered with the best food. At this period of the year this clover is dead and broken down and the earth is finely carpeted with this rich seed and the fine and broken clover stalks, upon which mules, horses, and cattle will fatten quicker than upon the wild oats of this country. The seed of this clover is inclosed in a burr of the size of a marrowfat pea, and the burr, with the seed, is as good as the best grain. We traveled this day about twenty-two miles, over a country beautiful and of very rich soil. At the Indian rancherias just above our camp we found wild mustard, hemp, and beautiful grapevines. These vines had covered the whole of many of the cottonwoods at the river, and formed beautiful canopies, sufficiently thick in foliage to afford protection from rain and sun. Here *también* we found the tame turkey sitting upon the ridges of the cabins and huts of the occupants.

[18]Probably the San Gabriel River.

Sept. 26. Arose early and called the camp, and went to
gathering dry weeds and *bois de vache*, or cow wood, for a breakfast fire. I found that the fog had clouded the heavens before
we went to our blankets and this morning we found our upper
blankets completely saturated with the falling fog, equal to a
drizzling rain of the north. After breakfast we started for the
long-sought city and traveled over a plain upon which there was
an abundance of clover, all broken and flat upon the ground.
At about 11:00 A.M. we followed the road over a small eminence
and at the distance of a short mile saw the City [of] Los Angeles[19]

[19]Los Angeles (see *Census of the City and County of Los Angeles for 1850,*
ed. Maurice H. and Marco R. Newmark [1929]) contained more than 3,000
people, and was "a place of considerable size, regularly laid out, with some
very good buildings. The inhabitants appear more energetic than any we have
seen on our journey. There are several American families in town." ("From
Texas to the Gold Mines," in *Southern Trails to California*, p. 277.) Bartlett,
Personal Narrative, II, 82, complains of the number of Indians seen lounging
about the streets, but he praises the agricultural potentialities of the Los
Angeles plain.
　Charles Edward Pancoast (*A Quaker Forty-Niner* [1930], pp. 270-72) says:
"We found it a dreamy old Spanish Town, more animated than some others on
account of the presence of numerous Emigrants. Its Location, Climate, and
Surroundings are the most enchanting I ever witnessed. It is situated on high
land at the head of a beautiful Valley that gradually opens out to the Ocean
(a few miles away but in plain sight) and is surrounded by low grassy Mountains. The Climate was so buoyant and inspiring that I could not imagine how
any Person could be indolent there; yet the place appeared to be decaying
with inertia, and what work they did perform was done in a most primitive
and slovenly manner. I did not see a Wagon in the Town, except those
brought by American Emigrants, and the light Carriages of the wealthy
Rancheros. Wood was dragged in by Jack Asses attached to the bundles by
rawhide thongs.
　"We found there an old Catholic Church, a few Stores, several Wine Houses,
and a dozen *Haciendas* with large and beautiful enclosed Gardens filled with
Figs, Pomegranates, Apricots, Oranges, Lemons, Almonds, Grapes, and other
fruits, with a Watch Tower in the centre, on the platform of which constantly marched a Guard with Rifle and Bayonet. The Town was owned and
governed according to the Mexican Policy of concentrating the ownership in
the hands of a few, thus raising up a powerful Aristocracy whose Loyalty
could be relied upon. . . . The City of Los Angeles was owned in the main
by about twenty Persons, occupants of the splendid Haciendas, some of them
also owners of large Ranchos in the Country. A number of Houses were built
to rent to poor People, Merchants, Doctors, etc.; but except for a few city
lots no land was for sale. The consequence was that although this Town was
said to be two hundred years old, possessed a most salubrious Climate, and was

on the banks of a beautiful and clear stream of water in the valley below us.

I was disappointed in the location of this place, having expected to find it on tablelands, which may be said to be so, for it is on the second rise of the land from the river, but here the bottoms of the stream are narrow. The buildings are principally of adobe, and only one house two stories high. The citizens of this place are all in possession of money and are well dressed and of much lighter complexion than the Mexicans. The city is also laid out without special regard to order. But one thing may be said for the citizens: they pay great attention to the cultivation of grapes, oranges, quinces, pears, and the grains of this country. Their gardens were all well inclosed with willow hedges crossed with other willows. I also saw several very ancient fig trees, affording shade and fruit to the owner. The population of this city is about three thousand, all of whom are handling money in greater or less quantity. On the brow of the highlands

surrounded by some of the most beautiful and fertile land on the Globe, it had only grown to be a Town of five hundred Inhabitants. . . . The People were courteous and clever, but, like all these Spaniards, never in a hurry, except on horseback."

"Los Angeles," said another visitor during the fifties, ". . . is justly celebrated for the beauty of its situation. I should not desire a more beautiful residence for myself and my best friends than such a one as educated and intelligent people might form on this spot. . . . the little town stands cleanly and elegantly at the foot of a hilly plateau, which abruptly terminates here, and, after the winter rain, is covered with grass and a rich flora of splendid flowers A clear mountain-stream gushes forth from a gully which opens in the hills behind the town. It has its rise in a majestic chain of mountains, forming the background of the picture, and its waters irrigate the gardens and vineyards, which constitute the wealth and chief attraction of the place. . . . At the time of my stay in Los Angeles, insecurity of life and bad morals prevailed to an extent by which the beauty of situation and climate, and other advantages of the place were counterbalanced, and quite a number of murders occurred in the short space of my sojourn." See Froebel, *Seven Years' Travel in Central America*, pp. 561-68. The best description of Los Angeles in the fifties and sixties is in Robert G. Cleland, *The Cattle on a Thousand Hills* (1941), chap. v. See also Harris Newmark, *Sixty Years in Southern California* (1930), *passim*. The architecture was predominantly Mexican—adobe construction with flat roofs. The chief hostelry was the Bella Union—"a one-story, flat roofed adobe, with a corral in the rear, extending to Los Angeles street, back of the city, are the remains of an old fortification,[20] upon upon which we saw an American flagstaff standing.

While in the city, I entered the baking and eating establishment of a German who has lately established himself among these people. Here I saw excellent pies, fine loaves of bread, and pyramids of sweetmeats; and a loaf of bread was bought at half a dollar such as are sold for *6d.* at home. I bought a pie for which the baker charged half a dollar. The flour purchased by us for the road cost $12 per 100 lbs. But we must again leave the city, and now—having first inquired our way out, the name of the next town of note, and having learned that Santa Barbara comes next, and is probably seventy-five miles from here—we will now turn this corner, and take a turn to the right at the next street, which will introduce us at the suburbs to a beautiful and extensive plain. But here we take the right-hand road, leading down the plain, at the foot of the high and rolling hills bordering upon our road. About two miles from the city we left this plain, and turning to the right over a more broken country at 4:00 P.M. we entered a canyon[21] and passed another spur of the coast range running due west. At the opposite side of this pass we encamped, and here met many Mexicans from the mines and now returning to their homes. Heavy fog and prospect of dew. Distance this day, about twenty miles.

Sept. 27.　On getting from under our blankets we found the fog had been so thick and damp as completely to saturate the outside of everything exposed. Left this camp and at the end of a mile entered upon a large and beautiful plain, upon which

---

with the usual great Spanish portal. On the north side of the corral . . . were the numerous pigeon-holes, or dog-kennels. These were the rooms for the guests . . . not over 6 x 9 in size. Such were the ordinary dormitories of the hotel that advertised as 'being the best hotel south of San Francisco.'" (Cleland, p. 108, from Horace Bell, *Reminiscences of a Ranger.*)

[20]Fort Hill, now near the intersection of Temple Street and North Broadway. Gillespie used the hill as a base during the first American occupation of Los Angeles.

[21]Cahuenga Pass, now the main highway to the San Fernando Valley.

we could see horses and cattle in every direction. Just where we struck this plain we passed a rancho inhabited by those having the care of the vast herds before us. This seemed to be the only employment of those residing upon this plain,[22] for there was no evidence of agricultural implements ever having been used. After passing down the east side of this plain we came to a small elevation of land covered something like a grove with black oaks and on its borders we found a spring of clear water but quite warm. Crossing over this grove we were in short time passing another break in a spur crossing our path, and once over, we found the earth black with recent fire, and the feed entirely destroyed for miles. This continued, and the country rolling and broken, until we encamped at 4:00 P.M. at the alum springs, where we found but little feed and that dry. On our route and in the canyons were growing the stately white oaks, and black walnut trees. Upon the white oaks hung in beautiful order long and green festoons of a species of the Spanish moss, but far more beautiful. Twenty-two miles this day.

Sept. 28. After another very damp night—that is, heavy dew—and a bitter breakfast, in consequence of the alum water, we left camp and traveled over a very hilly country until near noon, when we entered upon a small plain at a deserted ranch. Here horses and cattle were roaming over the plains, subject to any one who would kill or catch. At the upper end of this plain, in a beautiful grove of white oaks and near another alum spring, we halted and nooned it. After resting we moved forward and passed on to a large valley in which there were many cattle and horses, almost wild and without an owner. At the lower end of this valley we, after ascending a small mountain, found ourselves on the top of the highest and steepest mountain met with in California.[23] Our road led down this mountain in a spiral form, and for several minutes our mules could scarcely maintain their footing. With much care and attention we descended into the

[22]The San Fernando Valley.

[23]Conejo grade, leading down to the valley of the Santa Clara River.

opposite valley, one of beauty and many horses. Here we encamped near a rancho and had good grass and dry clover, fine
water and very good grapes. This day about twenty-four miles.
Found gray eagles numerous today.

Sept. 29. Left Eagle camp at 7:00 A.M. and traveled in
a northwest course over a beautiful plain for fifteen miles, with
the Pacific coast on our left, and 12:00 M. we arrived at Santa
Clara River, near the banks of which stream there is a ranch of
the same name. At this point the coast is only one league off
and can be distinctly heard at night (and when the wind does
not blow), and its roaring is music through the day. Here we
halted a short time, bought a piece of fresh beef and some bread.
We could not get flour at any price, and contented ourselves
with bread, one half pound at 12½¢. The timber on this stream
is (I think) black willow, not very large, but stands tolerably
thick. Water pure and clear and the road for several miles back
has been ankle-deep in sand. This ranch occupies a place in the
largest plain that we have yet met with, and produces wild oats,
clover and in places an abundance of mustard. After resting, we
again proceeded, and at the end of three miles came in full
view of the Pacific Ocean. The wind was low at the time, yet
the water seemed troubled, and was breaking in large white
bodies upon the beach, attended with a loud noise. Soon after,
we arrived at the mission of San Wan Buena Ventura, or St.
John's Good Venture, and encamped one mile above it, having
crossed four very good streams of water. At this camp we had
clover on the cliffs above us and the remains of a corn and potato
field, so our animals fared well. Here we also enjoyed a luxury
by way of a pot of potatoes, none of which we had seen since
leaving the Gulf of Mexico. These potatoes were of the white
kind, but proved to be very good, and when boiled and then
covered with gravy from the fryings of some fresh beef constituted one of the best meals in camp since leaving home.

The mission of San Wan is a goodly collection of buildings,
the main one of which is devoted to the school and church

purposes, and are all with pitched roof and covered with tile.

The inhabitants appear to be in easy circumstances and intelligent; nearly all of whom are, however, the descendants of Indians, educated at this school in days past by the Jesuits.[24]

Here the mountains began to close in upon the coast, and the valleys to disappear. In the gardens were trees of various kinds, among which I observed the palm and fig. The road today has been very good and we found water at convenient distances. The distance traveled this day is about twenty-four miles.

Sept. 30. Out at break of day and while breakfast was preparing we gathered in the mules, and at 7:00 A.M. were once more on the road, with the roaring ocean on our left. During our morning's ride, we came to places where there was barely room for our road between the towering cliffs on our right and the rolling waves on our left. At the end of fifteen miles we came to a stream of fresh water, and one mile beyond found good clover and nooned it. I picked several specimens of shells and we frequently found ribs and other bones of whales cast upon this coast. These were all very large, and occupied ground more elevated than that now reached by the waves or tide, and the bones look as if many suns had poured their rays upon them since they had been cast ashore. The porpoise we saw at almost every step, in large schools, and when lying still looked much like sticks of wood or other drift. But they were much inclined to play and kept up continual plunging. This afternoon we passed through several rancherias and crossed the dry channels of several mountain ravines, and after dark encamped, having traveled twenty-seven miles this day. During this afternoon we traveled through several small forests in which we found the red raspberry, wild gooseberry, and various other plants and shrubs incident to our northern climate. This change occurred suddenly, so much so as to create a feeling of surprise, and I thought that by some unseen agency we had suddenly been transported to our forests at home. The live oak, with its pendant

[24]Evans continually refers to the Franciscans as Jesuits.

moss, held its place among the trees and formed a beautiful and luxuriant shade. Wild clover covered the ground everywhere and made fine feed for our animals, and I never saw animals improve so fast both in flesh and strength. We travel twenty-five miles with much more ease on this feed, dry as it is, than we did eighteen on the best grass. Large flocks of seagulls, pelicans, etc., could be seen at any time.

This is Sunday, September 30, instead of yesterday being as I supposed the 30th. These errors will occur when traveling, as it were, without compass or rudder. But the reader will overlook this error and all other errors of this kind, and I am only surprised that we do not lose ourselves and, as the Yankee says, "our reckoning tew."

Here we lay in camp until 1:00 P.M. and then proceeded to the town of Santa Barbara.[25] This is a small semicircular seaport, not frequented by vessels much, but has more the apearance of an American village than any on our route. Here we found several neat cottages, and all the buildings were constructed with quarter-pitched roofs and those of tile. One half mile from the town is a large and ancient-looking building, one of the old missions, built by the Jesuits[26] and by them devoted to the education and religious reformation of the Indians in days past. Twelve American citizens from the States reside here, all in good and easy circumstances and surrounded by families. Their wives are of Spanish blood. Here we laid in more flour for the road, and here we left Dr. Bunnell, who stops for the double purpose of recruiting his purse and mules. Our mess now consists of five. After leaving this town we traveled three miles over a rolling country and near a small Indian rancheria encamped on good clover and water, having traveled six miles only.

[25]Another forty-niner remarked, "Santa Barbara is a pretty place on the seashore, and had it the advantage of a harbor, would doubtless become a place of importance. There is nothing but an open roadstead and vessels can only come in during mild weather. If caught here in a gale, they are sure to founder." The town housed many American businessmen. (Augustus M. Heslep, "The Santa Fe Trail," in *Southern Trails to California in 1849*, p. 384.)

[26]Santa Barbara was a Franciscan mission.

{ October, 1849 }

SANTA BARBARA TO MARIPOSA
DIGGINGS

Oct. 1. Left the Indian rancheria early and traveled until 4:00 P.M. on the tablelands bordering on the coast. During the afternoon we passed over the steep sides of many ravines which here cut the high lands frequently and make a hard and broken road. We passed several ranchos, in the mouths of the ravines, and encamped about a mile from the coast in a canyon and near a rancho. At this place we found pears, peaches, and apples, and have the promise of fresh bread and milk in the morning. We are now on our way across the mountains, which here bluff upon the sea and run out so as to make the distance by the wagon road fifty miles, when ten by the mule trail will accomplish the same distance; and we, being much inclined to curtail everything, take the nearest route if the same is steep and rugged. This mountain now lies before us, and promises, in appearance at least, one more hard pull for us boys tomorrow. Distance this day twenty-four miles.

Oct. 2. Left camp later than usual in consequence of some fresh beef, good California bread, and fresh milk for breakfast. The bread was baked for us by a lady at the ranch, and was very good indeed and made from flour imported from Chile, South America. For one league we had a good bridle- or mule-path and a fine stream of water passing down the canyon in which we were wending our way. After having attained this distance our path began to grow rocky and steep and two miles brought us to the top of this very steep mountain and two more landed us at the base on the other side. This mule path we found dangerous in places and found the remains of two mules which had been pushed by others over the steep sides of their dizzy path and dashed to pieces. We, however, ascended and descended without any danger or loss of property, and after a few miles more we came into the valley of Santa Ynes (pronounced "Sant Inez") and in full view of the mission bearing the same name. Here we found, upon inquiry, that we must retrace our path for a mile to good feed and water, where we encamped. We have therefore made at least fifty miles, though we traveled only ten. The timber on the north side of this mountain is much taller than any seen on our route. There are trees at our present encampment which measure in diameter from five to six feet and in length probably eighty feet. There are white oak, sycamore, and live oak; ebony, beech, and a species of black oak also grow here. The noble white oak in and about our present camp are hung with long moss, giving them a very venerable appearance, and the ground is covered with oats, ripe and ready for the sickle—which never comes.

Wolves, deer, etc., abound, and may be seen at almost any time by a practised hunter. Turkey buzzards and the raven are found in vast numbers at every ranch, and the corn and other grain fields are at all times under the charge of sentinels to keep these birds off. The California quail and the magpie are with us at every step. Who need perish by starvation in a land where all these blessings are so abundantly spread before him? There is no new country within the jurisdiction of our government that is blessed with so many resources as this, and it is only a matter of surprise that men of energy and enterprise have not long since availed themselves of the advantages here afforded.

Oct. 3. Started early, and traveled due west until 12:00 M., when we entered a small valley bearing off to the northwest. In this valley Mr. Kelley of our party killed a very fine black-tailed deer, which had discovered itself to us from the top of a very large and high hill on our right. This was a noble animal, but cost us much labor and exertion. We were still in full view of the Santa Rosa Ranch, which we left on our left on entering this valley.

After dressing and packing this meat, we turned into the canyon or pass before us, and shortly began the ascent of a small but very steep chalk mountain. We found this as hard as any mountain passed by us, on account of the loose soil in our path. But like all others we passed this and at sunset encamped at a water hole in the valley of Los Allamos, having traveled twenty-three miles.

Oct. 4. Soon after leaving camp this morning we passed Rancho Los Allamos and, keeping the wagon trail, found our road much improved. For a few hours we traveled over a country somewhat rolling and maintaining the same chalky appearance as of yesterday, the road in places being quite dusty and deep. About twelve miles from camp we entered upon a few of those sand hills so common on the desert, and thought that from the top of one of these, we could once more see the ocean. A few miles brought us to the border of a large plain heading towards the sea—west—and upon this there were acres perfectly bare, not even so much as a small bush growing upon it. These sand plains our road avoided, and after a tedious ride of eight hours we encamped upon a running stream of fine water, with the usual feed for our animals, having traveled about twenty-four miles. High wind on the plain.

Oct. 5. One and a half mile's travel this morning brought us to Ranch Nepomo, where we found an American selling goods. One of our party sold him a mule, and here we found a part of the wreck of the propeller, of New York, which boat went ashore five weeks ago on this coast. This propeller was in the government service, and happily there were no lives lost. This gentleman had brought in some of the irons of the boat and a portion of the main mast. He is now engaged in building a hewed log house, the first seen on our route since leaving Texas. After conversing with him a short time, we rode on and for a short time our road led over hills of deep sand, and then wound off among the hills to Aroyo Granda or Grand Ravine. This ravine we found a dense thicket of nearly all kinds of wood, weeds, and vines, in the middle of which ran a small stream of very cold water. After crossing this and meeting and passing seventy or eighty Sonorians returning from the mines, we found good clover and some grass and encamped, having traveled only thirteen miles this day. We are now only two miles from the deep blue sea, and shall be lulled to rest by its roar. More fresh venison at this camp, and deer abundant.

Oct. 6. After another night of heavy fog, a couple of boys belonging to our party went in search of more deer, and we did not leave camp until about 9:00 A.M. We found a hilly road, crossed by several fine but small streams of water, until we entered the valley of San Louis, after which the road was almost level. Five miles down this brought us to the Mission San Louis,[1] one of the same order of architecture already described. Here I met a Mr. Thomas B. Park, a Bostonian, from whom I obtained much information relative to the road, distances, water, etc. He has resided near this mission for thirteen years past, and told me that all these missions had been established by the Saint Franciscan College of Mexico under the patronage of the Crown of Spain, during the time that Spain governed this portion of the world. Mr. Park is very gentlemanly in his address and seems to be conversant with the history of this portion of the world as well as his own.

After making a few purchases of supplies, I bade him *adios*, and now, dear reader, if you have had the patience to follow our little band this far, I will once more introduce you to a canyon or pass in the coast range of mountains.[2] You know we have wandered together on the coast, and we have passed many mountains hand-in-hand, and we now go east of this range once more. This pass is, however, said to be an easy one, and the only hill of importance left for us to pass. Good news! Don't you think so? Traveled thirteen miles.

Oct. 7 (Sunday). Well, we have made another pass of the coast range of mountains, and are once more on the east side of this elevation. To gain this we had some work, and did we

[1]San Luis Obispo.   [2]Entrance to Gaviota Pass.

not puff some, Mr., Mrs., or Miss Reader, before we arrived at
the top of this mountain? There one of our party shot at another
fine deer, but missed it, and a little farther down the [hill] Mr.
Bruner shot one down, but the buck would not be satisfied with
his horizontal position, and jumped up again and toddled off.
After traveling over a rolling pine country and passing another
old mission,[3] we encamped, and at sunset Mr. Kelley brought
into camp another fine buck. This we dressed, and the meat is
now smoking on the rack. Traveled eighteen miles and found
but little grass.

Oct. 8.   Made an early move from camp this morning
and at 1:00 P.M. arrived at the deserted mission of San McGill.[4]
Here Laubenheimer, Parker, and myself left the packs, to wander
for a short time among the deserted buildings at this place. We
entered the church and found it a building worthy of the trouble
we took to reach it. The inside was neatly finished, with a gallery at the north end, and at the south end was the pulpit and
altar, and a statue as large as life, representing Christ at prayer,
was fastened over the stand. The fonts for holy water occupied
their places by the door, and the chair of confession was under
the gallery, and the incense urn was found by us in the middle
of the hall. To the left of the altar was a small door opening into
a room, the only tenant of which was a statue of Saint McGill
and the head of a wooden image. The statue of Christ was well
finished, being painted and gilded in fine style. This building was
covered with tile. Other buildings capable of accommodating
two or three hundred persons formed a square off to the right.
But notwithstanding all these preparations had been made to
live, there is now not a soul to be seen here but the passer-by on
his way to the mines. On emerging from these buildings we took
the mule path, and found that we had been separated from our
party, without bread or blankets with us. Impressed with the
belief that a few miles would bring us upon the same road, we

[3]Probably a building belonging to San Miguel Mission. The mission itself
was passed next day.   [4]San Miguel.

pushed on until night, and fortunately met a small party of Mexicans returning from the mines. By this party we were told that eighteen miles would take us to the road and we encamped with them and made our evening meal on a few roasted potatoes and lay cold all night. Twenty-nine miles this day.

Oct. 9. At daybreak we were once more in our saddles, and bidding our Spanish friends *adios* rode onward about seven miles and watered, having had none for some of our mules for twenty-four hours. Here we divided the last bread, being a cake of half a pound, and again pushed on, having to climb and go over a few very steep hills. During the afternoon we had a tolerably level road, and at sunset we found ourselves once more on the wagon road, but our packs far behind us; the road they had taken we found to be the farthest round, on inquiry. We had nothing to eat this day but the cake, until nightfall, when we were so fortunate as to meet another party of Spaniards, who invited us to their camp and gave us beef, which we roasted on the coals, and a small loaf of good bread. Traveled thirty miles this day. Game of every kind very abundant.

Oct. 10. The Mexicans camped with us during the night, left us this morning early; and after roasting a small piece of beef and one potato each, we saddled and took the back track about two miles to good grass and water, and here determined to wait the coming in of our company. About 9:00 A.M. we had the pleasure of seeing three packers coming down the road, and when they learned our destitute condition, [they] unpacked and invited us to cook and eat, which we gladly accepted, and once more had an excellent breakfast. These men were G. W. Arnett, T. M. Bridges, and William Coffee, and to them we are bound in gratitude for the generous manner in which they relieved our pressing wants and afforded us the comforts of life once more. They remained with us nearly all day, also waiting for companions who had taken the other road, but had brought their provisions with them. After breakfast I started out to kill a deer, and in attempting to get back from the bed of the river found

SAN JOAQUIN VALLEY

Reports of Explorations and Surveys . . . (Washington, 1856), V, plate III

myself almost a prisoner in a dense thicket of briars, weeds, willows, and young cottonwood. After laboring incessantly for one hour, sometimes on all fours, at others cutting the entangled weeds with my knife, I found myself out of the thicket and only about ten rods from the starting point. Here my hunt ended, having succeeded in nothing but starting an old bear from his lair. Game is very abundant, deer are seen on every hand, and yesterday we saw nineteen antelope in one herd. Crows, ravens, blackbirds, and quail are the most numerous kinds of the feathered tribe. The wild turkey has not been seen by us west of Texas, but bears are found numerous in the country passed during the last week, and the road is in places full of tracks resembling the trail left by a company of barefoot Negroes.

It is now nearly night, and I am looking for our companions with the packs. Being encamped off of the wagon road, it becomes necessary to have some one act as watch, and I am now on that duty on the hill near our camp, from which point I have a commanding view of both roads and the surrounding country. To our left is the coast range, very broken and but little timber growing on it. On our right is the river,[5] flanked with the high tablelands and of a dry and unproductive soil. This vicinity was once peopled, and the bones of many cattle are still bleaching on the plains, but Indian animosity has put an end to these things and the houses are without tenants. Several pack companies have just come in, and we have an invitation out to tea, which will be accepted as a matter of course. Dr. Riley and mess have invited us to take tea with them, and should our packs not get in this evening, we will still fare sumptuously.

The few trees growing on the sides of the ravines in these mountains are white and pin oak, bearing the one an acorn long and spindling, the other similarly shaped but larger in the body of the nut. The cups are small. This is food for the "varmints." Just as I wrote the word "varmints," Dr. R— called me to coffee, fried cakes, and tender beef, and, kind and indulgent reader, you

[5]The Salinas River in the vicinity of modern King City.

and I once more "lived." Our palates were once more tickled with the good things of this world. Well, it is an enjoyment that he who never goes hungry twice twenty-four hours never can realize or be a partaker of. Man never can know true, genuine happiness until he has been suddenly and unexpectedly relieved of starvation and thirst; and to do this he must become a "campaigner," and travel over the hot and destitute regions of the northern states in Mexico. After tea, I took my station and kept a lookout for the boys, but although many others came in, they were not of the number; and again we had to rely entirely upon our fire for warmth during the night. At 8:00 P.M. I returned to camp and about that time we had a slight sprinkle of rain. About bedtime the clouds broke away, and we spent the night with more comfort than was anticipated.

Oct. 11. Fine, cool morning and clear of fog. Breakfasted with Dr. R. The packers have all gone on, and there is now none but a wagon company and ourselves at this camp. We have been informed that our companions are near at hand and will in all probability reach here by 1 o'clock. We are therefore watching the road closely, and I am now occupying an eminence up the wagon road, and about one and a half miles southwest of our camp. Here I can see the approach of any person for miles on this road, and have also a view of the junction of the two roads on the banks of Rio Buenaventura, or River Good Venture. This wagon road winds down a canyon and enters a narrow and beautiful valley, and these terminate near our camp at the border of the *monte*, or plains, lying on and near the river. Upon these there is in a dry state grama grass in bunches, much esteemed by horses and mules. In the mouth of this pass, some person has in days past erected a *casa*, or house, and covered it with tile, but it now stands without a tenant. This small valley and canyon are better timbered than the sides of hills bordering the plains, but there is no water excepting the river within seven miles, and that a spring highly impregnated with sulphur—so much so that few persons can drink it. Night came on and our company did not arrive in camp, but we had a good supper prepared by a couple of packers who came into camp this evening.

Oct. 12. Breakfasted with our neighbors and saddled and took the road back, and at the end of a league met our packs. After mutual explanations and rejoicings, we turned our faces to the bleak plains before us and at night arrived at the ruins of Mission La Solidad.[6] Our road led through the middle of a vast plain bordering on the Buenaventura River and bounded on the west by the coast range of mountains; which plain is destitute of wood, water, and, with the exception of one place, of grass. Upon this there were many cattle. We camped this night without anything for our mules to eat, this place being on the river and as poor as poverty. Traveled thirty-one miles. La Solidad is a small place, part of which lies in ruins, and containing but few inhabitants.

Oct. 13. Left La Solidad early, after having spent a cold night with a light frost. Our poor mules stood shivering and hungry at the willows where we had them confined, and thinking to reach grass in a few hours, we crossed the river and pushed out upon a wide and beautiful plain. The first fifteen miles' travel was without grass; all that had grown upon it this summer had been eaten down close by the vast herds of cattle and antelope. These animals could be seen in every direction, but the most numerous herds were bordering on the mountains on our right. These herds, to procure water, must cross this plain to the river on our left,[7] many of them a distance of from eight to fifteen miles, and our road was crossed frequently by the deep and well-worn trails, all leading to water. Twenty-five miles must be traveled by us in order that we may reach water, and therefore we must "roll on." We had still reached no grass, and we

---

[6]Mission Nuestra Señora de la Soledad, about twenty-four miles southeast of the city of Salinas, was built in 1797, an adobe structure with a straw roof. Despite a period of early prosperity, the mission soon fell into ruins, and became a desolate landmark, fully living up to its name.

[7]Evans was following approximately the present route of the Southern Pacific Railway.

did not until 4:00 P.M., and, our mules having had nothing for the last thirty-six hours, we concluded to go to water without a halt. We therefore struck into a brisk walk, and at 5:30 P.M. arrived at the Ranch Natividad, which we found partly in ruins, particularly a large vineyard of healthy-looking grapevines. We here found clover and some dry grass, and our animals are again "rolling in clover." The water is also very good. Here is the first tanyard seen in the country, but the business is not conducted perseveringly, although one of the most lucrative branches of mechanical industry. Traveled this day twenty-five miles—and the last fifty-five without feeding, for want of grass.

Oct. 14 (Sunday). Left camp at 8:00 A.M. and marched over the mountain before us. This is a spur of the main range, lying on our right, and on arriving at the top one of the most sublime pictures was presented to our view that it has been my fortune to see. The valley of San Juan lay before us dotted over with the thousands of cattle upon it, and around us, above, and below us were the many large and small mountains, covered with clover, wild grass, and oats, and the rays of the sun fell upon them so as to gild and bronze in a most magnificent style. Never has it been my happy fortune to see anything so grand and magnificent as this! In this pass we were overtaken by four of the delegates. They last night signed the Constitution adopted by this Convention and closed their labors, and then the loud booming of thirty-one guns was heard at our camp (which was then distant thirty miles[8] from the city of Monterey).

There is much satisfaction throughout all the settlements passed by us, and much is expected from the next session of Congress relative to the mighty interests developed in the past few years in this territory. But to other matters again. At 3:00 P.M. we had accomplished the passage of the mountain, which we found steep on both sides, and entered upon the valley of San Juan, or San

[8]Nearer twenty. The constitutional convention met at Colton Hall, Monterey, called by Governor Bennett Riley, between September 1 and 9, 1849, and produced California's first constitution, which was amended by a second convention in 1879.

Wan El Baptisto,[9] and in a short time found ourselves in camp in an orchard of apple and pear trees, now neglected by the church, or mission, and open to the public. This has been a very valuable collection of fruit, and numbers about one thousand trees, all in bearing order, and from some of the pears we obtained all we could eat, and had several very excellent stews, and brought as many as we could carry away with us. Some of these pears were large and juicy, but the apples hard and small. At this place there are two stores, or retail groceries, and one hotel, and the old mission is still a place of public worship. Much attention is paid to the rearing and herding of cattle and horses, and the plains were covered with these animals as far as the eye could reach. Thirteen miles this day.

Oct. 15. Finding our mules much jaded and in want of feed, we packed and left the orchard camp and made our way towards the town of San Hosea[10] on the bay of San Francisco. Five miles up the valley brought us to good oats and water, and here we again encamped with the hope of improving our mules and resting them, there being now forty miles before us tolerably destitute of grass or other feed. Whilst our poor animals are enjoying their oats and resting, some of our company are ranging the hills around our camp in search of game, others are repairing saddles and washing clothes, and I have just finished my assistance of Mr. Parker in the preparation of a camp meal and baking bread. This has been attended with some labor in consequence of high and unsteady wind blowing the smoke in every possible direction. We are, however, rejoicing over our near approach to the mines, being now within two days of San Hosea and four days of our destination.

This affords us immeasurable pleasure, for after eight months spent in camp we are happy to know that daily travel and constant anxiety on account of grass and water for our animals will have an end, and that soon we will be where their services can in a great measure be dispensed with.

[9]San Juan Bautista.   [10]San José.

This camp is blessed with the kinds of timber already named, and to which catalogue may now for the first time be added the buckeye, which bears a more striking similarity to that in our own state, than any of the timber heretofore met with.

The white oak of California much resembles that in the north, but all other timber differs in some particular from the same in the north. There is timber used here in the erection and finishing of houses which resembles our red cedar, but is here called redwood, and I am not sufficiently acquainted with either, to determine their difference, if any exists. This wood is very lasting and works easy and smooth, having, when finished, a gloss equal to any other wood I ever saw, and it forms the bulk of lumber used for the purpose above named. The country improves as we go north, and the timber increases in size and quality; and I am happy to know that the Convention at Monterey has, in the Constitution adopted by that body, forever excluded involuntary servitude from its borders, being myself well satisfied that this beautiful and delightful country is in no wise adapted to slavery, and that institution would not only curse the owners of such slaves, but the country with them.

BOOK FOURTH

Oct. 16. Left our camp in the pass of the hills, and pushed out upon the plains. We met many persons returning from the mines. During our ride we were overtaken by Benjamin S. Lippincott, to whom I had been favored with letters, and from whom I have received valuable information. Lippincott was just returning from the Convention, where he had been as a member of that body; and several years' residence in this country qualified him to answer any question which might be asked touching the country and its resources. He informed me that the thirteenth day of November next was the time designated by the Constitution for the election of officers, and that there were many candidates already in the field, one of whom, Colonel Stewart, candidate for Governor, we had already had the pleasure of seeing. Before parting with Lippincott, a wagon drawn by four horses drew up to the tree under which they were dining, and among others who alighted from this vehicle was Captain Sutter,[11] a man with whom we had all been acquainted for, by, and through history for many years. We were all introduced to Captain Sutter, and enjoyed the meeting with this old pioneer very much. The Captain is a heavy-set man, with gray hair, fresh and unwrinkled face, and has spent sixteen years in this country. He told us that he expected his family in about eight months, and that they would have joined him long since if the country had not been so unsettled, but now that law and order had taken the place of disorder they would soon be joined together again in family bonds and unity, although separated for the past eighteen years. After conversing a short time with these gentlemen, we left them and turned to the left, to water and very poor grass. Here we encamped for the night, having traveled about twenty miles.

Oct. 17. Up and off early and drove over the beautiful valley of San Jose (pronounced Hose), and at 3:00 P.M. encamped one mile south of this Yankee town, on very poor feed, etc. After a few hasty preparations at the toilet Mr. Laubenheimer and myself strolled into town to see and be seen, and to acquire information, etc. We found a town regularly laid out, and several good buildings in a fair way towards completion.[12]

[11]John A. Sutter, builder of Sutter's Fort in Sacramento, on whose lands the first discovery of gold was made Jan. 24, 1848, by his mill employee, James Marshall.

[12]San José was one of the three pueblos established by the Spanish regime, and was founded in 1777. Bayard Taylor arrived near the end of 1849, two weeks after the town had been made state capital. The two-week period, he said, was "sufficient to have created a wonderful change. What with tents and houses of wood and canvas, in hot haste thrown up, the town seemed to have doubled in size. The dusty streets were thronged with people; goods, for lack of storage room, stood in large piles beside the doors; the sound of saw and hammer, and the rattling of laden carts, were incessant. The Legislative Building—a two-story adobe house built at the town's expense—was nearly finished."

207

There are many shops and stores, kept in tents or houses built of poles, with canvas roofs and sides—many of them entirely devoted to the sale of liquors [and] *cigarros*, and gambling. Vast fortunes are lost and made in this manner. All persons seemed to be rich, and watches and jewelry were sported by both American and Indian. Every article needed can be obtained at this place and at reasonable prices—with the exception of saleratus, which we found scarce, and for which we paid $1.50 per pound. Coffee and sugar, 18¢, bacon, 31¢, flour $20 per barrel and other things in proportion. We traveled this day seventeen miles, and tomorrow we expect to find grass.

Oct. 18. Left camp early, and drove into the town of San Jose. Here I mailed letters home, and after purchasing some supplies we left for the Mission of San Jose,[13] where we arrived at 3:00 P.M., having traveled over a very extensive and beautiful plain with the Bay of San Francisco lying on our left. After passing the Mission we turned to the right and entered a very narrow pass through the mountains before us, and at the end of two miles we encamped in the pass, on muddy water but good oats and some clover. I suffered much this day from colic and some pain in the temples, and was very glad to get into camp. We found a scarcity of wood in this camp, and some time was necessary for the preparation of tea. At the mission we found men from Michigan and Miami County, Ohio, who had gathered all they desired at the mines, and were now returning home, wealthy and healthy.

We drove our weary mules only sixteen miles this day, and

Hotels were springing up in all quarters; French *restaurateurs* hung out their signs on little one-story shanties; the shrewd Celestials had already planted themselves there, and summoned men to meals by the sound of their barbaric gongs. . . . The roads to Monterey, to Stockton, to San Francisco, and to the Embarcadero, were stirring with continual travel." Bayard Taylor, *Eldorado* (1850), I, 199-200.

[13]The Mission San José was founded by Father Lasuén in 1797. Although never a large establishment, it had at one time the largest number of neophytes of any mission. It was located thirteen miles north of the town on the east shore of the bay.

were happy to find such good feed at this camp, having had very poor grass for the past three nights. Our mules are very much jaded and worn down, but they must go through. I observed growing at this camp the snowdrop, full of very beautiful, almost transparent, balls or berries.

Oct. 19. Started early, and soon after leaving camp emerged from the pass upon a small plain, which we crossed and in a short time found ourselves in a second canyon of easy passage. Once through this, we crossed a larger plain, almost destitute of every kind of animal food, and no water, until we arrived at Robert Livermoor's ranch.[14] Here we found water and a little grass, and near the mountain, on poor grass, we again halted for the night. The immediate vicinity of this ranch is the most filthy of any passed by our party, and the young man who has charge of Livermoor's business does not injure his health by giving satisfactory answers to civil and polite questions. His name we did not learn, and I was disappointed in not finding Mr. L— at home. For fresh beef they charged us a shilling per pound, and asked 25¢ per pound for leaf tallow which had already tainted through the carelessness of the menials. Tomorrow morning we must pass another mountain, now before us. Once over that, we will find ourselves gradually approaching the San Joaquin River, which is yet distant thirty-five miles.[15] The country passed over today is not as rich and productive as that of yesterday, but, to persons fond of mountains, would be more attractive. Timber is scarce. Traveled this day eighteen miles. I have neglected to notice in this memorandum the California squirrel, a sprightly, active little animal much resembling the gray squirrel of the states, differing in two things only. This

[14]Robert Livermore came to the Santa Clara Valley in 1816 and in partnership with José Noriega bought the Rancho Las Positas. He developed fruit, grain, and vineyard culture in the area, and died in 1857. The present town of Livermore was not settled until 1869, long after Evans passed through, but as early as 1850 a settlement by the name of Laddsville centered the district.

[15]The town of Livermore is about twenty-five miles from the San Joaquin River.

little animal has a white ring around the neck, and knows no use for trees but burrows in large numbers in the ground. They have apparently many entrances or doors to the same house, and enter their houses in a winding way. Thousands of these are seen on every hand, and the hawk picks them up whenever he finds them too far from home, which is not often the case, for they are of a very timid nature, and seek their holes whenever [anyone] approaches. We have met a large number of persons today returning, some home and others to San Francisco in search of friends and provisions. From these we learn that our distance to the upper mines is yet an hundred and forty miles. This will place us on the Maraposa or Butterfly River, where the greatest profits are now made. It is yet uncertain whether we go to the Maraposa, but, reader, if our journey should prove interesting to you, we may yet wander there—but of that, more hereafter.

Oct. 20. Breakfasted soon after day dawned, and in an hour we were nearing the mountains, and at noon found ourselves on the borders of the Tulare Valley. The pass we found easy, and this valley very extensive and of rich soil. Soon after entering this beautiful valley, we saw the elk in large numbers on either hand and the wild goose and sandhill crane were almost constantly flying over us. Elk horns measuring, from head to tip, five feet were seen all along the road, and there is every indication of this valley being the best game region in California. At 2:00 P.M. we watered at a small lake; and at night encamped at another lake, or perhaps near a stream of water, though now without any perceptible current and much resembling a long, narrow lake. The next stream of any magnitude is the San Joaquin (or, as pronounced in Spanish, San Whakeen), which we cross after ten miles' more travel. Traveled this day, as near as we can estimate, twenty-three miles, over an excellent and level road. Grass and water good at this camp, and not a tree on our road and until at this camp; here there is plenty of oak and some willow.

Oct. 21 (Sunday). Up and off early, and after traveling

a few miles along the skirts of the timber found ourselves on the banks of the San Joaquin River. This is a narrow, but generally deep, stream of very clear water and fine sand bottom. The east side of this river was thickly grown with young willows. At this crossing we found a regular Yankee ferry, kept by a man by the name of Sparks, and who charges for his services in transferring persons from side to side, the moderate sum of $1.00 per head, man and beast. Thinking this rather too feeling, we took advantage of a ford a short distance above the ferry, and in five minutes were all safely over. Mr. S. has a victualling establishment, or traders' tent, and here for the first time we found hay in the stack, which will sell for about $100 per ton.

We had now passed the middle of the Tulare plain, and once more started for the next belt, or line, of timber, which we reached at the end of eight miles' travel. Here we found other traders' tents, and an end to grass—still five miles from Stockton. To give our mules the benefit of one more good feed of grass, we encamped, and on the morrow will go into town, lay in our flour and pork for the winter, and then move on to the mines; now only ninety-five miles to the Maraposa. There we think of establishing our winter quarters and engage in mining operations, provided we do not find it profitable to stop at either of the other mines through which we must first pass. We traveled this day only about fifteen miles, over a good road, and found good lake water frequently.

Oct. 22. This morning we moved into the town of Stockton.[16] This is a business place, few frame and but one adobe house; the others being all tents or frames covered with canvas or drilling. The town is located on a narrow inlet from the San

[16]Stockton was founded in 1847 by Captain Charles M. Weber, an acquaintance of Commodore Robert Stockton, commander of United States naval forces on the California coast during the Mexican war. By 1852 the population was 2,000, and the town was incorporated. It owed much of its prosperity to way-traffic from the southern mines. Bayard Taylor, there in 1849, said he found it "more bustling and prosperous than ever. . . . Launches were arriving and departing daily for and from San Francisco, and the number of mule-trains, wagons, etc., on their way to the various mines with freight and supplies kept

Joaquin River and in this water, just wide enough to admit a vessel, there were ships, schooners, and brigs floating, giving the place a commercial air. Here we found almost everything needed by the miner, excepting correct information in regard to roads— all being too busily engaged to answer Yankee questions. We immediately went to work and bought necessary provisions. For pork, we paid

by the pound		$ .21
Flour, per hundred	"	9.00
Sugar and coffee per	"	.15
Tea	" "	1.00
Salt	" "	.10
Boots	" pair	10.00
Shoes	" "	2- to 4.00
Marine shirts, *wool*		3.50
Potatoes per hundred pounds		35.00

For the above prices we got articles of the above names as good as any in the States. Besides the shipping, unlading of vessels, and the sale of goods, there was almost every branch of mechanism carried on. The barber and the lawyer domiciled together, and the sign and ornamental painter and retail grocer occupied the same tent. In order that we might take as much provisions to the mines as possible, we packed every mule and horse we owned, and at 4:00 P.M. started on foot for the southern mines,[17] driving our packs before us.

---

up a life of activity truly amazing. . . . A great disadvantage of the location is the sloughs by which it is surrounded; which, in the wet season, render the roads next to impossible. There seems, however, to be no other central point so well adapted for supplying the rich district between the Mokelumne and Tuolumne, and Stockton will evidently continue to grow with a sure and gradual growth." (Taylor, I, 98-99.)

[17] The "southern mines" were those lying south of the "ridge on the north side of the North Fork of the Mokelumne river" (Theodore H. Hittell, *History of California* [1898], III, 109), and they utilized Stockton as an entrepôt instead of Sacramento. In general, they included the diggings on the Mokelumne, Stanislaus, Tuolumne, Merced, and Mariposa rivers and their tributaries—the tributaries, in other words, of the San Joaquin River, whereas the northern mines found their placer deposits on tributaries of the Sacramento. Some of the famous camps which developed in this southern region were

At dark we encamped at a water hole in the plains, distant from our last camp, by the road, eight miles.

Oct. 23. We left camp at an early hour and crossed over the country about four miles to a middle road, which we reached during the forenoon. Once on this we moved on towards McIntyre's camp and well of water, where we encamped for the night, and had good well water and grass at a short distance. By the time I reached this traders' tent, my feet had become so sore that I fell in the rear of the train and was very happy to learn when I came up, that my companions intended to stay here during the night, for I could not have gone much farther. Here I shall probably make some arrangement to ride at least part of the time. Distance made this day only twelve miles—slow traveling, but sure in the end. This camp is still in the Tulare Valley, which is by far the largest passed by us in California, yet wholly unoccupied in an agricultural sense. The soil is rich, and produces in places grama, and generally wild grass.

Oct. 24. Started early, and continued a southeast direction through the valley, and at noon came to another traders' camp and well of water. Here we got all the water necessary for ourselves, but none for the animals. At sunset we crossed the Stanislaus River,[18] upon which millions of dollars in the precious

Drytown, Volcano, Mokelumne Hill, Angels Camp, and Sonora. The deposits, although rich at first, dwindled rapidly, and although rich strikes were made, these failed to maintain a steady production. The Mariposa diggings, where Evans and his companions worked, were in the extreme south of this southern district, and the camps mentioned by Evans were nearly all located in the famous "Mariposa Grant," a vast tract acquired by General John C. Frémont in 1847. During the 1850's Frémont unwisely attempted to evict the miners from his lands, and a squatter war resulted which eventually impoverished him and forced him to dispose of the grant.

[18]The chief camps on the Stanislaus River were Tuttletown, Jackass Gulch, Carson's, Angels Camp, Murphy's, Douglas Flat, Vallecito, and Columbia. The Morgan Mine near Carson's Creek was especially rich; "much of the gold was taken out by pounding the rock in mortars and not unfrequently there were so many bands or strings of gold running through the quartz that cold chisels had to be used to cut them apart. On one occasion one hundred and ten thousand dollars worth of gold was thrown down at a single blast." (Hittell, III, 120.)

stuff has already been gathered. But not content with the gold above us, and the grass, we filled our gourds and canteens with water, and pushed out from the river for grass, of which we found a little at night and encamped once more in a dry camp. At the crossing of this river there is a company of United States troops encamped, and all appear in good health. There is nothing in the shape of animal food growing on this river, and the officers' horses are subsisted on grass cut and brought from a distance, and barley. For the latter they asked us $2.oo per gallon. We are now fairly in the mineral regions—hence the scarcity of grass. Traveled this day twenty-one miles, and found it easier than yesterday, having a mule to ride a part of the day, through the kindness and obliging spirit of Mr. P. S. Kelley.

Oct. 25. Breakfasted early, and then went in search of our mules. We soon found all but my own, one of Mr. Bruner's, and Mr. E. S. Arnold's horse. From the rope trails we judged that they had all gone to the river during the night and had got separated, and a diligent search was immediately instituted and continued until dark without success. We searched the oak opening for miles around, and I came into camp worn down with fatigue and anxiety such as I never experienced on any occasion but parting with real friends.

This seemed the end of hope, and I had already cast about and selected a spot upon which to make a cache when my whole-souled companions told me to be of good cheer; for every pound of my pack and riding gear should be carried to the mines. This was a degree of comfort unlooked for by me, and the generous offer was thankfully accepted. Should we therefore not find the mules in the morning, we will push on as fast as circumstances will admit and hope that the evening of the third day will find us at the Maraposa mines in good health and renewed spirits. Reader, I hope your heart is lighter than mine; and now, good night.

Oct. 26. Breakfasted at dawn of day and while the boys were engaged at packing the mules I took one more look for my mules, but in vain. By the time I reached camp again all were ready to move, and in one hour we found ourselves beyond the low timber and again upon the plains. Soon after reaching these we turned from the main road and followed the tracks of three or four wagons leading us in a southeast course. The road for our afternoon's drive led among the round hills bordering upon the Towallamie River, which stream we crossed at 4:00 P.M. and encamped upon its beautiful wide bottom one mile above the ford. In trying to keep up with the mules, I did not succeed, but came into camp in half an hour after the boys, completely worn down and feet blistered. Locomotion became so painful that I could scarcely move at all; and when I came in sight of the camp I felt as if this day's labor had now nearly terminated. But we are on the Towallamie,[19] a beautiful river of pure and clear water with a rocky bottom. It is beautifully skirted with oak timber, has its source in the Serra Navada Mountains, flows a west course and discharges into the San Joaquin River. To-morrow we expect to reach the Mercea, and next day the waters of the Maraposa—the salmon trout and others of the finny race are caught in great numbers; and all are yielding gold in large quantities. Traveled this day twenty-two miles.

Oct. 27. Left camp at half past seven, and at the end of four miles turned to the right and left the Towallamie. At this turn of our road, we crossed the watering trail of the elk, and turning our eyes to the right we saw these animals quietly feeding on the hills. Judging from the tracks we crossed at this point, there must have been at least one hundred down to water during the morning.

Our road now wound among the hills all day. At noon we

[19]The Tuolumne diggings included Big Oak Flat, Chinese Camp, Jacksonville, Poverty Hill, Jamestown, Montezuma, Soulsbyville, and Sonora. Sonora was one of the largest towns in the southern diggings; gold was said to be so plentiful that "no attempt to accurately weigh or measure it was made: on the contrary a pinch, or so much as could be held between the thumb and finger, was considered and called a dollar, while a teaspoonful passed for an ounce, a wineglassful for a hundred dollars, and a tumblerful for a thousand dollars." Before the end of 1849 Sonora's population was 5,000. (Hittell, III, 125.)

found a water hole, and at 4:00 P.M. found ourselves on the waters of the Mercea,[20] a very rocky river, and within seven miles of the Mercea gold mines.

After crossing this stream we followed it up a short distance, and encamped, with the intention of instituting a thorough examination of these diggings; and, reader, I intend to keep you advised of our good or bad prospects. We traveled about twenty-three miles this day, and some of us came into camp almost worn out.

Oct. 28 (Sunday).   After breakfast I went up the rocky and noisy bed of the Mercea, whilst some of my companions strolled out on a visit to a camp above us. From this camp we soon learned that little was done in gathering gold on this river, and by 1 P.M. we were all in camp again, ready to move forward.

We traveled over some hard hills this afternoon, and at about sunset encamped in a small valley, with some grass and good water. I could not travel with my boots on, and to guard my feet against the sharp stones, I wrapped them in cloths and over this drew two pair of stockings. Thus equipped, I walked the nine miles of this afternoon with some ease compared with the constant rubbing endured from boots.

Oct. 29.   Left our camp early, and soon left the valley, after which we had high and low hills and mountains to pass during all the day. The whole of these hills were destitute of vegetation, and nothing but gold would ever have drawn men into this region. Towards night we entered the diggings of Aqua Frieo[21] and found the earth considerably torn up, and about three hundred men at work. We encamped near the cold spring, and thought this as wild a spot as it had yet been our fortune to

[20]The Merced diggings included Coulterville and Horseshoe Bend. Tributaries of the Merced River carved out the far-famed Yosemite Valley in the High Sierra.

[21]Agua Fría was also on the Mariposa grant. The Mariposa diggings, though rich and spectacular at first, proved to be shallow and quickly worked out. Mariposa, about eighty miles from Stockton, possessed an extremely rich quartz lode, and Hornitos, twelve miles west, contained rich placers and a fairly large population.

VIEW OF AGUA FRIA TOWN

From the original lithograph in the Huntington Library

stumble upon. The mountains rose high above us on every side, and in the bottoms of a few very narrow ravines men were searching in holes for the glittering metal. Of this they were getting but little, in consequence of a want of water to separate it from the dirt. After our mules were tied up for the night, we took a meal, set a guard, and all others retired, but were not able to sleep much in consequence of the constant noise kept up by gamblers and drunken men. In this way we passed an almost sleepless night, after having walked twenty-five miles this day.

Oct. 30. Breakfasted early and the mules were again saddled; and Messrs. Laubenheimer and Parker returned to Stockton for more pork and flour, etc. Soon after they left we— that is, Mr. Teats, Arnold Kelley, and myself—made an examination of the mines, and at night found ourselves the possessors of a few dollars of the ore each. Supper over, we found it clouding up, and considerable rain fell during the night. This is the first rain on us in California.

Oct. 31. Found our beds all wet this morning and a strong prospect of more rain, and did not go to mining until near noon. At night Mr. Arnold and myself had dug out half an ounce of gold. More rain this night, but we had spread our tent and slept dry, although under damp blankets.

❴ November, 1849 ❵

THE MARIPOSA DIGGINGS

Nov. 1. This day we had no rain, and but little sunshine. We worked all day in the mines, but met with nothing more than ordinary success; having panned out only $2.50 each. Towards evening the clouds broke away, and the night was clear and cold. I had the good fortune to learn that my mules had been placed under the care of Laub. and Parker by a Mr. Clark, who found them on the Stanislaus River some distance below our encampment. For his very generous services in taking up these animals and bringing me word, he charged $100 or my pack mule; and to these very moderate and modest propositions, I turned a deaf ear, but gave him an Indian pony for his trouble. This he did not much relish, and, making the best of it, he left our camp.

Nov. 2. Began work early, but with limited success, and at night found ourselves a few dollars richer only. The day was cloudy, and after nightfall the rain began to fall thick and fast, but we spent the night under our tent with a tolerable degree of comfort. I met with Mr. Haller, one of our old companions, in these mines and find that his fortune has grown at about the same ratio with our own. These mines, as well as all others, have been completely torn up, and if a man realizes a large amount of gold, it will be the result of accident. I also met with a gentleman from the city of New York, who informed me of the death of my friend William B. Gregory, of that place. Nothing could have come to my knowledge that so seriously affected my spirits, having parted with him in good health but a few days before leaving my home. But "death aims at a shining mark," and friend William was called to pass from a world of trouble to one of endless peace and happiness. A farewell to thee, for a few days only will separate us and then a peaceful union of parted friends and kindred will take place, and tears and parting shall be no more a matter of concern to the heart.

Nov. 3. This day opened with heavy rain, and continued so without intermission until late in the night. The ravines now have running water, and the business of gold picking has been profitable to some. J. Teats, of our mess, found a piece weighing just two dollars which had been washed out by the descending waters. Others found from 50¢ to $4.00. This is the result of picking alone. Several men were engaged nearly all the day in washing out dirt with the cradle[1] and some of them made as high as half an ounce. Night came on, and in wet clothes and damp blankets we passed it without much comfort.

Nov. 4 (*Domingo*). This is the first Sabbath for us in the mines, and I am happy to say that nearly all the miners have suspended labor, and there is order and decorum in camp. All my companions have gone to attend divine service at Fremont's Diggings, four miles east of this. 'Tis said that the chiefs of some

[1]The cradle was one of a number of devices used by placer miners to lessen their labor. The crudest method was pan washing, in which gold-bearing earths were agitated in a pan of water until the heavier gold sank to the bottom and the lighter detritus could be washed from the top. The cradle consisted usually of a long wooden box on rockers or a pivot, with riffles or cleats fastened to the bottom. By agitating the box, containing placer earth and water, the gold would collect around the cleats, and the waste could be poured off from the top. The long tom and sluice were merely extensions of the cradle which utilized a flow of water rather than rocking or agitation to separate the gold from the gravel. (See Owen C. Coy, *Gold Days* [1929], ch. vii.) One forty-niner described the cradle as follows: "it is very much like a baby cradle, which is the name they give it, only it is about eight feet long, on rockers, and open at the foot; at the head it has a sieve of wicker work, and is rounded at the bottom, and has three stout cleats nailed across. There were five men at work with it. One was shovelling up the earth close to the bank of the river, another was carrying it and throwing it into the top of the machine, while a third gave it a rocking motion, a fourth dashed water from the river over the earth, and the fifth attended the machine generally. The sieve caught the large pieces of rock gravel and gold, while the water, washing off the earth, left the greater part of the gold mixed with sand, is left in the bottom of the cradle. This is drawn off by auger holes into a pan, and dried in the sun, when the sand is separated by blowing it off." (Henry I. Simpson, "Three Weeks in the Gold Mines, or Adventures with the Gold Diggers of California," *The Magazine of History*, XLIV [1932; Extra Number, No. 176], 198.) See below, p. 233.

wild Indians are to be in at that camp, to enter into a treaty with the Americans. They seek to camp in some of these ravines during the winter months, and wish to first secure a peace with the palefaces now holding possession of their old winter quarters. These Indians have thus far been very troublesome to the miners, having stolen almost all the mules brought here.[2] I had the pleasure of meeting with a young sailor who was thrown upon this coast four years ago, by the wreck of an English brig bound from China to Oregon with a cargo of tea, etc. This young man with four others came ashore on one of the masts of the ill-fated brig and eventually made their way to San Francisco. Here he fell in with Captain Sutter, who gave him employment, during which time he and others discovered the existence of gold at Sutter's Mill. Upon this discovery, the young sailor went to Capt S— and told him he could work no longer, that he was going to work for himself. "Very well," said the Captain, "What are you going at, my lad?" "I am going, Sir, to dig gold, and with your leave will begin my work in your mill race." Captain S— gave him permission, and in a few months this young man found himself the owner of $17,000 and in one of the richest mines then known. He concluded that he was rich enough, stopped work, and fell into the hands of gamblers, who soon stripped him of every dollar he had. He again went to work, and in a short time had taken out nine pounds more; and to this he added until he was able to send home to his father $5,600. He gambles no more, and intends to go home in the spring and visit the roof from under which he absconded when a small boy; and his parents had never heard of their lost boy until they received his draft for the above

[2] These Indians of the Mariposa region were southern Miwoks, a tribe which inhabited the western slopes of the sierra and some valley land at its foot. Their culture, like that of most of the California Indians, was crude and simple. Houses were earth-covered affairs on the lower slopes in winter, bark lean-tos in the higher altitudes in summer. Clothing was almost non-existent, and the staple food was leached acorn-meal. It is possible, of course, that with the advent of the whites, other Indian tribes were pushed into the highlands and joined the Miwok in causing trouble. If others participated, they were probably Maidu, people who inhabited the slopes to the north. See Alfred L. Kroeber, *Handbook of the Indians of California* (1925), pp. 442-61.

amount of money. He is now the possessor of $1,500 in gold, a strong constitution, and robust health. If the history of the various men here met with were written out, it would perhaps be a book of the strangest and most startling character ever published. Two of the companions of this young man, who were saved on the mast, met with the same success in gathering gold; but the heinous vice of gambling led them on from crime to crime, and a few months ago both were hung at Stockton for murder.

Nov. 5. Rained the greater part of the day, and consequently there was little done in the way of gold hunting. People are flocking in from every quarter and the mines known as Fremont's Camp, distant four miles, bid fair to be depopulated, on account of the increase of water. At those mines they are compelled to dig from three to fifteen feet, and pumps become one of the chief instruments of the miner. Our work yielded an average of $3.00 to the man. Patience, that virtue we read of in the Bible, and hear taught from every desk, we are strongly called upon to practice under these adverse circumstances. Considering all things, however, we get along the path trodden by old Job tolerably well, strongly hoping that the large lumps of gold will soon appear in our holes. Quarrels and an occasional fight are the accompaniments of our nights, all originating at the gaming table. Monte,[3] a celebrated Mexican game at cards, has been here introduced, and large sums of money change hands whenever the "bank" is opened. I am thankful for my ignorance of Hoyle, and will make it the effort of my life to remain so.

Nov. 6. Cloudy, with some rain. Last night the Indians stole from this encampment eighteen mules and several horses, and strong efforts are now made to get up a force sufficiently

---

[3]Monte, or "Mexican Monte," was a banking game in which the players bet against the banker and his funds. The Mexicans who were most adept at gambling preferred it to all other games because they considered the player's chances to be more equal and the banker to have less opportunity for cheating. See Hubert Howe Bancroft, *California Inter Pocula* (1888), chap. xxiii.

strong to follow, kill, and plunder this thieving horde of savages. 'Tis said they number about 1,500 fighting men. Our little company gathered an average of $3.50 each this day.[4] Night set in with rain at intervals, and I was twice aroused from sleep by the quarrels of the monte players. About an hour before day the rain began to pour down, and so continued until day.

Nov. 7. Day dawned, and with it came one of the heaviest rains, which lasted without cessation until late bedtime. This caused all work to stop and we got no gold this day. Our boys are not yet in, and we begin to look with interest to their return. More gambling and drunkenness, and much noise and confusion in this part of the diggings.

Nov. 8. Cleared off and the rays of the sun once more visited the earth and cheered us poor diggers with their genial warmth. To work we went, and at night averaged about $2.50 each. In the afternoon I sent to Stockton a letter to my wife, containing specimens of the riches of these ravines. The clouds again covered the heavens, and we had a fair prospect of rain, but none came. The boys are not yet in from Stockton, and it is now too late to expect them this evening.

Nov. 9. Day clear and pleasant and our work paid a little better. Panning out gold is slow work. Mr. J. Teats is making a cradle or rocker, and when that machine gets to work we expect to realize more from our labor.

Nov. 10. Rained by light showers all day and part of the night. Consequently our labor did not more than pay expenses. People are crowding in every day, and an Irish trading tent has been established within ten feet of our own. Our nights are therefore much disturbed, and the last night was one of particular note. They began their infernal orgies early in the evening, and a constant howling and fighting was kept up during the long night. At one moment they were swearing eternal fidelity and friendship, and the next the whole hive was swarming,

[4]Takings varied widely in different parts of the diggings. Clarke, mining on the Tuolumne River, for instance, claimed that his companions made an average of one ounce ($12 to $16) per day (*Travels in Mexico*, pp. 135-36).

and they were fighting promiscuously. This disturbance will not continue an annoyance to us long, for we will move a short distance from such a hell.

Nov. 11 (Sunday). The day opened clear, and the Irish boys are up and drinking again. The Chilian Indians[5] also became very mellow during the day, and the sun set casting its last rays upon the gamblers still busy at their damnable work. Many were entirely helpless and some dead drunk. The guardian of morality finds few stepping stones in this part of the world.

Nov. 12. Breakfast over, I wandered over the ground occupied by traders and camps, and at the outskirts came to a camp of Chili Indians, one of whom had paid the debt of nature last evening. He was a small man, and as soon as death had taken place the attendants wound his blanket around' him, planted the cross at his head and six candles set to burning around him. His feet pointed to the south, with the heels against each other and the toes pointing in opposite directions. In this manner the corpse lay, and a silent watch was kept during the night. Two of the candles were still burning after sunrise this morning. In the afternoon the church (Catholic) ceremonies were gone through with, and the remains deposited in a grave near by. Jacob Teats dug from an arroyo $21 in lumps and gold dust,[6] and Mr. Kelley killed three deer, all of which meat sold at 37½¢ per pound. He therefore made about $60 this day. A force consisting of seventy men left camp in pursuit of a body of thieving Indians. The weather has been beautiful, and our packs have not yet reached here, probably in consequence of high water.

[5]The *Chilenos* formed an appreciable percentage of gold-rush society. News of the discovery was brought to the west coast of South America as early as September, 1848, by Colonel Mason's messenger taking the news to Washington by way of Cape Horn, and many Chileans and Peruvians flocked to California. They scattered through the mines and settled in colonies in San Francisco and the larger towns. Evans' reference to "Indians" probably refers to mestizos.

[6]Mason's report of Aug. 17, 1848, noted that gold dust was used as currency at the rate of $12 to $16 per ounce. This value fluctuated, of course, according to time and place. Coy, *Gold Days*, p. 333.

Nov. 13. Began raining last night and continued all the day. The first election for officers under the Constitution for California took place this day. We did not do much at digging.

Nov. 14. Morning clear, with a cold wind. The mountains in our immediate vicinity were covered with snow, and ice was formed in our ravine. The most violent wind came hurling in every direction, and, with the rain, made the past night exceedingly unpleasant. Jacob and myself took out $9.00 in gold and Mr. Kelley killed another deer. The provision train has not yet reached us, and we are beginning to be apprehensive of trouble to the boys.

Nov. 15. No rain this day, although it was cloudy towards evening and threatened more *agua*. I arose from my bed this morning with an aching head, and only worked until noon, having realized just $5.00 from my morning's work. Jacob Teats worked nearly all day and at night had $13 in gold dust. The boys are not yet in.

Nov. 16. Went to work early, and at noon came in with $2.00. Jacob, blessed with good luck, brought $28.25 in from his morning's work. Mr. W. A. Haller found a piece near Mr. Teat's work which will weigh at least one ounce; and at the same time others were delving with all their strength and ingenuity, and realized almost nothing. But luck will strike us yet, and we are only called upon to exercise patience and our strength.

Nov. 17. I went to work early and labored hard all day, and about sunset came into camp with $13 in gold. This I washed out of a sticky, brick-colored clay. When I came in I had the pleasure of seeing Laubenheimer and Parker, who had just returned from Stockton with provisions. They brought with them my two lost mules, and I had the satisfaction of knowing that I still owned two mules, although at a cost of $36 charges. Letters I received none, and still know nothing of the home cares.

Nov. 18 (Sunday). This morning Mr. Bruner and myself started back to Burn's Ranch with the mules, and after toiling all day over the boggy road reached that place in the evening. Here we left a part of our animals, and bought pork at $110 per barrel and flour at $62.50 per hundred, and packed back six mules loaded with this addition to our table comforts. Had some sea bread, bear's meat, and coffee for supper.

Nov. 19.　Left camp at 10:00 A.M. and drove on our mules through [a] very bad road and almost constant rain until we got over the worst mountains. It then cleared up and the afternoon proved more comfortable, and just in the dusk of evening we once more entered camp, after having plunged for twelve miles through mud and mire. One heavy rain will in these mountains make mud and mire enough to swallow up any mule.

This peculiarity of soil exists throughout the territory, and is one great objection to California. Whether a man is overtaken on the plains or mountain top by the rainy season, the result is the same, for he will be exceedingly fortunate if he is not bogged at least at every low place or break in his path. Little gold taken today.

Nov. 20.　Breakfasted, and Mr. Parker and myself went to chopping and getting in logs for our palace in the Maraposa mines. Night found us just finishing off the foundation, which measures ten by thirteen feet, with a parlor at one end—formed by pitching our tent at that place. The entrance is a door two and a half feet wide; stone chimney, and a fire place measuring four feet by three. When this is once finished, reader, you may enter and again look at our internal arrangements for comfort and convenience.

Nov. 21.　Work same as yesterday. Teats and Laubenheimer found a little gold this afternoon.

Nov. 22.　Carried logs in the morning, and then Parker and myself went to work, one on the house and the other on our chimney. Laub and Teats got about $8.00 this day by digging.

Nov. 23.　We this morning carried more logs, and soon had the satisfaction of seeing our house gradually nearing completion. In the afternoon Laub and Teats gathered about an ounce of gold. The Indian hunters and gold prospectors came into camp this evening without having effected anything but a treaty with a small party of Indians. They represent these Indians as a tribe of well-formed, athletic men, and withal intelligent, disposed to be friendly and on good footing with whites.

Nov. 24.   Worked at stone work—that is, built part of a chimney—this afternoon. Laubenheimer worked on the roof, consisting of a tent fly, Parker upon the woodwork of our palace, and Jacob worked in the mines and brought in one ounce of gold this evening.

Nov. 25 (Sunday).   This has been a day of various events. Near our new house a party were selling every variety of articles at public auction. Others were digging gold, and others hunting, whilst some worked on their log cabins.[7]

Nov. 26.   This day worked on our house, with Jacob in the mines. In the evening he came in with $32.50 in gold.

Nov. 27.   Worked same as yesterday. Amount of gold gathered this day $18. Rain nearly all night.

Nov. 28.   Finished chimney. Jacob's work amounted to between $5.00 and $6.00, having only worked a part of the day. This night I spent in the new house alone.

Nov. 29.   All our things having been moved yesterday, we finished "daubing" our house, and set up the tent to be used as a parlor addition to the main building. In the afternoon I began and by sunset had a bedstead ready to lie on.

Nov. 30.   I passed the last night on a bedstead, the first I have slept on since leaving the gulf of Mexico, and, though hastily made and rudely constructed, it proved a luxury. Mr. Laubenheimer also finished his, and enjoyed the exalted pleasure of reposing off of the damp ground. Every man must be his own mechanic, and he who fails in this had better be in some other

[7]The literature of the gold rush is vast, and many items give excellent descriptions of living conditions in the mines. See, for example, Bancroft, *California Inter Pocula*, J. D. Borthwick, *The Gold Hunters* (1922), E. Gould Buffum, *Six Months in the Gold Mines* (1850), Alonzo Delano, *Life on the Plains and Among the Diggings* (1854), Francis S. Marryat, *Mountains and Molehills* (1855), Taylor, *Eldorado*, Hittell, *History of California*, and Coy, *Gold Days*.

part of the world. All things necessary for the construction of such articles as bedsteads, stools, tables, doors, etc., have to be taken from the stump—excepting rawhide, which is taken from the market tent (or the animals suffered to starve, in this region of no grass). This day we concluded to use as a day of rest; consequently, we employed ourselves as we chose and got no gold.

{ December, 1849 }

THE MARIPOSA DIGGINGS
(CONTINUED)

Dec. 1.   A heavy frost visited us last night and the night before, and the oak trees are shedding their leaves fast. After breakfast Laub, Teats, and myself went "prospecting"—that is, we looked for other and better diggings, but found the ground nearly all occupied, and we returned at night with but little more in our pockets than we had started out with. But 'tis said that a bad beginning makes a good ending, and this month may yet be productive of much good to us. The population of these mines has increased more in the past week. There are now at least a thousand men in, dependent upon the proceeds of their labor. One man found a piece of gold valued [at] $1400 this week.

Dec. 2 (Sunday).   I this day wrote to Colonel Green of the *Defiance Democrat*, but know not when an opportunity will occur to send it to either of the offices. I was very fortunate today in procuring a pint of vinegar, for which I paid $1.50. Day cloudy and damp, and a cold on my lungs and in my head, no better. Three auction sales this day.

Dec. 3.   After breakfast Laubenheimer, Teats, and myself went into the mines, leaving Parker at work on a cradle which had not yet been finished for service. In the evening our day's work weighed out $29.37, Teats having found a piece weighing $20.50. Day cold and very unpleasant, and at dark began to rain, which soon turned to snow.

Dec. 4.   On getting from bed this morning we found the ground covered with snow and the weather quite cold. Breakfasted, and then turned our attention to making doors and such other arrangements as would add to our comfort, and at night found our hole of entrance filled with a comfortable door, constructed of wood frames and rawhide panel.

Dec. 5. Worked in the mines and brought in about $18. The day has been cold and cheerless. Dr. Bunnell called on us.[1]

Dec. 6. Mined this day. I dug out a piece worth $3.87— the largest yet found by me.

Dec. 7. Heavy frost last night, and when the sun had attained considerable height this morning I went to work and until noon made nothing. In the afternoon I picked and washed out $5.00 in gold. Jacob had $5.25, Laubenheimer $9.00, and Parker 25¢. The weather was mild and pleasant, and the days during clear weather are rather warm, but the nights cold.

Dec. 8. After the frost of the night began to yield to the rays of the sun, I took my pan and knife and went to work. I washed some dirt thrown out by the Mexicans, and at sunset found myself the owner of $16 in gold, or, in the parlance of the mines, I had made an ounce this day.

Laubenheimer had made about half an ounce; Parker and Teats made but little. For this ounce of gold I washed probably twenty-four pans of dirt which had been looked upon as valueless by all who saw it and by those who had so carelessly thrown it there. This, added to my labor of yesterday, makes $21 out of a very small heap of castaway earth, and proves how easily men are or can be deceived. Towards evening it clouded up and became windy.

Dec. 9 (Sunday). Very mild morning, with a little sunshine; about noon the sky became clouded over and rain threatened, but none fell during the day. We had a visit from Parson Hill, one of our fellow travelers. He just came in from the

[1]Lafayette H. Bunnell later played an important part in the mining history of the Mariposa region, and was credited with the opening of the Sherlock's Gulch diggings. He accompanied Major Savage's expedition of 1851 which explored the Yosemite Valley, and is said to have been the first to suggest that the name of the Indian tribe which inhabited the valley be perpetuated. The original spelling was Yosemity, later modification replacing the *y* with an *e*. See Newell D. Chamberlain, *The Call of Gold: True Tales on the Gold Road to Yosemite* (1936), pp. 28-32, 46-49; also Lafayette H. Bunnell, *Discovery of the Yosemite . . .* (1911), and Howard A. Kelly, "Lafayette Houghton Bunnell, M.D., Discoverer of the Yosemite," *Annals of Medical History*, III, 179-93 (1921).

Towallamy diggings, and reports rich prospects for the coming summer. Spent the day in writing letters to my family and brother.

Dec. 10. Worked at mining as usual and ended the day's work by having found $6.25 in gold. Weather clear and pleasant.

Dec. 11. Worked at mining, but not with the same success, having only made $3.25. Weather cold and blustering, cloudy, with stormy appearance.

Dec. 12. Cloudy and stormy. I went to work, but had to quit in an hour on account of the rain and sleet, which began to come down fast. I therefore only made $1.00 out of my morning's work, and believe if the rain had held off during the day, I would have made an ounce of gold. I am now at home, comfortably seated by my fire, and must again travel back and bring up the rear, or, in other words, sum up the distance traveled by our little company since leaving home. This has already been done in part, and the task is not therefore a hard one. It will be remembered by the reader that we left home in sleighs and by this mode of conveyance came to Finlay, a distance of fifty miles, and next morning by wagons to Carey on the railroad, and from thence by said road to Cincinnati, Ohio. Making, from Defiance to Cincinnati, 225.

From Defiance to Cincinnati	225	miles
" Cincinnati to mouth Ohio River	700	"
" mouth Ohio River to New Orleans	1000	"
" New Orleans to Port Lavacca	375	"
" Port Lavaca to Chihuahua, Mexico	1015	"
" Chihuahua to Los Angelos, California	1066	"

Making the distance from our home, or

From Defiance, Ohio, to Pueblo Los Angelos, Cal.	4381	miles
" Pueblo Los Angelos to Pacific Coast	82	"
" first view of coast to La Solidad	249	"
" La Solidad to San Jose	80	"
" San Jose to Stockton	77	"
" Stockton to Maraposa Mines	100	"

Making the distance of

4,969   "

From Port Lavacca, Texas, to these mines we traveled overland, meeting with a diversity of climate, landscape, scenery, etc. After having fairly entered the Mexican territory until we emerged again from its borders, we were never out of sight of some mountains or highlands. The northern states of Mexico traversed by us have little land susceptible of cultivation, compared with any state in our own union. The traveler passes through small valleys and over high ridges and mountains, and those valleys only are cultivated, and many of them support a large population upon much less than is frequently and generally raised by a farmer in the United States upon one hundred acres of land.

Leaving this land which seems to exist and have a place among the nations of the earth without God's blessing, we entered into California, a country more prosperous and better adapted to the agricultural improvements of the age. This country is not so thickly sprinkled with mountains, although there are many, and some of these towering to the skies and covered with snow at all times whilst at the same time the valleys below are green with wild grass and in places blooming as a garden. Among the pleasant and rich spots of this country may be reckoned the valleys of Aqua Callientas, William's Ranch, or Rancho Del Chino, the country bordering upon Puebla Los Angelos, and the numerous valleys found bordering on the Pacific Coast. Some of these receive considerable agricultural attention and in almost all of them we found the California grape, a delicious fruit, and here also the wild clover, oats, mustard, etc., seemed to grow without the attention of man. This clover and oats is found in great abundance in some of those valleys and even on the tops and sides of the highest mountains, and afford rich food for the thousands of cattle, horses, antelope, and deer seen on every hand. Leaving the coast, the traveler is, at the end of a day's ride, thrown again among the mountains and hills, but nearly all of which are of easy passage, although presenting a bold front. The valleys gradually become smaller and the mountains higher as you advance into the country, and as you approach the mineral region of this oriferous land, the grasses or animal food is diminishing, and finally, when you are at the mines, there is nothing for a horse and mule to live upon. Here you find yourself hemmed in by mountains, some large and high, others small, but all of conical form. Those in the immediate vicinity of the mines are covered with a dense growth of some wild brush called temescal. This grows about four feet high, and men and animals avoid passing through if there is any passage around it. At the foot of all these mountains are ravines or gulches, from some of which gold is taken in greater or smaller quantities.

These mineral mountains are also in places covered with quartz, and [in] the ravines from which the most gold has been taken, or in which the ore abounds, this stone is found in great quantities. It is in fact the "gold blossom," and is the guide to the miner.

Dec. 13. The rain of yesterday continued at slight intervals during the night, and it has rained hard this day. Knowing that it would wash the ravines, and believing that gold might be picked up, I went out and in an hour found a piece worth $1.88 and several smaller particles. This will just pay expenses for this rainy day.

Dec. 14 The rain held up this morning about daybreak, and after breakfast I went to mining and continued at this until the rain drove me in. I only realized $4.63 this day. The rain continued at intervals all day, and at sundown the air became colder and a very violent hail storm set in, but soon changed to snow. The rainy winter of California is now upon us, and it sets in rather strongly and makes no very pleasant impression.

Dec. 15. I judged it necessary to take mercury, to arouse the action of my affected liver, and do therefore not work today. The storm of last night abated, and this morning the sky was unclouded and the ground considerably frozen. I have in a hurried manner described the land of California and named some of its productions and given a short history of this branch of the

SACRAMENTO IN 1849

From a reproduction in the C. C. Pierce collection

"Maraposa" or Butterfly diggings, and it only remains for me to name the instruments used by the miner in his work of separating the gold from the dirt. To make work convenient, the gold hunter must provide himself with a good, but light, pick, a round, pointed shovel, a light crowbar, a pan or a light cradle, a short, strong knife, and a horn spoon, and, when thus equipped, he is ready for the work. The cradle needs a description in these pages, for it is not the machine used by mothers to lull their children to rest, although bearing a striking resemblance. This is a machine from three to five feet in length, and from five to eight inches deep, the bottom of it crossed by cleats, called bars. On the head of this cradle or rocker, and sloping backwards, is a box, generally four inches deep, on the bottom of which is nailed a piece of sheet iron, zinc, or copper, punctured full of holes. This is the sieve. Under this sieve is a board or slide, also inclining backwards, which receives the dirt, gold, and water from the sieve and throws it into the bottom of the cradle, and when the gold reaches the bars it lodges and is saved to the laborer. To be worked with speed, one man should rock and another dip on water, yet one can do both. The horn spoon is part of the horn of an ox, opened, the pith taken out, and considerably pointed at one end. This is then spread out according to fancy and looks something like a large oyster shell in shape. This instrument and the knife are found very convenient in searching the pockets and getting out the dirt and gold. Besides these things, the miner must have a good store of pork and beans on hand, and then he can expect to lay up money if he is industrious and saves his earnings.

By the use of the rocker, pick, and knife, Messrs. Parker and Teats made this day the sum of $41—having found a few rich pockets or holes in the slate.

Dec. 16 (Sunday). The day was clear until near night, when it promised more snow. This day was again devoted to the transfer of property from the hands of the auctioneer to those of the purchaser. Many persons are selling out and leaving for the settlements, with the hope of doing better but, as I think, to fare worse. San Francisco, Stockton, Sacrimento City and all other points must be densely populated and overrun with men of all professions. Labor, or its value, must become reduced under such circumstances, and many will reach those points but to be sadly disappointed and find too late that they had better remained here where a day's labor would pay from three to twenty dollars.

Dec. 17. Did not work until late in the afternoon, and made but little gold. Some rain in the morning, and it again opened upon us at sunset.

Dec. 18. Heavy rain during the whole of the night; at about the dawn of day it cleared up, and we have had a very pleasant working day. I made this day only $5 washing out dirt. The quality of the gold taken by us is good, but the most is in very fine particles called "dust."

Dec. 19. Attended an auction and purchased some vinegar, tobacco, etc. The day was cloudy and at 8:00 P.M. some rain mixed with snow fell. I did not dig gold but collected in some money which I had out on interest and sold one of my mules to Parson R. H. Hill, who intends opening a trading tent in these "diggin's."

Dec. 20. Rained all night, and has not abated for twenty minutes this day. The water has soaked through and now runs in a constant stream across our ground flour. This has been attended to, and we have the prospect of being relieved of this most unwelcome visitor. No mining this day, for should it clear up now the streams would still be foaming with the descending waters from the mountain sides.

Dec. 21. Breakfast over, we all set out to hunt gold (the rain having abated), and at 10 A.M. came in wet to the skin, rain having again set in. My pickings amounted to $1.25 only. Various sums were found during the day, ranging from one to four dollars. Mr. Kelley found a beautiful specimen weighing $3.25, perfectly solid, smooth, and beautifully bright. Mr. Parker picked up pieces worth about $1.00. The rain continued all day, with short intervals, and during each suspension of the storm all the miners were out in search of such pieces as had, during this long rain, become exposed to view. In this way probably $800 or $1000 have been added to the gathered ore now in the pockets of the miners.

Dec. 22. The rain ceased during the night, and the morning opened clear and beautiful. After a late breakfast we went to work and at night found ourselves in possession of more of the ore. I made about $5.00 and lucky Jake $16.50, he having the advantage of a rich hole and a rocker to work with. This day remained almost unclouded and warm as an April day. Towards evening the clouds encircled the tops and peaks of the surrounding mountains and a beautiful picture was presented. Standing on the top of a high hill, I could look down and see the clouds in the form of a beautiful wreath, almost entirely concealing the valley below me—magnificent, lovely picture, drawn by an artist never excelled.

Dec. 23 (Sunday). Three auction sales on this beautiful and pleasant day of rest. In my strolls through camp, I saw men engaged in all kinds of work, and there were also those to be seen who had not forgotten their Bible or the manner in which this day is passed at home.

Dec. 24. Beautiful, clear, and warm day. We went to work after breakfast, and at night returned with the following sums of money: Jake had $2, Parker, $10, Laub, $15—and I had $9.25, being a little better than for the several past days. There is something new in the way of excitement up the creek about one mile. An almost constant firing has been kept up since dusk or for the past half hour, and I must go and learn the cause of it. The camp may have been attacked, as Indians have been seen close in this day. Ah! the mystery solves itself, for tomorrow is Christmas, and this accounts for the firing and general rejoicing. We rejoice because we have pleasant weather and a supply of something to eat, and that the coming day is the anniversary of our Saviour's birth and the opening of the promise made to the prophets of old.

Dec. 25. Beautiful weather. Washed out $6.oo, and wrote another letter home.

Dec. 26. Prospected nearly all day and found but *tres pesos*. Weather warm and pleasant, cloudy towards evening, and a slight sprinkle of rain in the night.

Dec. 27. Continued my "prospecting," or hunting a new and better place to work, but without much success. In the performance of this work, I followed up several gulches or ravines and found them poor in gold but full of granite rocks, and in places forming no inconsiderable cascades, and might yield good pay to him who would go into them and remove many of those rocks and boulders and work in the water.

I had been suffering for the past day and night with bilious colic and did not wish to expose myself further and returned to camp. Here the pain of my distemper increased, and I had to resort to such remedies as I had with me for its alleviation.

Dec. 28. Suffered at times during the night intense pain but was relieved this morning by the quick action of medicine and now feel much better, but weak and sore. I shall not be fit for labor this week, and shall have nothing to do, unless I stroll over the diggings in the company of the reader of these pages; and whilst we are thus engaged, we will take note of the appearance and doings of those placed in authority over us, and first inquire how they became rulers of this isolated community. R. H. Driggs, the present incumbent of the alcalde's chair, is the first man we meet on setting out on our journey through camp; and while you are viewing the diminutive creature in buckskin breeches, I will relate the manner of his elevation to office. This took place shortly after our reaching these mines, and at the *card table*, as I have been well informed. On that night the assembled sportsmen, without the usual public notice, proclaimed Driggs alcalde of Aqua Frieo, and the gamblers had the power in their own hands, and this professor of Hoyle was the lawgiver and the judge of the rights of all who came into these mines. And now, reader, you have seen the man and others have not, so it becomes necessary to give a description of the man. In stature he measures about five feet, dark hair and black eyes (bloodshot, and seemingly trying to escape from the sockets). His dress consists of buckskin coat and pants, shoes (or boots, for he has a pair of each), a small cap, from under which a cotton handkerchief is always disclosing its presence. His hair is never combed and the beard is suffered to grow on unmolested, and he is the owner of a slave. You can now know him whenever you meet Alcalde Driggs. In his habits he is slovenly, and he generally gambles and drinks all night and sleeps away the day. The labor of his slave supports him at times only, for he is generally *broke*, losing all the Negro can make and he win.

The Americans scarcely ever brought suit before His Honor, and those he did adjudicate were between Mexicans, and his fees were an ounce for every decision rendered, and half an ounce for the sheriff or marshall.

This officer (the sheriff) is the next individual we have to deal with, and his name I have never heard. He is a young man of very important feelings, and can be seen strutting about in high boots, brown pants, yellow or clay-colored overcoat, and black, slouched, broad-rimmed wool hat, and white hair [and] light whiskers of nearly the same. He also lives upon chance, or, in other words, upon his winnings at the gaming table. His honors were conferred and he received his diploma from the same professors, and at the same gambling table at which Alcalde Driggs arose to distinction. Another means of knowing him is this: he is always talking, and laughs immoderately at everything he is foolish enough to utter, and reminds one of a guinea hen in the noise he is constantly making. We have now seen the important men of these mines, and it is only necessary to say that the people have taken this matter into their own hands, and that a notice is now stuck up requiring the people to assemble on next Sabbath at the forks of the stream and then and there elect an alcalde and sheriff for this branch of the Maraposa Mines.[2] There are also three more auction sales advertised for the same day.

We will now wander up the main stream, and the first place we arrive at is Hawkin's store; a few hundred yards above this is a Mexican trading post, and still further up is Rusia's store, and one mile beyond we come to Captain Ozier's trading house. All these stores are making money hand over hand, and are kept in tents, and each [is] supplied with a gaming table, excepting the first. Between those points, the hills and banks of the river are dotted over with tents and huts of every description, occupied by the miners, who have in many places wholly changed the channel of the stream, which is now being dug up and every stone turned over. In this way some are making money, whilst others, less fortunate, barely make expenses. We might now go up the other branches of this stream, and find nothing new to record, and it only remains to say that the miners are camped in every direction for five miles from the common center and that their system of operations is about the same and their success equal. So far I have not yet heard of any man who has by a lucky stroke suddenly enriched himself this winter.

Dec. 29. In company of Mr. Parker, I went to work on an arroyo, or ravine, this morning, and in a few hours we changed the channel of the water and prepared it for digging on Monday next. What progress we shall make, or the amount of gold we are to get for this labor, remains for the future to reveal, but our prospects can be said to be as flattering as were those who have gone and done likewise and have been well rewarded. Got but a few specks of gold, and suspended all labor after the water went galloping down the new canal.

Dec. 30 (Sunday). This day has been beautifully clear and calm, and several sales and the election have passed into the

[2]The crude but effective application of democratic procedures to mining-town government amazed foreign visitors and was a matter of pride to most Americans. For a full discussion of miners' governments, etc., see Hittell, *History of California*, III, chaps. x, xi, xii, xiii.

things that were. William L. Scott, an elderly gentleman and a man of much experience of the pioneer kind, was elected alcalde, or chief magistrate, and M. F. Barbour, of Fort Wayne, Indiana, sheriff of these diggings. Mr. Scott had a majority of thirty-eight votes over Dr. E. Stone, and Barbour beat the old sheriff, or guinea fowl, just ten votes. This result is very satisfactory to the people, and everything passed off quietly and without a word of contention, showing that the men engaged in business here are lovers of peace and are willing to submit any difference of opinion or right to the arbitrament of their own chosen servants.

Dec. 31. Worked in the newly-opened mines, but was compelled to desist on account of an increase of pain in the chest and stomach. I, however, had the fortune of digging up some very handsome pieces of gold, and, should it hold out, we may yet be recompensed for our labor in turning the creek.

This is the last day of the year 1849. Tomorrow ushers in a new year, and with it another and a different date; and who can tell the events with which it is pregnant. Men are firing guns and loudly rejoicing over the closing hours of the old year, and welcoming the approach of the new. This question, and one of importance to every man, should be well considered before we give a loose rein to our pretended or real feelings: "Have we done all the good we were capable of rendering our fellow beings in the past twelve months?" If this can be answered affirmatively, then we have discharged an obligation of binding force and there exists no reason why we should not rejoice upon the birth of another period of time. Time is given for the discharge of every duty. In this, the Creator has left man almost unlimited; but if we neglect to use the time given to or set apart for the discharge of those duties, we are but spendthrifts and squanderers of an important part of our patrimony, and when thus lost it never can be regained. Time is money, and we are bound to economize it, and being so bound are accountable for its use.

〖 January, 1850 〗

THE MARIPOSA DIGGINGS
(CONTINUED)

Jan. 1. Cold, rainy, and dismal day—cheerless without and uncomfortable within. The rain commenced falling at 9:00 A.M., since which time it has almost incessantly been pattering upon the roof of our humble dwelling. A New Orleans Frenchman died last night, and will be interred today—disease, affection of the lungs, ending in bronchitis.

In consequence of the continued rain, I have had time to devote to reading, and have enjoyed the inestimable privilege of perusing the biography of those eminent statesman and distinguished patriots who signed their names to the immortal Declaration of Independence; and in all my past life, and with my years of reading, I have never enjoyed a treat like this, although I had perused this same book before. For this I am indebted to a young man in an adjoining tent, who kindly loaned me this valuable collection of biographies. This enjoyment was heightened, undoubtedly, by a want of something to read, although [I was] tolerably well acquainted with the history of the repeated wrongs heaped upon the colonists by George III and his ministry, and [with] the lives of those eminent men who so boldly asserted their rights and the rights of millions yet unborn, and for the just maintenance of which they solemnly pledged unto each other their lives and sacred honors. Glorious and immortal band, your efforts proved successful, and you can now look from your exalted rest, from the Heaven of Heavens, upon the millions in the full enjoyment of "life, liberty, and the pursuit of happiness."

Of that noble and resolute band I have read much before, but never with that heartfelt interest experienced in the mountains

240

of California, and a brighter page can never be opened to man than that which discloses the characters of such men as John Hancock, Dr. Franklin, John Ross, Charles Carroll of Carrollton, and their illustrious associates.

Jan. 2.   The rain held up after breakfast and I went out to look for gold. Of this I found, in small pieces, about $1.50 or $2.00. Towards evening a heavy thunder gust came up, and after a few loud peals the rain descended copiously. Soon after, Messrs. Laubenheimer and Teats came home from Burns's and Widner's ranch and brought with them all but three of our mules. Among those missing is mine, and I am again without animals, and feel poor, because mules are now worth from one to two hundred dollars; but I have one consolation, and that is, if I have nothing to ride, I can walk. My pack mule I sold to Mr. Hill, and he was fortunate enough to get that one, but my favorite, Jim—old, yellow Jim—is among the missing.

Jan. 3.   Worked in the mines and brought in only about $3.00. The day was very pleasant and warm about noon.

Jan. 4.   Worked until the rain set in, about 10 A.M., and realized but a small amount of gold. During the afternoon I was summoned to appear before the alcalde as a juryman in the case of the People *vs.* a Spaniard.

Jan. 5.   Appeared before the court, and was struck from the jury list and appointed by the Court counsel for the defendant. Under this appointment I entered into an investigation of the charges preferred against the prisoner, and at 10:00 A.M. the prisoner was placed at the bar and the trial proceeded. This Spaniard was charged with stealing a pound and three quarters of an ounce of gold ore, and a gold thimble and key, and $2.50 in coin. In the trial the prosecutor failed to prove the larceny of the ore, but established that of the thimble, key, and coin, and the jury found him guilty of petit larceny and he was remanded to the custody of the sheriff for future sentence and punishment. After this had been laid aside, I was called upon a jury and declined another fee as attorney because I had already been sworn as a juryman. This was an action of debt, and required but a short time to determine it upon merits.

The day and past night have been excessively stormy and much water has fallen and all streams are high. A description of our courthouse and the other arrangements for the due administration of justice may be interesting. The sitting of this court was held in a small trading shanty, for this day's term, which was constructed of upright forks, crossed with poles, filled in with stone and mud, and the roof was of slate and sloped but one way. One corner of this was occupied by Dr. Stone as a grocery, and a rawhide table served as a bench for the jury and a smaller one covered with slabs of slate was used as a writing table for the judge, sheriff, and members of the bar. The alcalde sat upon a pole, the upper side of which was slabbed off, and the bar was accommodated with stools of frail workmanship, and barely supported the weight and dignity of the law. The sheriff acted both in the capacity of executory officer and clerk of this court, and, when ordered, called the jury and counted the number at the same time. With such instruments as these, and thus circumstanced, the court moved on in even tenor, and the day and its important events passed to the satisfaction of all persons—save, perhaps, the prisoner found guilty of petit larceny.

Jan. 6 (Sunday). No rain, but cloudy a great part of the day. I found a copy of the Constitution of the new and growing state of California in camp today for the first time and think, after a careful perusal of its pages and investigation of its provisions, that it rivals those of many of the older states; and while it confers liberty and power upon the citizens, it also guarantees them the protection necessary in the exercise of the privileges granted. It is based upon democratic principles, leaving the election of state officers in the hands of the people, forbidding involuntary servitude, and granting to no association banking privileges or the power to issue notes as a circulating medium. It is truly refreshing to meet with any good publication in these wilds, as it serves to while away a weary hour and, if good in its tendency, adds to the reader's stock of information and knowledge. It is, however, much to be regretted that books are few, and newspapers or letters seldom, if ever, reach us, and this is a perpetual source of annoyance to him who has the welfare of his family at heart, or wishes food for the mind.

I have now, since the day of my arrival at the Pueblo San Jose, been constantly knocking at the door of the postoffice at San Francisco and at Stockton, and all my efforts to get letters or papers have so far proved abortive. For this I can not assign a satisfactory reason, and cannot tell when I shall have the exalted privilege of again hearing from my family, from [whom] I have now been separated nearly twelve months without a single letter, paper, or other evidence of their being alive.

It is a trial, it is perplexing and harassing to the mind, to be kept in this state of suspense, and particularly when you know that letters have been written, and that, judging from the treatment some have met with at the office, you are equally certain that they are there and of right ought to be delivered.

'Tis said that a change of postmasters takes place every month at the former office, and this may serve to explain the irregularity in the distribution and delivery of letters and back mails; or, for instance, it is now January, and unless you politely request it, the mail of December last will not be referred to, and if that of January has nothing to your address you will be told, "No, sir, nothing for you," when at the same time there may be in the office a letter or letters to your address for every month since you left home. But we are in the mines, and to them it is a matter of little importance whether we hear from home or not, and *we* must endure this perplexing state of things with philosophic fortitude. The time is fast approaching when this nuisance will be removed, for communities will not suffer so flagrant an usurpation of their just rights and abuse of the privileges conferred upon the mail company. Endurance ceases to be a virtue when such rights are trampled upon by those who deem themselves the only ones entitled to carry the mail from San Francisco to New York.

Jan. 7. Morning dawned clear and pleasant. I went to work and at noon found myself in possession of $8.00 of the ore, but made nothing further during the day. Mr. Parker had the good fortune to find his lost mule in the hands of Mr. E. T. Holloway, who returned it to him in good order and fine condition.

Jan. 8. Clear morning, and I went to work but was compelled to suspend at noon in consequence of the fall of more rain. I had, however, taken about $2.00 of the ore, and this I picked from the crevices of the rocks.

Jan. 9. Was called by the sheriff to assist in searching for stolen property, and night came without having found any of the pork which had been taken from Mr. Petty. Rained hard during the forenoon. Up to this date there has been ice but one night this winter, and men now wade all the creeks in their path without so much as feeling chilly. The winter has this far been exceedingly mild, and the trees are yet green as midsummer, and grass and bulbous plants have already shot forth to the length of three inches or more. To a person accustomed to the cold and dreary climate of the north, this seems strange. This climate is truly a delightful one at all times in the year, and, were it not for the heavy fall of rain in the months of December, January, and February, we might live comfortably with no other covering than that afforded by a tent, or even in the open air; but when this season opens, a log house well covered or roofed becomes, in the eyes of the occupant, a perfect palace, not so much for the warmth it affords as for the water it turns off. Few have this comfort in these mines, as a large majority now live in tents.

Jan. 10. Rain in the morning, but about noon cleared off and the sun shone out very warm until towards sunset, when the heavens again became overcast and it rained slightly. During this interval between rains I occupied myself in picking gold from the crevices in the rock, and obtained about $3.00 of the ore in this manner. In this way thousands of dollars are picked up after each rain, and [this] fully justifies the opinion that the soil contains this metal and it is only dislodged by the action of water and eventually deposited in the gulches or ravines from which it is taken by the miners. It is hard to come to any definite conclusion as to the origin of this gold, but nearly all the miners agree upon one thing, and that is, that this country is volcanic in its origin. This opinion is sustained by the nature of the soil, by the growth of the timber, and in a particular manner by the ore obtained and the occasional finding of a stone bearing a striking resemblance to lava. Almost every particle of gold taken from these mines present[s] strong indications of having in times past undergone the action of heat and in its cooling moments became or partook of the form and shape of the cavity into which it fell while in a liquid state. This fact or opinion is more strongly fortified by the ore found adhering and firmly fixed in quartz; of which many pieces have been found this winter.[1] No one can doubt, after having fully examined these specimens from the smallest to the greatest, that this gold has passed the fiery ordeal, and that this country was thrown from the sea by convulsions of nature.

As to this country being an offspring of the sea, and raised out of the ocean by the force of internal commotion, there need be no doubt in the mind of any one, for there is abundance of evidence to sustain this position. In these pages I have already mentioned the variety of sea shells found on the desert, and the large beds of oyster shells, of immense size, over which we passed on the seventh day of October, 1849. These shells have been barely alluded to, if at all, and will admit of further notice in this place. They were, to all appearance, oyster shells, but very large, and I had the curiosity to examine a hole dug into the bank, and found them occupying a depth of several feet, and the bottom of the bank had not been reached by the person who had dug

---

[1] The gold-rush years decimated the placer deposits so greatly that almost all subsequent production depended upon quartz mills and stamps.

the hole. Some of these shells measured eight, and a few specimens twelve, inches in length, and from six to eight in breadth. The variety of shells found on the desert and this ancient deposit of oyster shells, are the only witnesses in connection with the foregoing deemed necessary to' be brought forward by me to prove that this oriferous land is a child of the ocean.

Jan. 11.　Storm and rain during the whole night, and continued up to this hour, 10:00 A.M. The waters are again very high, and gold digging is once more entirely suspended, and now it is that the mind wants food and hungers because books cannot be found. I have just finished an hour's reading of a work styled *The Pirates of Cape Ann*, which task I found a pleasant one. With this opportunity I was kindly furnished by Sheriff Barbour, and to him I owe the pleasure of passing a few hours whilst the descending rain was pattering upon our canvas roof. But, like all other books in my reach, it has been read through, and I have not another to begin upon. This rain will prevent Mr. Laubenheimer's coming home from a hunting expedition he joined on Tuesday last, and knowing that packing in game was out of the question I purchased this morning a little fresh venison, for which I paid 37½¢ per pound. Potatoes are now selling at Stockton for $18.75 per hundredweight, a reduction of one half from the price sold at in the fall. Speculators are for once foiled. Expecting to realize large profits from the sale of this article, they had shipped from the coast large quantities of this vegetable, and while the market was supplying, the price of packing was rising, and miners could not afford to eat potatoes at $1.18 per pound; consequently they remained upon the hands of the speculators, and hence the present low prices. Men are sometimes caught in their own nets, or under their own deadfalls, and when this is the case, they get little sympathy from the consumer. Flour is now selling here at $1.00 per pound, beans the same, and everything in the same proportion. When these things are contrasted with home prices they appear astounding, yet here we are forced to acknowledge them just, and men are made happy by having an opportunity of obtaining provisions even at these prices.

Jan. 12. Prospected again, and found the water so high in all the gulches that little could be done. In my rambles I came upon one of the most interesting ravines in California, and passed an hour very pleasantly in viewing its cascades, waterfalls, jets, and spouting fountains. One of these cast its water to the height of about two feet, and, when it had attained its full elevation, broke off and fell over both ways. The other was much smaller in the volume of its water and spouted forth and fell in the form of a bow. The rocks in this beautiful and romantic ravine were of the gray granite, and formed a continued succession of cascades or falls. This ravine had its source in a high mountain east of us.

Jan. 13 (Sunday). Beautiful clear day. I saw in the hands of Mr. C. Speeker a piece of gold which he had taken out weighing $139.50. So much for being one of the fortunate!

Jan. 14. Rained slightly during the past night and this morning the adjoining mountains are white with snow. A heavy frost settled about our camps. Found but little gold this day. Laubenheimer is out hunting and sent us in a fine quarter of venison.

Jan. 15. "Now comes the winter of our discontent"; all outdoor employment has ceased, in consequence of the falling snow, and the miners are shut in and forced to pass this gloomy day in such manner as will best accommodate their tastes and conveniences. The snow is still falling and the evidence of the continuation of this storm favorable. About noon this storm changed from snow to rain and continued through the day.

Jan. 16. Cloudy, with intervals of rain. Jacob and Parker are both on the sick list, and we are doing nothing in the way of mining.

Jan. 17. Suffered much during the night and day from a renewed attack of my old malady, being confined to my bed a greater part of the day. Parker and Jacob are better today.

The day has been cool and beautifully clear, and the ground is
still hove up by last night's frost. No news from Laub since
Sunday, and the express has once more returned from San Francisco without letters for either of our party. Sheriff Barbour
received two letters from home by this express, and bearing news
of such a character as are alarming to me. The cholera seems
to have visited all the towns on the Wabash and Erie Canal, and
who knows but my little family has had this terrible disease to
contend against. God in mercy grant that those spared to me
on leaving home may still be living, and that I may once more
meet them on earth. With the night came F. Laubenheimer and
P. S. Kelley from their hunting ground, but there was one of
this little band who did not nor ever will return. This young
man was A. G. Yotter, a resident of Belleview, Erie County,
state of Ohio. With this young man I was but partially ac-
quanted; but Mr. Laubenheimer was well acquainted with him,
as they both a few years ago lived in the same town. I will try
to give the particulars of the death of Mr. Yotter as they were
detailed to me by the two returned hunters. It seems that Kelley
and Yotter started from camp early yesterday for the purpose
of hunting, and whilst out four large brown bears came upon
him suddenly, and one of them knocked or pulled him down,
bit him in the thigh and sides of the throat. The wound on the
thigh bled profusely and was the cause of his death, as an artery
had undoubtedly been opened. At the time of the attack, Mr.
Kelley was distant from Yotter and the bears about three hundred yards, and by the time he was able to reach the spot, the
bear left his victim, soon after which Yotter got up, replaced his
fallen hat, and walked off about twenty yards, and fell on his
face. Mr. K— approached, raised him to a sitting posture, and
asked him if he was badly hurt. An affirmative nod of the head
was the only answer, and soon after he expressed a desire to see
Mr. L— and told Kelley to go to camp for him and he would
remain there until L. came. When Kelley and Laubenheimer
returned to the fatal spot, they found Yotter a corpse. They had

been previously joined by another hunter, and these three men, with no other instruments than their jackknives, dug a grave by the side of a projecting rock, and in it deposited the mortal remains of Yotter. This unfortunate termination of this day's hunt induced our men to return home, glad to escape from the thousands of dangers by which they were constantly surrounded. Three men belonging to these diggings have during this winter been torn and dangerously wounded by the denizens of these mountains, and escaped with their lives, but cripples for life, and now we have recorded the fatal termination of a fourth attack.

Jan. 18. I this morning appeared before our court as solicitor for F. Laubenheimer on behalf of the estate of A. G. Yotter. Mr. L— was appointed and qualified as administrator on said estate, and immediately took charge of such goods and chattels as were found belonging to said estate. The amount of property found will not exceed $150 in value, but there is actual cash to the amount of about $140 or $150, which money has not yet been found, and the whole matter is wrapped in mystery. There is full evidence of Yotter's having this money on the evening before he left for the hunt, for on being asked by his late partner whether he intended to carry his money with him his answer was, "No! I have left it up here," accompanied with a nod of the head. Before his interment, his clothing and body was examined, but only the sum of $4.35 found upon his person, and there is no clue as to the place of his deposit, or to the person he might have left it with, and the probability is that it will be lost to his heirs.

The day has been stormy with occasional snow showers, and from indisposition I was confined to the house.

Jan. 19. Again I am confined to the house, unable to work, caused by a deeply-seated cold, extreme soreness of all the bones of my mortal frame, and attended with the evils of a constant diarrhea. I am, however, in the company of Jacob, who has been worse for the past two days, a part of the time in high fever, and also suffering under a very violent cold in the head and on the lungs. I have acted in the capacity of his physician, and yesterday administered cathartics and am now giving quinine to break the fever, which is periodical in its visits. The day is beautifully bright and clear but withal a little cool. Laubenheimer and Parker are at work, and when they return we can give the result of their labor. This is easily done, for they only found $3.75, but have a fair prospect of doing better.

Jan. 20 (Sunday). Almost sick enough to be confined to my bed. My disease has changed to camp dysentery, and I am almost at a loss for remedies. The mercurial medicines resorted to have salivated me slightly, and this morning I resorted to a mild pill to assist the stomach and cause a removal of the disease, which seems to be on the coatings of the stomach and intestines. How often in my sick and solitary hours has my mind reverted to the tender care and unceasing attentions received from loved hands at home; and after wandering over these pages of memory until I seemed to enjoy them over again, it suddenly turned to the heart-sickening circumstances by which I am now surrounded. Like green and pleasant spots in an arid waste, the heart leaps for joy at the remembrance of the past and pants for a hasty release from these storm-locked hills to revel once more in scenes like these, to be again where physicians are qualified to administer remedies for the diseases flesh is heir to. Imprisonment here is tolerable until sickness prevents work and you are confined to the inside of a house; then this world becomes dreary and life almost a burden. But I would not murmur against the decree of God.

Jan. 21. Still on the sick list, and J. Teats but little better. The fever has been checked, but the camp dysentery still hangs to both of us and is attended with great pain. Yesterday the goods and chattels belonging to Yotter's estate were sold by the administrator, and today he, accompanied by John Houghton and Sheriff Barber, set out to visit the place of interment of the remains of the deceased, for the double purpose of reintering the body to secure it against the prowling animals of the mountains and instituting an examination for the lost money, which has not yet been found. They have arranged to meet Mr. Conklin and Mr. Sharp in the vicinity of the grave, who have kindly volunteered to assist. These two men came from, and when at home reside at, Belleview, Ohio, and were friends and neighbors of the deceased.

Mr. Parker, an excellent and attentive nurse in sickness, and a good cook, baked us some apple pies, the first we have had in this country, and the only food relished by me for the past four days. These pies could not have been better if baked at home, and Mr. P— has my most hearty thanks for his kind attentions from the beginning of my malady. Alcalde Scott has just sent me over a fine piece of corned beef, already boiled and of the choicest quality, also a handful of dried sassafras roots, brought by him from the state of Missouri. My best thanks, kind friend, for these rarities—things I have often wished for, but knew not where to get them.

Snow and hail is again rattling on our roof, and a cold storm hanging over us. Snow fell during all the evening.

Jan. 22. Morning dawned, and I arose from my bed much refreshed by a peaceful night's repose. On looking out, I found the ground covered about three inches deep with snow, and the air chilly. The sun rose clear, but had little effect, excepting on the exposed side hills. During the day my disease returned again, and I must again resort to pills.

Jan. 23. Cloudy this morning, with a sprinkle of falling snow. Heavy cargoes of provisions came in yesterday, and flour is now offered in this market for 75¢ per pound, and vinegar for $5.00 per gallon. Goods of every description are falling—and so is the snow. The day has been tempestuous and the snow now lies to the depth of several inches. Mr. L— and his companions came in this evening. On nearing the place of sepulture of A. G. Yotter, they discovered that some wild animal had already dug for the remains but had effected but little. A new grave was sunk, the body taken up, re-examined, and again interred and

251

further security placed over it against the depredations of the bears and wolves. The lost money and a silver-cased gold pen was found in a side pocket of the deceased's pantaloons and taken in charge by the administrator, and the party returned to camp this evening, fully satisfied that everything that could be done, had now been effected, and that all cause for suspicion touching the money was now forever removed.

Jan. 24.   Still snowing hard at daylight, but melting at the same time; consequently, but little deeper than last night. At about 8:00 A.M. the storm changed to violent rain, which continued until late in the night. My malady is not so bad today and I firmly hope that it will gradually disappear. Our boys were caught here with their horses during this storm and had to feed each at a cost of $3.33 for one feed only.

Jan. 25.   Cloudy and misty. Parker has just started with the horses for the ranch, and I have been engaged all the morning [in] drawing up and preparing the administrator's account and report for the court in behalf of Yotter's estate. Mr. Reed came in and paid $36.50 due us on a packing contract of last fall, and there is yet $73 due from him.

Jan. 26.   Feel much revived and invigorated by my undisturbed night's repose, and believe my disease getting better. Cloudy weather, with occasional droppings of rain, and if I had but one of the many books at home, how infinitely I would be blessed. The sheriff again called for me as juror in a civil suit between M. F. Boalt, plaintiff, and Thompson and —, defendants. This matter was quickly disposed of, and each juryman was paid the sum of $6.00.

Jan. 27 (Sunday).   Feel much improved in health and once more entertain strong hopes of going to work in the course of a week. Mild and beautiful day, but find the air from the snowy mountains chilly and damp. I find many persons complaining of dysentery in camp and one man is now lying very low with this and fever combined. Little hopes of his recovery are entertained by his friends. New cargoes of provisions came in yesterday, and flour is now selling for $75 per hundred pounds and pork for $62.50. All kinds of provisions are becoming lower, and we will soon be able to live as cheap here as at Stockton, or proportionately so.

Jan. 27. Fine, clear weather, strongly resembling the first day of a pleasant April, but how long this may continue to us is quite uncertain. This has a bracing influence upon my weak frame, and I much wish for a continuance of warm, dry weather. I was engaged today as attorney for Francis Ligeness *vs.* James Fitz Harris and had three officers in pursuit of the defendant at an early hour in the evening. Damages claimed in this suit $2,674.50.

Jan. 29. At 11:00 A.M. the officers came into court and returned the body of Fitz Harris, defendant. The alcalde then adjourned to Stone's store, which we found occupied by a set of intoxicated men, and accordingly His Honor opened court on the sunny side of a neighboring hill, and the trial opened. I presented my case, and sustained it by the papers or notes in my possession, and recovered a judgment for $2,474.50, and found nothing excepting an old horse and saddle to make even a part of the cost from. The day was remarkably pleasant, but with the night came clouds and rain. On the 24th an express (private)[2] left these mines for the postoffice at San Francisco, and in a few weeks we *may be* in receipt of letters.

Jan. 30. Clear morning, but cloudy evening; and being still unable to labor, time passes heavily. L. and B. are at work, and have of late been poorly recompensed for their toiling. I have this week lived on roasted mackerel and cheese, and find this the best diet for my complaint. Cheese, $2.00 per pound, and the fish, 75¢ each. Strong indications of snow.

---

[2]The express business was a highly profitable one in the mines, although its participants were poor insurance risks. Many men preferred the excitement and action of an expressman's career to the plodding labor of the diggings. See Oscar Osburn Winther, *Express and Stagecoach Days in California* (1936); Ernest A. Wiltsee, *The Pioneer Miner and the Pack Mule Express* (1931); and Neill C. Wilson, *Treasure Express: Epic Days of the Wells Fargo* (1936).

Jan. 31. Suffered much through the night with pain in the head. The chilly, damp weather seems also to exercise an influence upon my rheumatic bones, and I am again forced to stay within doors, although the weather promises to be delightful. Through the politeness of Mr. Sullick, of New York, I have been favored with files of the *Tribune* and *Herald*, being the first news of tangible form and character met with in California. These papers bore date November 13, 1849, but did not allude to Ohio politics or her late election, and with the exception of New York, Louisiana, Massachusetts, Maine, and Georgia, I am still left in comparative darkness as to the general result of elections in the Union. The foreign news I found full of interest and was sorry to lay down the last paper, for want of further details.

On Tuesday last a party of twelve men by accident came in here, in a starving condition. This party belonged to a train of thirty wagons; [they] arrived at Salt Lake some time in the month of August last, and at that place recruited their cattle for a few weeks. On leaving the lake, they traveled almost due south for about three hundred miles and then bore west, and soon found themselves in the great American Desert, near the west side of which the most of the party burnt their wagons and packed their cattle, with the intention of crossing the Sierra Nevada Mountains wherever they should reach it. A separation of the party had already taken place, and the fragment now in had reached Owen's Lake and here met with a party of Indians who directed them to go south along the mountain until they reached Walker's Pass and through it pass to the west side. Following these directions, and subsisting upon acorns, mule meat, and a few fish obtained from the Indians, they happily reached these mines without the loss of a man, after having suffered intensely. These men think the other party about twenty days behind, and what renders this more painful is the fact that there are women and children suffering with those behind. The Mormons at Salt Lake are to blame for this disaster, for it seems they urged to these strangers the many advantages of this route, and recommended it as far superior in all advantages over that of the north; and all this for selfish motives, for it seems that the Mormons have long cherished a wish for some party to open a wagon road from the lake south to the old Spanish trail and thence west to the California settlements. This seems to have been their motive, and one, too, of which they boasted in the hearing of some of this party. God only knows what will be the final result of this unjust and selfish counsel, and it only shows the disposition of men and communities to adopt any means, however unjust, to further their selfish and ingenious designs.[3]

[3]Evans here refers to the Jayhawkers of the famous Death Valley party. Captain Jefferson Hunt, of the Mormon Battalion, contracted to guide a group of emigrants from Salt Lake to California via the southern route. Halfway to California the party split, the majority favoring a doubtful cutoff which led directly west toward central California. Hunt refused to take chances, and all but seven wagons deserted him and became trapped in the fiery wastes of Death Valley. This ill-advised group split a second time, into the Jayhawkers and Bennett-Arcane party, and plodded slowly across the deserts with terrific hardships and tremendous losses. Hunt, meanwhile, pursued the regular Spanish Trail through Cajón Pass and arrived safely in southern California. See William Lewis Manly, *Death Valley in '49* (1894); John W. Caughey, "Southwest from Salt Lake in 1849," *Pacific Historical Review*, VI (1937), 143-81; and Carl I. Wheat, "Trailing the Forty-Niners through Death Valley," *Sierra Club Bulletin*, XXIV (1939), 74-108.

THE MARIPOSA DIGGINGS
(CONTINUED)

Feb. 1. Beautiful, mild day. As the weather changes, so changes also the severity of my rheumatism, but I have been enabled to crawl up and down a small ravine running in front of our cabin and extract from its rocky bed a small quantity of the ore, and from this am led to hope that better days are in store for me.

Feb. 2. Delightful day. I wandered to the old arroyo, a mile from camp, and picked up several pieces of gold, and then returned, almost worn out with the pain and fatigue of my walk. Laub and Parker yesterday made $27 and today $12.50.

Feb. 3 (Sunday). Pleasant forenoon, but cloudy towards night. Were visited by Mr. Jimison, Mr. J. Lott, and Mr. Burns, the first from Sherlock's and the others from Fremont's camp. They report the snow at those diggings two feet deep yesterday, whilst here there is no snow, and beautiful weather, a part of the time at least.

Feb. 4. Weather mild and clear until night, when rain again threatened. I went out to work and found gold enough to pay expenses. My labor was, however, attended with much pain in my diseased joints. There is a rumor in camp to the effect that Great Britain had declared war against the United States, and that all the ports on the Pacific coast in our territory were now in a state of blockade. I cannot credit this report yet, although there are those here who believe it true and look forward to the troubles that must consequently follow such a state of things. New York papers of Nov. 13, '49, do not allude to any cause for such a rupture; and I cannot yet think it true.

Feb. 5. Clear and beautiful, warm as May and very calm. Our neighbor, mentioned on Sunday, January 27, as being sick and not expected to recover, died last night [and] was buried to-day on the hill in front of our cabin. He has left a family some-where in the state of New York, and was from France. We have no confirmation of the report alluded to yesterday, but, by a gen-tleman arrived from San Francisco, learn that provisions or their prices have a downward tendency, and he heard nothing of the British blockade. I am again confined to the house by the severity of my rheumatism.

Feb. 6. Confined to the house as usual, the tedium of which was much relieved by a visit from Mr. Record, late attor-ney-general to the king of the Sandwich Islands. I found this gentleman intelligent, and his history of adventures, professional and otherwise, full of interest. He is a native of New York, and has passed through many of the vicissitudes of life, and finds him-self now a digger and delver in these mines, instead of being in the full enjoyment of a salary of $3,000 per annum with house and servants paid for by the government of the islands.

Feb. 7. Almost unable to walk at all from the violence of the pains in my legs and hips, and am almost ready to sink under the ennui now so wholly in possession of my mind. I had another consoling and refreshing visit from my new friend, Mr. Record. Laub and Parker made today $28 and Jacob $11 and I am forced to sit here unable to earn my board by digging. God's will be done.

The news of the blockade of our ports has not yet been con-firmed, but a report has found its way here to this effect, that a joint resolution to organize this territory had passed, and that the newly-appointed territorial Governor had reached Califor-nia. This is taking a constitutional course in this matter, and if true all the doings of the statesmen of California will be as void or voidable things, and in one year from this time, the state of California will become an integral part of our Union, upon a constitutional application for admission.

Feb. 8. Clear at sunrise, but soon became cloudy and continued so until night. The damp condition of the atmosphere did not contribute much to the dispersion of the aches of my body, and my sufferings were at times almost intolerable. Attended court as juror in conjunction with my brother chip, Mr. Record, in the case of Perry *vs* Parker: replevin; verdict for plaintiff; fees paid jury, $6.00 each.

Feb. 9. Cleared off as the sun rose, but towards night became cloudy again, and once more threatened rain. Laubenheimer and Parker have gone over to inspect the mines at Fremont's camp, Colorado diggings, and also Sherlock's—all within a day's travel—with a view of finding and locating in a richer "placer" if possible. Prospects are not very promising and men are becoming dissatisfied, and seeking other and better locations. A few days more, or perhaps weeks, will end my stay in this branch of the Maraposa Mines and it is now utterly impossible for me to say what steps I shall take after arriving at San Francisco, to which city I shall go at an early day, unless I find by letters from home that no necessity exists for my visiting that place.

This memorandum of travels and transactions closes the fourth book and contains no variety for the reader, although, should life be prolonged, it will serve to brush the cobwebs from the tablets of my memory in after years and guide my imagination along the same perilous path again. Reader, with your consent we need not part company yet, and if you think these notes worthy your attention, you are invited to turn to Book Fifth.

BOOK FIFTH

Feb. 10 (Sunday). The weather much resembles April, and is particularly delightful today. I had the pleasure of a long conversation with my friend and fellow miner, Mr. Sullick, of the city of New York. Seated upon a wagon tongue near the alcalde's tent, we canvassed political subjects, more intimately connected with California than otherwise, and the prospects of the present and the future, and came to the sage conclusion that few men would or could amass a fortune in the mines without the investment of capital, and a residence of several years at least. To the latter I do not wish to submit, for a few thousands would not tempt me to forgo the pleasures of home and its society. The twentieth instant is fast approaching, and it ends one year of misery to me at least—without so much as one letter up to this date to acquaint me with the situation and condition of things at home.

But there is still *hope*, the last to forsake the human breast, that the express to arrive here on the fifteenth instant may bring me the ever-welcome messages from home. But I am again running into murmurings, and will briefly state that a fight of a very serious character took place last night up the creek, one man badly wounded on the head by a stone thrown by another, and a second repeatedly knocked down and badly bruised. Some individual or individuals also stole $400 from a Spaniard yesterday. Some of these outrages will yet be productive of the use of the hempen halter to the perpetrators. Ten men, belonging to the train mentioned as being yet in the desert beyond the mountains arrived here last night, having left the main body some three hundred miles from here, all in a starving, and some in a perishing condition. The Indians met by these men were very friendly and rendered them every assistance in their power, and it is to them they owe the safety of their lives at this moment. Several of those still in the rear could not keep pace with the train, being so much reduced for want of food, and at every encampment it became necessary for some of the advance to return and bring in those who had given out and fallen by the wayside. The women and children endured it best and are still urging forward.

Feb. 11. Every exertion is now being made to send relief to the unfortunate emigrants, and strong hopes are entertained that they may yet be found and saved from absolute starvation. When this last fragment of this forlorn band broke off, there were those in the train who had not tasted bread of any kind for the past thirty days, having subsisted entirely upon

dried beef of very inferior quality. I drew up several appeals
to the humane of Aqua Frieo, which are designed for general
circulation on tomorrow. I was again called as a juror in a civil
suit, Bruner *vs.* Sontag: verdict for plaintff, $20. Weather
pleasant.

Feb. 12. Still unable to work. I have applied one of the
remedies furnished by nature; to wit, a plaster of gum of the
pine, but have not yet experienced much relief to my aching
back and joints. New diggings have been opened on the headwaters of the San Joaquin River, and for the past two days there
has been a general rush from these mines to those new deposits.
How rich they are, remains for time to develop. The weather
is beautiful.

Feb. 13. Weather comfortably warm, but hazy during
the most of the day. After drawing up some papers for my
esteemed friend, A. D. Selleck, I was called as commissioner by
the Alcalde, to co-operate with a gentleman by the name of
Metcalf, authorizing and empowering us to purchase provisions,
hire mules, and send forward to the relief of the destitute and
starving emigrants. Although exceedingly lame, I cheerfully
entered upon the discharge of this duty, and with the prompt
assistance of others when called on, we made out six loads of
bread, pork, beans, flour, coffee, tea, etc., weighing in all 1,041
lbs. From the scattered condition of the donations, the day was
passed without getting the mules and packs off. These diggings
are now being almost wholly deserted, and things are fast assuming a Sunday appearance—quite the reverse from that worn a
month since. I suppose that one hundred mules, well packed,
have this day left here for the new diggings.

Feb. 14. My disease is no better, and I applied to Drs.
Hoar and Meridith, who pronounced my case scurvy, that bane
of these mountains. They advised me to get all the vegetables
afforded by these hills and use [them] as long as I remain, but
go to the coast at the first opportunity. To put their prescrip-
tion into practice, I sent up the side hills and had some wild cab-

bage and a small wild onion brought down, and purchased a bottle of lime juice, and a few Irish potatoes. All these vegetables I use raw, with the juice of lime, and most sincerely hope this change of diet may be productive of a cure.

The provision train started early and are now speeding on their errand of mercy; and may they quickly reach the sufferers. This cabbage found growing here tastes like cress, and resembles the plant found in the gardens of our German population at home and known by them as kale. The only difference is in the leaf, which is much smaller. It makes, however, a most luscious salad, with the lime juice and a little sugar.

Feb. 15. The state of the weather still continues remarkably pleasant. Up to 3:00 P.M. I have anxiously watched the pass for the appearance of our letter express, but so far have been sadly disappointed. No arrival yet, and still that feverish anxiety relative to letters from home must have its sway. If not this evening, tomorrow it must get here, and then something must reach me.

Mr. Parker, Kelley, and myself were called as jurors in the case of Atwell *vs.* Hill and had to dispose of conflicting testimony. Verdict for Atwell, $321.42. 10:00 P.M., and no express in yet.

Feb. 16. My health is improving. A sudden change of diet is fast removing the cause of my dismal aches, and I shall yet take the liberty of describing all the symptoms of this terrible disease. No express in yet, and now 9:00 A.M. At intervals during the winter a solitary frog has kept up his serenade in front of our cottage, and recently I noticed the addition of another voice, and now a constant chorus sounds through the night. To these sounds have now been added that of the small owl and the large hooting owl, and occasionally the mountain wolf sends forth his notes to apprise us of his presence. The sky, today, is clouded over, weather cool, and vegetation pushing forward rapidly, everything indicating a warm and early spring. From these early indications here in the mountains, we may safely say that many of the early plants and shrubs of [the] plains below are now decked in their most lively colors. This evening after dark, friend Barber came to the door and announced the arrival of the express. This glad news brought us all on our feet and we rushed into the open air, where I was immediately seized by the arm and asked to what point I was destined. I was then told that it had stopped something over a mile from us, and that I could not walk that distance, which was but too true, and reluctantly I once more entered the boundaries of our cottage, anxiously awaiting the return of those who had gone to the office.

Here, and alone, I fell into a singular train of reflections. The incidents of the past year crowded into these few moments and familiar faces once more were smiling around me, and then again I was breaking the seals of the various letters upon our table. Ah! little did I dream of the trouble so soon to sound upon my ear, and cause the brain to whirl! The boys came, but not a letter, no, not one, for me. Mr. Parker, however, was more fortunate, having received one from his wife, and its pages disclosed to me the death of my loved and revered father from cholera and also the death (from [the] same disease) of Uncle Lee and his son and daughter. This was the amount of heart-rending news to me from that single letter, and I retired at ten o'clock with heart full of misery, doubt, and uncertainty—uncertainty because no mention was made of my wife, child and others.

Mrs. Parker lives about twelve miles from Defiance, Ohio, and knew my father, he being a physician, but was not acquainted with my own little family; hence the uncertainty about them.

Feb. 17 (Sunday). I found Mr. Haller, one of our party, had also received a letter, and he had the kindness to send it to me and from it I gathered that the cholera had not visited Defiance and that my wife had received one of my letters from Mexico. This removed a mountain of troubles, and I had the satisfaction of knowing that on the eighth day of November last all were alive, save those mentioned yesterday. I feel thankful to God for these mercies, and pray Him to hold them in His arms of love and to watch over, guide, and direct me in all my endeavors to do good, and to support all in affliction. The weather was warm, but the sky overcast with thin clouds.

Feb. 18. Weather same as yesterday. I busied myself in closing and settling up all open matters, and particularly affairs as Commissioner of [the] Benevolent Fund, and am now fully prepared to wind up all things having connection with that fund, and then I am off for the coast. My reflections are of a deep melancholy character and spirits exceedingly depressed by the sad news from home, and I can scarcely content myself until the arrival of the packer, who has gone to the relief of the suffering emigrants. This evening the clouds became heavier and at bedtime a few drops of rain descended; and during the night we had a refreshing spring shower, which lasted some time in duration.

Feb. 19. Glorious morning, plants are dressed in lively green, birds are warbling forth their notes of joy, and happiness seems to reign in every breast but mine. There is still an aching void, which one single letter from home would fill, but that remedy is not at hand and I am doomed [to] endure the suspense for some time to come; to occupy (as it were) a dreary and a dreamy circle—a path clear of all companionship save visions of a melancholy nature.

F. Laubenheimer, who had gone down to the ranch for the mules, returned this evening without having found my favorite, Jim, and I now consider myself without a mule, and wholly dependent upon such conveyance from this place as may fall in my way. Jacob says he has made $200 in the past three weeks at mining, which has been profitable.

Through Mr. L— I received the payment on a small note I held against L. H. Bunnell, but Hill and Young have not yet paid me for a mule sold to them on the nineteenth of December last. To get this, I suppose a trip to the Towallomne diggings will be necessary, and if so, it will be at a heavy cost to them.

Feb. 20. Cool and cloudy weather, and the day unpleasant. Many left here today for the new diggings; amongst others, our alcalde and sheriff. So the court is gone, and my profession is at an end. I met with Dr. Woodward, Mr. Manoah, Mr. Godfroy, and Harvey Kimber—all Maumee boys. Glad to see them and sorry they, too, are on the move. So we go. Just one year ago this morning I bade adieu to my family and friends in Defiance, and this year has passed on the wings of time without even a letter from my loved ones. Sad news, melancholy tidings of the death of my loved father, have reached me and I have nothing for my mind to feed upon but the contents of Mrs. Parker's letter to her husband. In this there is enough to furnish food for bitter, wretched reflection. Time! Time—whose every footstep is deeply imprinted on the hearts of man—has again strongly admonished me of the shortness of human life—of the absolute certainty of death.

Feb. 21. On waking this morning, I found the snow falling fast, and the ground covered to the depth of a little over an inch. Shortly after sunrise, it began raining, and the snow was fast disappearing when the wind once more chopped round, and snow again descended during the evening.

Feb. 22. Sun shows out occasionally, warm and pleasant, and the snow is fast disappearing. Some eight or ten ox teams left this place, all designed for the road. This will reduce the freight on transportation of goods still lower. The mountain mist indicated clear weather and this storm may be looked upon as the clear-up shower. Arrivals from the new diggings do not give so flattering an account as previous reports. High water prevents a full investigation, and it is extremely difficult to determine the extent of the San Joaquin mines. The gold found there up to this time is very fine, and requires the aid of quicksilver to separate it from the sand.

This is one of the great days at home, a day which calls forth eulogy upon the character of Washington, the Father of our Country; yet here, in these labyrinths of wilds, no stirring events or soul-cheering music strikes the ear, and the only change perceptible from the usual monotony, is an increased number of bets and bystanders at the montebank, and a little more drunkenness.

Feb. 23.   Weather more pleasant, bidding fair to grow better as it grows colder. Many persons are returning from the new diggings, and those who had made their arrangements to leave here are again settling back to their old holes and commencing their work again. Many persons are now doing better or realizing more from their labor than has been realized during the winter at any time.

Feb. 24 (Sunday).   Weather again clear and becoming milder. The day has again shown an increase of population at these mines, as many of the persons who had left for the new diggings have again returned, well satisfied that they can do as well here as any other mines until the water recedes. Considerable gambling and plenty of liquor drank. On man lost, in about twenty minutes, nineteen ounces in bets at the montebank.

Feb. 25.   Clear, and warm sunshine which continued until towards night. Thin, fleecy clouds then veiled the sky, and about bedtime rain commenced falling and at intervals during the night was heard pattering upon our humble roof.

Feb. 26.   Ground covered to the depth of about one inch at daylight, and the snow is still falling abundantly; now 10:00 A.M., and the storm promises no cessation at present. A train of seven large wagons, all drawn by oxen but one, came into camp this morning, just arrived from Missouri. Among the individuals composing this train were four or five American women, who accompany their parents and brothers to these wilds. They locate for the present at Fremont's diggings. They brought with them a large drove of sheep, which they sell readily for an ounce per head, and the consumer pays 50¢ per pound of meat from the market. The snow continued to fall during the greater part of the day and after night the clouds broke away and we had the faint prospect of this being the end of this storm. But snow again fell during the night, so heavy as to break down our tent with its accumulated weight.

Feb. 27.   Still snowing at intervals, and attended with

high wind—a thing quite unusual in California. The snow is now about six inches deep, and I think that snow to the depth of about ten or eleven inches has fallen since the storm began but is constantly melting at the bottom. The diggings at Sherlock's must be covered to the depth of several feet, because they are much more elevated or higher up the mountains than these, and snow falls in that vicinity when there is none here. Should this be a general storm, much suffering will be the consequence at the diggings on the Sacramento River and its tributaries. Night came on and snow falling rapidly.

Feb. 28. Several inches of increased snow, the fall of last night, and this morning we have another slight prospect of clearing off. All mining operations are suspended, and traveling at an end for the present. I expected to be at San Francisco by this time, but am still a denizen of these mountains with better health than usual but still vast room for improvement. The sun shone out during the middle of the day and the snow was fast yielding to the influences. At bedtime, clear as a bell. Several of the miners from Sherlock's region have come in here seeking refuge from the violence of the snowstorms.

{ March, 1850 }

THE MARIPOSA DIGGINGS TO SAN FRANCISCO

Mar. 1. Weather clear, and the snow fast melting away. F. Laubenheimer has gone, first to the mouth of the Merced River, and from thence to the Ta-walla-mne diggings, expecting to meet Young and Hill at the latter place. Mr. Parker and I wrote home, sending by Mr. Wyckoff, of Pittsburg, Pennsylvania, and should he arrive safely at Cincinnati, Ohio, our letters will be sure to reach their destination.

Mar. 2. This day opens cloudy, strongly threatening another storm. This winter has thus far presented a series of contradictory weather, and the season presents the appearance of a quarrel between storm and sunshine, each claiming and contending for the mastery. During the afternoon it rained and snowed alternately, and snow fell to the depth of four inches during the night.

March 3 (Sunday). Almost cloudless during the day, and the warmth of the sun's rays had a melting effect upon the snow.

Mar. 4. A friend brought me several copies of the *Boston Olive Branch, New York Tribune*, and *Herald*, of late date, and I was much pleased to learn from the *Tribune* that the Ohio Legislature had at last organised, but sorry to see the attempts of the long-haired ass of Fairfield (Whitman, of the Senate),[1] to create disturbance and to tyrannize over the members. Such men are not qualified for the stations to which they are called through mistake, and instead of giving dignity and honor to a legislative body their brainless acts are constantly acting as a drawback, and finally fill up the days of the session with blots and blemishes throughout its record. Shame upon the party hack!

[1] Henry C. Whitman, leader of the Locofoco faction in Ohio.

There has also been the usual amount of "tempest in a tea pot" in the U. S. Senate, the most of it emanating from Senator Foote[2] of Mississippi on the subject of slavery in the proposed admission of California, Deseret, and San Jacinto, all of which territory has ever been free, and which is declared so, as far as California is concerned, by an actual vote of the people residing in the territory.

Mar. 5.   Open, clear weather, and the snow is fast going into water. The snow is reported to be four and five feet deep at Sherlock's diggings, and many of the miners have taken up their homes here until the winter closes. The day has continued calm and warm, and the snow has in places been wholly thawed away. 'Tis now sunset in our camp, but his departing rays still linger around the tops of the mountains east of us. In that horizon are also thin, fleecy clouds, premonitory of another storm, which sign (I hope) may fail.

Mar. 6.   Clear in the morning, but clouds came over us and the storm wind again swept through the natural channels formed by the mountains, and again warned us of its near approach. Mr. R. Bell of Wisconsin called in today, and I am invited to dine with him on tomorrow. The past heavy fall of snow is fast leaving us and I humbly hope it may be the last link of winter's chain, which has so long confined me to these mountains. I much, most ardently wish to breathe the pleasant air of the valleys below and once more have something other than mountains to rest my eyes upon. Almost anything would prove a relief, and this prison-like life would be at an end. Yet I am truly thankful that my situation is no worse. Rain fell towards night, and in a few hours the snow had entirely disappeared.

Mar. 7.   Rained nearly all day, and one of our neighbours came in and we spent several hours at a social game of euchre. Still cloudy, though wearing a more promising face for dry weather. The rain prevented my dining at my friend's house, and as soon as an opportunity offers I shall pay him my promised

[2]Henry Stuart Foote (1804-80).

visit. Etiquette is observed here; consequently, we never enter a tent or house at general mealtimes, because good manners would make it necessary for the master of the house or tent to invite you to a seat at the table; but where an express invitation has been given, we always answer it by actual presence at the appointed time unless prevented by health or bad weather. Rained during the evening, but the wind came in gusts and soon dispersed the storm.

Mar. 8. Clear, beautiful morning. After the storm broke away last night it froze quite hard, and several hours will be required to dry the surface of the earth. The day passed almost unclouded.

Mar. 9. Pleasant morning, with an unclouded sky and pure, bracing atmosphere. Laubenheimer has not yet returned from the lower diggings, but is expected in this evening, and a few more days may pass before I get off to San Francisco.

The hour of twilight has passed, and had Mr. L. returned, I would have been on my way to S. F. tomorrow. Should he not get in this evening, I will be compelled to wait for the next train down, which may and may not go next week, and I will be unable to transact my business in time for the departure of the next steamer. Mr. Pattey, our neighbor, leaves in the morning for Stockton, and I am vexed at the obstacles preventing my going with him; yet the Good Book says all is ordered just right and, if so, I can in no event be the loser.

Mar. 10 (Sunday). This has indeed been one of the noted days at these mines. Gambling has seemed to chain the most of men to the Juggernaut, and as usual the poor dupes have "paid too dear for the whistle." A very large amount of money has changed hands this day, and many who came with bags of gold and silver returned to their cabins and tents penniless. Mr. L. has not yet returned and I am still "a looker-on in Venice." Cloudy this evening, and another snowstorm indicated.

Mar. 11. Cold and cloudy, with some rain, and high wind in the evening. The gamblers were tapering off their game of yesterday, and one man bet to the amount $1,003 and lost every penny. This was between gamblers, and he is not worthy of sympathy.

Mar. 12. Wet, dismal day, and last night proved the storm of storms in the way of high wind and rain. Continued rain for several days and nights in succession is peculiar to this season in California, but high wind and storm seldom ever occur. Mr. L. has not yet returned, and his task has become onerous indeed. Whilst rain is falling here, snow is descending upon the top and side of the mountain a few miles from our cabin, and presents to the eye a curtain of mist.

Mar. 13. Heavy rain during the greater part of the day.

Mar. 14. Still cloudy, with occasional rain. Sold flour this morning at 40¢ per lb. Received a paper, by way of a friend, which announces the nomination of Hon. Reuben Wood for Governor of Ohio by the Democrats. Rained very hard during the evening. Mr. L. not yet returned.

Mar. 15. Still raining at short intervals. Mr. Laubenheimer has not got home from the Ta-wall-umne diggings yet, and I am getting apprehensive of some ill luck having befallen him. More rain in the afternoon.

Mar. 16. Morning dawned clear and beautiful. At 9:00 A.M. the wind commenced blowing and occasional clouds passed over us. The day continued pleasant. Mr. L. is still among the missing.

Mar. 17 (Sunday). Beautiful day, and the passion for gaming stronger than ever. There is a similarity between the banks of some of the states, and the montebanks of California, and this similarity becomes striking when heavy draws are made upon either, and especially has this been done by the "buckers" in the past few days. Banks are tumbling and crashing on every hand. Last night one of these gave up the ghost and this morning at an early hour another, with but two or three gasps, sunk deep into the pockets of the bettors. Intense excitement, visible in every face around the board, attends the steps of the "tapper."

The dealer sits on one and the "payer" on the other, or opposite, side. Between these two are stacks of dollars, dubloons, and eagles, and bags or papers of dust, and this is *the bank*. The "buckers" are standing around the table. The dealer shuffles, and one of the buckers cuts, and then come two "layouts," and upon these the bets are made. Some one of the buckers, with more luck than his brethren, we will suppose, has by his bets won from the bank $500, and now the exciting time is coming on. The dealer makes another *layout*, and the fortunate bucker turns one of these down, and taps the bank. If his bet is successful, he takes all the money and the "bank is broke." So the gaming of directors of banks often produces a perfect parallel to the doings of our montebanks, with this in favor of the latter: when they break, the people are not the losers.

Whilst [I was] penning the above hasty lines, Mr. Laubenheimer came in, much fatigued but quite successful, and I was truly glad to see him. A gambler by the name of Platt attempted to commit suicide by cutting his throat and shooting two balls into his body. He is still alive, but death must ensue.

Mar. 18.   Express came in this morning and I am happy to say that I have indirectly heard from home. Wife and child in good health last fourth day of June, thank God. I am now making every preparation to leave in the morning for San Francisco, and think I shall get off. I find by a letter from home that my wanderings in California are wrapped in total mystery at home up to January 3, 1850, although I have dispatched the fourteenth letter home. Inquiries for the lost one are made, and I am perfectly astounded at the repeated failure of mails. But it must be endured, however trying and vexatious to the soul.

Mar. 19.   Clear morning, and at 10:00 A.M. the wagons came along and I was once more on the road, my whole movables consisting of a bag of clothes and my bed. We literally fill the commands of the Good Book—that is, "take up thy bed and walk." Traveled ten miles and camped.

Mar. 20.   Weather pleasant, after a cold night in the

mountains. We are now in camp, a few rods from the spot on which our little party camped on the night of the 26th October last. The grass is abundant and flowers cover the entire valley. Just in sight is the California Ranch, and there I expect to leave my present mode of conveyance (spring carriage drawn by four good mules), and on the back of another of these faithful animals will proceed to the next river, and from thence in a boat, barring disappointment. George Lichliter, my driver, has been kind and very attentive. Distance today eighteen miles, and fare thus far $5.00. Roads boggy in places.

Mar. 21. I am now at the California Ranch, kept by Messrs. Evans and Davis, and find a very companionable man in the person of my namesake, Mr. R. E[vans]. They set a very excellent table, and Uncle Dick, as we all call him, is a man six feet, six inches in height, well proportioned, and full of fun and anecdote. Dr. Riley, whom I expected to meet here, has not yet come in, and I am anxiously waiting for him, at an expense of $4.50 per day. The day has been warm, but clouds are showing their heads in rainy quarters.

Mar. 22. Here I am, still seeking an opportunity of getting down. Riley has not yet got in, and were it not for Uncle Dick I would almost die of ennui. No rain this day, but strong indications for the future.

Mar. 23. On awaking this morning I heard the heavy drops of a warm shower falling upon the roof of our canvas hotel. Birds were warbling their morning praises in sweet notes, and although [the sky was] cloudy, these sounds were cheering. No means of getting off yet. At noon a small train came along and in company with Judge Inghram and Daniel Triplett, moved down the banks of the Merced River ten miles and encamped at Scott's Ranch.

Mar. 24 (Sunday) Left this ranch early, and at noon crossed the Tuolumne River and at night encamped on the north side of the Stanislaus River, at Cotton's Ranch, having traveled thirty-six miles over a country full of beauty.

Mar. 25. Left Cotton's Ranch early, and after twenty-five miles' travel reached the public house of Lebarn and Company at the French Camp, five miles from the town of Stockton. I have been much relieved in this journey by Messrs. Inghram and Triplett, and am indebted to them for all the opportunities of riding. Here we leave our mules and proceed to Stockton in the morning by water.

Mar. 26. Started in a small boat propelled by oars, and, after a journey of three hours through the Tulares, arrived safely at Stockton and "put up" at the Branch House, where we had the best the market affords for $1.00 per meal. The steamer "Mint" came in this evening.

Mar. 27. Business prevented our leaving on the "Mint" this morning, and the "Captain Sutter" comes in this evening. We have therefore deferred going. Accompanied by Dr. Ward, of Stockton, I visited the fashionable gambling houses, where "piles" of dust and dollars were displayed upon every hand; and here a new and novel sight presented itself—women were betting, but I am proud to say that but one of these was an American.

Mar. 28. Precisely at 8:00 A.M. the steamer "Captain Sutter" whistled up her passengers, and the lines cast off and we glided down the Stockton Slough, and in a short time found ourselves on the waters of the San Joaquin River. At 8:00 P.M. we touched the wharf at San Francisco.[3]

Mar. 29. Waked up in the city, and a breakfast on shore after the beautiful scenery of yesterday served to render satisfaction. Much has been said of this city, and much remains to be said, but it also belongs to some other pen to say it. Should I enter into a full and perfect description of the city today, six months hence and my saying would be a misrepresentation;

[3]For descriptions of riotous San Francisco during the gold-rush period see Frank Soulé, John H. Gihon, and James Nisbet, *The Annals of San Francisco* (1855); Hubert Howe Bancroft, *History of California* (1886-90) and *California Inter Pocula*. There is also an excellent chapter in Robert G. Cleland, *A History of California: The American Period* (1927).

and for these and other reasons I shall not say anything today, only that I have not received a letter from home yet.

Mar. 30. The Democrats hold a convention and the Jack Hays party go in procession. At 2:00 P.M. a large assemblage of the friends of Jack Hays, the Texas Hero, took place in Portsmouth Square, and several speeches were made. At 7:30 P.M. the Democrats took the field, and after marching in torchlight procession were addressed by Colonel Holt and John W. Weller of Ohio, and, that over, the parties declared themselves ready for the election, which takes place on Monday, April first. The officers to be chosen are for the county, from judge of the courts down to assessors. The contest is, however, wholly waged upon the strength of the candidates for sheriff. Townes is the Whig nominee, Colonel J. J. Bryant, Democrat[ic] nominee, Colonel Jack Hays, Independent nominee.[4]

Mar. 31 (Sunday) Church bells calling the flock to the house of worship, and at the same time the gambling houses are opening their morning ceremonies—and thus the day of rest is passed in the city of San Francisco. I am now boarding at a house kept by several Chinese, and, should I become better acquainted with their manners and customs, I will attempt a description. One thing I can say in advance, they are good cooks and set excellent tables—charges, $1.00 per meal. I mailed, per steamer "California,"[5] a letter to my wife, one to General O. Evans, and one for J. W. Goodson, of Belleview, Ohio.

[4]For an account of this campaign, see Soulé, Gihon, and Nisbet, *Annals of San Francisco*, pp. 269-72.

[5]See Victor M. Berthold, *The Pioneer Steamer California* (1932).

❴ April, 1850 ❵

SAN FRANCISCO

Apr. 1. Day dawned, and with it came the mighty rush for the several wards of the city; banners and our own noble stripes and stars were flung to the breeze, and at 8:00 A.M. Pourts̄mouth Square was at times nearly jammed with the multitude seeking access to the ballot box. The contest thickened, and at an early hour the friends of Colonel Bryant gave up all hopes of his being the first sheriff of San Francisco. The gallant Hays bore down all opposition, and at the close of the polls was nearly a thousand votes ahead of all opposition. Whenever the Colonel made his appearance, shouts long and loud went up. Townes, the Whig candidate, scarcely touched bottom, and Bryant was not much ahead of him. About sunset one or two fights took place, and with this the great contest ended, and the judges sealed up and went off to count the votes.

Apr. 2. Weather milder, and were it not for the cold sea breeze, this would be a pleasant climate. The precise result of the election of yesterday has not yet been ascertained, only as to the shrievalty. Hays is sheriff by about nine hundred majority. The vote is large, over four thousand having been cast in this city, and the judges are still engaged in counting (now 8:30 P.M.).

I had appointed to meet Henry L. Dodge, Esq.,[1] this evening and am compelled to say that I did not find him at his office, business of more importance having detained him. My Chinese host has taken a notion to go to the mines this week, in consequence of the continued pressure in business here. A sensible reaction has already commenced. The price of real estate is going down, and lots are now bought for the amount they rented

[1]Probably H. L. Dodge, a Vermonter who came to California during the gold rush and became prominent in San Francisco business and civic affairs. He was clerk of the court and council in 1849-50, and later became superintendent of the mint. See Bancroft, *History of California*, VII, 168 n.

for two years ago. Men who were regarded as immensely wealthy a short time ago are now insolvent, and one attempt at suicide has resulted from this inflation. When this convulsion in trade has once taken place and things have, like water, found their level, then, and not till then, will a safe business be transacted in this new portion of our glorious Union. But until this mighty moving mass has become permanent, and the wholesome laws already adopted are fully recognized by the people, there will be no stability in trade, and California speculators must expect to be subject to disappointment.

Apr. 3. This morning I had the honor of an interview with Colonel James H. Collier of Ohio, collector of customs for this port, and I was much pleased with this gentleman and the prompt measures he adopted to enforce the strict observance of our revenue laws. He is kind and affable in his deportment, and makes a person at once "feel at home" when in his presence. Any and all infractions of the law, or the onerous duties of his office, are met with promptness and the penalties inflicted whenever found necessary. Gambling is carried to an excess in this city. Monte tables and heavy banks are found in every public house and these are closely followed by the multitude. The Empire Hotel is constantly crowded and few houses are found set out with richer furniture and paintings than may now be seen in this city. The population is composed of men and women of almost every clime, and is fast thinning out by an almost constant movement towards the mines; consequently, there are many houses empty, and it may safely be said that one half of the city is now offered for sale or rent. But business is still very brisk, and the winter's accumulation of gold at the mines is just beginning to come in. The steamer "California"[2] sailed on Monday evening with a full load of passengers and a very large amount

[2]See John Haskell Kemble, "The Genesis of the Pacific Mail Steamship Company," California Historical Society *Quarterly*, XIII (1934), 240-54, 386-406, and "The Panama Route to the Pacific Coast, 1848-1869," *Pacific Historical Review*, VII (1938), 1-13.

of gold. Adams and Company[3] sent from their Exchange House nearly $200,000 of the riches of these hills and gulches, and at the same time similar shipments were made by Burgoine and Company and other houses. I shall probably make preparations tomorrow to return to Stockton, and possibly as far south as the Tuolumne River diggings.

Apr. 4. Agreeably to appointment, I met Colonel Collier at 9:00 A.M. at his office and was immediately sworn in as inspector for the harbor of San Francisco, and in an hour afterwards I was introduced on board of the bark "Minerva," lying out in the Bay, as a customhouse officer, clothed with full power over every article on board. I am still on board, and have thus far met with kindness from all on board, and have the prospect of remaining here several days to come, commanded not to leave the vessel at any time until the cargo is all discharged or until ordered to do so at headquarters. My situation is far more pleasant to me than on shore and the fare is equally good, and this seeming imprisonment is acceptable.

Apr. 5. Pleasant morning, although cloudy. About 11:00 A.M. the wind freshened up, blowing from the west, and the noble little "Minerva" began to exhibit her airy form, and to grace the city with her nodding salutations. At 2:00 P.M. the bay became rough and up to this hour we are kept in a bounding motion, although at anchor about a mile from the city. A scene full of excitement to a "landlubber" took place this afternoon. As soon as the wind began to blow, a fleet composed of ships, barks, and brigs came driving into the harbor, several completely loaded with passengers. The sloop of war "Plymouth" anchored near Goat Island, and two large Hamburg ships took stations near the "Minerva." A Yankee who was one of the first to let go his anchor had scarcely furled his sails before a large ship came up with sails spread, intending to stop near by, and when in the act of rounding came so close under the Yankee's stern as to carry away his yawl and some of his yards, and almost dis-

[3]See Winther, *op. cit.*, for an account of the Adams stage and express lines.

mantling his little craft. The ship received but little damage, but moved farther up before she let go her anchor. Among the vessels in today I recollect the name of the Hamburg ships, "Elizabeth" and "Anna." Considerable rain has fallen during the afternoon and the wind is still blowing into the harbor very heavy.

Apr. 6. Cloudy and damp, with wind still blowing off. At 6:00 A.M., being the hour of slack water, our captain came off and the work of mooring ship was commenced, and at 8:00 we had again dropped anchor, within pistol shot of the dock, and were ready for the discharge of cargo. My duties now commenced, and baggage of passengers was examined. I found some contraband articles and sent the owner on shore to clear before landing.

Apr. 7 (Sunday)   The hatches having been unsealed and opened, and no locks with which to secure them, I was compelled to stay on board this day—not much against my will, for it rained nearly all day. The mate, a clever fellow, and myself hung out some hooks and lines over the stern and caught a young shark, measuring nearly four feet in length. The rascal's mouth, young as he was, exhibited a strong set of teeth, and several rows of them. Nothing of interest passing in the city. The "Vandalia," Captain Gardner, sloop of war, came in yesterday, instead of the "Plymouth," as above stated. The weather continues wet and stormy.

Apr. 8.   The clouds have passed away, and the vessels are all engaged in drying canvas. Many have and are almost hourly coming into port and the customhouse officers are constantly on the move. We discharged from the "Minerva" today 125 bags of flour, containing 100 lbs. each, besides passengers and baggage. Captain Tucker spends nearly all the time on shore, coming off to meals. We shipped a new cook, and gave him charge of the shark, and he has promised us a meal from his lordship's sides this evening. Wind blowing into the harbor at a stiff breeze. I am getting better of my scurvy every day; my cold upon the lungs is also easing off, and I am inclined to believe my appointment to be the best thing that could have taken place in my present situation.

.Apr. 9. Mild and pleasant day. At 10:00 A.M. a large lighter came alongside and we commenced discharging flour. Four hundred bags of flour were loaded, and one hundred bags of barley, and we have the promise of more of the same kind of work for tomorrow.

Apr. 10. The day opened clear and warm, and at flood tide, the lighters were alongside, and in them we sent off two hundred bags of flour. Our hooks and lines were also in luck, and we caught two fine shark, and after having got them on deck they were placed in the hands of the cook with orders to dress and prepare for the tea. This gentleman, who is an indispensable on board, severed the heads—jaws, teeth and all—from their bodies, and opened their paunches, from one of which he took seven young sharks—one of which was immediately transferred to the water, and as quickly disappeared beneath its surface, showing every qualification to take care of himself, even if "his anxious Ma did not know he was out." After we got through discharging flour a spacious awning was spread, and under its cool shade, with book in hand, I passed the day pleasantly. Of books there are many on board, and I have not, since leaving home, spent time more pleasantly than on board of the "Minerva." Captain T. remains on board this evening.

Apr. 11. Early this morning our late captain and mate were paid off, and although [we were] sorry to lose the company of these men their places have been supplied by the appointment of Mr. Harvey L. Casswell, a man who is in the full sense of the term a gentleman. As soon as he came aboard as Captain Casswell, the men before the mast were instructed to obey his orders, and the immediate answer was "Aye, Aye, Sir." Sailor's discipline produces this answer. Every order is promptly obeyed, and with seeming desire on the part of men before the mast to outdo each other in its execution.

Apr. 12. Weather cool, with some wind. A heavy fog

bank is gradually extending itself into the bay, through the *Golden Gates*,⁴ and indicates a curtain without, through which the stoutest and most daring seaman will not venture his vessel but had rather stand "off and on" until the wind shall cause the fog to rise or disperse. At 11:00 A.M., on casting my eyes over the shipping in the harbor, I discovered the cross of St. George and many of the Stars and Stripes floating at half mast, indicative of the death of someone in the harbor. Death finds us everywhere; yet there was solemnity in this scene, in this display of colors, such as is seldom felt on the mere announcement of its occurrence in [a] community. There we are generally informed of our neighbor's illness; here nothing is known until the flags at half mast inform us that a fellow being has been released from sickness and pain and now lies cold and motionless in yonder ship.

Apr. 13. Morning dawned clear, and warmer than yesterday. Yesterday and today a material increase of water was perceptible, being high or neap tide, and the currents setting in and out of the bay are much increased in velocity. No part of our cargo discharged today. Another death occurred this afternoon from diarrhea. This evening the sea breeze brought upon its wings a heavy fog and the shipping in the harbor is enveloped in this curtain of mist, which is damp. I was visited this afternoon by a brother officer now stationed on board of the brig "Chili." After an hour's pleasant conversation he departed and I went to tea.

Apr. 14 (Sunday). Day raw and rather unpleasant. At 12:00 M. the loud-mouthed cannon announced the approach of the steamer, and on looking out we saw the "Tennessee"⁵ gliding into the harbor, her decks covered with a multitude of human beings. She brought over three hundred passengers and all the mail now due. I am happy to say that my health is much improved. I devote all my unoccupied time to reading and thinking

⁴"Name of the entrance to this bay"—Evans' note.

⁵The "Tennessee" was a $300,000 Pacific Mail steamer; she went down off San Francisco in 1853—the company's one great disaster during the early years of its existence.

of those so dear to me; and although in the full enjoyment of everything desirable (excepting the companionship of my loved ones) there is still a strong desire to revisit my *home*, to mingle once more in their society, and to dream of dangers past, and look back upon the past as upon matters of no importance and just such as everyone must expect to encounter who takes it into his head to go campaigning. To the arrival of that happy moment I look forward with renewed interest.

Apr. 15. The wind has been blowing hard all day and withal quite cool. The climate here is not as pleasant as in the gold region, being warm, sometimes hot and sultry, from sunrise to 10:00 A.M., when the sea breeze sets in and at this time (4:00 P.M) makes overcoats and firesides pleasant companions. An order from the consignees of this vessel came off for the whole of the flour on board, and a few days more will end my sojourn here, and I shall probably be placed in charge of some other vessel, and compelled to form new acquaintances and brought in connection with new associations. Such are the ways of man, guided by the hand of God and impelled by destiny.

Apr. 16. Coffee served at six, and 8:00 A.M. breakfasted. Launches alongside early, and at sunset we had discharged 695 sacks of flour, making now nearly half of the cargo out. Tomorrow they have promised to take the remainder, and then I shall probably go aboard of some other vessel. Received a paper, off [ship], containing a list of passengers, but my friend Tellign did not arrive as expected.

Apr. 17. Warm until 10:00 A.M. and then wind arose to a perfect gale. Only fifty sacks of flour discharged today. Another death announced by flags at half mast.

Apr. 18. High wind, and very chilly. Discharged 470 sacks flour and spent the evening writing to brother Frank.

Apr. 19. Cool and windy weather, with occasional showers of rain. Discharged 366 bags of flour and barley, and one day more will complete my labor on board of the "Minerva." The ship "Architect" came up this morning, forty-seven days from

Valpirazo, with flour and lumber. She is truly "a model of a ship" and employs twenty-five sailors exclusive of her officers. Few ships can cope successfully with the "Architect" for speed.

Apr. 20. No cargo discharged this day and all hands were set at work stowing empty water pipes below, after which the decks were cleanly washed down and everything put in readiness for the Sabbath.

Weather moderately warm, affording much comfort to those on board of vessels. Captain Caswell announced that we would be visited on tomorrow by ladies and gentlemen of his acquaintance, and the steward immediately set to work to provide a good dinner for the occasion.

Apr. 21 (Sunday). Beautiful, clear, and bland morning. Coffee was served a moment after leaving our beds and 8:00 A.M. breakfast was announced. At 1:00 P.M. the Captain was seen coming off in the long boat with his visitors and a few moments after they stepped on deck, dinner was announced, and we adjourned to the cabin. After being seated soup (macaroni) was first served, then came John Bull's delight, a handsome cut of roast beef. The next was macaroni custard, followed at short intervals by a cut of the best fruit pie and nuts, accompanied with bumpers of port wine, and the whole dinner closed with a general smoke—gentlemen of cigars, and the ladies *cigarettos*. These visitors were Spaniards[6] of superior breeding and this was but the second time during my long journey that accident brought me into the society of Spanish ladies, and for both occasions I can say that they exhibited by their general conduct a perfect knowledge of the rules of etiquette. With this visit I confess myself perfectly satisfied, and if time and opportunity permit will call in answer to their pressing invitation to that effect. These visitors are Chileans[7] by birth, but cheerfully drank a bumper to "long live the Union of States." An hour after dinner, and a cup of coffee was served; after which the guests of our Captain departed to their homes and I was left to pen this

[6]Latin-Americans.   [7]Evans wrote "Chilianians."

memorandum of pleasant events once met with in California. Nothing was wanting to heighten the pleasure but the presence of my own little family, and a perfect knowledge of the Spanish tongue.

Apr. 22. Beautiful weather and but little wind. Spent this day in reading and the unbounded pleasures of writing to my wife.

Apr. 23. Clear and pleasant morning. The consignee of this vessel came on board this morning and tomorrow will take with it, in all probability, the last of her cargo. At 11:00 A.M. the wind came off, and during the afternoon and evening blew a perfect gale. Six or eight vessels have come in, from various parts of the world, in the past few days.

Apr. 24. Pleasantly warm during the forenoon, but had another stiff blow landwards, which winds are cool and very unpleasant.

Contrary to expectation, the launch failed to come off, and the remainder of our cargo still remains on board; and this sufficiently accounts for my being still on board of the "Minerva." The "Greyhound," another splendid ship, came in with a large complement of passengers from Panama. The steamer "Panama" is also in the harbor and leaves again on the first of May. She also brought a full load of persons in anxious search after fortunes. I finished my letters to my family and brother Frank, and hope to get on shore tomorrow.

Apr. 25. Pleasant weather, with lighter wind than usual. Wrote to William Rush Evans.

Apr. 26. This forenoon a small sloop came alongside, and in a few hours the last of the "Minerva's" cargo was discharged and I made immediate preparations and went on shore. My first visit was to the post office, and I had a letter handed me, and having found a quiet corner proceeded to open the letter, not doubting for a moment the handwriting and from whom it came. Judge, then, my surprise when I found it dated St. Louis, Missouri, and signed by a Miss Henry, with whom I

283

never have had the slightest acquaintance. I could scarcely credit my own eyesight—I thought it a dream of the most tormenting kind—but was compelled to acknowledge that it did not *mean me*, and having carefully sealed and returned it, I hastened from [the post office] with feelings of bitter disappointment such as I had never yet experienced. I then wandered into the office of Adams and Company and left in their care, for transmission to New York, eighteen ounces and eleven pennyweights of dust— proceeds to be sent home by draft—also one pound for my friend M. F. Barber. This done, I felt a relief from a great measure of responsibility. Also sent letters to White and Barnes relative to the gold, and one to my wife. God in mercy grant that the steps taken to secure its safe delivery may be successful. I also made out my final report to the customhouse, and again go on shore in the morning for further orders. What is to follow I cannot even guess at now.

Apr. 27. After breakfast went on shore and reported myself at the customhouse and was immediately ordered on duty. I was placed in charge of the British bark "Change" of Panama. Judge of my very agreeable surprise on meeting with Dr. John M. Fletcher and Dr. Lewis of Fort Wayne, Indiana. This meeting gave me sincere pleasure and I felt as if once more among men with whom I had met before. M. F. Barber, our old acquaintance at the mines, also called, and after a short conversation with these old friends, I proceeded to the discharge of the baggage of 129 passengers. The evening I passed with Dr. F. and at bedtime retired to rest, gratified and thankful for these events.

Apr. 28 (Sunday). All the passengers gone but Dr. F., and we have spent the day pleasantly. The wind has been very high all day, but served to bring into port several vessels. The day cold and the ship kept rolling.

Apr. 29. This has been one of those cold, stormy days without any comfort excepting the arrival of the "Goldhunter" steamer this afternoon. Such arrivals are comforts because here is another opportunity to hear from home.

Apr. 30. No mail per steamer "Goldhunter," and, having ascertained this fact and discharged cargo from the "Change," I made my report, and was immediately transferred to the American brig "Oniota," Captain Keene, all from Philadelphia, Pennsylvania, originally, but now from Chili with an assorted cargo. I was taken with the dysentery today, and am using every means to check it.

{ May, 1850 }

TO SACRAMENTO AND BACK
BY RIVER

May 1. Orders came off today for my appearance at the customhouse, and after reaching that place was ordered to proceed with the brig to Sacrimento City and to remain on board at that city until all the cargo is discharged. I pocketed my instructions and proceeded on board and tomorrow we sail for that city. My disease is not yet entirely hushed, but have laid in some medicines for this dangerous disease.

May 2. At 1:00 P.M. the pilot came on board, the anchor hove short, and sail made when we swung into the bay and headed off for the bay of "San Pablo," or St. Paul. Having a fair wind, we sailed onward rapidly and passed the steamer "William Robinson" bound to Stockton, soon after which we entered the straits of Benecia and rounding the point, came at once in full view of this naval depot. Here we found the frigate "Savannah," the sloops of war "Preble" and "Warren" at anchor. Without halting we entered Suisun Bay and at dusk came in sight of the city of New York[1] and its shipping, and soon after ran aground in two fathoms of water, the brig drawing twelve feet three inches. All sail taken in, and consequently we rest here; fifty-five miles today.

May 3. This morning we found ourselves a short distance below the entrance or mouth of the Sacrimento River,

[1]Another argonaut in November of 1849 wrote: "New York on the Pacific now has three houses and is situated at the junction of the San Joaquin and Sacramento rivers. A large plain is in the rear of a rich prairie soil back to the mountains or rolling hills a mile or two from the shore; there are seven square-rigged vessels lying here aground and are used only to eat and lodge in. It may be a place of great importance but it hardly looks like it at present." ("Diary of Nelson Kingsley, a California Argonaut of 1849," *Publications* of the Academy of Pacific Coast History, III [No. 3; 1914], 88, 322.) See also James L. Tyson, *Diary of a Physician in California* (1850), p. 54.

having about two fathoms of water for about 150 yards astern, proving that we had taken ground several minutes before the vessel stopped. The kedge anchor was got out but did not hold and then the larboard anchor was taken out and long hawsers rove on and we waited for the high tide at 7:00 P.M. At that hour the windlass was put in requisition and shortly after the brig gradually went astern, much to the satisfaction of all on board. An hour's work and the brig was lying in three fathoms of water, and ready for the morning's wind.

May 4. Beautiful and warm morning, but no wind, and we lay quietly at anchor until noon when the wind sprang up and we weighed and stood up stream. The brig made slow progress and I had constant opportunities of looking over the adjoining country from the rigging. This river is a beautiful stream, studded with various small islands and the banks lined with a growth of small but bushy trees. The depth of the channel varies from two to seven fathoms. The wind lulled at 8 o'clock and we cast anchor near the mouth of Cash [Cache] Creek, a tributary of the Rio Sacrimento.

May 5 (Sunday). Day warm and pleasant but no wind until noon. The timber growing on the banks broke the wind and we made but little progress, passing, however, all the shoals and now have deep water to sail in. We are now entering a slough or cutoff, saving about twenty miles of travel. Mosquitoes are somewhat troublesome. By a small schooner from the bay, we were informed of an extensive fire at San Francisco on night before last, which is reported to have destroyed a large portion of the city. This conflagration originated upon the same ground as did that of last winter and has laid in ruins nearly the same portion of the city.[2]

May 6. Began "warping," a term used by sailors, and sig-

[2]This was commonly known as the "Second Great Fire," and occurred in the early morning hours of May 4. It consumed three blocks of buildings in the area between DuPont, Jackson, Montgomery, and Clay streets and caused great damage. The first fire Evans refers to occurred on December 24, 1849. See *Annals of San Francisco*, pp. 274-75.

nifies pulling by ropes, and our progress has been painfully slow. We are now nearly through the slough which is six miles in length, and the bordering land on both sides wholly submerged and covered with tules—a species of "flag." It is amusing to hear Captain K. giving orders, contrasting his pronunciation of words with our own. As an instance I will transcribe some of the terms found in the mariner's vocabulary. "Forty-gallon mas" for foretop gallant mast, "men mas"—forty royal—"clew lin" besides the various names for the thousand and one ropes composing a ship's rigging. "For sal," "men sal" are terms used to denote foresail and mainsail. The distance for today will not exceed six miles, with constant and hard work.

May 7. Weather pleasant, and after a hard day's work arrived near the upper end of the slough. Land still in a submerged condition.

May 8. The wind was favorable this morning and at 9:00 A.M. we found ourselves at the river and at 11:00 A.M. we were sailing again upon this beautiful stream. At the junction of the slough and river there are several "squatters," who have laid claim to the only high land in that vicinity, and several of their houses were entirely surrounded by water. As we passed up, several more new farms opened to our view and the land became higher and the timber (oak) better. At 1:00 P.M. we were again in sight of the snow-capped Sierra Nevada. Wind fell at sunset and we again let go our anchor.

May. 9. Warm and pleasant morning, and no wind. At 11:00 A.M. it freshened up and we made all sail upon the brig [and] at 2:00 P.M. had passed through the "Devil's Reach"— so called on account of the difficulty met with by vessels. The river here turns west southwest, and the wind almost dead ahead, but [it] being strong, we passed without the necessity of warping. This accomplished, we made good progress, and during the afternoon passed several neat little farms and the town of Sutter's ville, located on the east bank, and contains probably a population of fifty souls. At 8 o'clock we let go our anchor at the foot of "K" Street, Sacramento City, in front of the Sutter House, from which issued the sounds of sweet music by a brass band. Shipping lines the whole front of this new but important business city of California, and everything wears an aspect of thrift, although the city is but a very few inches higher than the surface of the river at this time.[3]

May 10. Pleasant weather and steamboats coming and going. Among those from below were the "Senator," "McCim," and "Eldorado," and the "Yuba," "Lawrence," and "Excelsior" from the upper-river navigation. All these gave a business appearance to this city and a daylight view of the place confirmed my first favorable impression. This is decidedly a business point and one of interest to the various settlements in the upper or northern diggings, but is at present subject to overflow from the river. This the city is guarding against by the speedy erection of a levee.

During the afternoon we moored on the left bank of the river, where a new town, known as Washington City, has been laid out and promises to become a place of some note. Here the banks are higher, free from inundation. From this point we have a view of the mouth of the American fork of this river, which empties its waters just at the upper limits of Sacrimento City. This stream has the appearance of being narrow and is not navigated by any of the steamers.

[3]Sacramento City was a busy place during the gold rush, and was already assuming metropolitan characteristics. Statements of two travelers follow: "Sacramento City, at the period of which I write [1849], contained a floating population of about five thousand people. It was first laid out in the spring of 1849, on the east bank of the Sacramento River, here less than one-eighth of a mile wide, and is about a mile and a half west of Sutter's Fort. Lots were originally sold for $200 each, but within a year sales were made as high as $30,000. There were not a dozen wood or frame buildings in the whole city, but they were chiefly made of canvas, stretched over light supporters; or were simply tents, arranged along the streets. The stores, like the dwellings, were of cloth, and property and merchandise of all kinds lay exposed, night and day, by the wayside, and such a thing as a robbery was scarcely known. This in fact was the case throughout the country, and is worthy of notice on account of the great and extraordinary change which occurred. There were a vast number of taverns and eating houses, and the only public building was a theatre. All these were made of canvas.

"At all of the hotels and groceries, gambling was carried on to a remarkable

May 11. Very warm, and much annoyed by mosquitoes in the evening. In the afternoon the public had an opportunity of attending the "Circus" of Rowe and Company.

May 12 (Sunday). Continued warm weather. The music of every variety of instruments is heard emanating from the various gambling houses of the city.

May 13. Sun shone hot but [we] were much relieved by a gentle breeze which lasted throughout the day. The first steam ferryboat commenced her regular trips, plying between Washington and Sacramento cities. She is a scow with engine attached to each wheel, and answers a good purpose.

May 14. Still warm. The past night was less oppressive and the mosquitoes less troublesome. The new steamer "Gold Hunter," left here this morning for San Francisco and the propeller "Hartford" has just arrived with a large load of passengers. As an evidence of the increased attention to agriculture, I will state that a large number of cattle and sheep have been crossed on the new ferryboat and destined for the farms in this region. Lettuce, radishes, onions, and other products of the garden make

extent, and men seemed to be perfectly reckless of money. Indeed, it seemed to have lost its value, and piles of coin and dust covered every table, and were constantly changing hands at the turn of a card.

"At high water the river overflows its banks, and a notice of a dreadful disaster of this kind will appear hereafter. For a mile along the river lay ships, barges, and various water craft, laden with merchandise and provisions. Trade was brisk, and prices exorbitantly high.

"On the north side of the city is a large and deep slough, in which cattle frequently mire and perish, and at this time the effluvia arising from their putrid carcasses was almost insufferable. A little beyond the slough the American River empties into the Sacramento. This river is not navigable for vessels. The Sacramento River, though affected by the tide, is pure and sweet, and generally is better to drink than the water of the wells, some of which are slightly brackish." Alonzo Delano, *Across the Plains and Among the Diggings* (1936), pp. 109-10.

"Stages run regularly to the mines; steamboats run on the river; a theatre, church and several large handsome hotels with billiard saloons and bowling alleys and all the fixings, have been put up. Even a couple of girls are around with a hand organ and tambourine. Civilization is making rapid strides. . . . I like the climate situation and the people here first rate and I believe it is bound to *blaze*. This and San Francisco will be *the places* in California.

"The city is laid out one mile square. The streets 80 feet wide, crossing each their daily appearance in this market. The business routine of this city is about the same on each day. The ringing of auction bells and the outcry of the auctioneer, interspersed with the music of the various bands, and an occasional fight, are the only things which break the monotony of the warm days we are doomed to pass. Wrote and sent a letter to the office yesterday, directed home, having been under the impression that a mail would go with the steamer of the fifteenth, which is, however, not the case.

May 15. A little warmer than usual. By the "Gold Hunter" we learn that an accident happened to the machinery of the "Senator" on her downward trip which will keep her out of the line a few days.

May 16. Very warm and nothing new. No cargo discharged yet and some time will yet elapse 'ere I will return to duty on the bay. The mines are yet under water and must remain so for several months in consequence of the heavy fall of snow in the mountains.

May 17. Not quite so warm as yesterday. Thermometer yesterday stood at 90° in the shade. Nothing of consequence has taken place today.

May 18. Cool wind blowing up stream and the small

---

other at right angles. They have spared most of the noble white oaks that line the banks of the river so the streets are all set out with trees full grown. The streets are lettered up from the river: A, B, C, etc., and numbered parallel with it: 1st, 2nd, 3rd, etc. We are on H Street, between 5th and 6th. Right below our store is one of the most busy scenes you ever saw. It is a large livery stable where they sell horses, mules, oxen and carts at auction. The auctioneer gets on the animal and rides him up and down the street, shows him off to the best advantage and frequently four or five are selling at once. Such a Babel of sounds! There is always a large crowd and some rare sport. You know I always liked riding on horseback and if I only had time I could have enough of it here. We bought a fine riding horse for $109 at auction, bought from the Snake Indians with saddle, bridle, spurs alone six inches long, all complete. Everyone rides on horseback as carriages are scarce.

"Out of the town the country is one level prairie, a grand chance to ride. . . . Out about two miles stands Sutters Fort, quite a large establishment." Franklin A. Buck, *A Yankee Trader in the Gold Rush*, ed. Katherine A. White (1930), pp. 51-52.

sloops laden with provisions are moving out of port at all hours. The "El Dorado," "Hartford," and "Gold Hunter" steamers left this city for San Francisco and the "Lawrence," "Yuba," and others came down. I am now engaged in writing home, a package to be sent by next steamer.

May 19 (Sunday). Beautiful weather and warm. Thermometer at 80° during the day and usually at 60° at night. Finished my package to my family, containing 512 lines of written matter, and averaging a few over six thousand words.

May 20. This morning we once more moored ship and we are now lying at the foot of J Street, Sacramento City. Business tolerably lively. Tomorrow we commence discharging cargo and I hope and expect to get back to San Francisco in time for the departure of the mail.

May 21. The "Gold Hunter" left here this morning and the propeller "Hartford" came up, with many passengers and bundles of New York and New Orleans papers, all of which sold freely at $1.00 each. We began discharging cargo and Captain K. purchased a small sloop at $800 which he calls "Emma," after his wife. She is intended for the up-river trade.

May 22. Not so warm as yesterday, and we discharged 1,671 sacks of flour, and in the evening enjoyed a short walk and then a look at Bennett's *New York Herald*.

May 23. Discharged today 1,803 sacks [of] flour and 107 bags of barley. Weather pleasant and business lively. We expect to accomplish the final discharge of the brig's cargo on tomorrow.

May 24. Discharged today 590 sacks flour, 263 sacks barley, and 810 boards. There is yet another day's work on the cargo, and I will not get away from here until Sunday.

May 25. At 10:00 A.M. we had accomplished the final discharge of all our cargo, and I made out my account of all labor and dues from the brig "Oniota," preparatory to leaving for San Francisco on the steamer "Hartford" tomorrow. I have made acquaintance on this brig long to be remembered on account of its pleasantness, much enhanced by the very gentlemanly deportment of Captain Keene, C. W. Bewley, and G. R. Burton.

May 26 (Sunday). Bade the "gude folks" goodby, and at 6:00 A.M. the "Hartford" was making rapid progress down the Sacramento River. On board I found a pleasant company, one of whom was Mr. Bartlett of Lagrange, Indiana, now on his return home. I gave him a letter to my mother-in-law, and he promised to call on my family as soon as he reached home. At the hour of sunset we landed at San Francisco and I took lodging at the Bay Hotel, a quiet and pleasant retreat. This hotel is kept in the hull of an old ship moored along the banks and is neatly arranged and well kept. The bar is kept by a Mrs. Miller, a lady of some beauty and remarkable taste in dress.

May 27. Reported at the customhouse and, this over, I was ordered to go on board of a vessel, the "Le Monde" from Guiequail,[4] and as a matter of course obeyed. By this order I was deprived of calling at the postoffice and am still lamenting the absence of letters from home. Out of a crew of fifteen men there is but one who speaks the English language, they being French and Ecuadorians. The mate, and a young gentleman who is interested in this ship,[5] are the only persons who can speak a word of English and the following conversation with the mate will enable the reader to judge of the perfection to which they have attained. I observed some hens walking over the deck, and remarked that, they seemed very tame. "Oui, sir, ver tam ver. Vat you call von cook? no! me no mean cook, vat you call—ah—ze husband of ze hen." "Oh! " I replied, "We call him in English, Cock!" "Oui sir, ze cock—ze husband of ze hen." I could not repress a laugh, and this conversation will do as a parallel to that told of the "mayor," the "vife of the horse."

May 28. This day has passed as usual, warm in the morning with cold and strong wind during the afternoon. No cargo discharged, which consists of lumber and will not sell for more than first cost.

---

[4]Guayaquil.   [5]Probably the supercargo.

May 29. Cool day and less wind than yesterday. Tomorrow the mail closes, and my correspondence is now ready for delivery.

May 30. Very windy all day and cloudy. Wrote to sister Lucy and mailed a copy of the *Pacific News* to Cornelia. Once more my heart aches with disappointment, having received no letters per the "Oregon," arrived the twenty-first instant from Panama. This is truly inexplicable, and brings no consolation with it. I doubt not they think me dead.

May 31. This month is now about to be numbered with the past, and it has thus far had but one or two green spots in it for me. By the sailing of the "Panama" on the first instant, I sent home a little over $300, and lived in the gladdening hope of being able to transmit $200 more by the steamer "Oregon" on tomorrow. But this consolation is denied me. The great mail closes today and our wages cannot be drawn until tomorrow, just one day too late to send treasure home by this steamer. 'Tis said that "to endure with patience is a virtue," but this is a little too much endurance.

The porpoise is paying us a visit in the bay, and may be seen floundering and plunging on every hand. Whilst lying at Sacramento City I saw many salmon weighing from five to twenty-five pounds. They are excellent, as I can well attest.

{ June, 1850 }

REMOVAL TO SACRAMENTO

June 1. The clouds dispersed early, and the sun's rays shed a more benign influence upon us shivering mortals than usual. This evening I was engaged in my usual occupation of pacing up and down the deck when I was suddenly aroused by the loud roar of a signal gun, and on looking up beheld the noble steamer "Oregon" just gliding from her berth and rounding off for the troubled waters of the sea. But hark! another loud, mounted cannon announces that she is off. As she glided by with her decks swarming with passengers, I fervently prayed, "God speed her, and may she carry joy and gladness to many anxious hearts." I kept my eyes fastened upon this noble vessel until she faded from view and had entered the Golden Gate, and with another fervent wish for her safety, I again resumed my usual promenade and fell into my usual melancholy train of thought, but consoled myself with the reflection that in twenty days another steamer, and perhaps letters, will arrive. Heaven grant it.

June 2 (Sunday). Did not leave this ship, although permitted to do so on the Sabbath under the regulations, and I passed the day under exceedingly depressed feelings. My thoughts were constantly of home and its endearing ties, and I could not shake off the dread of some misfortune attending my loved ones. How inestimable would a few lines of good news be at this time, what a load of care would they remove from this surcharged heart! Nearly sixteen months have I been noting my daily doings, and during that long and painful period I have not had a single letter from home. The wheel of fortune is turning backwards as to me.

June 3. Pleasant morning, with no wind to trouble the bay and nothing but "ground swell" perceptible in the water. The wind began blowing violently at the usual hour, and at

1:00 P.M. the waters of the bay were in a more perturbed state than I have ever seen them. The large porpoise could be seen in its apparently rotary motion on every hand. No cargo discharged today, and I am apprehensive that I may have to stay on board much longer than I desire. The people on this ship are kind and attentive, but their customs are so materially different from our own, that their kindness becomes burdensome. The cooks are slovenly, and our cabin boy spreads the table and passes the dishes with one hand, whilst the other is diligently and nimbly arousing the inhabitants of his hair or, in a more homely phrase, "stirring up the insects."

If the cooks would cultivate a greater regard for water and occasionally bathe their limbs in this purifying element, the result of their efforts to appease our appetites would be received with greater favor. Were they females, they would perhaps have more regard for water, but being Spanish boys, I am probably asking o'ermuch.

The captain and his officers are kind, generous, and cleanly in person and do not seem to regard things in the same light I do. I have said that their customs and our differ. Two meals a day are furnished in the cabin; breakfast at 8:00 A.M. and supper at 5:00 P.M. The breakfast consists of beefsteak and bread for the first course, wine is then drunk, and if any cold meat remains, it follows as the second. The plates are then all removed and a cup of coffee closes the first meal, one cup only.

Supper, a meal composed of, first, soup and boiled meats and bread and wine, followed by a cut of roast beef, and then the usual measure of coffee. These dishes follow each other at intervals allowing sufficient time for appetite to renew her strength and lay hold on the succeeding course with increased energy. Our dinner consists of what is embraced in the very comprehensive term of "lunch." Tea is a stranger who never appears on board.

June 4. This is the anniversary of the birth of my wife, and her portrait lies open before me almost speaking, almost breathing my name. Oh, how I love it, in my isolated condition—how inestimable the pleasure it affords—how pleasing to scan the features of absent loved ones, in their reflected images!

I received a call from J. T. Ackley, U. S. Appraiser of Customs, and he informed me that the citizens held an indignation meeting last night to give vent to their collected passion on account of the large salaries voted themselves by the city fathers. By this vote the mayor receives $10,000 per year and each alderman $6,000, which would "bleed" this young and healthy city freely in her infancy—a new practice for doctors to engage in.

June 5. The long expected steamer, "Sarak Sands," came into port this morning, with but a portion of her former number of passengers. Many of these had left her at some port down the coast and arrived here several weeks in advance of this very slow steamer. High wind blowing nearly the whole day. Several vessels have departed for foreign ports, expecting to return with a cargo of something for this market.

June 6. Discharged 13 barrels eggs, containing 500 dozen, sold for 75¢ per dozen. Also 18 cases sardines and 19 cases champagne. The propeller "Columbus," of Philadelphia, came into port this morning, with a large number of passengers. Several brigs, schooners, and barks have left port, most of them outward bound.

June 7. Windy day. A small propeller, said to be from New Orleans, took her departure from the bay and seemed to be destined for the Stockton trade. She outruns every other propeller now on the rivers and will be the favorite. Her name I did not learn. I had a short quarrel with the captain and mate, they contending that I am too strict in the enforcement of unnecessary rules and regulations. The only satisfaction I gave these French gentlemen was to tell them to "help themselves and be careful not to violate the law." The captain became very angry and I silently permitted him to utter his "sacrés" and his "futas," to his heart's content.

June 8. The captain has gone on shore, and the mate and

men are engaged in stowing lumber below. As soon as this is finished I shall put the hatches "under seal,'" and go on shore tomorrow. The steam propeller "Columbus" left this morning, outward bound.

June 9 (Sunday). Very warm, and no wind until 2:00 P.M. Several vessels departed with the first favorable breeze. The steamer "Gold Hunter" left for Mazatlan, San Blas, and of course, "intermediate ports." I sealed the hatches this morning but did not go ashore as contemplated. Tomorrow or day after, this vessel leaves port for Panama, an event clothed with pleasure to me, come when it will. The sailors are changing their old clothes for new, and consequently the lice are becoming more generally distributed, so much so, indeed, that I yesterday found them marching over our greasy cabin table. The utmost personal attention is requisite to keep myself free from this loathsome vermin.

June 10. Very warm, but enjoyed more breeze than yesterday. The hands are preparing the vessel for sea, and she will probably depart tomorrow, with the first favorable breeze. Joy go with her! I will not.

It appears that the "Gold Hunter" only went on an excursion of pleasure, as she is now again in her berth, and steam up for Sacramento City. She was advertised to sail and we may now safely conclude that advertisements mean nothing.

June 11. Warm in the morning, but heavy wind during the afternoon. Captain King, Assistant Inspector, came on board with orders for me to report, as the ship was now ready for sea. Tomorrow at 8:00 A.M. I leave her, conformably with this order. Wrote a letter of two full sheets to G. B. Way, judge of my own dear circuit. In this I gave him a limited and brief history of events, scenes, and doings in California. I have reason to believe that my present employment will end with tomorrow, as no vessels from foreign ports have come in for the past week, and should this prove to be the case, I am off for the diggings.

June 12. Reported at the customhouse and, as expected, I

was paid off with many others, and have now made arrangements to leave tomorrow for Sacramento City. Lodged with my old friend, Captain Tucker.

June 13. Gathered my matters into as small a compass as possible, and having bought a ticket for passage on the "Senator" ($25), at 4:00 P.M. I was fast leaving the scene of my past employment and once more launching out into unknown and untried ground, but full of hope and vastly improved in health, and therefore [I] felt better qualified to take this step. I have already described the scenery, towns, etc., along this route, and it is not necessary to say more to the reader than that we passed the wreck of the propeller "McKim," sunk in San Pablo Bay, near the Straits of Caraquinas, by coming in contact with the steamer "Gold Hunter" night before last. After being struck she went down in ten feet water in less than ten minutes; fortunately, no lives lost. The "McKim" had no lights up, and undertook to cross the bows of the "Hunter," instead of laying her course to the right of the "Hunter's" lights, and this error in judgment may be assigned as the cause of the collision.

June 14. This morning I found myself at daylight crawling from between the folds of my blankets, which I had spread upon the cabin floor of the "Senator" and which bed was shared with me by a Mr. Gray of New York City, whom I found a stranger just arrived in the country, and wholly unacquainted with the ways of California life. On leaving the cabin I found that we had arrived at Sacrimento City, and, in company of my friend [I] sallied out on a walk. After returning I crossed the river and was soon after once more shaking the hand and receiving a kind welcome from Captain Keene on the decks of the brig "Oniota." On board of this vessel I passed the day.

June 15. Passed the day between the brig and the city very pleasantly, but have not yet determined what course to pursue. Business I find very dull, and gold advancing.

June 16 (Sunday). Day warm but pleasant and passed on board the brig in company with Captains Keene and Thompson.

June 17. Received papers from San Francisco detailing the particulars of another very extensive conflagration by which another large portion of that devoted city has been reduced to ashes.[1] This is the third calamitous fire visited upon the city of the bay, and many are again cast upon the world in poverty who the day before rolled in wealth and opulence.

June 18. Pleasant weather, and have to note the return of Mr. Bewley, who has been to San Francisco and purchased a bark, and Captain K. goes in her to Chili. Preparations for his departure are now in progress, and tomorrow I lose the company of a friend.

June 19. Captain Keene left on the "Senator" and I am now occupying his place on the brig "Oniota," having been placed in full charge this morning at $100 per month. This day has been windy and there is quite a gale blowing this evening. Business is improving.

June 20. Called on by Captains Tucker and Flavell, and they stayed on board with me this night. Weather comfortably warm. Slept on deck, in consequence of the cabin having been painted.

June 21. Discharged 150 half sacks of flour and delivered to Cavert and Hill. Captain Tucker left for Marysville.

June 22. Remained on board all day, and discharged 201 sacks of flour.

June 23. Very warm, with a light wind in the afternoon. Began writing home.

June 24. Discharged 157 sacks of flour, and found the day extremely hot.

June 25. Weather very warm, and spent the day in closing my letters home and one to G. B. Way, Esq.

June 26. Warm, as usual. Thermometer at 78° in the cabin. Attended auction and tried to get a letter upon the arrival

[1]The "Third Great Fire" began at eight o'clock in the morning of June 14, and, driven by a high wind, swept over the area bounded by Clay, California, and Kearny streets and the waterfront. See *Annals of San Francisco*, pp. 277-78.

of the mail, but failed. Goods sold high. Lard at 25¢, sugar at 32¢, loaf at 45¢ per lbs. Potatoes low at 12¢ per pound.

June 27. Very warm. Captain Tucker has returned from Marysville, and is now on board with me.

June 28. Very warm. Thermometer standing at 75° in the shade. Business lively.

June 29. Exceedingly warm, with thermometer 81° at 6:00 P.M. I was overcome by this very great heat. Met with Colonel Jones of Fort Wayne, Indiana, and had a pleasant day with my old friend at the Sutter Hotel. His headquarters is at the city of Fremont.

June 30 (Sunday). On board all day; weather very warm.

{ July, 1850 }

SACRAMENTO CITY

July 1. This morning Captain R. Tucker left here for the Trinity diggings, having purchased an interest of one half in a drove of cattle destined for that market. After breakfast I went over to town, attended auction, laid in a few supplies, and at 3:00 P.M. returned on board, and found the thermometer at 90° in the cabin.

July 2. Mr. Jordan, of the firm of Osborn and Company, Marysville, left here this morning, and Captain Thompson is in the city. Not so hot as yesterday, a brisk wind. Preparations for a celebration of the fourth are making on both sides of the river, and our nation's birth will be celebrated, perhaps for the first time on the Pacific Coast.

July 3. Went over to town this morning but consummated nothing. After returning on board, we overhauled the halyards and attached the stars and stripes of our beloved country, and everything is now ready for tomorrow. We have 81 flags to unfurl to the breeze on board of the "Oniota." Weather pleasant and considerable wind. Several cannons have been fired off on trial.

July 4. We were aroused from sleep at daylight by the report of cannon fired, and immediately began dressing the brig in her rich attire. The ship's flag was run up to mainmast head, and with smaller flags we decorated her standing rigging. During this time the cannon were sending forth their loud welcome to the opening of the anniversary of our national birth. The day was passed with such patriotism as might be expected of the descendants of our noble sires, without a single accident to mar its pleasures.

July 5. Stayed on board during the day.

July 6. In town most of the day. High wind, and goods sold low.

July 7 (Sunday). Wrote another letter to my family.
The day was quite warm, with no wind for relief, and from
appearances I judge that the majority of the denizens of our
cities had laid aside all other business and gone to church.

July 8. Delivered my letters to a gentleman who has
kindly offered to deposit them in the postoffice at New Orleans.
He leaves in the steamer of the fifteenth instant. I also was informed that a mail would be carried home by this steamer.

July 9. At auction, goods sold low. Weather not quite
so hot.

July 10. Went into the city and attended auction. At a
sale by J. B. Starr and Company a large invoice of watches, some
of which were gold, was sold at various prices and after the sale
it was found that one of the best watches had been taken off by
some one well versed in thieving. I saw a poor-looking man
walking along Front Street carrying in one hand a piece of fresh
beef. He stopped on the corner of Front and J Streets and picked
up a pair of old pantaloons, and said he had a poor messmate
at home, whose "trousers" were worse than these, and money
was scarce, and he felt himself called upon to take this castoff
garment home to his friend. I remarked to him that here money
could be made and no man need want an hour. He replied that
they had made much and had also spent it, and then, with his
breeches in hand, walked off, muttering "Times are hard, and
money scarce." I admired the noble feeling that prompted this
fellow to assist a fellow mortal in time of need. One poor fellow
paid the debt of nature last night, from fever and want of timely
application of medicine. Another was badly and mortally
wounded by a mad bull.

July 11. This is, or has been, the happiest day to me in
California. I received a letter from my wife, the first from home,
and full of kind feelings and wishes to the wandering husband.
The details are full of comfort, and amply repay me for all I
have suffered from not hearing from home at an earlier date;
and this proves to be the twelfth letter written, and the only one

received. I now know that *they*, upon whom my heart's deepest affections are centered, were enjoying good health on the first day of April last, and I now feel a contentment of mind such as I have not known in California before, and thanks to Him who rules us mortals here below for this supreme blessing.

July 12. Spent part of the day in town. Left a letter in the postoffice for the arrival of my brother-in-law, John Davis, who left Ohio for this place sometime in March last, as I am informed. I also mailed one to him at San Francisco, and should he arrive at either place and get either letter, he will be able to find me. He is the bearer of my little son's miniature, and I am now anxiously expecting to meet him here.

July 13. Some wind stirring, and the day is not so hot. There is a growing desire on my part to return home, and had I been fortunate in laying up even a *small fortune*, California would not hold me another hour. But I must hush my impatient spirit and submit to a longer imprisonment than is or ever will be desirable. Another steamer, the "Captain Sutter," has come upon these waters, and the papers announce that the "New World" will in a few days take her place in line with the "Senator." The "New World" has just arrived in the bay below.

July 14 (Sunday). Considerable wind during the after part of the night and during the day, and consequently not so warm. Remained on board all day. Amused myself in the evening by dangling a hook and line around the vessel and captured several beautiful fish called "shiners" and much resembling herring. They are numerous and easily taken.

Wrote a letter to Laubenheimer and Parker, conveying them some information received from home by my wife's letter. Oh, how much, much pleasure that single letter from home has given me!

July 15. Last night, about 1 o'clock, we were aroused by the violent ringing of bells and the cry of "fire." On gaining the deck, I found a light almost strong enough to "chase darkness away," and a building on N Street enveloped in flames, and in a very short time it was reduced to ashes, and the fire over. Had this occurred on J Street, no power on earth could have stayed the destruction of a large portion of the city. The day has been moderately warm, with a light but balmy breeze.

Auction sales confined to real estate.

July 16. Warm. Spent the forenoon in town and found trade active and much property changing owners. Met with Messrs. Taylor and Barnett of Philadelphia, who have just arrived in the country.

July 17. Quite warm. Met with Mr. E. Briggs, of Wayne County, Ohio, who has just arrived in the country, overland, entirely destitute. I immediately procured work for him and at night he came on board, stating that he had earned his $5.00, being $1.00 for each hour's work. I provided him with a place to sleep, and gave him tea and breakfast.

July 18. Went on shore, and whilst there purchased a very fine rifle, hoping to make something in the speculation. Friend Briggs procured employment in an auction house and left us this evening. The day has been excessively *hot*.

July 19. This is the anniversary of my birth, and I am now 31 years old. One year ago this day, we—that is, the reader and I—were in camp in the state of Chihuahua, Mexico. In this brief period many things have transpired. Our hopes, then resting upon future success in getting to this country, have been realized, and a portion of this fabled land has been seen, its trials and troubles tasted, its cup of bitterness quaffed, and still we are looking forward with *hope* as large as ever. We will now hope for the blessings of Him who rules to rest upon us and *ours*, and with such a Friend, we will never reasonably want. Tomorrow will end a period of seventeen months since the reader and I set out for this land of promise, and during that long and eventful time we have heard from home but once; yet that one letter shed a new and almost holy feeling abroad in our sinking hearts,

and we can this evening look with pride upon all we have encountered and endured and still hope to be speedily united to
those so inestimably dear to us.

July 20. The brisk wind blowing prevents this being a
very hot day. As it is, there is warmth enough for any man's
comfort. The mail from home has not yet reached port, and it
is anxiously looked [for] by many who desire to hear from
absent friends.

July 21 (Sunday). Another funeral from shipboard. I
find that sailors do not stand the assaults of diseases incident to
this climate and several have already been borne to their last
homes from the ships that brought them from their earthly firesides to die in a strange land.

This day appears *most* like the Sabbath.

July 22. Tolerably warm. No mail in from the States yet,
though due two days. Sold a rifle and made something on that
purchase. My next operation may not be so successful.

July 23. Large and extensive sales at auction today. Wind
higher than usual, and the weather consequently cooler. Captain
George Bragdon of the brig "Shadduck" was found dead yesterday and buried today. All the vessels in port had their flags at
half mast. This man had been sick for some time and yesterday
went to the city, and was found dead near his vessel, which he
never lived to reach.

July 24. Warm, and mosquitoes very numerous in the
evening.

July 25. Received letters from home, O. Evans, and
White and Barnes, New York. What blessings such monitors
bestow! How pleasant to commune with our loved ones at home!
Weather very hot, with little wind.

July 26. Quite warm and but little wind. Business exceedingly dull.

July 27. Finished my correspondence for this mail, having answered the letter of Messrs. White and Barnes of New
York; and sent an additional draft for $50 drawn on the Bank

of America, New York, payable to Mrs. C. M. Evans. Draft drawn by Messrs. Hensley, Merrill, and King, of Sacramento City. This morning some Spaniards have been engaged in catching wild cattle, tieing their legs, and dragging them on board of the ferryboat for crossing. On landing them in the city, they loosed the cattle, and a large crowd of persons had assembled to see them. One of the bulls became furious and gave chase to the assembled people, and killed one man and two horses. It is hoped that this will prove a lesson for idlers in future, and that on the landing of cattle hereafter, people will not gather around them and by shouting and hurling missiles, provoke them to madness. The bull was shot down before he could do further injury. Have been engaged in discharging the remainder of the flour on board, and the company has also taken off all the vinegar and onions belonging to Captain Keene. Received $40 due the captain, of the "Washington Lunch" proprietors. This day has so far been very hot. A cargo of *ice* from Boston is said to be within a short distance of this city. Just in time. Worth now about 80¢ per lb.

July 28 (Sunday). Mosquitoes very thick this evening and but little wind. Wrote to General O. Evans. The brig "Cornelia" arrived here this evening and I was truly glad to see that others admired this cherished and much-loved name.

July 29. Lively breeze, and not so warm. Mailed my letters to Cornelia, General O. Evans, and White and Barnes. Also sent one to Colonel Colier[1] at San Francisco. Finished discharging cargo, and commenced the operation of clearing ship.

July 30. After an early breakfast, I took a boat and went over to the city. Rambling down Front Street I happily met with J. Davis, just arrived, after 78 days' journey on the plains. After a warm greeting, we went into a shade and then I put into requisition the Yankee mode of questioning and soon had a full and perfect history of all the news from home. Poor fellow, he too seemed happy and we both enjoyed the meeting much.

[1] James Collier was appointed collector of customs in November, 1849.

He brought me a perfect likeness of my dear wife and boy, and this has been another *happy* day to me. Another *letter* and a perfect *picture* of my *dear little family*. Who would not be happy under like circumstances? Now this world wags right again, and my "dottings" are of a more pleasant character.

July 31.   J. Davis and myself traveled over a large portion of the city inquiring into the rents of property, and intend to open some business as soon as a good location can be made. The result of this day's travel has been to find rents enormously high and the houses generally poor.

{ August, 1850 }

SACRAMENTO CITY
(CONTINUED)

Aug. 1. Continued our investigations, and with no better success. The future may open richer. Weather warm, with cool nights.

Aug. 2. This morning John Davis and myself went over into the city, and he having received an offer of $140 per month, we concluded to suspend intentions of going into business and labor to acquire further capital before opening on our own hook. We adopted this as the safest course. The day has been moderately cool, thermometer at 78° in the cabin.

I have realized much pleasure in meeting my brother Davis in this strange land and few can imagine the pleasure I enjoy in reading my wife's letters, and looking upon the *almost living* and *breathing* pictures of my dear, absent wife and child. The picture is indeed a good one, and heightens my longing desire to *go home* and see the loved originals.

Aug. 3. This morning I received two letters from my dear wife, full of kind and tender feelings—dated in February last and sent to Stockton. For these I had sent by Beresford and Company's express, and they were actually in their office during the last two months of my stay at San Francisco, and often inquired for by me. If men could realize the pangs of heart caused others by their neglect, they would not be thus careless of others' feelings, but until the heart of man is changed we must look for disappointments. Oh! what happiness these missives of love confer.

Aug. 4 (Sunday). On board all day. Passed pleasantly, having letters from home to read and their pleasing contents to meditate upon. What a contrast to the weary hours passed in time gone by. Mr. Jerry, from the house of D. W. B. of this city passed the afternoon and took dinner with us, and I was highly complimented on the soup and tea and other edibles prepared for this occasion by me.

Weather warmer and yet quite pleasant.

Aug. 5. In town a few hours witnessing the excitement consequent upon the failure of Barton Lee, who was supposed to be worth nearly half a million. Took a very heavy cold which settled in the head.

Aug. 6. Very unwell all day. Devoted some time to writing to my family in answer to the letters recently received.

BOOK SIXTH
Notes in California.

Aug. 7. Suffered very much from a heavy cold, seated on the lungs and brain. I thought last night that my days for this world were about closing.

Aug. 8. Felt much better this morning. The "New World" did not enter her appearance this morning, from some unknown cause. J. Davis is again with me, and through his exertions a fine mess of fish was served up for supper.

Aug. 9. Intended to mail my letters today, but, on learning that a regular mail would leave on the fifteenth, did not do so. One poor fellow lost at the gaming table today $2,144 before he left the table. No letters by the mail to Davis or myself and I now rest upon the hope afforded by the coming of the express tomorrow. I met with Mr. Carpenter of Perrysburg, Ohio, and Mr. Hudson and Mr. Manning of our own town. I was truly happy to meet them. The two latter took dinner with John and myself.

Aug. 10. No letters by this mail. Weather tolerably pleasant. Thermometer at 80°.

Aug. 11 (Sunday). This day I closed my home correspondence in a letter to C. of four sheets—sixteen pages closely written, containing 4,320 words. The mail closes on Tuesday next. J. Davis is making arrangements to go to the mines, and should he find good quarters I will shortly follow. Very warm, with but little wind.

Aug. 12. Davis, Manning, and Hudson left here this morning for the mines on the American River. A large sale of real estate took place this morning in this city, and to draw a comparison of prices now with the offers made for this same property, I will state that the highest price bid for the Sutter Hotel today was $24,000. Sixty thousand was offered for this stand last February and refused. The adjoining property sold for $11,000, and now rents at $1,100 per month. For this the owners refused $25,000 last spring. There is a downward tendency, and the end is not yet. Quite unwell, with a heavy cold.

Aug. 13. Mailed a letter to Cornelia and then returned to the brig—a much cooler and more comfortable place for my aching frame. The weather for the past few days has been cool and pleasant, and considering the heat, dust, and general exposure but little sickness has yet appeared amongst us.

Aug. 14. This morning I began the work of varnishing the decks of the brig, and found it a warm piece of work. For some weeks past some excitement has existed in this city relative to the rights of real estate, the "squatters"[1] claiming that they have rights in the land in this city, and that those claiming under Captain J. A. Sutter are not the owners of the soil. Various meetings of the squatter party have been held, and yesterday one of this party was tried and imprisoned for some violation of the law. This afternoon the party assembled under arms and openly attempted to force the authorities to release the prisoners. The Mayor (Bigelow) headed the citizens, and when these parties met some firing took place. Pat Maloney, the leader of the squatters, fell dead, having received eight balls in his head and body. Mayor Bigelow fell, supposedly mortally wounded

[1]The "squatters" were settlers who disputed Sutter's claims to title of land in and around Sacramento. The courts favored those holding titles cleared by Sutter, and the dispute was between these two groups. An account of the squatter riots of August 14 can be found in *Annals of San Francisco*, pp. 284-86.

with two shots. A gentleman by the name of Woodland was also killed. His wife was confined last night and now she is a widow and her new-born babe fatherless. This is truly a hard, a deplorable, state of things. Several others, some mortally and others have been slightly wounded. The city is under guard tonight and God only knows the end.

Maloney was an Irishman by birth, who distinguished himself in Mexico at the battle of Fort Brown, and it is truly a pity to know that he has fallen while openly resisting the law.

Quite an unexpected change in the weather has taken place in the last few hours. At about sunset, purple clouds began to appear from the southeast and grew thicker and darker as the rays of the setting sun were withdrawn. 'Tis now about 10 o'clock in the evening, the heavens are overcast and a better prospect for rain I have not witnessed since last March. Cool and light breezes.

Aug. 15. No new outrages today. The Mayor is better and hopes of his recovery are entertained. Woodland's funeral took place this afternoon, attended by the military and a large concourse of citizens. The squatters are said to be organizing and equipping their forces twenty-five miles above this city, with the expressed intention of forcing the city authorities to give up the prisoners. 'Tis said they number eleven hundred men. Should this be true, "the end is not yet." Arms and ammunition were sent up from the naval depot on the "Gold Hunter" and men are to follow by the "Senator" tonight. The report of firearms is constantly sounding and things wear a fearful aspect. Every preparation for defense is being made, but, after all, the security of life and property is extremely limited. I was informed by a friend that a lady, Mrs. Alexander of this city, had actually kept watch during the past night with a drawn sword in her hand, firmly resolved to do all she could to resist an invasion of her premises by anyone. Here was heroism. God grant that this outbreak of wicked passion may speedily end without further violence to life or property.

Aug. 16. I began my notes yesterday with the declaration that there had been no new outrages, and I am truly sorry to say that I was wrong, that I erred in this because ignorant of what was then being transacted in this world of strife. Gloom has again come over this city; the Angel of Death has again unfolded his wings, and the voice of mourning is again renewed. Scarcely have the remains of those [who] fell a sacrifice on the altar of duty been inclosed in the tomb before fresh victims are called to bow before the same Almighty Power. McKinney, sheriff of this county, was shot last night by the squatters. He who so nobly periled his life at the first slaughter lived but to fall a few hours later. His remains were interred this afternoon. One other person on the side of law and order fell with him, and four of the squatters were killed and several taken prisoners. Troops have arrived from below and our city wears a gloomy and a martial aspect. We will trust in God for better times. Mayor Bigelow is pronounced better but still in a very critical situation. Again cloudy, after a very warm day.

Aug. 17. This day opened warm and a dead calm continued until late at night. The troops from San Francisco left for their home on the "Gold Hunter," the difficulty and dangers from the squatters having subsided. Their presence here had a very salutary effect. The squatters dispersed and are now hidden in the recesses of the mountains, and it is hoped that law and order once more prevail and that lawless and murdering disposition has been finally and forever suppressed. Bigelow and his wounded companions are getting better. In a few days I again change my business, and I am now only awaiting the arrival of a letter from John Davis.

Aug. 18 (Sunday). Pleasant breeze now blowing inland, and the day promises to be one of greater coolness than yesterday. Joseph Lloyd of Phlladelphia came up yesterday and intends opening a store in this place. He is a Quaker and a very pleasant old gentleman, and well acquainted with many of my old neighbors in Pennsylvania. The old gentleman is strictly a

313

Quaker of the orthodox faith, and consequently one of that numerous class always found in opposition to every vice, and has done all in his power to put down the traffic in human flesh, and looks upon those going to war and in action slaying their fellow men as "legalized murderers." "Peace and liberty to the world" is his motto, and could all feel this and by their acts acknowledge its force, how much this world would be benefitted. He is a man of almost unlimited knowledge, and one blessed with a retentive memory, having the full [ability?] of giving date[s] for many transactions of the past, and his reading has been well digested, his criticisms close and to the point. To such men there is a pleasure in listen[ing], and [I] left him feeling in my heart that much is gained by drinking in the truths falling from the lips of Joseph Lloyd.

Aug. 19. Finished varnishing the decks of the brig "Oniota," and this day closes the time of my stay on this vessel. I have passed many hours pleasantly here, and it seems like parting with an old and much-esteemed friend to leave her, but by so doing I hope to better my fortune. The war has closed, it is hoped, and this day has passed quietly, with a very cool and refreshing breeze towards night.

Aug. 20. In town as usual, but did nothing of consequence. J. D. returned from the mines and reported so discouragingly that I am now taking time to deliberate before going further. Weather warm.

Aug. 21. The mail from home has not yet reached here. The disturbances which so recently distracted this community have settled down, and quiet and peace is again restored. Weather hot. Purchased goods at auction on speculation.

Aug. 22. Friends Lloyd and Boulden left, with the intention of visiting the neighboring mines. No mail in yet.

Aug. 23. Again in the city early, but the mail had not yet arrived; consequently nothing new from home. Weather very warm in the city, but cooler on the water under the shade of the vessel's awning. Opened my home correspondence yesterday and hope to have letters to answer by the return mail.

Aug. 24. Went into the city, after hoisting the brig's colors to half mast, commemorative of the loss our nation has sustained in the sudden death of President Taylor. On reaching the express office, I found a letter from my wife and again I am happy indeed.

Aug. 25 (Sunday). Spent the day on board with J. Davis, engaged in writing home. Weather tolerably warm.

Aug. 26. Day pleasant. Towards evening a cool and strong breeze sprang up and we were sheering all night. At about 10 o'clock the "Gold Hunter" and "New World" came up.

Aug. 27. I leave the brig in the morning, as she has been sold, and once more I am without an income and open for bids. Received a letter from P. Palmer, Esq., of Lockport, N. Y., and answered it this afternoon.

Aug. 28. Left the brig "Oniota" this morning, with such feelings as old friends experience on parting. I am now an inmate of the cabins of the brig "Tecumseh," and a guest by invitation of friend Boulden—out of employment but not bereft of *friends*. I have not determined yet on my future course, leaving all things of this character in the hands of God, who watcheth over us all.

Aug. 29. Very warm, and did not go to town, as usual, but spent the day in writing to friends at home.

Aug. 30. Warm and little business doing.

Aug. 31. Have thought seriously of taking a tour through the mines this fall. Weather warm and roads very dusty. Hazy sky towards evening but not one drop of rain. Mailed letter to C., and P. Palmer, Esq.

❴ September, 1850 ❵

SACRAMENTO CITY
(CONTINUED)

Sept. 1. Weather very clear and warm, without the usual sea breezes. John Davis, Manning, and Hudson were here this morning and stated their intention of going into the Yuba River diggings. They leave in the morning and in a few days I expect to follow them. Very warm indeed—it may safely be said hot weather.

Sept. 2. Warm, with light winds. Business tolerably lively. J. Davis and his companions started for Yuba River this morning. I was much amused at the narrative of friend Lloyd's journey to the mines, and laughed heartily at the expressions of the old Quaker. It appears that his horse, purchased by him for the journey, was one that had seen hard service and in days past "made friends with the whip," or, in other words, was broken down and broken hearted. The old gentleman however, used persuasions as long as Christian forebearance ruled, and in these persuasions used the following kind words: "Now, Sarah, why don't thee go along? Now thou hast got into the dust and are shuffling it up at a monstrous rate. Will thee get along now before I use my spur or whip? I don't wish to treat thee badly, yet this moping rate will never do, Sarah. Get along! Will thee not get along?" But all his kind words did not accelerate his speed or cool his rising impatience, and he then whipped and afterwards spurred, but still with no good effect, and he would melt into expressions of a tender nature and say, "Poor beast, though hast had thy heart broken," etc. After his return, he had the unwilling Sarah turned out to rest and pasture.

Sept. 3. Business dull, and the weather very warm. It seems a collision took place between the "Senator" and a brig. "Senator's" damage slight.

316

Sept. 4. Business looking up, and the sun pouring *down* its melting rays.

Sept. 5. Many goods sold at auction, but at exceedingly reduced prices. Mr. Lloyd promises again to visit us soon. No letter yet from J. Davis.

Sept. 6. Heavy auction sales. Mail has arrived from home but is not yet fully distributed. Hope to get further advices from home. Mayor Bigelow was removed to San Francisco a few days since, with a view to being benefitted by the cool sea breezes. Since his arrival there he has been getting better, and has had his arm amputated.

Sept. 7. This day received two letters, one from my brother Frank and wife, and the other from General O. Evans, and from the pages of these I gathered much welcome news. None received from my wife and sister Lucy. These I may certainly expect by next mail. I should have stated in my notes that the death of President Taylor was commemorated in this city on Thursday the fifth instant by a large concourse of people—civilians and soldiers. The procession was a long one and presented a mournful and imposing appearance.

Sept. 8 (Sunday). Spent the day on board, and for dinner had an excellent soup; the afternoon was spent in writing home and reading letters and other good ways. Cool and very stiff breeze blowing all day.

Sept. 9. Wind still continues to blow and clouds begin to gather. Bought good[s] at auction.

Sept. 10. Cloudy, with considerable wind. Received another very welcome letter from my wife, to which was appended a P. S. by brother James Cheney and one by sister L. W. Cheney, and these I must now answer.

Strange as it may seem, we had quite a clever little rain today, sufficient to lay the dust in some measure, and make the air cool and damp. It "astonished the natives" and they lay it to the presence of the Yankees. We are truly a great people! Finished my home correspondence by answering letters from Orlando Evans, F. T. Evans and C[ornelia] M. E[vans].

Sept. 11. Cool and windy. The light rain of yesterday seems to have expended its greatest force in the mountains and hills. Attended auction this evening, and whilst [I was] at the door, a horse attached to a buggy ran away and turned over at my feet, slightly injuring a lady. Her attendant had jumped from the vehicle and left his lady to escape, if possible, the peril of her situation. Carriage broken into pieces.

Sept. 12. Did not do much. Business lively and weather cool.

Sept. 13. Found John Davis and A. Hudson in town this morning, having just returned from the Yuba River diggings, without having accomplished anything. They leave again in the morning for mines on the American River. At noon I went into the service of Reed, Grimm and Company, an auction house.

Sept. 13. Worked very hard this day in passing goods in and out, having to prepare for a large sale on tomorrow.

Sept. 14. Up at daylight, distributed bills, and at 9:30 A.M. opened sales. Sold goods at about $5,000 in amount this day and delivered the whole amount, closing work at 8:00 P.M. I met with my old messmates, Laubenheimer and Bruner, and through them learned the whereabouts of all the Defiance boys. Strange as it may appear, none of them had ever received a letter from home, and Laub was overjoyed to learn the news I had in store for him.

Sept. 15 (Sunday). Laubenheimer and Bruner left this morning for Placerville, alias Hangtown, and I am here in the store to record a dinner on the brig "Tecumseh." Cloudy weather, prospect for more rain, and continued cool and vigorous winds. At 8:00 P.M. thunder and lightning set in, and heavy rain fell for about an hour.

Sept. 16. Had a large sale and handled a large quantity of goods. Cloudy and warm.

Sept. 17. Sold a heavy lot of goods and labored until

late at night. The contrast between my labor here and that performed by me at home is truly great.

Sept. 18. Held another heavy sale today and changed a heavy lot of goods, and made further arrangements for a sale on tomorrow. Steamboat fare between this city and San Francisco has suddenly fallen from $15 to $1.00, the effect of the opposition and hard times.

Sept. 19. Very warm, and no wind until evening. Sold a very heavy assortment of goods. Went into the family of Mr. Price to board, and find a good table, very kind landlady, and a talkative, but not very handsome, daughter.

Sept. 20. Held another sale, and when night came on I was almost broken down by the excessive labor of the day, and the heat.

Sept. 21. Changed all the goods in the house, and gave it a general cleaning up, and in the evening received a kind and warm letter from the partner of all my joys and cares. This letter bears date, July 12, 1850, and was due here two weeks past. I am truly thankful for the good tidings it contains, and the comfort it conveys.

Sept. 22 (Sunday). Dined on board of brig "Tecumseh" and came over after a pleasant visit with friend Boulden.

Sept. 23. Sold a heavy lot of goods, and wound up the day with another heavy rain. The mail has not yet come in.

Sept. 24. Held no public sale today, and did I enjoy perfect health, I would not complain of dismal aches, etc., for my labor today was comparatively nothing.

Sept. 25. In consequence of the nonarrival of goods we had no sale. Weather very warm. My health is gradually being undermined by the over-exertion arising from the labor I have to perform.

Sept. 26. No sale. Weather hot. I had some fever in the night and feel much prostrated.

Sept. 27. Sold a heavy lot of goods this morning and at

noon I quit work, being wholly unable to labor any longer. I went on board of the "Tecumseh," where I have always found open doors, a kind welcome, and generous heart in my friend Boulden. Took a dose of medicine this evening.

Sept. 28. Had a high fever during the night, and renewed my medicines again this morning. This evening I feel much better and am still under the influence of medicine.

Sept 29 (Sunday). Escaped all fever last night and suffer nothing but weakness and general prostration now. The steersman of the steam ferryboat was drowned last night. It is supposed that he was taken with an apoplectic fit and fell overboard. His body was recovered this morning.

Sept. 30. No return of fever, and all fever symptoms are subsiding. Sent a letter over to the office, to be mailed home. My dear wife's letter per last mail has not yet come to hand. Weather quite warm and at present very dry; little moisture during the night. Were it not for the weakness and prostration, I might now resume my labor but I deem it advisable to allow the body to recover strength before commencing active labor again. I much wish to be at work, for I am now on expenses and realize no income. To be sick in California is one of the hard things of this world, for want of proper attention and nursing, and on account of the ten-dollar visits of the worldly and gold-seeking physician.

{ October, 1850 }

SACRAMENTO CITY
(CONTINUED)

Oct. 1. Weather seems to be increasing in heat. In the town and on all traveled roads, the dust is very deep, and for want of free wind, it at times becomes a part of the atmosphere. My fever has left me, but an occasional potion of medicine is still necessary.

Oct. 2. Very warm. Had access to the postoffice but got no letters. My health is again improving, and hope soon to be able to resume my labors.

Oct. 3. Quite unwell all day, and concluded to keep quiet and take more rest. This is truly hard upon me, but God's ways are not mine and to his care and guidance I surrender myself, assured that it will be well for me in time to come. Weather very hot.

Oct. 4. Very warm, and my health is again improving. The brig "Tecumseh" was sold today at $1,200 private sale, and she, too, will soon pass into strange hands and no longer be a home to me. On Monday next I hope to be able to resume my labors and once more begin to make more than it costs me to live.

Oct. 5. Very warm, and but slight breezes. Remained on board of the brig. During the evening the candidates for state offices were haranguing the people and telling them how to vote.

Oct. 6 (Sunday). Boiled a fine beef soup and Mr. R. Williams, of the house of Reed, Grim, and Company, dined with us. In the evening we strolled into town, and found the dust thick and the fleas very active.

Oct. 7. This is election day, but little excitement. I did not go to work as expected, feeling too weak for the required labor. More than usual wind, and weather just moderately warm.

Oct. 8. No reliable information as to election results.

Received a good and kind letter from my wife this morning, and at the request of the agents of the California Trading Company I took charge of their office as guard during their absence to San Francisco. Health improving, but slowly.

Oct. 9. Suffered from another attack of diarrhea, and do not feel as well as yesterday. I have, however, not been confined to room yet, and hope it will pass off without further trouble. Engaged most of the day in writing home, not knowing what may come to pass between now and the fifteenth at which time the mail goes out.

Oct. 10. Not quite so hot. Dust a little thicker, and rain much needed. The agents of this company have not yet returned and I am still a denizen of their office. Received per mail a letter from my wife, dated Aug. 17, also one from brother Thomas, all giving good and cheerful accounts from home.

Oct. 11. Day opens warm. My health is slowly gaining. Sultry and dusty, with fleecy clouds.

Oct. 12. This day they have been engaged in removing the contents of the postoffice, and on Monday next we have the promise of better arrangements in this department.

Oct. 13 (Sunday). Finished my mail correspondence and am now ready to send my letters to my *home*, where my heart is. John Davis dropped in on me, and looks healthier than I ever knew him.

Oct. 14. Once in the city, I went to the new and extensive postoffice buildings, K and Second Street, and found everyone delighted with the new order of things. Instead of having to stand "in the line" for hours, you could now reach the window in a short time, and my soul rejoiced over this "crumb of comfort." I mailed my letters and wished them and myself an early arrival *at home*. Cloudy and high wind, threatening rain, but only a few drops fell. Fell in with Colonel Jones this morning.

Oct. 15. Pleasant weather. Assisted friend Boulden in selling goods and begin again to realize something in the way of an income. My health has and is still improving rapidly.

Oct. 16. Sold a large lot of goods and made fair wages today.

Oct. 17. Heavy sales, though not as good as yesterday. Saw Thomas and John Davis today. Weather pleasant, but roads very dusty. Several murders and robberies have recently occurred in this city, and as an evidence of the watchful care of the city police, I need only mention the fact that the prison ship has now a large crew of these midnight assassins on board.

Oct. 18. Very warm. The brig "Tecumseh" was passed over into other hands this morning and my home on the waters closes after this night. Friend Boulden and myself have arranged to lodge over his store and will have a good little room, yet it will not be that cool, pleasant, and retired place we used to have on board of the dear old brig. The best of friends must part.

Oct. 19. This morning, a few hours before day, we were aroused from sleep by the heavy booming of cannon, and on ascending to the deck, we found the steamer "New World" just coming into port, attended with the discharge of her cannon and the display of fireworks. A few moments' reflection settled the reason for all this rejoicing. The mail from *home* had arrived, and the cheering and welcome news of California's admission into the Union as a State was now shouted in our ears, and right happy were we poor *hombres* that the Union still stood unshaken and unbroken, and that *we* were now enjoying once more the protection of our glorious confederacy. Left the brig this morning, and we are now domiciled in the dusty city of Sacramento.

Oct. 20 (Sunday). A large meeting assembled last night, at the foot of J Street, which was addressed by several gentlemen. During the speaking, cannon were fired at regular intervals and the boys were also very active in the display of firecrackers, and we found this part of the evening exercises very annoying. This day has been comfortably hot, and having the late *Tribune* and *New Orleans Delta*, I gleaned from them the transactions of our people at home. Tomorrow I hope to get my letters. From these papers I gleaned the fact that California had become a

State, that Professor John W. Webster had paid the penalties of the violated law, and that a large portion of our country at home had been visited by severe storms of wind and rain, and that the cholera was fast disappearing from the land. This last item is of very gratifying character.

Oct. 21. Very warm, and business limited on account of the appearance of cholera in this city. Several cases have already been reported—fatal—and several new cases have arisen. Received no letters from any person by this mail, and am greatly disappointed.

Oct. 22. Captain Janvier of the schooner "Naomi," just arrived from home, was taken with the cholera yesterday morning and died last night at 11 o'clock. Several other deaths occurred last night. Mr. Coman, of the firm of Reed, Grimm, and Company, is now lying at the point of death with this dreadful disease. Sick are reported from every quarter of the city and the disease is spreading.

Oct. 23. Mr. Coman died last night. Yesterday he was actively engaged in writing home to his wife, and told her with his own hand that the cholera was on him and he must die, and left this sad letter to be closed, after the curtain had dropped upon his earthly career, by his partners. This sad duty will be performed by his partners, and woe and sorrow will soon reach an anxious and confiding wife and loving children. God's ways are not ours. The deceased has proved himself a very worthy citizen during his brief stay among us and every kindness and attention was shown him in his expiring moments. Weather very warm.

Oct. 24. The cholera is abating, and cloudy weather setting in, with strong indications of rain. Another captain of a neighboring vessel fell a victim to this disease last night. This is the only death I have heard from today. Received another welcome letter from home this morning and, were I differently circumstanced, I would start home by next boat.

Oct. 25. Seven deaths from cholera yesterday, but the

report of only one for today, yet many more may have occurred. Business is quite lively and many goods are changing hands. Worked hard, and took in over $500 for goods sold today. Began writing home yesterday, but do not intend to mention the cholera, as it will confer no benefit upon my wife and child.

Oct. 26. Very warm and almost sultry weather. Nineteen deaths yesterday and several reported this morning. Disease on the increase. I am myself quite unwell, with dysentery, and pain in the head. Doing all I can to prevent the cholera. To show others (who may read this notice of the mortality of our city) the light in which some view this visitation of Providence, I will state that I this morning saw a large handbill posted up at the corners of our streets, announcing to the public that on Sunday evening next a grand masked ball would come off at the "Bella Union," dancing to begin at 7:30 P.M. Oh, God, withhold Thy chastening rod, and let Thy holy spirit work a reformation in the hearts of men!

Oct. 27 (Sunday). Cool, brisk wind from the southwest. No new cases of cholera reported yet. I have now only two days more to live when a full year for me in California will have rolled into the past. On the thirtieth day of October, 1849, I began the first labor in this country, and on an investigation of my accounts I find them to stand thus: Whole amount made in twelve months last past—

		$871.23
Sent home	$523.23	
Now on hand	226.62	
	$749.85	749.85
Expenses in one year		$121.38

Aside from expenses, I have therefore made the small sum of $62.48 per month, which I consider very favorable under the circumstances, and had I been able to labor during the entire year, I would have been better off. But I am truly thankful for this favor, and have the further satisfaction of having been able to send home more than it cost me to reach this country.

Oct. 28. Changes are constantly arising in this community, and on tomorrow we move again. Messrs. Barton and Boulden purchased the business of Messrs. Reed, Grimm, and Company, and now we move again, with the hope of better business to all concerned. Having long been associated with Messrs. B. and B., they have offered me a place and good salary, and I go with them having once more something like the assurance of steady employment at good wages. This is pleasing to me, having had no steady employment for several months, in consequence of sickness. I have finished, or am nearly ready, with my home correspondence, and I have seldom had more gratifying information to impart to my family than this letter contains, because, if health is continued, I am almost certain of continued employment to the first of March, when it is my purpose to leave for home.

Oct. 29. This day I enter the service of Messrs. Boulden and Barten, successors to the late firm of Reed, Grimm, and Company, Auction and Commission Merchants, and I have been actively engaged all day at removing goods and making out invoices.

Oct. 30. Sold at auction a very large lot of goods, and when night came I was pleased to enjoy its rest. Sales exceeded $3,000.

Oct. 31. Weather much cooler, cholera on the decrease.

{ November, 1850 }

SACRAMENTO CITY AND THE
END OF THE TRAIL

Nov. 1. Sold again a large lot of goods, but it is very evident that the cholera has its effect upon every branch of business. It is said to be on the decrease.

Nov. 2. Held no public sale, but disposed of many goods on private contract. Very high wind and constant clouds of dust. Cholera said to be less violent.

Nov. 3 (Sunday). Seven corpses had passed over the road to their long homes up to 8:00 A.M. today, and the extent of mortality shows itself this evening to be great. Probably not less than forty or fifty have gone to their last home this day. Fever has again come upon me, and now I am under the necessity of taking more medicine. I am at times sorely troubled about my future state of health.

Nov. 4. After another feverish night, I arose and went to work, but under severe pain. Sold at auction a large lot of goods.

Nov. 5. Great suffering from pain over the whole body, and applied to Dr. Hardenstein, homeopathic physician.

Nov. 6. Fever abating, but dysentery threatens, and I have resolved to rest this afternoon. Quit board at the Brannan house, for the simple reason that such diet as was ordered by my physician they would not provide.

[George Evans died at Sacramento City, Dec. 16, 1850, aged 31 years.]

BIBLIOGRAPHICAL NOTE

THE LITERATURE of the gold rush is so vast that no attempt will be made to present an exhaustive bibliography. The following items, however, are of assistance to one wishing to learn more of Evans' route and the type of country he encountered.

THE TEXAS-MEXICO ROUTE

LORENZO D. ALDRICH, *A Journal of the Overland Route to California! and the Gold Mines* (1851)

JOHN WOODHOUSE AUDUBON, "Illustrated Notes of an Expedition through Mexico and California 1849-50," *Magazine of History*, XI, 1-83 (1936; Extra Number 41)

JOHN R. BARTLETT, *Personal Narrative of Explorations and Incidents in Texas, New Mexico, California, Sonora, and Chihuahua, connected with the United States and Mexican Boundary Commission, during the Years 1850, '51, '52 and '53* (1854; 2 vols.)

FRANCIS BAYLIES, *A Narrative of Major General Wool's Campaign in Mexico* (1851)

A. B. CLARKE, *Travels in Mexico and California* (1852)

ROBERT CREUZBAUR, *Route from the Gulf of Mexico and the Lower Mississippi Valley to California and the Pacific Ocean . . .* (1849)

WILLIAM HEMSLEY EMORY, *Notes of a Military Reconnaissance from Fort Leavenworth, in Missouri, to San Diego, in California, including parts of the Arkansas, Del Norte, and Gila Rivers* (1848)

Exploring Southwest Trails, 1846-1854 (1938; Ralph P. Bieber, ed.; Vol. VII of "Southwest Historical Series")

JULIUS FROEBEL, *Seven Years' Travel in Central America, Northern Mexico, and the Far West of the United States* (1859)

"From Texas to California in 1849; Diary of C. C. Cox," Mabelle Eppard Martin, ed. *Southwestern Historical Quarterly*, XXIX, 36-50, 128-46, 201-23 (1925-6)

Journal of Cave Couts, 1846. (MS in Bancroft Library)

MABELLE EPPARD MARTIN, "California Emigrant Roads through Texas," *Southwestern Historical Quarterly*, XXVIII, 287-301 (1925)

SAMUEL McNEIL, *McNeil's Travels* . . . (1850)

WILLIAM MILES, *Journal of the Sufferings and Hardships of Capt. Parker H. French's Overland Expedition to California* . . . (1851)

CHARLES EDWARD PANCOAST, *A Quaker Forty-Niner* (1930; Anna Paschall Hannum, ed.)

Pioneer Notes: the Diaries of Judge Benjamin Hayes (1929; Marjorie Tisdale Wolcott, ed.)

Southern Trails to California in 1849 (1937; Ralph P. Bieber, ed.; Vol. V "Southwestern Historical Series.")

FREDERICK ADOLPHUS WISLIZENUS, *Memoir of a Tour to Northern Mexico, Connected with Col. Doniphan's Expedition, in 1846 and 1847* (1848)

CALIFORNIA IN 1849

BARBER AND BAKER, *Sacramento Illustrated* (1855)

J. D. BORTHWICK, *Three Years in California* (1857)

History of Sacramento County, California (1880)

FRANK S. MARRYAT, *Mountains and Molehills* (1855)

One Man's Gold: the Letters and Journal of a Forty-Niner, Enos Christman (1930; Florence Morrow Christman, ed.)

FRANK SOULÉ, JOHN H. GIHON, AND JAMES NISBET, *The Annals of San Francisco* (1855)

BAYARD TAYLOR, *Eldorado* (2 vols:; 1850)

JAMES L. TYSON, *Diary of a Physician in California* (1850)

LATER ACCOUNTS

HUBERT HOWE BANCROFT, *California Inter Pocula* (1888)

———— ———— ————, *History of Arizona and New Mexico* (1889)

———— ———— ————, *History of California* (7 vols., 1886-90)

———— ———— ————, *History of the North Mexican States and Texas* (2 vols., 1884-9)

NEWELL D. CHAMBERLAIN, *The Call of Gold: True Tales on the Gold Road to Yosemite* (1936)

OWEN C. COY, *Gold Days* (1929)

—— — ——, *The Great Trek* (1931)

JOSEPH J. HILL, *History of Warner's Ranch and its Environs* (1927)

THEODORE H. HITTELL, *History of California* (4 vols., 1892)

FREDERICK WEBB HODGE, *Handbook of the American Indians North of Mexico* (1907)

ROBERTA EVELYN HOLMES, *The Southern Mines of California* (1930)

JOSEPH HENRY JACKSON, *Anybody's Gold* (1941)

ALFRED L. KROEBER, *Handbook of the Indians of California* (1925)

APPENDIX

The Evans Family Record

Births

Caroline Cheney was born Jan. 6, 1843

Roswell Willard Cheney, son of R. and L. Cheney, Nov. 6, 1844

Helen Cheney was born May 19, 1843

Roswell W. Cheney was born Aug. 16, 1844

Cornelia Mary Cheney was born Jan. 1, 1847

George W. B. Evans was born July 19, 1819

Cornelia M. Cheney was born June 4, 1823

George Cheney Evans was born Oct. 29, 1843

Margaret Abigail Evans was born Aug. 24, 1845

Franklin James Evans was born June 13, 1847

Roswell Cheney was born May 17, 1789

Abigail Willard was born Dec. 6, 1793

Caroline Maria Cheney was born Sept. 19, 1813

Roswell Willard Cheney was born Jan. 21, 1816

James Cheney was born Dec. 15, 1817

Cornelia M. Cheney was born June 4, 1823

Marriages

George W. B. Evans and Cornelia M. Cheney were married Feb. 1, 1843

Charles G. Baker and Cornelia M. Evans were married June 21, 1853

Roswell Cheney and Abigail Willard were married Dec. 13, 1812

R. W. Cheney and Susy Daniels were married Oct. 9, 1837

James Cheney and N. B. Evans were married May 2, 1842

Deaths

George Cheney Evans died Oct. 1, 1844, aged 11 months 1 day

Margaret Abigail Evans died Aug. 24, 1845

George W. B. Evans died in Sacramento City, Dec. 16, 1850

Roswell Cheney died Jan. 22, 1846

Roswell Willard Cheney died Aug. 17, 1844

James Cheney died Dec. 13, 1903

INDEX

Adams and Company, 277, 284
Ackley, J. T., 297
Acorn flour, 166-68
Agriculture, in Mexico, 76, 83, 87, 88, 98, 104, 114-15, 117-18, 129, 135; in California, 170, 172, 173-77, 182, 205
Agua Fria, xvii, 216-71
Agua Prieta Creek, 147
Aguas Calientas, xvii, 168, 170-72, 231
Alamo, xv, 26, (well), 163
Altarias Creek, 71
Alcalde of Agua Fria, 236-37, 239, 241-42, 251, 253, 260
American Fork of Sacramento River, 289
American Hotel (in Chihuahua), 97, 122, 125
Amigo Springs, 91-92
Amusements, in Mexico, 98; in California, 270-71
Apaches, xvi, 104, 107, 113, 115-16, 148, 161
Architecture, in Mexico, 79, 88, 95, 97-101, 107, 144, 149; in California, 188-89, 192-94, 202, 207-8, 225-28
Arkansas River, 8
Arnold, E. S., 214, 217
Arroyo Grande, 197
Aztecs, 134-35

Balize, 14
Barbour, M. F., 239, 246, 248, 250, 262, 284
Barranco, 136-37, 138
Baton Rouge, 10
Battle of New Orleans, 23
Bay Hotel (in San Francisco), 293
Bears, attack on miner, 248-49
Benicia, 286
Blackwater Creek, 144
Boulden, 314, 315, 322, 323, 326
Boulden and Barton, 326
Branch House (in Stockton), 273
Browning, Mr., 148, 176, 185
Bruner, Elias, 3, 43, 96, 110, 121, 167, 214, 224, 318

Brush fire (in Mexico), 50
Bryant, J. J., 274, 275
Bunnell, Dr. Lafayette Houghton, 27, 28, 32, 43, 47, 65, 72, 96, 106, 111, 112, 113, 121, 129, 148, 149, 151, 152, 156, 157, 161, 182, 194, 229, 263
Burns' and Widner's Ranch, 241
Business, in Sacramento, 317-27

Cache Creek, 287
Cactus, 146, 149, 150, 155
Cahuenga Pass, 190
California, xvii, xix, 24, 41, 51, 102, 128, 160-327; Colorado River, 160-62; San Felipe, 168; Aguas Calientes, 168-69; admission to Union, xix, 257, 323-24; Warner's Ranch, 171; Chino (Williams') Ranch, 174-86; Constitutional Convention, 184, 204, 206-7; Los Angeles, 188-90; San Juan Buenaventura, 192-93; Santa Barbara, 194; San Luis Obispo, 198; Soledad Mission, 203; San José, 207-8; Livermore's Ranch, 209; Stockton, 211-12; Agua Fria, 216-71; San Francisco, 273-85, 293-99; Sacramento, 288-92, 299-327
California Ranch, 272
"California" steamer, 274, 276
California Trading Company, 322
Cameron, Milton M., 3, 40
Cameron, S. L., 3, 40
Cape Horn, 11
"Captain Sutter" steamer, 273, 304
Carmel, 133
Carmel River, 133
Carmen River, 131
Carpenter, O. H., 21, 26, 29, 30, 43, 72
Carquínez Strait, 299
Carrizeta, 164, 166, 167
Casas Grandes, xvi, 135-36
Casas Grandes River, 135-36, 138, 139
Cassiano, 23
Casswell, Capt. Harvey S., 279, 282
Castroville, xv, 31
Catholicism, xv, xviii, 79, 95, 99-101,

335

107, 123, 125, 133, 134, 138, 192-94, 196, 198-99, 203
Cattle ranching, 176-77, 180, 186, 190, 203, 231
Cattle, wild, xvi, 144-45, 307
Cave-in-Rock, 6
Cedar River, 140
"Change" bark, 284
Chase, J. Holland, 43, 96, 99
"Chief Justice Marshall" steamer, 4, 8, 11, 16
Chihuahua, xvi, xvii, 26, 29, 40, 49, 67, 72, 75-78, 80-82, 84-85, 89, 92, 96, 97-127, 128, 130, 131, 138, 140, 143, 154, 178-79, 230, 305
Chile, 195
Chilenos, 223, 282-83
Chinese, in San Francisco, 274-75
Chino (Williams') Ranch, xvii, 174-86
Cholera, xiv, xv, xviii, 12, 14, 30, 32, 43, 248, 262, 324-27
Churches, 26
Cibolo Creek, 22
Cincinnati, Ohio, 3-5, 68, 230
Clark, Charles, 26, 54, 57, 66, 72
Clark, George W., 40
Cleland, Robert Glass, xx
Cleto Creek, 21
Coast Range, 198-99
Coco-Maricopas, 150, 155, 161
Coleto River, 18
Collier, James H., 276, 277, 307
Colorado Diggings, 258
Colorado River, xvii, 160, 162, 166-67, 173, 178-79, 183
Comanches, xvi, 35-36, 74, 85-86, 116-17
Concepción, Mission, Texas, 34-35
Conchos River, xvi, 78, 84, 86, 98, 124
Conejo Grade, 191
Constitution of California, 242
"Convoy" steamer, 9
Cooke, Philip St. George, xvi, 141, 143, 145-46, 148, 151, 154
Corralitos, 138-39
Cotton's Ranch, 272-73
Coyame, 86-89, 93, 113
Cradle, 219, 222, 228, 233
Crittenden, Hiram, 3, 21, 40
Customhouse in San Francisco, 276-99

Cypress River, 48, 50, 53

Davis, John, 304, 307-11, 313, 316-18, 323
Day, Captain, 158
Death Valley Party, 254-55, 259-61, 263
Defiance, Ohio, xiv, 3, 230, 262, 264
Devil's Reach, 288
Dodge, Henry L., 275
Doniphan, Col., 124, 128
Dress, in Mexico, 43-44, 77, 85, 106, 109; for trail, 120
Driggs, R. H., 236-37
Dry Creek, 18
Durango, 96

Earthquake, 151
East, Dr. (of Chihuahua), 117, 124-25
Elections, on the trail, 29; California, 224; mining camp, 236, 238-39; San Francisco, 274-75
Elk, xvii
El Paso, 24, 82, 108, 131, 143, 148
El Yseta, 165-66, 178
Emigrants, 144, 146, 148, 152, 154, 158, 170, 208, 265
Emory, William H., 167
Encinillas, xvi, 129, 131
Equipment, 48, 68
Evans, Cornelia M., xiv, 262, 294, 296-97, 303-4, 307-9, 311, 315, 318-19, 320
Evans, George W. B., departure, 3; Ohio to New Orleans, 3-13; by boat to Texas, 13-15; in Texas, 15-38; in Mexico, 38-161; in California, 161-327; in Mariposa Diggings, 216-71; in San Francisco, 273-85, 293-99; in Sacramento, 288-92, 299-327; death, 327
Evans, Rinaldo, 3, 21, 26, 40
Evans, William Rush, 283
Evansville, Illinois, 6

Fannin, James, xv, 19
Fight, on trail, 126-27
Finlay, Ohio, 3
Fire, in San Francisco, 287, 300; in Sacramento, 304-5

Flotte, Lewis, 136-37
Fog, 184
Food, in Mexico, 40, 78, 94-95, 102-3, 106, 110, 119-22, 127; in California, 179, 181, 192, 195, 200-202, 225
Foote, Henry S., 268
Fort Hill, 190
Franciscans, 198
Fredericksburg, 108
Fremont, Col. John, 180, 184
Fremont's Camp, 219, 221, 256, 258, 265
French Camp, 273
Frío River, 36
Fumaroles, 167
Funeral, Mexican, 40-41

Galeana, xvi, 131, 134-35, 136
Galveston, xiv, 14, 15
Gambling, 6, 220-21, 236-38, 265, 269-71, 273, 276
Gavia Pass, 76
Gaviota Pass, 198
Gila Rver, xvi, xvii, 11, 108, 121, 130, 141, 148, 152-60, 166, 179, 180
Gilboa, Ohio, 3
Glanton, John, 133
Gold, 88, 90, 148, 163
Gold mining, 216-17, 219, 220-30, 232-36, 238-40, 244-45, 247, 256, 264
"Gold Hunter" steamer, 298, 299, 312, 313, 315
Golden Gate, 280, 295
Goliad, xv, 19, 20, 24
Gómez, Apache chief, 113, 134
Gonzales (of San Antonio), 82
Government, mining camp, 236-39
Graham, Maj. L. P., 139, 142, 167
Gregory, William B., 218
Guadalupe Pass, 82, 141-43, 179
Guadalupe River, 17, 18
Gulf of Mexico, 15, 192, 226

Haller, Wesley A., 3, 43, 102, 218, 224, 262
"Hartford" steamer, 292-93
Hawkins' store, 238
Hays, Jack, 274-75
Helena, Arkansas, 8
Hidden River, 38-39

Hidden Spring, 90
Hill, Rev. R. H., 82, 148-49, 157, 229, 234
Hondo River, 34
Houghton, John, 250
Houses, Texas, 18, 32; Mexico, 76; California, 186-87, 191
Huaqui River, 143-44
Hutchinson, Dr. Benjamin F., 3, 20, 29

Indians, xiv, xvi, xvii, 32, 37-38, 44, 55-57, 59, 61-63, 71, 74, 81, 85-86, 90-93, 96, 103-4, 107-9, 111, 113-15, 122, 131, 133, 138, 141, 143, 148-55, 164-70, 172-74, 176, 182-83, 194-95, 201, 219-20, 225-26, 235, 254, 259
International Boundary, xv
Iron, 87
Irrigation in Mexico, 117-18

Janos, 96, 121, 131, 138-39, 178
Janos River, 138
Jayhawkers, xviii
Jewett, Helen, 23
Johnson, S. P., 43

Kearney, General, 167
Keene, Capt., 299, 300, 307
Kelley, P. S., 148, 199, 214, 217, 224, 234, 248, 261
King, Thomas Butler, 184
Kinzer, D., 43

La Bahia, 19
Lafitte, Jean, 15
Laubenheimer, F., 3, 29, 43, 55, 64, 80, 108, 112, 148, 156, 157, 182, 199, 208, 217, 218, 224, 225, 226, 228, 229, 235, 241, 248, 250, 251, 253, 257, 258, 263, 267, 269-71, 304, 318
Lee, Barton, 310
"Le Monde" vessel, 293, 296-97
Leona River, 36
Lichliter, George, 272
Lipans, xvi, 74
Lippincott, Benjamin S., 206-7
Litigation, mining camp, 241-42, 252-53, 258, 260-61
Livermore, Robert, 209
Livermore's Ranch, xvii, 209
Lloyd, Joseph, 313-14, 316-17

337

Los Alamos Ranch, 197
Los Alamos Valley, 197
Los Angeles, 102, 178-79, 185, 188-90, 230-31
Louisville, Ky., 3, 4
Lynch, Mr., 70, 71, 73, 82, 109

McCauley, J. G., 3, 43, 102
McIntyre's Camp, 213
"McKim" propeller, 299
McKnight, George S., 11,29,43,65,96
McKnight, Robert, 136
McKnight, Terry, 23
McNeil, Capt., 103-8
Madison, Ind., 4
Maguey, 141
Maricopas, xvi-xvii
Mariposa diggings, xviii, 214, 230, 233, 258
Mariposa River, xvii, 210, 211, 215
Marriage customs, Mexico, 111-12
"Martha Washington" steamer, 4, 8
Matagorda Bay, xiv, 15
Mazatlán, 97, 102
Medina River, 31, 32
Medio Creek, 31
Memphis, Tenn., 7
Merced River, xvii, 215-16, 267, 272
Mescalero Apaches, 74, 85, 90
Mesquite, 139, 159, 166
Metropolis, Ill., 6
Mexicans, 22, 44-45, 56, 92, 93, 97-102, 106, 109-12, 117, 123, 126, 131, 135-36, 150, 153, 163, 170, 174, 182, 189-90, 200, 229, 237
Mexican War, xv, 26
Mexico, xiii, 38-161, 231, 262, 305, San Fernando, 39-42; social classes, 44-45; Santa Rosa, 42-48; San Carlos, 76-77; Presidio del Norte, 78-79; Coyame, 87-89; San Gerónimo, 94-96; Chihuahua, 97-127; Encinillas, 129-31; Galeana, 134-35; Casas Grandes, 135-36; Barranco, 137; Corralitos, 138; Janos, 138-39; Gaudalupe Pass, 142-43; San Bernardino, 144; Santa Cruz, 147; Tucson, 151; Pima Villages, 150-54; Gila River, 152-59
"Minerva" bark, 277, 279, 281, 283

Mining, Mexico, 136-37
"Mint" steamer, 273
Mississippi Mining and Trading Company, xv, 37, 39, 43, 111
Monte Bank, 98, 221, 270-71, 276
Monterey, xvii, 184, 204
Mormons, 254-55
Mules, 26-27, 185-86,208-9,214-15,218

Napoleon, Ark., 8
Natchez, Miss., 9, 10
Natchez California Company, 49
Natividad Ranch, 204
Negroes, xiv, 13, 14, 44, 45, 81, 237
Nepomo Ranch, 197
New Albany, Ind., 5
Newburgh, Ind., 5
New Madrid, Mo., 6-7
New Orleans, xiv, 5, 10-13, 68, 230, 240, 303; negroes, 10; cemeteries, 11; All Saints' Day, 11; cholera, 12; St. Charles Hotel, 12
New River, 163
"New World" steamer, 304
New York on the Pacific, 286
Nueces River, 36, 38

Ogburn, Dr., 112, 148-49
Ohio Company, xv, 43, 60, 63
Ohio River, 230
Old Spanish Trail, 255
"Oniota" brig, 285, 299, 302, 314, 315
"Oregon" steamer, 294-95
Owensboro, Ky., 5-6
Owens Lake, 254
Ozier's Trading Post, 238

Pacific Ocean, 181
"Palmetto" steamer, 11, 13-14
"Panama" steamer, 294
Park, Thomas B., 198
Parker, A. T., 3, 43, 55, 64, 66, 68, 80, 96, 112, 148, 199, 205, 217, 224-29, 233-35, 238, 244, 247, 250, 252, 253, 257, 258, 261-62, 267, 304
Parras, xiii, xv
Paso del Norte, see El Paso
Peach Creek, 35
Peons, 182
Perrysburg, Ohio, 11
Pickpockets, 5

Pimas, xvi, 149-51, 152-54, 161
Pima Villages, 96, 149-51, 153, 156, 166, 178
Pinole, 33
Placerville, 318
Plantations, 8-9
Pollard, W. T., 148
Porter, James D., 4, 5
Port Lavaca, xiv, 11, 15, 16, 230, 231
Portsmouth Square, 274, 275
Postal service, in diggings, 243-44, 262; in San Francisco, 283-84, 295, 303-4
Presidio del Norte, xvi, 78-82, 89, 92, 96, 98, 108
Prices, mining camp, 246-47, 253, 265, 270
Puerco River, 94, 96

Quihi Creek, 33

Ranches, in Mexico, 84-85
Rangers, Texas, 36
Reed, Grimm, and Company, 318, 321, 324, 326
Richardson, George, 47-48, 109
Riddells, Bennet, 124-25
Riley, Dr., 64-66, 70-71, 73, 90, 272
Riley, Capt. James, 64
Rio Grande, 11, 38, 78, 79, 82, 139
Robinson, Richard P., 23
Rocker, 235
Rocky Mountains, 130-31, 135, 141, 158, 179
Rondé, M., 136
Routes through Mexico, 96-97

Sacramento, xviii, xix, 234, 286, 289-91, 294, 298, 299, 307
Sacramento, Battle of, 124-25, 127-28
Sacramento River, 266, 286-87, 293
Sacramento Valley, Mexico, 127-28, 132
Saguaro, 150
St. Charles Hotel (in New Orleans), 12
Salado Creek, 24
Sabinas River, 47, 53
Salinas River, 201-3
Saltillo, xiii, xv, 49

Salt Lake City, 254
San Antonio, Tex., 16, 20, 23, 24, 26, 30, 34, 40, 108
San Antonio River, 23, 25, 174
San Bernardino, Mexico, 144-45
San Carlos, xvi, 67, 69-71, 75-77, 82, 98
San Carlos River, 76
San Diego, 171
San Felipe, 168, 178
San Fernando, Mexico, 39, 40, 88
San Fernando Valley, 190-91
San Francisco, xviii, 102, 110, 156, 171, 180, 185, 210, 220, 234, 243-44, 253, 258, 266, 269, 271, 273-76, 293, 304, 319, 322; second great fire, 287; third great fire, 300
San Francisco Bay, 205, 208, 277
San Gabriel River, 187
San Gerónimo, 82, 88, 90, 93-95, 96, 107
San Joaquin River, 163, 180, 209, 210, 211, 215, 273
San Joaquin Valley, xvii
San José, California, xvii, 205, 207-8, 230, 243
San José Mission, California, 208
San José Mission, Texas, 34
San Juan Bautista Mission, 204-5
San Juan Buenaventura Mission, 192-93
San Juan's Day, 98
San Luis Obispo Mission, 198
San Miguel Mission, 199
San Miguel Ranch, 172, 173-74
San Pablo Bay, 299
San Pedro, Mexico, 145
San Pedro, California, 180
Santa Ana del Chino River, 174-76, 231
Santa Anna, Antonio López de, 35, 85, 130
Santa Barbara, 194
Santa Barbara Mission, 194
Santa Clara River, 191-92
Santa Cruz, 146-47, 178
Santa Cruz Peak, 145
Santa Cruz River, 148
Santa Fe, 131
Santa Rosa, 42, 45-46, 47-48, 74, 78, 82

Santa Ynez Mission, 196
Santana Pass, xv, 50, 53-62
Sauz, xvi, 128-30
Sauz Lake, 131
Sauz River, 131
Scott, Capt. George, 71, 90
Scott, James, 148
Scott, William, 148
Scott, William L., 239, 251
Scott's Ranch, 272
Scurvy, xiv, xviii
"Senator" steamer, 299, 312, 316
Serranía del Burro, xv
"Shadduck" brig, 306
Sheriff of Agua Fria, 237-39, 242, 244, 246, 248, 250
Sherlock's diggings, 256, 258, 266, 268
Shipping, at Sacramento, 289; in San Francisco Bay, 277-85, 293
Shrieves, Mr., 102
Sierra Madre, Mexico, 43, 57, 128, 146
Sierra Nevada, 178, 215, 254, 288
Silver, 62, 75, 87, 90, 136-37
Slaughter of beef, 176-77
Soapweed, 140
Soledad Mission, 203, 230
Sonora, 146-47, 178
Sonorans, 198
Southern mines, xiv, 212
Spafford, A. J., 43
Spanish dagger, 14
Spanish moss, 18
Sparks' Ferry, 211
Speaker, Charles, 3, 43, 102
Spring Creek, 21
Springfield, Ohio, 3
Squatter riots, xix, 311-13
Stanislaus River, xvii, 213, 218, 272
Starr, J. B., and Company, 303
Steamboats, 8
Stockton, 211-12, 222, 224, 230, 234, 243, 269, 273, 277, 286, 297
Suisun Bay, 286
Supplies, 120, 123
Sutter, John A., 207, 220, 311
Sutter Hotel, 301, 311
Sutter House, 289
Suttersville, 288
Swiss colony, 32

Teats, Jacob, 3, 19, 38, 43, 51, 55, 64, 66, 80, 110, 148, 217, 219, 222-29, 233, 235, 241, 247, 249-50, 257, 263
"Tecumseh" brig, 315, 318, 320-21
"Tennessee" steamer, 280
Terry, John C., 3, 40
Texan Republic, 34
Texan War for Independence, xv, 35
Texas, xiii-xv, 14-38; Galveston, 14-15; Port Lavaca, 15-16; Victoria, 17; Fannin's Battleground, 19; Goliad, 20; San Antonio, 25-29; Castroville, 31; Mission Concepcíon, 34-35; Rio Grande, 38
Tippin, Judge, 82
Torrey (Mexican trader), 85
Towns in Mexico, 84
Traders, 89
Trias, Angel, xvi, 130
Tucson, 82, 147, 149, 151, 157, 166, 178
Tulare Valley, 210-11, 213
Tuolumne diggings, 215, 230, 267, 272, 277
Tuolumne River, xvii

Vicksburg, Miss., 9
Victoria, Texas, xv, 16, 17, 76, 94
Victoria California Company, 76

Walker's Pass, 254
Wamsley, Asa S., 3, 16, 40
Ward, Col., 102-3
Warner, Jonathan T., 171
Warner's Ranch, xvii, 168, 171
Washington City, 289
Watson, Col., 69, 81, 88, 90, 110, 127, 129, 149
Weller, J. B., 180
Whitman, Henry C., 267
Williams, Isaac, xvii, 174-77, 179, 181, 231
Wool, Gen. Joseph, xv
Word, Col. C. G., 28, 66, 82, 102, 110, 111, 148, 150-51
Worth, General, 24

Xenia, Ohio, 4

"Yacht" steamer, 14
Yotter, A. G., 248-49, 250
Yuma Indians, 161-62, 167, 183

PRAISE FOR THE ORIGINAL EDITION

"This well designed and executed volume [gives an] account of a little-known route to the gold fields, [Evans'] day-by-day entries on the results of actual mining, and sheds light on bay and river life and the hubbub of early Sacramento."

—*Pacific Historical Review*

"With its unexpected color and the author's literate style…this book is a surprise and a delight…one has the feeling of being there."

—*California Folklore Quarterly*

"[This] is the journal of a tenderfoot who 'saw the elephant' on a strange trail, who faced death by disease, starvation or thirst more than once, whose single desire was to gain wealth enough in the gold fields to permit him to return to his family in Ohio, and who, failing to attain this desire, died at an early age a few days after the journal ends."

—*Southwest Review*

MORE WESTERN HISTORY TITLES FROM
HUNTINGTON LIBRARY PRESS

The Butterfield Overland Mail by Waterman L. Ormsby,
edited by Lyle H. Wright and Josephine M. Bynum
$12.95 paper 179 pages 978-0-87328-095-2

The Cattle on a Thousand Hills: Southern California, 1850–1880
by Robert Glass Cleland
$24.95 paper 368 pages 978-0-87328-097-6

Charles F. Lummis: Editor of the Southwest by Edwin R. Bingham
$19.95 first paperback edition 240 pages 978-0-87328-221-5

**Ho for California!: Women's Overland Diaries from the Huntington
Library** edited and annotated by Sandra L. Myres
$14.95 paper 320 pages 978-0-87328-119-5

The Irvine Ranch by Robert Glass Cleland
$11.95 paper 180 pages 978-0-87328-015-0

Juan Rodríguez Cabrillo by Harry Kelsey
$12.95 paper 276 pages 978-0-87328-176-8

**Land of Golden Dreams: California in the Gold Rush Decade,
1848–1858** by Peter J. Blodgett
$20.95 cloth 978-0-87328-183-6; $14.95 paper 978-0-87328-182-9

A Mormon Chronicle: The Diaries of John D. Lee
edited by Robert Glass Cleland and Juanita Brooks, with a new foreword by
Andrew Rolle
$35.00 paper 868 pages 978-0-87328-178-2

**Uncle Sam's Camels: The Journal of May Humphreys Stacey
Supplemented by the Report of Edward Fitzgerald Beale** edited by
Lewis Burt Lesley with a new foreword by Paul Andrew Hutton
$24.95 first paperback edition 324 pages 978-0-87328-220-8

**A Victorian Gentlewoman in the Far West: The Reminiscences of
Mary Hallock Foote**
edited with an introduction by Rodman W. Paul
$16.95 paper 420 pages 978-0-87328-057-0